D1598857

WE WILL

DANCE OUR

TRUTH

WE WILL DANCE OUR TRUTH

Yaqui History in
Yoeme Performances

DAVID DELGADO SHORTER

UNIVERSITY OF NEBRASKA PRESS

LINCOLN AND LONDON

Portions of chapter 5, "Hunting
for History in Potam Pueblo,"
previously appeared in *Folklore*
118, no. 3 (December 2007):
282–306.

All photographs by the author.

Library of Congress Cataloging-
in-Publication Data
Shorter, David Delgado.
We will dance our truth : Yaqui
history in Yoeme performances /
David Delgado Shorter.

p. cm.
Includes bibliographical
references and index.
ISBN 978-0-8032-1733-1
(cloth : alk. paper)
1. Yaqui Indians – Folklore.
2. Yaqui Indians – Rites and
ceremonies. 3. Yaqui Indians –
Social life and customs.
4. Folklore – Performance
– Mexico. 5. Oral tradition –
Mexico. I. Title.
F1221.Y3S47 2009
305.897′4542–dc22
2009012604

Set in Arno by Bob Reitz.
Designed by Nathan Putens.

I DEDICATE THIS BOOK
to the loving memories of
Antonia Flores Buitemea and
Ignacio Amarillas Sombra.
Their *tu'i hiapsim*, or "good
hearts," provided the basic
understanding that right
relations precede all else.

Contents

Illustrations

Acknowledgments

As any ethnographer will attest, trips to the field and time to write are expenses often afforded by the generosity of institutions and agencies. In chronological order, I would like to thank the Whatcom Museum Society for a Jacobs Research Grant in 1999. The University of California at Santa Cruz's Department of History of Consciousness gave me a dissertation year fellowship in 2001. An Andrew W. Mellon Postdoctoral Fellowship enabled me to spend two wonderful years at Wesleyan University from 2002 to 2004. The Hemispheric Institute of Performance and Politics was seminal in starting my digital research with their 2004 Cuaderno Development Grant. At Indiana University, I received great support from the Office of the Vice President and Office of the Vice Provost of Research in the forms of Exploration Traveling Grants, New Frontier Grants, Summer Faculty Fellowships, and an Institute for the Digital Arts and Humanities Institute Fellowship. A grant from the National Science Foundation's Cultural Anthropology Program enabled me to complete the research for this book in 2006.

This book is the culmination of many years spent learning in both pueblo and academic communities. My Yoeme friends in Arizona and Mexico have always welcomed my visits, questions, and appetite for learning more from them. In particular, I want to thank Felipe Molina, Mini Valenzuela, and the families of my "kompae into komae" in Potam Pueblo. As a means of recognizing the value of many conversations over the past decade, I want to thank some of the people who have directly helped me think through various aspects of this research: Henry Glassie, Gary Lease, Octaviana Trujillo, Diana Taylor, Armin Geertz, Kimberly Christen, Gloria Matuz, Robert Berkhofer Jr., Joseph Wilder, Betsy Brandt, Richard Bauman, Aracelli Amarillas, Hayden White, David Hoy, Angel Flores, Enrique Espinoza, Larry Evers, Ignacio Amarillas, David Burkhalter, Guillermo Flores, Pravina Shukla, Neferti Tadiar, Steven

Amarillo, Don Brenneis, Marshall Anstandig, Guillermo Delgado, Lori Felton, Annie Lorrie Anderson, Olga Nájera-Ramirez, David Turnbull, James Mahoney, Jason Baird Jackson, Joel Gereboff, Raymond DeMallie, and Sylvia Marcos de Robert. I owe a substantial amount of gratitude to James Clifford, who took me on as a graduate student and helped this project take shape in fundamental ways. I received much research assistance from Alan Ferg at the Arizona State Museum Archives. Kenneth Morrison has been a mentor and scholarly role model, landlord, roommate, indexer, and the voice in my head reminding me that "all writing is rewriting."

While a postdoctoral fellow at Wesleyan University's Center for the Americas, I rewrote much of this material through the thoughtful advisement of Ann Wightman, Elizabeth McAlister, Kehaulani Kauanui, and Colleen Boyd, and the insightful readership of an advanced seminar on Ethnographies of/as Colonialism. At Indiana University's Department of Folklore and Ethnomusicology, I benefited from supportive colleagues, many bright graduate students, and a rigorous writing group that included Lynn Hooker, Greg Schrempp, Nina Fales, and Ruth Stone. At the University of California Los Angeles, I have found a camaraderie with all my colleagues in World Arts and Cultures, particularly Al Roberts, Mary (Polly) Roberts, Janet O'Shea, Victoria Marks, David Gere and Don Cosentino. I thank Dean Chris Waterman for his support, and Peter Nabokov for his generosity in both time and spirit. Working with the University of Nebraska Press, I was gifted the careful readership of the anonymous reviewers and the shepherding of Gary Dunham, Elisabeth Chretien, and Ann Baker. Matthew Bokovoy has been a phenomenal colleague in the process. For the conversations about and the use of his art on the book's cover, I owe a genuine "chiokoe" to Mario Martinez.

Although my research practices affected all of my personal relationships, I particularly want to thank a group of people who have actively helped me finish the book with integrity: Edwin Acosta, Karen Phelan, Dorothea Ditchfield, Kate Kordich, Tarajean Yazzie-Mintz and the Yazzie family, David Bleecker, Rebecca Niday, Sara Friedman, Steve Quattrocchi, Sheila Peuse, Heidi Quattrocchi, Mary Jane Quattrocchi,

Laura Munoz, Beth Anstandig, Sam Cronk, Matthew Guterl, Sandra Latcha, Randy Lewis, Circe Strum, María Elena García, José Antonio Lucero, Andrew Storrs, Carrie Hertz, Raquel Chapa, Denise Cruz, and Jordan Blackman. For their assistance with the details of translations and citations, I greatly appreciate the help of Lorena Alvarado, Rachel Gonzalez, and Gabriel Berlinger. Elaine Durham Otto and Cyndy Brown proved supportive and disciplined copy editors. Both Kiara Bahn and Timothy Peace advocated for my health and sanity at crucial moments in the writing of this book. Henry and Pravina embodied the grace and passion that I hope to emulate in my scholarship. Kathryn Lofton gracefully played the roles of honest editor and dear friend, a difficult combination to balance. Offering the sort of support that entails sitting with me for hours on end, my dogs JD and Riley generously sacrificed many a Frisbee game. Nicholas Quattrocchi showed up and provided the much needed love and patience to help make an academic life more livable. No one has known my highs and lows as much as my parents. I want to thank my mother, Helen Viscarra Reno, and my father, Steve Shorter. My stepfather, Richard "Andy" Viscarra, was important to my achieving my academic goals, although he passed away before seeing me finish this book. Along with Paula Valle, Mary Maes, Ignacio Amarillas Sombra, and Antonia Flores Buitemea, I think of Andy as being there from the beginning and for all of my beginnings. I thank all my relations.

WE WILL

DANCE OUR

TRUTH

Introduction

TALKING ABOUT WHERE YOEME HISTORY BEGINS

Potam Pueblo, November 2, 1999. After I returned from the cemetery, Ignacio Sombra allowed me to record him talking about animam miika, *the ceremonial feeding of the departed souls. I retrieved my recording equipment from the truck and returned to the room where Ignacio, his wife, his son, and my friend Felipe Molina were sitting. Sitting upright, clearing his throat, Ignacio began, his voice more monotone than usual, his phrases paced and rhythmic:*

Kompae, ka religionta hiakim tekipanoa'u
[The religion that the Yoeme people work with,]
wohnaiki pueplo santiklesiam
[the eight holy pueblos]
hoka ve'ekatana
[from where they sit]

Inika pasion pahkota weye'epo
[this passion play that is happening]
animam pasionta weye'epo
[the passion of the soul]

Si'ime pueplo wohnaiki pueplo
[all the eight pueblos]
santiklesiam hippueme
[the ones that have the holy churches]
inika wepulsi a tekipanoam
[the ones who work it as one]

Into inian a naatek vattukariampo
[they started it like this in yesterdays]
dia primeropo natek ian vea woi
[it started on the first of the month, but today is the second,]
yoko vea vahi miisa ultimo
[tomorrow is the third, last mass.]

Ian navuhti vicha vea wa si'ime pueplo
[Furthermore, it is like that in all the pueblos]
vea nuen aa tekipanoa
[like this they work it]
wa vato'ora inim aneme
[the baptized ones that are here.]

Inian a ta'a, iat nah kuakteka hiapsa
[They know it like this, they walk about here, alive]
malampo natekai achaimpo.
[starting from the mothers and the fathers.]

Now as I lie in this Esperanza motel room, listening to the tape and writing of the day's events, I am struck by Ignacio's description of animam miika. I thought the recording would be good material for my research on Yoeme rituals for the deceased, but now I realize its relevance to my larger research. As I follow Ignacio's recorded voice and Felipe's translations of the tape, I begin to understand how Yoeme elders represent their culture in similar terms: religion is "work" for Yoemem; "people" are synonymous with the eight holy pueblos; "holy" stresses the authoritative sanction of their towns. Those Yoemem doing the work, tekipanoa or religious labor, in the pueblos are "the baptized ones that are here," the contemporary Yoeme Catholics. They distinguish themselves from their relatives, the Surem, who live immortally outside the pueblo (civil society) and yet inside the landscape. The deceased villagers are considered present, "walking about here," a type of movement in a specific location. Mixing Spanish and Yoeme, Ignacio situates his description within a set of spatial, temporal, and religious references that are particular to his community's historical understanding of itself.

The tape continues. Ignacio repeats these ways of talking about his culture and religious practices, references you can hear in almost any formal talk by a Yoeme elder. You see these articulations in Yoeme rituals, in their contents and forms. Although I hadn't asked him for a "formal" presentation, Ignacio clearly gave me a gift tonight, not just in his description of animam miika. His talk evidenced a distinctly Yoeme way of thinking about, historicizing, and continuing tribal religious identity.

The faint mechanical sound of the recorder's turning spindles and the audible movements of the microphone accentuate the contrast between being there with Ignacio and hearing the by-product of that moment, the recorded talk. Records, things we keep, proof of events that "really" happened, documentation — a complex chain of relations links common notions of evidence to certain forms of representation. Ignacio's voice, in a serious and subtle way, asserts that indigenous communities have relied on practical and logical representative forms. His words "make sense," since they recall and reassert Yoeme ways of knowing the world. As I contemplate how I can share this evidence of Yoeme autoethnography with others, I have to laugh. As a scholar, I'll have to take this live talk and turn it into text. How do I re-create the mud and cane walls, the smell of coffee spilled on burning embers, the ambient sounds of sleeping children breathing heavily in adjoining rooms? What have I not sensed about Ignacio's presentation? And how do I relate what I have sensed? In these cases, translation is literally transformation. I do not tell, dance, or sing Yoeme history as most Yoemem do. Rather, I write about how Yoemem understand and share their history in active, embodied, religious ways.

Journal entries like this one reflect a certain type of personal experience, moments when connections are made, insights gained. These notes from the field derive from my years of collaboration with Yoeme individuals. This particular field note was written after I had been visiting Potam Pueblo for more than five years. I start with it because it evokes the cornerstone of my larger research and offers the reader insight into the making of ethnographic knowledge. This book is thus a study of a people, but also a study of the ethnography of a people. I have been mindful to focus on the Yoeme ways of knowing, not swaying too far toward anthropological theories. Some readers may deepen their analysis by reading the books and articles listed in my endnotes. Because I hoped to write a social science that emphasizes the intersubjective and social dynamic between me and community members, I include field notes within chapters and transcribed interviews between chapters.

Writing ethnographic accounts became much more complicated after the "writing culture" debates and the larger crisis of representation. Although I will not rehearse those debates here, many readers will rightfully sense that these contexts surrounded the beginnings of my fieldwork and graduate training. Until now I have remained conscious that all ethnographers employ particular strategies to assert authenticity and authority. Accordingly, I have read texts and produced this text with authenticating strategies in mind. One strategy, for example, is to use my field notes, which intentionally dispute some of my own cultural interpretations. In exchange for such fractures, this ethnography keeps the dialogical process central to the project of rewriting Yoeme ethnographies. Without the real face-to-face conversations, which sometimes wander and diverge, no true cross-cultural understanding can emerge.

This book explores many facets of Yoeme religious life in Potam Pueblo, in the northern Mexican state of Sonora, and I want to begin our time together as writer and reader by explaining why I wrote this book. Based on archival, field, and ethnographic studies, I express the spatial, performative, and religious ways that many Yoemem sustain their collective identity. I also contend that these acts provide alternatives to Western academic ways of thinking about history and writing. While these linked arguments speak to multiple conversations within the study of indigenous religions, each of the chapters develops the central claim for a performative approach to understanding Yoeme place-making. Like much recent anthropological scholarship, I remap the boundary between the ethnological categories oral and literate and expand Western notions of historical expression to include nonliterate representations of "local" history through various oral and ritual practices. By focusing on place-making, my work takes Yoeme values as the starting point, since tribal identity is narrated in terms of a specific geographical territory. Using Yoeme myths and ceremonies as ethnohistorical representations will enable me to ground the various chapters in the symbols, forms, and logic that are recognizable to many Yoemem, especially those from the Yoeme homeland in Mexico. One of my main goals is to produce scholarship that makes sense to native communities. And as many scholarly readers will find, through Yoeme acts of inscription I argue not so much to replace but to expand the categories of "writing" and "history."

I want to address how my work relates to previous ethnographic accounts of Yoeme identity before outlining how each chapter develops themes of place-making and local historicity. This review of the relevant literatures provides readers with a baseline perspective on studies of the Yoemem in terms of their land and their sense of "otherness." Following the lead of Yoeme historical narratives, I pay attention to Yoeme relations with those who have shared and disputed rights to that geography. I examine the scholarship of Edward Spicer (1906–83), who devoted his life to interpreting Yoeme ethnicity and who developed a dynamic approach to studying identity. I also explain how the present study creates new approaches to specific theoretical and methodological issues in the study of indigenous religions. These discussions connect my work to previous scholarship and reveal the directions taken in subsequent chapters.

Previous Yoeme Studies: Names, Places, and Perspectives

My use of "Yoeme/m" rather than "Yaqui/s" distinguishes my study from the majority of written descriptions of the communities. The origin of the name "Yaqui" has long been a topic of conversation among scholars and community members, demonstrating a diversity of views regarding historical self-representation. While they are most widely known as "Yaquis," the Yoemem are referred to in some Mexican scholarship as "Cahitans." But this term is considered by many to be disrespectful, since the Yoeme words *ka hita* literally mean "not a thing" or "nothing." According to one of Spicer's earliest ethnographies (1954, 23), community members with whom he worked preferred "Yoemem." He later writes that a form of "Yoemem" was recorded in the only seventeenth-century description of their language. Although he gives no reason why he used "Yaqui," he suggests that "Yoeme" was used solely in the context of Yoemem speaking about or among themselves (1980, 306). According to Yoeme writer and deer singer Felipe Molina (Evers and Molina 1987, 43), "We call ourselves 'Yoemem,' Mexicans and Spanish are 'Yorim,' and Whites are 'Riingom.'"

Most Yoemem on both sides of the U.S.–Mexican border, however, refer to themselves as "Yaquis." I have heard people refer to me as "the professor who calls us 'Yoeme,'" which I consider a compliment, particularly from elders. Whether they use "Yaqui" because of its widespread presence in the anthropological literature (and perhaps to facilitate Yoeme communication with outsiders), or because Yoeme language use is declining, I cannot say for sure.[1] Perhaps they are attached to a well-established name. Clearly these matters can be complicated. On both sides of the border, for example, official/legal discourse refers to "the Yaqui Nation" or "la Tribu Yaqui." Yet in Potam Pueblo one can go for days without hearing the word "Yaqui" outside of that nationalist discourse. I use "Yoeme" because my Yoeme friends do so when talking about themselves. I also take as my lead the first Yoeme-authored book, which Herminia Valenzuela (Kaczkurkin 1977) titled *Yoeme: Lore of the Arizona Yaqui People*.[2]

As with other Native American tribal names, "Yaqui" may be a term initiated by outsiders. Some community members claim that "Yaqui" originated from a misunderstanding: when a Spaniard first approached the Yoemem and asked who they were, the response was "ya aqui," "already here."[3] Another commonly heard story is that in the early years of Spanish contact, Yoemem associated themselves with the name of their central waterway, the Yaqui River. This river, called in Yoeme the Hiak Vatwe, is such a centerpiece of Yoeme history and myth that the entire area of the homelands is often called the Hiak Vatwe or *hiakim*. In both folkloric and historic accounts, Yoemem represent themselves in ways that are based on landownership and indigeneity. According to one of the first documented Jesuit accounts of the Yoemem (written by Andrés Pérez de Ribas in 1645), the people said, "Don't you see we are *hiaqui*, 'the ones who make sounds'?" I have also heard that a lone Yoeme walking through the desert eating organ pipe cactus fruit was asked by a Spaniard who he was, and confusing the question for what he was doing, responded, "*Aakim*," meaning "organ pipe cactus." These clearly do not exhaust the supply of "folk" etymologies. I feel more confident with the simple translation Yoemem = People, and I thereby join a recent cross-tribal move to refer to tribes by names in their respective languages. For consistency I retain the use of "Yaquis" in the contexts of proper place-names, previously published quotes, and titles, while I use "Yoemem" in my own analysis.[4]

The Hiak Vatwe, or Río Yaqui, remains a fundamental point of tribal reference in both the pueblos and ethnographic descriptions; it is the central landmark of collective identity for many Yoemem. From its 9,000-foot-high source in the Sierra Madres, this river flows south through the mountain ranges of eastern Sonora, widens downstream, and enters what Yoemem call *hiakim*, their homeland. From the mountain country to the level coastal plains bordering the Pacific Ocean, the Hiak Vatwe is the northernmost of five rivers that drain the mountains of what was once called New Spain and is now Sonora. Considered one of the most productive agricultural regions in the world (Dunbier 1968; West 1993), both Yoemem and newcomers knew that this land, as James Mahoney (1994, 7) wrote, "has held the sweetest promise of prosperity." Yoeme settlements are cradled by these mountains, sustained by these waters, and nourished by these fertile lands.

Known as the eight holy pueblos, five towns lie north of the Hiak Vatwe (Veenem, Wiivisim, Rahum, Potam, and Torim) and three towns (Vikam, Vahkom, and Ko'oko'im) lie south.[5] Although the river's course has changed over the centuries, its symbolic role defines Yoeme territory and joins its agricultural role as a vital part of ethnic solidarity. The Mexican government has attempted to diminish, if not extinguish, tribal unity by redirecting the river. Both before and after the construction upriver of the Alvaro Obregón Dam in 1952, the Mexican government aimed to decrease the water's flow to the Yoeme pueblos. Although this activity has destroyed entire villages, one is still struck by the beauty and fertility of the hiakim. But note, we are already caught in the links between land and history: to discuss the Hiak Vatwe necessarily involves mentioning the eight holy pueblos, which leads to issues of identity and a distinct retelling of the past.

Both Yoeme and non-Yoeme historians narrate three general phases of the Yoeme past: the religious syncretism that began in 1617, the geographic dislocation that started around 1766, and the cultural revitalization of the 1900s (Molina, Salazar, and Kaczkurkin 1983; Spicer 1954, 1980). While this characterization of Yoeme "eras" sweeps too briefly to account for the particular places, individuals, and events that constitute a tribal history, the consensus among most published and internal historical narratives does suggest that the three-part periodization roughly approximates the stages of postcontact interethnic relations.

The Yoemem defeated Spanish armies at least three times between 1533 and 1609 and therefore negotiated a contact situation on their own terms. Their engagement with the newcomers was selective and tactful. Yoemem invited Jesuit missionaries to their pueblos in 1617 and kept the Spanish conquistadors at bay at the same time. Yoeme strength clearly controlled the influence of Catholicism on precontact traditions. Like other early colonial encounters, this control included a significant amount of indigenous agency and maneuverability. Yoemem enforced and strategically maintained their territorial and cultural boundaries and sustained sovereign control of their land from pre-Columbian times through the period of Jesuit collaboration.[6]

To understand Yoeme cultural dynamics, we must grasp that roughly 30,000 Yoemem decided to befriend five or six Jesuit missionaries, ultimately choosing which aspects of Christianity and European life were sensible and adoptable.[7] Yoemem also decided which practices were to be rejected. Control maintained continuity in a time of change. During 150 years of Jesuit collaboration, Yoemem consolidated hundreds of settlements into the eight central pueblos around the Hiak Vatwe and constructed churches and plazas. They also sought to learn agricultural methods, governmental duties, and languages from the missionaries. As most academic and community historians agree, the Yoeme-Jesuit relationship must have been one of give-and-take, not of domination. If either group had the upper hand in terms of power, however, the Yoemem dictated and managed the conditions. This foundational control of missionization clearly shapes any interpretation of Yoeme culture: Yoeme tradition is based on a religious syncretism constructed of pre-contact worldviews and a Catholic cosmology.[8]

Any sense of sharing and mutual commitment to peace that characterized the Jesuit period slowly dissolved from the early 1700s to around 1767, when the Spanish expelled the Jesuits from New Spain. In the years before expulsion, changes in Jesuit leadership demonstrated a preference for the Mexican *encomienda* landholding system and a general distrust of Yoeme-elected religious/governmental representatives.[9] After the Jesuits departed, Yoemem once again were sole caretakers of their homelands, but now they possessed livestock, irrigation systems, metal tools, and European-influenced architecture. Some spoke and wrote in Spanish and, for a few, Latin. In the 1820s, the Mexican government began to deport Yoemem to mining camps and sugar plantations across Mexico, the Yucatan, and what is now the southern United States.[10] Mexican government officials also began allotting Yoeme lands to Mexican agriculturalists, who for 150 years had been hearing Jesuit reports about the fertile lands surrounding the Hiak Vatwe. As Mexicans waged a war for independence in the early to mid-1800s, some Yoemem fought against the Creole elite in New Spain and some against the Spanish. The continual slave raiding and outright brutality against the villagers, however, led many to migrate to areas near Sonora and the southwestern United States. We can trace these historical diasporas on a map, following the lines of train tracks, footpaths, and boat travel that led Yoeme slaves to Yucatan plantations. We can imagine the paths of migration to surrounding tribes or north into present-day Arizona. After the Jesuit era, Yoemem created another fundamental aspect of their identity: tribal life in a transnational context both in Mexico and the United States.

After President Lázaro Cárdenas established favorable agricultural policies in the 1930s, Yoemem began to repopulate their original pueblos in the Hiak Vatwe valley. Along with the establishment of a Yoeme "zone," these policies supported cultural revitalization. From the early 1900s, Yoemem had already formed permanent communities around Tucson and Phoenix. They thus began to define their territories in binational contexts. In Mexico, the Yoemem were the first federally recognized indigenous tribe, but in the United States they held private lots and trust land, as well as the Pascua Yaqui Reservation. Speaking with tribal members on both sides of the border would lead one to conclude that a total Yoeme population count is comparable to the 30,000 estimated at first European contact. Most still live in communities along the Hiak Vatwe, while 11,000 live in the four communities around Tucson or in the town of Guadalupe near Phoenix (Evers and Molina 1987, 19). As testimony to their sense of tribal sovereignty, some Yoemem during the late 1990s sought to issue their own passports to tribal members to allow restriction-free travel across the U.S.–Mexico border for religious purposes. By crossing this border, some Yoemem attempt to connect their northern and southern communities through indigenous paths of migration that respect no national jurisdictions (Norrell 1998, 47).

This brief outline of Yoeme postcontact history suggests that Yoemem cannot be easily included within common representations of the Native American colonial experience. Unlike many other tribes in Mexico and the United States, the Yoemem controlled substantial amounts of their own lands and community activities; only later did they come under Mexican domination. In contrast to forced conversions, we know from both Yoeme and Spanish sources that Yoemem invited the Jesuits into their territory using envoys sent to surrounding missions to observe possible benefits of missionary collaboration. This phase was not a moment of defeat but a shifting story of struggles and negotiations. The Yoemem were not displaced from their homeland or left alone by Mexican colonizers. Perhaps because of their sociohistorical predicament, their experience attracted attention from anthropologists. The name most reasonably associated with the ethnological study of Yoeme people and culture is that of Edward Spicer.

Approaching Yoeme History

Edward H. Spicer provides an invaluable foundation for any understanding of Yoeme culture. He pioneered what Raymond Folgelson (1974) calls "ethno-ethnohistory," or "other"-centered interpretations, by documenting Yoeme history through long-term relations with Yoeme people on both sides of the border. Between 1939 and 1950, Spicer lived sporadically in Yoeme communities; he spoke Yoeme and Spanish and wrote nine books (four solely on the Yoemem) and countless articles. His long-term research with Yoemem led him to an unparalleled depth and innovative concept of cultural processes. Spicer's earlier publications (1954, 1958, and 1961) placed him at the forefront of ethnic studies as well as American Indian studies.

In her epilogue to Spicer's posthumously published book, *People of Pascua* (1988), Kathleen M. Sands appreciates his theory of ethnic persistence as a watershed understanding of collective identity. She notes, "As a cultural anthropologist with early training in culture and personality scholarship, he remained inclined to look at ethnicity in terms of ethnic group members' historical, social, religious, and personal relations with other groups" (1988, 306).[11] In contrast to other cultural anthropologists of his time, Spicer demonstrated how ethnicity results from increased contact with other cultures, not from relative isolation. This "interactionist" approach to ethnicity (Spicer 1962) anticipated Fredrik Barth's claims that people define themselves mostly in terms of who they are not. Sands commends Spicer for initiating a movement from a functionalist approach to a more contextual and dynamic understanding of identity. After working extensively in the Arizona State Museum archives researching Spicer's unpublished papers, I would add that he has provided me with much of what I have learned about fieldwork: from organization of notes to compilation of data, Spicer left a model for any anthropologist. Moreover, based on what Yoemem and non-Yoemem who knew him have said, I know that he possessed, as they say in Yoeme, *tu'i hiapsi*, a "good heart." Spicer's work is essential for any research on Yoeme ethnography and historiography.

I specifically build on Spicer's theories of culture and ethnic identity. Spicer and Robert Redfield, his thesis advisor, shared the view that culture resided in objects, symbols, and the acts and behaviors associated with them (McGuire 1989, 165). Spicer's "interactionist" model of ethnicity emphasized that identity persistence was, at least for the Yoemem, a result of external contact. Spicer, in fact, preceded Barth in arguing against "isolationist" theories of ethnic identity that assumed interethnic contact would eventually lead to culture loss and assimilation. The combination of his behavioral view of culture and his interactionist view of ethnicity provided the reasoning for his focus on religious and political life (Sheridan 1988, 178, 184). Since Spicer understood that political and religious organizations engendered the most symbolically expressive aspects of Yocme identity, his works progressively developed the thesis of *The Yaquis: A Cultural History* that religious symbols and rituals are requisites for enduring cultures.

I follow Spicer's lead in my methodology by drawing on fieldwork and contemporary ritual practices to better understand Yoeme history. As Thomas Sheridan notes in his critical comparison of Spicer and another historian of the Yoemem, Evelyn Hu-DeHart (1981, 1984), Spicer moved beyond simply reading the reports of Spanish and Mexicans who wrote firsthand accounts of the Yoemem. Knowing that these documents contained obvious biases and with few exceptions lacked native perspectives, Spicer brought his "modern linguistic and ethnographic research to bear upon at least some of those documents" (Sheridan 1988, 184). The difference between Spicer's and Hu-DeHart's histories of the Yoemem reveals the problems associated with both his "cultural" approach and her "narrative" approach. Whereas Spicer's work leaves many historical periods undiscussed or brushed over quickly and with little detail, Hu-DeHart's descriptions of Yoeme culture are quite often flat and incomplete because they are derived from non-Yoeme sources (Sheridan 1988; Voss 1981, 144). I draw on both historical approaches, and based on these key works, my research methodology resembles the work of Spicer most closely.

I agree with Spicer's "up-streaming" or "direct historical" approach, which is that contemporary Yoeme voices and practices can inform and fundamentally shape our historical accounts. I rely on both non-Yoeme written sources and Yoeme "writings" as they are inscribed in religious performances. Since nonliterate documentary styles live and change, I pay attention to current Yoeme expressive forms as clues to better understanding events in the past, much like Spicer.

Unlike Spicer, I see Yoeme oral traditions, dances, and processions as ways of understanding historic events and manifestations of Yoeme historical consciousness. The distinction is slight yet important. Yoemem do not just express their perspective on history; they practice in particularly Yoeme ways to develop a historical consciousness. Through embodied action, the Yoemem theorize, map, inscribe, and document their history. Even though my research goals coincide with Spicer's aim to better understand Yoeme social cohesion, I also want to examine how Yoeme historicism provides a means to expand Western notions of writing and the contours of historical discourse itself.

March 19, 2001. Sitting in the cold reading room of the Arizona State Museum Archives, I come across a field note written by Spicer on March 18, 1942.

Bets, Juan Valenzuela, the Rahum maestro capilla, and I sat for a while in the afternoon in Juan's ramada before beginning work on the copying of his texts. He said, "Have you been working with Juan [Uhyollimea] on this history?" I said, "He seems to know nothing about it. He knows only about the church and Yaqui religion today." Juan said, "Well, religion is the base of all the history. You have to know about that. But there are many things which have been forgotten and which are not practiced now since the guerra. The people have lost many things, but when they were in the sierras they kept their religion, too. No matter where they were in the sierras they had a misa when it came time. They also had the visperas. That is the way it was. The maestros took their books into the sierras. As you know, the people have always kept their religion, as in Arizona. But there were formerly other things besides the matachinis and what they have now. The Aguilenos are very much apart from us, but still they have their pascolas and their matachinis.

They haven't lost these things. You should take up the religion point for point to write your history." I agreed.

I have spent many a day in this room, searching through Spicer's field notes, photographs, and correspondence for materials that might help me better understand Yoeme history. Today, in particular, I feel far away from Potam Pueblo, where I was last week and where I will return next week. The combination of archival research and fieldwork is taxing. Perhaps I should have decided to just do one or the other. But I remain optimistic that working in the archives will provide a rich resource to accompany my trips to the hiakim. And on days like this, when I find a note card like this one, the work seems worthwhile. Then I notice today's date. I look again at the date on Spicer's field note. Almost sixty years ago to the day, Edward Spicer was sitting with Juan Valenzuela and discussing my research, as I would pick it up later.

Looking at that day's notes, I realize that Valenzuela tried to help Spicer, but not by supplying him with more data. Rather, Valenzuela clearly provided Spicer, a non-Yoeme, with an insider's perspective on Yoeme history: "You should take up the religion point for point to write your history." Perhaps it was Valenzuela's status as a community elder of Rahum pueblo or that he soon became Spicer's good friend and principal collaborator. And Spicer agrees: in the subsequent forty years, he works continuously to understand Yoeme history and identity as an outgrowth from and contribution to religious practice.

My research similarly starts from Valenzuela's perspective that "religion is the base of all the [Yaqui] history." And after speaking with Yoemem on both sides of the border, I feel as though Valenzuela may have inferred a possible destination or at least one of the benefits of the journey: "But there are many things which have been forgotten and which are not practiced now since the guerra." Could he have been suggesting that a religious studies approach to Yoeme history might offer insight into Yoeme endurance? I heed Valenzuela's call and explore various ways of understanding Yoeme identity as grounded in religious acts. In their oral traditions, written histories, and ritual performances, the Yoeme people of Sonora, Mexico, continue to perceive of their land as aboriginally inherited and themselves as sovereign protectors. As Valenzuela told Spicer in the Lenten season of 1942, "They haven't lost these things."

Mythology, Prophecy, and "Religion" in Indigenous Studies

A small number of scholars have written thousands of pages on the Yoemem, and few have attempted to appreciate myth and ritual as forms of historical consciousness. A number of studies provide fruitful data and analyses regarding Yoeme history, culture, dances, and folklore (Bogan 1925; Evers 1981a, 1981b; Fabila 1940; Giddings 1959; Griffith and Molina 1980; Hu-DeHart 1984, 1995; Kaczkurkin 1977; Sands 1983; Spicer 1980, 1984, 1988; Wilder 1963). Others focus specifically on certain aspects of Yoeme life: land management, localized politics, and biographies or auto-biographies (Kelley 1978; Mahoney 1994; McGuire 1986; Moisés, Kelly, and Holden 1971; Savala 1980). These topics are often shown to have deep roots within Yoeme religious cosmology, and scholars of Yoeme culture rarely utilize mythology and ceremony as interpretive lenses to view nonliterate historiography. (Erickson 2003, Evers and Molina 1987, and Morrison 1992b are exceptional on this matter.) The resulting scholarship presents a picture of Yoeme society where religious perspectives and practices become reduced to "modes of thought," "religious arts," or, in one case, "secondary attributes of Yaqui identity." Without serious consideration of Yoeme mythology as historical, researchers fail to consider native ways of understanding themselves.

In stark contrast, Larry Evers and Felipe Molina give primary importance to such considerations as myths and prophecy in their 1992 collaboration, "The Holy Dividing Line: Inscription and Resistance in Yaqui Culture." Yoeme worldviews are most fully articulated in the Testamento, a collection of stories about the *vatnaataka* (the beginning or times long ago). These stories include a global flood, the establishing of tribal territory by prophets and Yoemem "singing the boundaries," the confirming of bow leaders as territorial protectors, and the formation of the eight pueblos along the Hiak Vatwe. Evers and Molina's research demonstrates that the Testamento continues to circulate in written and oral form in Yoeme communities. If Evers and Molina are correct, a careful analysis of this storytelling tradition must inform any aspect of Yoeme historical studies. By relating the Testamento to other widely referenced stories of the "talking tree," we will be able to appreciate Yoeme historical practices as recognizable and relevant to Yoemem themselves. For these reasons, my research centers around the Testamento, the talking tree stories, and how Yoeme performances of history are embodied within their religious performances and their written and oral traditions.

I pay considerable attention to the form and function of Yoeme myth. I agree with Armin Geertz that mythology is the "narrated tradition that codifies, coordinates, and sometimes systematizes interpretive frameworks and categories in terms of stories about beings and events that are of primary significance to a given culture" (1994, 3). Geertz's definition notes the importance of storytelling within a particular community. Geertz avoids defining myths solely in terms of religious or phenomenological beliefs to keep the "real, experienced" world firmly within the scope of myth and to articulate how myths convey local ways of knowing. Myths are cosmological narratives that explain past events and provide models for interpreting and creating contemporary realities (Sahlins 1985). Myths change as often as their tellers themselves respond to changes. As Jerold Ramsey has pointed out, literatures converge when cultures converge (1977, 444). Kathleen Sands follows Ramsey's cue and joins other scholars to show how through the reshaping and synthesizing of myths, known as mythopoesis, storytellers are "claiming and making knowable and tolerable the strange and exotic . . . by alleviating culture conflict" (1983, 356). My work uses these studies of myth and mythopoesis to establish that both change and persistence define a people's tradition.

The prophetic aspect of the talking tree myths is central to my study of Yoeme culture because the prophecy makes sense of Yoeme religiosity and relations with their land. In the time of the Surem (the short, immortal, telepathic ancestors of the Yoemem), a tree began making noises that were understood only by a young girl. The girl told everyone the tree's prophecies: the coming of the Jesuits, baptism, new technologies, and Spanish and Mexican territorial encroachment. The tree's messages led to a constitutive division between those wanting baptism and other social changes (Yoemem) and those who would move into the surrounding landscape (immortal Surem).

In the separation between Surem and Yoemem, the talking tree stories provide a model for simultaneous processes of accommodation and continuity. I will not seek to answer the epistemologically harassing question of how a tree can talk. Rather, my work more closely resembles that of Johannes Fabian or Michel Foucault, since I retrace and recount Yoeme prophetic discourse as a means of discovering more about Yoeme social praxis within specific temporal and spatial contexts. As a discursive social practice, Yoeme prophecy is told to someone or some group at specific times by someone for particular purposes: entertainment, religious, political, and so on. As Geertz has said, prophecy is "a way of articulating and defining contemporary events within the context and language of 'tradition'" (1994, 7). I understand Yoeme historiography through the lens of prophetic traditions and recognize that this is one approach among many. Yoeme myth, however, offers a clear conception that some native histories are distinctly religious in form and content.

For tradition to change yet remain meaningful, traditional stories through symbol or metaphor must reference a central narrative that accounts for assimilation and nonconformity. Geertz argues persuasively that prophecy enables such references to change *and* to continuity. Prophetic flexibility in the Yoeme case enables us to see how telling stories of the talking tree preserves indigenous values within a context of cultural adaptation. Peter Nabokov speaks to this issue directly: "Prophecy is a subset of mythic narrative by which Indian tradition assumes a sort of predestined superiority over historical events yet to come. . . . By its claim that the future is theirs to know and outsiders' to find out, prophecy offers Indians an important conceptual weapon in the power struggles between indigenous and invasive world views. They can stay a step ahead of the history which volatile interaction with Europeans has kicked into accelerated motion" (1996, 17–18). Nabokov explains that these "retroactive" prophecies underscore the "emphasis on the dire consequences of European contact" (18). I concur with Nabokov's description of "prophecy" in Native American contexts and show how for many Yoemem prophecy supports a practical appreciation of cultural continuity in the face of external changes.

The scope of this book does not supply the various definitions of religion. However, I think it may be important for some readers to know that my approach considers both indigenous views of religion and a critical use of scholarly definitions. No Yoeme word directly translates to "religion"; however, the word *kohtumre* is close. While resembling the Spanish word for "custom," *kohtumre* can also be translated as "religious society" or "religious tradition" and sometimes as "authority." When speaking formally, Yoemem refer to religious practices either using a loan word, *religionta*, or in their own language as their *tekipanoa*, their "work." The sense that religion is work cannot be taken too lightly. Yoemem use *tekipanoa* constantly to describe community responsibility, and such work is thoroughly exhausting. I have attempted in this book to demonstrate how much labor goes into the preparation and completion of ceremonies, or as Kirstin Erickson (2008) aptly calls it, the "everyday production" of Yoeme identity. Another Yoeme word, *weyeme*, can be used for "custom," "tradition," and even "culture." Most Yoemem refer to "religious knowledge" as *yoem lutu'uria*, Yoeme truth, or *yoo'ora lutu'uria*, elders' truth (Molina, Valenzuela, and Shaul 1999). Clearly none of these terms corresponds to common academic or Western definitions of religion because most religious scholarship continues to theorize religions as belief systems. The alternative to defining religion as "belief" would be to understand indigenous religious systems as epistemologically actualizing. Such philosophical terminology might seem tedious, but we should not glaze over what sits at the core of this book's argument: indigenous performances and rituals are epistemological because they make knowledge and set the standards for what counts as truth. Moreover, such knowledge making is neither "as if" or "sort of" like scientific reasoning; rather, these activities are actual, effective, and internally logical. Indigenous groups rely on oral traditions, hunting rituals and native dances because they are practical ways of knowing themselves, their environments and their histories.

In conversations with Yoeme deer singer and language specialist Felipe Molina, I asked why the Yoeme language did not include a word for "religion" as an aspect of society. He responded that for traditional Yoemem the entire world is related: each rock, each planet, and each bug. As I understood his comment, Yoeme religion is a causal reality that deals with activities, ideas, and relationships between humans and other-than-human persons.[12] For some Yoemem at least, one's work, culture, environment, and family relationships could be considered religious. And yet for others, "religion" may simply designate their affiliations and devotions to Catholic ceremonies and cosmologies.

Much difficulty exists in finding one word in Yoeme to describe ways of making sense of the world. This is to be expected when most indigenous communities, at least in precolonial times, did not interpret social relations as distinctly economic, political, or technological. My research confirms the ways that many native peoples have conceived of their worlds as a single interrelated network of social relations that include other-than-human persons. If the Yoeme have no indigenous word for the cultural category of religion, then in precontact times and still for some, they have not understood their world as having split into sacred and profane realms.

Without such a split, indigenous religions have remained elusive to the academic study of religion because, with few exceptions, academics continue to define religion as either a belief system or a way to manage some form of a sacred-profane dichotomy. The ramifications of such thinking are paramount because by equating native lifeways with other religions, indigenous intellectuals and scholars are complicit in the loss of land and even tribal status. To fully have that debate here would turn this book into one about scholarly concerns rather than about the community that hosts me, another persistent problem in academic representations of native communities. How does one write a book about indigenous peoples without the subjects becoming objects, without the living people becoming things to study in order to test academic theories?

At an earlier stage of this research, I asked Greg Sarris, the well-known indigenous writer, to help me conceive of a book that would satisfy both the academic community and the native readers. It seemed to me that he had come some ways in achieving such a text with his wonderful *Mabel McKay: Weaving the Dream*. His response was quick and clear: it cannot be done. As he saw it, the two communities have differing notions of responsibility that could not be reconciled within the pages of a single text. Either the academic community would be dissatisfied that such work is valid or tenure-worthy, or the native community would feel used and objectified. At the time, I was frustrated by his resolve on the matter, but I remained also intellectually stimulated and challenged.

My response to the challenge is this study of Yoeme lifeways. By "study," however, I do not mean objective and distanced. More so perhaps than a scholar should, I downplay when the Yoeme materials fuel an academic debate and leave many (though not all) of those discussions suggested in the endnotes. I use the Yoeme material to critique notions of "conversion," and I evaluate professional histories of Yoeme-European contact according to how such histories account for Yoeme prophecy.[13] At one point in the text, I step back to reframe the discussion within philosophical debates and contemporary indigenous struggles elsewhere. Since this is a book about the Yoemem, I do not give that one section the status of a chapter. Some readers may even choose to skip that interchapter. Additionally, I supplant each chapter with an almost direct transcript from my field interviews. Within the intersections of the chapters and the interviews lies a critique of the ethnological sciences, but again, one that I intentionally choose not to make explicit, or this book would be another sort of book. The interviews remind us of the difficult and suspicious work of turning travel into cultural interpretation. And they keep us mindful that not all cultural insiders are wise, not all "outsiders" are ignorant, and some questions elicit responses but not necessarily answers. Still, we must be committed to the dialogue.

Preview

This study frequently refers to the general worldview or topology of the Yoeme people. Chapter 1 surveys this cosmology in specifically spatial terms, particularly in my discussion of *aniam*, Yoeme "worlds of being." Although I hesitate to suggest that all Yoeme people have one view of the world, I am confident that the maps I sketch reflect a way of knowing the world shared by elder, conservative, and/or most southern Yoeme people. Just as differing individual interpretations of "tradition" exist in all communities, some Yoemem may think that the aniam I describe belong to a more ancient time and that my descriptions only continue the "spiritualized" representation of Indian peoples. Indeed, there is considerable force to Sherman Alexie's argument that the market of non-Indian readers leads many writers to continue representing Native Americans in romantically religious terms (Brill de Ramirez 1999). I can only refer such critics to the people from whom I learned these ways: the families in Potam Pueblo, Las Guásimas, and Marana Pueblo and the ritual performers with whom I have associated since 1993. I also concur with Juan Valenzuela, who told Spicer to focus on the religion in order to understand Yoeme history. Finally, as I have come to understand it, "religion" is not some underlying "spiritual" essence but a dynamic process, inscribing histories in specific places and valuing actions and texts within relations of power. Since the remaining chapters make references to the various aniam, or states of being, in Yoeme topology, I begin with the unfolding of a religio-spatial map.

Chapter 2 moves from a general consideration of Yoeme cosmology to an analysis of Yoeme territory. Specifically, this chapter focuses on the Testamento as a primary corpus of Yoeme myth and history. Since previous scholars have examined the Testamento in great detail, I dwell on the implications of understanding this narrative for a reexamination of Yoeme ritual and land rights. No other scholar has placed the Testamento in conversation with other Yoeme myths as a means of inferring Yoeme cosmologies before European contact. My use of "in conversation" is intentional here and describes an important process in the interpretation of a community's oral and written traditions. To understand the dynamics between two or more forms of communication, we must listen to what they say about each other. The work entails listening to written texts and reading spoken texts. In the Yoeme context, we see that some of their traditions of writing include a performed or spoken section. Similarly, some Yoemem clearly intended their oral stories to be written and disseminated by literate communities such as academics. Writing, like any form of memory and representation, is strategic.

Chapter 3 develops the argument that talking tree stories are ways of historicizing Yoeme agency in early contact zones. The chapter analyzes nine versions of the talking tree myth in order to show how Yoeme prophetic stories complicate commonplace notions of Native American history. First, by explaining how the tree foretold the coming of the Spanish, Yoeme historical discourse displaces a Euro-centered story where narratives of native pasts are subsumed under the dominant historic trope of progressive/tragic European expansionism (Dirlik 2000, 28–30; J. Smith 1978, 295). Second, by understanding how the tree's prophecies led to a split between proto-Yoemem who move to accessible underground worlds and Yoemem who decide to stay and accept the European cultural syncretism, we are offered a model of indigenism that allows for both aboriginal continuity and cultural adaptation. Talking tree stories are examples of a non-Western, nonlinear history: a local consumption of the global (Sahlins 1994). Yoemem subsume the all-encompassing European historical trajectory in their prophetic anticipation of Western peoples and knowledge. Yoeme mythology emerges as a native historiographic practice, since Yoemem make internal sense of changes from the outside world.

In chapter 4 I demonstrate how the core narrative components of the talking tree myth offer a Yoeme-centered approach, inflecting the histories written by the two best known historians of Yoeme culture, Edward H. Spicer and Evelyn Hu-DeHart. Building on recent work in American Indian studies, this chapter reassesses the contact histories provided by Spicer and Hu-DeHart and demonstrates ways that notions of "conquest" and "conversion" may not adequately represent Yoeme-European relations. By reading the talking tree myth as primary historical evidence, we gain perspective on Yoeme agency and ingenuity within both the early contact zone and contemporary sovereignty movements.

The second half of this book moves the discussion of Yoeme identity into contemporary ethnographic contexts. In a theoretical interlude, what I call an "interchapter," I develop an argument regarding the need to move away from restrictive definitions of "writing" when working with non-Western historiography. Much canonical literature assumes writing to be a fundamental component of "civilized" societies, a notion that has long negatively affected indigenous peoples; this chapter suggests the very real implications of this prejudice in courts of law. At the heart of the larger ethnography, this interlude expands notions of inscription to include speech and ritual acts. Consequently, my argument presents a truncated critique of the civilizational and absolutist dichotomy, oral and literate. Here I prepare the ground for the following two chapters, which examine the performative and inscriptive ways Yoemem understand themselves and their histories.

Chapter 5 centers on the often described and studied deer dances. Along the Mexico–U.S. border, the image of the deer dancer appears as a symbol of Indianness. A shirtless Indian figure with a deer head strapped on top of his own head, holding gourd rattles and wearing butterfly cocoons strung around his calves, the image speaks to aboriginal "tradition" in ways similar to the *katchina* image for Pueblo Indians or the totem pole stereotype of Pacific Northwest tribes. In popular ethnographic literature, the deer dancer is characterized as the most "ancient" of the Yoeme expressions. Based on this exoticism, more descriptive attention has been given to Yoeme deer dancing than to any other aspect of their culture. Assessing this previous research, I add my own ethnographic descriptions of deer dances and advance the claim that these dances embody Yoeme views of knowledge and truth. Tracing the ties between contemporary deer dances and precolonial deer hunting rituals, we are able to see how Christian personae such as Jesus and Mary make sense according to indigenous concepts of kin solidarity. Building on the interchapter's theoretical framework, chapter 5 demonstrates how deer dancing explains Yoeme-Catholicism as a process where native cosmological ethics remain unconverted.

In chapter 6 I return to my initial spatial focus, examining the performative ways that Yoemem historicize and map their territory and identities. This chapter looks closely at funerary practices and Sunday church processions. Using "place-making" to describe the ceremonial, embodied grounding of local history, I attend to how these acts include boundary-marking processes. The animam miika ceremonies, or offerings to the departed, provide a context for understanding the ethnic boundaries demarcated by differences between Yoeme and Mexican cemetery activities. Since the departed souls come back to earth to visit the living for the entire month before animam miika, chapter 6 also describes how some Yoemem conceive of their cosmological boundaries as permeable, both Catholic and indigenous in nature. The books of the dead, called animam, are written in and read from during this ritual. As family books, these animam underlie the importance of Yoeme writing traditions, now connected with genealogies. At the same time, cosmological references to heaven, hell, and seven indigenous realms provide a rich context by which to understand the dimensional boundaries within Yoeme Catholicism. As noted in the description of the Testamento above, in "singing the boundaries," prophets visit Yoeme territory after a flood and lead Yoeme survivors in processions across the land, establishing the boundary, or "holy dividing line," of Yoeme territory. Resembling this myth, large groups of Yoemem still escort Catholic statues in Sunday processions, called *kontim*, around their pueblos during the Lenten season. These embodied movements through the desert link Yoeme collective identity with their land and create a sense of belonging to a cosmologically designated place. Synthesizing the previous chapters, I describe ritual action as the inscriptive acts by which Yoemem narrate their historic relations with ancestors, with non-Yoemem, and, perhaps more fundamentally, with their land.

Understanding Yoeme processions as religious acts of place-making enables me to benefit from works in the study of indigenous religions as well as the growing body of literature in cultural geography. In the field of religious studies, the literature on native religions provides a wealth of tribal case studies and theoretical approaches (Joseph Brown 1977; Capps 1976; Geertz 1994; Hultkrantz 1981; Williamson 1984). Whereas some of these works address the complexities of religious change and continuity (Deloria 1994; Treat 1996; Vecsey 1990, 1991), and some link native identity with land (Feld and Basso 1996; Gill 1982, 1998), none seems to be asking how indigenous ritual performance, as spatial practice, mediates the syncretizing effects of colonization and missionization. I hope to fill this interpretive gap by considering Yoeme ethnic endurance as an active, embodied fusion of religious and geographic sensibilities.

While other scholars have focused on concepts of place in their ethnographies (Basso 1996; Classen 1993; Cruikshank 1998; Deloria 1994; Farrer 1991; Geertz 1984; Harrod 1987; Irwin 1994; Sullivan 1989), only a handful have offered in-depth analysis of how native regard for place is religiously grounded through maintenance of ethnic boundaries (Erickson 2008; Kugel 1998; Meyer 1994). The Yoeme context is unique due to their relative control of colonial contact zones and missionary practices, their long history of north/south travel and the resulting binational configurations, and their mythistoric models and practices of border creation and maintenance. Yoeme rituals reflect cosmological models of cultural solidarity as well as their transnational status. Drawing from and contributing to conversations in anthropology, ethnohistory, and religious studies, I show how one indigenous community uses religious rituals to inscribe localized selfness within and across surrounding ethnic and national boundaries.

My Yoeme friends, collaborators, and ceremonial family members in Potam Pueblo heavily influence the approach I take. My relations with Yoemem began in 1993 when I met Felipe Molina. He was raised deeply aware of the mythology and ceremonial activities of the tribe. He was once the governor of Marana Pueblo, and he coauthored the watershed text *Yaqui Deer Songs/Maso Bwikam* with Larry Evers. He has written community oral histories and a couple of Yoeme language dictionaries. Although he is only one of my collaborators, his influence on my work cannot be overlooked. For the beginning years of fieldwork, he was my translator. Throughout the last nine years, Molina has accompanied me on many of my visits to Potam as a translator, interpreter, scholar, and as one of my dearest friends. His family members around Tucson have welcomed me into their homes and at times have traveled with us to the Hiak Vatwe. In the southern villages, Molina's relatives have invited me to stay in their homes, they have nursed me through colds and other maladies, answered my stream of questions, shown me around the hiakim, fed me constantly, and invited me into their kinship as a *kompae* (godfather).[14] As with other authors, his last name, Molina, appears throughout the text, although I refer to him in field notes as "Felipe."

Since 2002 I have also begun filming in the pueblo. Ten years after first working with Potam residents, I welcomed their invitation to begin recording dances and ceremonies. Since non-Yoeme academics are rarely invited to live within the pueblos, I have been gifted a certain access to Yoeme cultural interpretations and religious performances. Readers hoping to see examples of dances and hear clips of the music described in the following pages can visit my Web site, http://hemi.nyu.edu/cuaderno/yoeme/content.html.

As with all ethnographies, I have my blind spots. I cannot speak with any qualification about women's religious societies or the secretive men's *fariseos* and coyote groups. These are just two of the many absences from a total picture of Yoeme lifeways, as though such a composite were possible. Since they are instructive cases, and will be glaring to those familiar with Yoeme culture and literature, I should say a bit more. In this text, I refrain from discussing or even using the Yoeme word commonly used to describe the large, masked, "folded nose" ceremonial society. Although this society is not what we might technically call a "secret society," some Yoeme collaborators have said that I should only hear about their group from actual members, and several respected elders have gone as far to say that even their formal name should not be said outside of Lent. My conversations with members of that group lead me to trust the statements of the elders and not write anything about them. Likewise, I had a chapter drafted about the Coyote Society, or Wiko'i ya'ura. Although that research enriched my project overall, I came to a point where I realized that writing about the Coyote Society endangered more than it helped contemporary political situations.

There are other areas of research where I chose to draw the line, or where I followed the advice of my Yoeme collaborators rather than the advice of my academic advisors. A final disclaimer is that I do not speak for Yoemem on the north side of the U.S.–Mexico border, although some of the material here draws from and contributes to their collective history. Simply put, I am a non-Yoeme American academic who has ceremonial relations with people in Potam Pueblo. In more ways than any ethnographer cares to admit, my complex identity prevents me from gaining access to certain activities, dialogues, and associations. I try to keep these limits in view by using "some" or "many" when describing worldviews and activities. Additionally, my field notes demonstrate my partial and situated perspectives. My Yoeme collaborators in this research include elementary schoolteachers, ceremonial performers, linguists, fieldworkers, basket weavers, and college-educated intellectuals. I invite my collaborators to review my "data." I also invite them to shape my methods and theories. Such important work deserves more recognition than "anonymous respondent," which I use throughout my transcribed interviews. Yet anyone familiar with contemporary tribal politics and violence can attest to the importance of keeping certain sources confidential. By combining these collaborations, my fieldwork, archival research, and a careful review of previous ethnographies of Yoemem, I am able to confirm and amplify Edward Spicer's claim that the Yoemem are a remarkably "enduring people" (1980: 330–62). A quarter century after Spicer wrote that, I show here how that endurance continues, just not in ways or for the reasons previously described. Yoeme stories of homeland, kinship solidarity, prophecy, ceremonial dances, burial rites, and processions are both historiographic and ethnographic.

1 Geography of Yoeme Identities

Hakwo ketun Itom Ae Mariata into Jesusta inim bwiapo am ho'ako ian um Hiak bwiapo wa huya ania kaita kawekantea. Senu taa'apo Jesus Itom Aetau o'omtek hita vetchi'ivosu humaku'u. Jesus Itom Aeta tehwak ke apo au hoarata tosimvaetia. Itom Ae intok hiokot au hia ka sim'i'akai. Apo ala haivu au tu'uten huya aniau vicha wevaekai. Itom Ae into aa asoawa sak tuhta nuteriak. Itom Ae uka sak tuhta vemela, ka haitimachi tahorimpo aa vihtariak hunakvea ili kutat a sumak Jesusta henomet a weiyane vetchi'ibo.

Jesus vea vo'ota nuka huya aniapo weamak. Haiki taewaimpo apo huya aniapo weamak hunaksanvea ume tahorim siutitaitek. Hunama ili siutaipo u sak tusi yeu wotitaitek um bwiau kom vicha. Huna sak tusi hunak bwiau kom wotekame san ume kawim ian itom vicha'um.

[When Our Mother Mary and Jesus lived on earth in the present-day Yaqui country, the wilderness was without mountains. One day Jesus got mad at our Mother for some reason. Jesus told Our Mother that he was going to leave home. Our Mother tried to discourage him from leaving. His mind was already set on going, so he readied himself for the departure into the wilderness. Our Mother prepared her son some lunch, which was *sak tusi* (cornmeal). Our Mother put the sak tusi in a new clean cloth and tied it into a bundle on a stick so that Jesus could carry it on his shoulders.

Jesus left on his journey and wandered in the wilderness. For many days he traveled in the wilderness, and his cloth bundle began to tear. From this small tear the sak tusi began to spill out onto the ground. So all the sak tusi that fell to the ground at that time formed the mountains we see today.]

PAULA CASTILLO VALLE, as told to her son, Felipe Molina

In the story presented here, "How the Mountains Were Created," Paula Valle provides a beautiful example of how Yoemem tell stories of Jesus, Mary, and their land that combine the times and places of the past to validate a grounded identity that is felt today (Evers 1981b, 211). Valle's story stresses the humanity of Mary and her son, Jesus, while locating their lives in the Hiak Vatwe. Listening to the story helps us understand the depth to which many Yoemem fuse indigenous identity with Catholicism in the communities: Catholic personae live in the Yoeme homeland before Yoemem build pueblos. Jesus, more like a stubborn trickster than an all-knowing God, accidentally helps create the world. Valle's story offers an appropriate beginning for this chapter, since it speaks clearly about Yoeme memories and is centrally concerned with religiously transformed space. Beginning with a review of cultural differences between temporally and spatially informed identities, I examine how Yoeme ritual activity proceeds from an indigenous Catholicism that annually re-members (bodying again) precontact worlds to celebrate Jesus's life and death.[1]

Many Yoemem identify as Catholic Christians, and some refer constantly to Mary, Jesus, and the saints, thinking of heaven as a place where their good deeds are taken into account. On that level, the Jesuits seemingly succeeded in changing an indigenous culture, shifting a worldview from its spatial foundation to a new, temporal basis. Many Yoemem do seem to understand sin as an individual matter and separate the lone person from eternal glory. Many also understand Jesus, Mary, and the saints as ultimate benefactors and themselves as undeserving supplicants. In these ways, some Yoemem engage notions of ultimacy and transcendence that suggest Yoemem have undergone a radical conversion. These factors reveal a sense of the religious that is other than oriented to the here and now. But there is no line between the two worldviews that can be drawn easily in the Yoeme case.

Yoemem remember their cultural inheritance in ways that are focused on particular places and specific movements through those places. Among people I have worked with in several Yoeme pueblos, the world is multidimensional, and this multidimensionality — the creation, recognition, and access to both different and overlapping states of being — grounds their rituals and identity. In spite of the genocidal brutality, dire poverty, and results of colonization, Yoemem survive strongly and devote large amounts of resources on ritual ceremonies that involve thousands of people and stretch over many months. These ceremonies are dramatic performances; they almost always entail masks, costumes, music, singing, oratory, and unimaginable physical labor. By seeing Yoeme collective identity as embodied in these ritual performances, we see that many Yoemem spatialize their cosmology into multiple worlds, or *aniam*, and that these places provide Yoemem spaces to enact their identities and share them with their plant, animal, and ancestral families. Danced at the climax of their Easter celebrations and during all-night ceremonies for saints' feast days and for relatives' death anniversaries, for example, the deer dance features some of the more aboriginal elements of Yoeme expressive culture. The deer dance brings the aniam into the present for the performers and audience and creates a distinctly Yoeme space. These indigenous worlds provide context for Yoeme identity and lay the groundwork for other relationships between these worlds and the Catholic dimensions of heaven, hell, and, to a lesser extent, purgatory.

This hike seems longer than most of the others. It also feels hotter than our earlier trip to the Hiak Vatwe, and we have been at three pueblos since sunrise. Felipe leads, while I drag behind, carrying the camera cases and our lunches. At practically every stop, a Yoeme family prepares us a meal upon arrival and usually one for the road if we accept their offers. I look at the small salads that were prepared for us in Las Guásimas and think about how hungry I will continue to be even after eating. It won't be enough for us, especially considering the fatigue that we're building from hiking, all because I told Felipe that I wanted to see if the legend was true that Jesus's handprint was somewhere among the pueblos.

Looking ahead, I see three mountains, the first small, then a larger one, and the third larger still. When we reach the top of the first hill, we rest by a four-foot cross that has been secured there with a pyramid of rocks. Felipe decides that this will be a good place to rest and eat the salads. I take off my cowboy hat and place it next to the camera bags. Felipe reminds me that Yoemem place their hats on their tops, so that the opening is facing upward. "That way, it will collect the flowers." I turn my hat over and smile, too tired to reply or to ask further questions. I hand Felipe his salad and begin to remove the plastic wrap that is covering mine. Without utensils, I immediately start shoving pieces of lettuce and carrots into my mouth. I can't remember enjoying a better bowl of shredded vegetables. Glancing back at Felipe, I see that he has yet to taste his lunch. Instead, he is taking a couple of pieces of each vegetable and placing them in a pile at the foot of the cross. He blesses the food by making a cross motion over it, and then he says a short prayer. Shamefully I swallow the food in my mouth, stand, and move to place some of my salad next to his pile.

Sitting back down, I take notice of our view. Looking to the east, I see miles and miles of green land, covered with large trees that extend all the way to the mountains. The mountains themselves appear lush with vegetation. They must be at least thirty miles away. To the north lies a huge stretch of crops, the lines of growth extending miles within their individual squares. I see the southern slope of the hill we are on to my right, leading to a smaller section of green farming land. I look behind me, and there is Felipe, sitting in front of the willow cross and the two larger hills to the west. A cool breeze caresses my face and dries the perspiration on my forehead. I feel the wind blow through my sleeves, slightly lifting the shirt away from my back. An unknown smell of some tree drifts sweetly in the air. Perhaps I smell a flower in bloom. We sit there in silence while finishing our lunches. I then take our Styrofoam bowls and stuff them into the camera bags. Felipe asks me if I am ready to move on, and I put my hat back on and sling the photo equipment over my shoulder. Just smiling, I start leading the way.

Climbing the second hill, Felipe asks me if I knew that Jesus had walked the Yoeme land a long time ago. Still in motion, I remind him that we looked for Jesus's footprint on our last trip down here. As if I hadn't said a word, Felipe adds that in certain places there are traces of where Jesus stopped in his travels *through the pueblos to heal people. Felipe says that Jesus left his handprint in the rocks somewhere on the third hill. Remembering my frustrated search for his footprint by the Hiak Vatwe the year before, and expecting more of the same, I tell Felipe that it would be great if we saw them up there. When we reach the downward slope of this second hill, Felipe directs my attention to the third and largest hill ahead of us. The entire upward slope is covered with massive boulders, black, like volcanic rocks with smooth surfaces. I can't help but think that they would make perfect homes for snakes. Feeling energetic, I move ahead anyway, jumping onto the first boulder in my path.*

Felipe takes his own path about fifteen feet away. We both climb faster than before. At times we are on different sides of the hill, both jumping from boulder to boulder. Some of the rocks move under my feet, forcing me to balance quickly with every leap. I can tell from the sounds of Felipe's footfalls that he has gained a lead. I unload the camera bags on the first flat rock I can find and start taking larger jumps. Reaching the top, I see that Felipe is walking around, searching the boulders. One large tree grows from the center of the hilltop. Although the tree must branch out at fifteen feet above soil, boulders surround the trunk for twelve of those feet, creating a silo of rocks with one lone tree trunk rising up in the middle. Felipe and I start heading to the top of the stones surrounding the tree. He says, "People have seen the handprint up here, but I am not sure exactly where it is." I silently hope I'm not being dragged on another fruitless expedition for evidence in the "field." About to give up hope, I look over at his face and realize that Felipe enjoys these adventures — and not egotistically because I respect him as a cultural insider. By continually asking to see the many respected places of Yoeme folklore, I invite Felipe to search for himself, to plan, pursue, and relive his previous adventures. Or perhaps my ethnographic work provides a reason to see something himself for the first time. No longer just for me, I join his search, stepping from boulder to boulder on the other side of the tree.

"Oh, wow! Here it is!" I turn around before the words completely escape Felipe's mouth. I jump, stone by stone, over to the rock next to the one Felipe is standing on. I peer down into the well formed by the wall of boulders around the tree. There it is, a right handprint. It must be ten feet down, but it is easy to see. It seems to be glowing. I ask Felipe if we could climb down in there. Felipe

reminds me of the possibility of snakes and adds that a fall would make the rest of the trip more difficult for one of us. I agree. Then, three seconds later, I grab one of the branches and swing myself down between the rocks and the tree. Using the stones and the side of the tree as opposing ladders, I slowly move downward until the handprint is at eye level. I place my feet on the rocks and straighten my legs so that my back is flush with the tree and my weight is supported by the tension of my outstretched legs. I look up at Felipe, and he smiles with slightly feigned astonishment; it must have taken me all of a minute to get there. I surprise myself by mouthing a "thank-you" to the powers that be. I reach out my right hand and place it on the print in the stone.

To my amazement, my hand sinks slightly into the rock. The print is actually an indentation. The seeming glow comes from the shape's contours reaching into a deeper surface of the boulder, exposing a crystalline texture. Felipe asks me if my hand fits perfectly. I move my hand to match the palm, my fingertips just slightly reaching past the end of the print. I yell up to Felipe, "Almost! Jesus must have been shorter than six-foot-one, or at least he had a smaller hand!" After I say another prayer, more of a body reflex than a conscious will to communicate, I start heading back up to the top. Felipe grabs the same tree branch I did and moves toward the print. By the time I get fully out of the hole, Felipe is already placing his hand in the rock. He yells up, "My hand fits perfectly!" He looks up, grinning, and I can't help but laugh at the small ways we have grown competitive in our friendship. While Felipe stays down there in silence, I look down the slope of the hill and see my camera equipment. I question my own desire to document the handprint. Was I trained somewhere to want evidence beyond my own experience? What would a photo prove? To whom? Without saying a word, I wait for Felipe to climb out. We look at the land around us, we look down at the handprint one last time, and we start heading down the hill. I grab my camera bags on the way down. Reaching the bottom of the three hills, I ask Felipe if he thinks I should take a picture of the three hills in the sunset. He says that it would make a beautiful picture.

Singing and Dancing Worlds of Meaning

The watershed text in Yoeme autoethnography and collaborative scholarship on Yoeme musicology is Larry Evers and Felipe Molina's

Yaqui Deer Songs/Maso Bwikam. They translate deer songs into English and interpret these songs for their readers. Before doing so, however, Evers and Molina prioritize questions about the origins of the deer songs, where the singers learn the songs, and how the ability to sing well comes from specific dimensions within Yoeme cosmography. The authors direct attention to the spatiality of deer ceremonies by titling the chapter "Yeu A Weepo/Where It Comes Out." Evers and Molina relate a time when a tree talked to the immortal Yoeme ancestors, called Surem: it spoke in a foreign language to a young woman who translated the prophecy to community members. She told them of the future, about the coming of the Europeans, their practice of baptism, and their worship of God. The tree sang about the end of one way of life and the beginning of another, one that would include mortality. The Surem-Yoemem division and cohesion literally ground a belonging in the Sonoran desert. Yoeme ancestors could remain in the geography by declining baptism; contemporary Yoeme kinship extends literally into the ground and the surrounding landscape. The contours of this dynamic must be understood in order to make sense of all Yoeme myth, ritual, and worldview. The rituals within the communities work effectively with the simultaneous movements and staying of Yoeme ancestors.

In every account of the singing tree, we are told that the Surem held a meeting in which they divided themselves into two groups: those who would choose baptism and this new life, and those who would maintain their pre-Christian lives and so remain immortal. This latter group "stayed around and went into the ocean and underground into the mountains. There in those places the Surem now exist as a knowing, powerful people. Those who stayed behind are now the modern Yaquis, and they are called the Baptized Ones" (Evers and Molina 1987, 38). Evers and Molina note that the "relation between these two parts of the Yaqui world is complex and reciprocal, and it bears directly on our understanding of deer songs" (1987, 38). Evers and Molina enable us to see that all interpretations of Yoeme deer ceremonies must recognize the division between the baptized ones and the Surem.

Yoeme ritual performances, like written and oral traditions, are acts of memory, reconstituting and re-membering the spaces of a shared Yoeme past. By looking at how people make space, or spatialization, I support the view that cosmological and geographical maps stand as primary indicators of cultural identity since they delineate the world of possibilities for human existence. Yoeme spatiality consists of interrelated realms, some more pre-Christian than others, but all combined to form a cohesive Yoeme worldview.[2] To gain understanding of these domains and dimensions, I follow Evers and Molina, who write that these aniam "are visible only in the private eye of dream and vision, and they are made public only when they are put into words in stories individuals tell of their own experiences and those of others. The actions of the *pahko'olam* and the deer dancer during a *pahko* may be thought of as reflections of experience performers have had in one of the other worlds" (1987, 45). Stories are persuasive, ontologically effective, and create truth. Not wanting to take this epistemological claim lightly, nor wanting to divert focus from Yoemem, I proceed from the notion that primarily oral communities define and create truth through socially performed labor, not limited to but including the verbal arts. I look at the places remembered in deer dancing and singing and contextualize these places by reviewing the stories told about them. Connecting the work of Evers and Molina with Edward Spicer's concerns, I demonstrate that in these acts of remembering such places Yoemem maintain a unique and "enduring" identity.

Evers and Molina wished to understand the creation of deer songs, and they sought out a respected and knowledgeable Yoeme elder, Don Jesús Yoi Lo'i. Asked about the beginning of these songs, Don Jesús referred to the first Yoemem, the Surem, "a race of people of small stature, 'little people,' who inhabited what are now the Yaqui lands in the days before European contact. Yoemem widely understand the Surem as people of great knowledge, attuned to all the ways of the Sonoran desert and the living things in it" (1987, 42). The Surem live in a world known as the huya ania, roughly translated as "wilderness world." While the Yoeme term *huya* can be used to designate a branch, a whole plant, or the entire desert, Evers and Molina stress that an adequate translation of huya ania must include "a rich poetic and spiritual and human dimension of the area surrounding the Yaqui villages as well" (1987, 44). The huya ania was all the Surem knew, since the missionaries had not yet arrived to help form the eight pueblos. Evers and Molina say that the huya ania includes the spiritual and human dimensions of Surem life, and many Yoemem say that the sea ania and yo ania are considered emerging within the huya ania.

The relationship between deer performances and the place called *sea ania*, or flower world, is centered on the word *seyewailo*. Appearing in almost all the deer songs that Evers and Molina recorded, seyewailo designates "that convergence of time, place, direction, and quality of being that is for Yaquis the essence of what they call the sea ania, the flower world, the convergence at which Wok Vake'o found the little fawn and the inspiration for the first deer song" (1987, 51). Every act of deer singing, then, since Wok Vake'o's first, describes the sea ania and through the labor of the singers and dancers re-creates this place of flowers that grows from and contributes to the communities' shared inheritance of the aniam, the aboriginal dimensions or states of being.

In singing the deer songs, Yoemem are not only commemorating the first song sung in the sea ania but also opening the doors of the world through which saila maaso (little brother deer) passes into the dance area, making the dance area the seyewailo. The sea ania is described by most as the huya ania in bloom, a perfect image of the beautiful outside world. Located by most Yoemem in the east, beneath the dawn, the sea ania refers to the world of flowers, the beginning of life, and the result of hard work. The sea ania is the home of the actual embodiment of sacrifice, the deer. When Muriel Painter, a collector and publisher of Yoeme perspectives on their own culture, asked Yoemem if it is a mythical world, she was told that "it is real" and "it is the living beautiful part of our present world" (Painter 1986, 18–19). A Yoeme writer, Refugio Savala, also tells of the presentness of the sea ania in his autobiography when he writes: "Again, Tucson was pretty on my side of town. The irrigation canal from Silver Lake Dam went through, so the *seya aniya* was lively and lovely, and there was a willow tree grove across from our house" (1980, 27). In consideration of Painter's collaborators and Savala, then, we must see the sea ania as a real and present aspect of the huya ania — that place in the huya ania where deer live, that area of the *pahkom* where deer dance, and that realm of the world where Yoemem understand perfect sacrificial beauty being born.

By this point it should be fairly clear that to study either the physical landscape or the cosmic dimensions would be to see only part of Yoeme religious identity. The aniam, or worlds, are areas of the physical landscape, yet some also consider them states of being. Yoeme aniam reference both physical and cosmic realms. As not-simply-physical spaces, aniam help Yoeme spatial identity endure. Rather than being separate aspects of Yoeme space, the geographical and the cosmological can be understood as one and the same: the huya ania is the wilderness world *and* the range of beings in that world and their related powers. The sea ania is the wilderness world, blooming in the east, *and* it is the world that is reestablished anywhere a pahko begins, the mythistorical home of our brother deer. By locating Yoeme spatiality as cosmic dimensions with physical references, it follows that diasporic movements, loss of land, and changes in sustenance have failed to diminish the strength of Yoeme identity. If the important places of Yoeme culture are re-created and re-membered through ritual performance, then distance from the Hiak Vatwe does not prevent Yoemem in Arizona from entering these places every time they dance deer. While older Yoemem might spend warm evenings recounting the prediasporic days of worry and wonder, the sense of loss is lessened by the ever-present experience and knowledge of being at home. In Yoeme communities both north and south of the U.S.–Mexico border, many Yoemem, particularly elders, perceive other worlds, beneath the dawn, a flower world, a world within the land and waters.

The yo ania is a perfect example of a place that many Yoemem locate geographically in the physical landscape, while also a precontact world — a world still very real and powerful for some visitors. The yo ania is the home of the Surem, located by some in mountain caves that open to the west. The yo ania is not only the strongest tie between

Yoemem and their Surem ancestors but also the realm most shaded by scholarly doubt and misrepresentation. Perhaps, as Evers and Molina note of the aniam, "Some feel that it is not appropriate to discuss some aspects of them with outsiders at all" (1987, 45). In light of many conflicting stories about the yo ania in Painter's book, *With Good Heart*, many Yoemem she questioned gave intentionally misleading descriptions of the yo ania, or they spoke in terms — anthropological language or Christian concepts — that they thought Painter would understand.[3] However, as will be clear in this study, when knowledgeable Yoeme elders speak about the yo ania, they designate this world as the most respected and indigenous of Yoeme places.[4]

Evers and Molina expertly describe how the yo ania relates to concepts of space, place, and aboriginal identity. Locating the yo ania as "another space within the huya ania," Evers and Molina offer the following etymology of the term *yo ania*:

> *Yo* is another Yaqui word that is not easily translated. The verb *yo'otu* means "to grow old" and the verb *yo'ore* "to respect or venerate." In Yaqui communities an old and respected elder is called *yo'owe*, and in these contexts, *yo* may itself be translated as "old." But especially when it is used with *ania*, *yo* suggests not just "old" but the oldest old, the ancient, the primordial. The yo ania is an ancient world, a mythic place outside historic time and space, yet it can be present in the most immediate way. *Yo* refers to the essential and originative quality of being in that time and place. Both Felipe's grandfather, Rosario Castillo, and Don Lupe [respected Yoeme elders] translated *yo* as "encanto"; we translate *yo* as "enchanted." (1987, 62)

The yo ania clearly embodies the most ancestral ways of life for Yoemem. In the above quotation, Evers and Molina help outline the difficulties involved in translating *yo ania* as "sacred" or conceiving it as referring solely to a physical place. Wanting to avoid Judeo-Christian concepts that burden our interpretations with ineffective and in some cases detrimental dichotomies (sacred/profane, holy/mundane, spiritual/physical), I have many concerns about the use of words that signify something "mysterious" and therefore out of the realms of understandability. In my own writing, I am wary of how the word *enchanted* plays into common associations with *magical*, and therefore I utilize *respected* more so. Evers and Molina tell us that yo ania is the oldest of the old, but they specifically say that world is present, living, and available; the yo ania is "mythic" only because it is a place outside of place and time, and yet it can be immediately available in the here and now.

Deepening their readers' understanding of the relation between the yo ania, the sea ania, and the huya ania, Evers and Molina cite a Yoeme elder explaining how saila maaso comes out of the yo ania, an actual home inside the sea ania, which is in the huya ania. We can also understand how the worlds interrelate by listening to what is always the first song of the pahko ceremonial dances, "Sewailo Malichi." Translated by Molina, the deer singers sing, "Flower-covered fawn went out, enchanted, from each enchanted flower, wilderness world, he went out" (1987, 88). The first verse, then, of the first song, at every pahko, is an act of spatialization, since it creates a space for the deer to be born, a space that is in the wilderness, among the flowers. Bringing all three worlds together — huya ania, sea ania, yo ania — the deer singers introduce the deer and his worlds to the ceremonial participants and audience. Since the deer dancer brings the lyrics to life, Yoemem dance deer to reestablish themselves in relation to these worlds, especially the most ancient, the yo ania. The performance is at once an act of memory and a ritual sharing of identity, grounded in remembering and re-membering the places of their ancestors. In the starkest terms, they make the old new once again.

As both a geographical and a cosmological state of being, the yo ania is also connected to the art of dancing deer and pahko'ola in that it provides the power and talent to perform the rituals. In ways similar to vision quests in other southwestern indigenous cultures, Yoemem sometimes search out the yo ania in order to gain the ability to dance beautifully. Molina notes that "when someone has ability from the enchanted homes and the enchanted world, he can dance well" (1987, 101). Yoemem may stumble upon the yo ania by virtue of having a good heart, out in the wilderness, at the right time, in the right place, "with good heart" being a widespread description of those who embody self-sacrifice and thoughtfulness toward others in the community. There are Yoemem who tell stories of reaching the yo ania by achieving a proper state of mind, as in a state of meditation.

Telling Stories as Making Place

To demonstrate the pervasiveness of yo ania tales and their actuality in Yoeme culture, I turn now to the storied ways of knowing the yo ania. In *Yoeme: Lore of the Arizona Yaqui People*, Herminia Valenzuela asks Yoeme elders about the special places, and three of her contributors discuss the yo ania in Sikili Kawi, Red Mountain. Although more of a hill than a mountain, Sikili Kawi is within walking distance from Torim Pueblo, on the way to Vicam Switch, another pueblo in the Hiak Vatwe. Valenzuela is told the following description of the yo ania: "There is one spot on the mountain, an indention, which leads into a large cave inside. At high noon you can stick your head in and hear beautiful supernatural music coming out of it. This is the *Yo-Ania*, an enchanted world where you can pick up a talent, like playing a musical instrument, singing, without having to practice" (13).[5] In the story that Valenzuela is told, Yoemem locate the yo ania at an actual physical location, accessed through an opening in the mountain. Inside are Surem holding pahkom who will take their guest on a tour though the yo ania, eventually testing the visitor's strength, courage, and heart. If humans fail the test, they may go crazy or die. If humans succeed, they can choose the talent or power they would like to take back to the realm of Yoeme community life.

In Valenzuela's book, Carmen Garcia tells a secondhand account of someone who goes to the yo ania through the passage in Sikili Kawi. A well-loved Yoeme elder, Garcia, tells Valenzuela that "back in the old days when your Pa Grande Rosario was young, he and a friend were able to enter into Sikili Kawi. Your Pa Grande Rosario's friend chose the gift of making himself invisible at will" (13). Looking at Muriel Painter's compendium of Yoeme stories, Garcia's claim is one of many, not only about Sikili Kawi but also about mountains across the Sonoran desert.

Since the stories of the yo ania are also stories of the physical landscape, like the mountain Sikili Kawi, we are able to see a relation between the people, their land, their stories, and their deer dancing. We see that the Yoemem of Arizona make themselves at home on a land that provided sustenance for their ancestors, and the Yoeme ancestors are still living in the hills, providing gifts and talent to contemporary deer dancers, singers, and pahko'olam.

In another section of Valenzuela's collection, Carmen Garcia shows that sometimes people experience the yo ania by simply passing by the right place. Garcia told Valenzuela of a pahko'ola who was a terrible performer, unable to dance well. This pahko'ola was traveling alone to dance at another pueblo when he was met by the yo ania. Hearing beautiful music coming from the hills, the pahko'ola wanted to dance, but thought himself too poor a dancer to do so. Garcia continues, "And he stood there, listening, and wishing with heart and soul that he were more graceful" (14). Just then a goat came out of a cave, licked the man all over, urinated on his legs, and returned to the hills. Garcia says that the music stopped. After that point, many people considered that pahko'ola the funniest clown and the best dancer in the pueblos. In this story Garcia highlights another type of yo ania experience, the unexpected appearance of a gifted and sometimes gifting animal.

Many of Painter's Yoeme contributors agree with Garcia that the yo ania refers to all the animals and beings of the respected world (1986, 19–28). These accounts demonstrate that the Yoeme concept of space includes the yo ania as an other-than-human subject who has agency. In this way, yo ania decides when and where to meet humans and in what form. That in Garcia's story a goat appears is not surprising, since the goat is a central character in pahko'ola art and performance. These accounts also speak to the veracity of the yo ania, rather than an "as if" or make-believe status.

The yo ania is a real space, experienced by friends, family members, and ancestors. According to Yoeme elder Christina Valenzuela, the yo ania gave a pahko'ola named Vakot Pahko'ola the ability to shrink to any size. She knows the story is true because, as she tells Valenzuela, "My mother saw Vakot Pascola when I was a young girl, about fifty years ago. Vakot Pascola died an old, old man while I was still a young girl" (15). Others know that the yo ania exists because they see the Surem walking around, and they hear the beautiful music coming from cemeteries or mountains in the desert. Also, two well-known Yoeme elders, Don Jesús and Refugio Savala, both knew that a Yoeme, José Kukut, once gained from the yo ania the ability to fight well in battles. According to Don Jesús, Kukut got angry once and returned to the yo ania. "He lives there where they call it Pilem. Near Ortiz, he lives there. Whoever wants to see him, they look for him at high noon, twelve o'clock, they talk to him in the mountains. Then he will come out, they say. Those who know of him say that he is over there. Around twelve o'clock he is seen sitting outside on some big rocks" (Evers and Molina 1987, 211–12). Savala's story varies little from Don Jesús' description of what happened. Their stories share many interesting aspects, like Kukut being a respected elder, or *yo'owe*. Central to our understanding of Yoeme spatiality is the fact that Kukut is immortally present in the yo ania and that stories locate exactly where Kukut still comes out to talk with Yoemem. Don Jesús and Savala swear that the yo ania is an actual world, home of the immortals, visible and accessible at the right places, to the right people.

As my interest in the yo ania grows, I ask Felipe if we can travel to the Hiak Vatwe and speak with someone about this world that still exists in the mountain caves. I even ask if we can visit some of the rumored openings into this respected place. Felipe responds that the best person for me to talk with about the yo ania is José Kukut. Noticing the confusion on my face, Felipe asks me if I know who Kukut is. I tell him that I remember reading about him in Deer Songs, *but that I forgot exactly where he lives and why he would be the best source of information on the yo ania. Felipe reminds me that Kukut is a man who lives in the yo ania. I cannot believe what I am hearing. Felipe is suggesting that we visit with a person who currently lives in the yo ania and appears at twelve noon to speak with people. Before we leave for Sonora, Felipe shows me the maps, and with his finger he traces the road we should take to get to Pilem, "Los Pilares" in Spanish, or "The Pillars" in English. "If we leave early* enough from the pueblo," Felipe tells me, "we should get there in time for you to meet José Kukut at noon."

We leave the pueblo for Pilem in the early morning. With two excited elders from Las Guásimas in the back seat, Felipe drives while I examine the map. Leaving the main highway that cuts through Yoeme land, we follow a dirt path toward the Vakateteve Mountains. We have to stop at several points to open gates or to reexamine the map. We drive for several hours, seemingly in circles. I feel the suspicion in me rise: another journey for some revelatory experience, something I can call personal documentation, the sense of being too goal oriented. Moments like these make me chuckle, since they accentuate my own struggles with "Indian time" and how I've come to know it as "the failure to meet non-Indian rigidity regarding appointments and schedules." In this case, though, the expectation was not mine alone: an immortal yo'owe appearing at twelve sharp on a rock formation in the wilderness is enough to have all of us in the truck excited. The older men in the back point to the spot in the distance where we should be heading, but the supposedly right path twists and turns upon itself, pointing us in the direction from which we came. We stop at a lone house out in the desert. We are directed by a Mexican man to retrace our journey a couple miles and to turn off a smaller path. By this time it is after noon: I have missed my self-designed appointment with the yo ania.

Stopping to take a break, Felipe and I separate from the other two and walk along a barbed-wire fence. After some small talk, we conclude that we are lost. Felipe tells me that the land has fooled us and the road has misled us. "What did we do wrong?" I ask Felipe. He tells me that we forgot to ask permission to enter the huya ania. He says that we should have said a prayer or made an offering to the wilderness world upon entering the desert this morning. I now realize what is meant when people say the land has agency and that it can trick you. Walking back to the truck on different paths, Felipe and I silently ask permission to go further. We try to excuse our earlier absentmindedness. The four of us get back in the truck and try again.

As the sun begins its afternoon descent, we begin anew. Immediately there is a difference in our progress. Within twenty minutes we are driving beside a mountain range. To the right, caves line the side of the mountain. The caves are dark and appear deep. Inside one of the caves we see the head of what *appears to be a large buck. While Felipe drives, I take pictures outside the passenger window. We turn around a hill and find ourselves completely surrounded by bright colors. In every direction, flowers are exploding in bold hues. The ground is covered with orange blossoms; Felipe calls them sevoa'aram, also known as mallow. From one to ten feet high, the bushes are covered in little yellow flowers called hachihtiam. Even on top of the organ pipe cactus, or aakim, large yellow flowers surround the resting vultures. Driving slower, we fall silent in awe of the beauty before us. I ask Felipe if this is "like the sea ania." He responds, "This is the sea ania."*

By the time we reach Pilem, it is sunset. Walking alongside the small creek, the walls of the riverbed reach up into the sky for twenty-five or thirty feet. Although darkness is slowly surrounding us, the full moon makes the riverbed shine. The four of us walk through sand beds and over boulders until we get to the first pillar. Separated from the sides of the canyon, a rock formation stands like a marble column, more than forty feet tall. If I have ever been to a place that felt deserving of respect, it is here. I am in awe of the geological characteristics; only long-term, high-pressure flows of water could have eroded the base of the pillar in such a way. And what kind of meteorological events cause all of the surfaces to take on such a sparkle, as if the entire area had been lightly spray-painted with silver and white glitter? On the other hand, beyond the physical appearances, what leads this particular place to accumulate all the stories over generations? Something had to have happened here at some time, perhaps many times. The pillar is truly spectacular as a focal point of folklore, myth, and the other ways we label truth-making narratives.

The other men are pointing to the top and speaking in Yoeme while I start experimenting with the camera, attempting to use a flash and the moonlight to photograph the silhouette of the pillar. After only five minutes, the men start heading back down the canyon. Trailing behind them, Felipe urges me to hurry up because soon it will be too dark to find our way back home. As I step up the side of the bank, practically climbing the pillar for one last photo, I hear a noise echoing from up the river canyon. It sounds like footsteps on the river rocks. I can't discern whether I am hearing a coyote or a person. I realize simultaneously that the footsteps seem to be approaching quickly and that Felipe and the others are somehow quite far away, around at least several bends in the arroyo. I fumble for the camera equipment and yell, "Hey, wait for me! Esperen, hombres! I think I heard something! Algo viene!" My heart races from the sense of everything all at once: approaching footsteps, the light at dusk, seemingly glowing river rocks underfoot, tall cliffs all around, fumbling and unsure of my place. Frankly, everything is unearthly. I start running toward the others and am surprised by how far ahead they are. Were they running? Are they afraid of something?

By the time I reach the others, everyone is taking very large strides to get back to the truck. Several Mexican ranchers are waiting to ask us our business. A rifle hangs across their truck's back window. Perhaps we have trespassed on their property. I think suspiciously of what historic events would lead to Mexicans owning the landscape where Yoeme ancestors appear. Explaining that we are from Arizona and without mentioning anything about José Kukut, Felipe tells them that I am from a university and that I would like to return. At times like these, I am thankful that Felipe has a way of talking that is polyvalent, since I do want to return, alive, to Arizona, as well as return to Los Pilares. The ranchers chuckle to themselves and respond in Spanish: "Sure. You come back and stay with us. That way, you can spend the night and get to the pillars by noon." At that moment, I felt that I was part of a story that repeated itself every so often, a story that is told and retold to those wanting to know more about José Kukut. I also feel that Felipe has given me my own story of the yo ania.

Mapping with Stories

Accounts of the yo ania, like all ania stories, enable us to think about the ways Yoeme places contrast with Catholic cosmography. The addition of heaven and hell to indigenous concepts of the aniam can be associated with moralistic tendencies to link the sea ania with heaven and the yo ania with hell. Indeed, some Yoemem portray yo ania visions and visits as moments when people sell their souls to the devil (Painter 1986, 19–26). Encountering a plethora of these interpretations, Painter writes, "Almost without exception, power-seeking through *yoania* visions is considered evil. It is said that no one will admit to having gone to the caves, and it is evident that some informants are uneasy even when discussing it" (21). However, Painter went to a Yoeme elder for clarification, a man well versed in Yoeme culture and deer singing. This Yoeme man told Painter that the yo ania was "a natural way to excellence," leading Painter to write that "the names of a number of participants in *yoania* visions have been given confidentially, and it is contemporary and real to all with whom the writer has talked.... A feeble attempt is sometimes made to equate the *yoania* with hell" (1986, 21).

Many Yoemem conceive of heaven and hell as separate from the aniam. From the information provided by Painter's collaborators, heaven, hell, and even purgatory exist for some Yoemem, but they are purely cosmological spaces with no geographical or, more specifically, earthly location. The words used to refer to the Christian places are often borrowed from Spanish: *santo cielo* for heaven, *infierno* for hell, and *purgatorio* for purgatory. Sometimes descriptive words are used to name these places, such as *teeka*, meaning "sky," *vetukuni* for "below," or *ka maachikun*, meaning "place without light" (Painter 1986, 89; Molina and Shaul 1993, 117). The indigenous places, the aniam (huya ania, sea ania, yo ania, and so on), are described as having physical locales here on earth, whereas the Catholic spaces (heaven, hell, purgatory) are never located in the surrounding landscape. Only after death, a temporal condition, does one gain access to these Christian worlds. Additionally, some elders express a "traditional" understanding that although most Yoemem are buried in front of the church in white sheets, there are some "who have dealt with the wilderness world," who will go to the respected homes after death (Maaso, Molina, and Evers 1993, 315).

Yoemem rarely if ever emplace Catholic geographies in their indigenous landscape. Painter as well as Evers and Molina address this issue in their respective works. Painter writes, "Heaven is visualized as a place full of flowers, rivers, forests, and green meadows, bathed in holy light. ... The words used to describe heaven are often the same or similar to those referring to the *sea ania*" (1986, 89). Painter is quick to note, however, that using the same descriptive words does not constitute the same referential place; in fact, she stresses the presentness of the sea ania and the temporal distance of heaven as the distinction between the two realms. "The road to heaven is thought to be narrow and rough, thorny and almost impassable, as not many go there. It leads to the east, which is also the direction of the legendary flower world. Informants, however, do not equate heaven with the flower world and say that there are no legends to indicate that it was a pre-Spanish idea of a hereafter" (1986, 89). Evers and Molina note a cosmological combination of the two places when they demonstrate that in some deer songs the words for "flower-covered cherished enchanted world" are sometimes replaced by the words for "flower-covered holy heaven" (1987, 54). But like Painter, Evers and Molina conclude that Yoemem fuse the two places together only in flower symbolism, rather than actually thinking of them as the same place.

Still, as with stories of Jesus forming mountains with leaked cornmeal, Yoemem have clearly combined an indigenous worldview with Catholicism. St. Michael takes the "flowers" from the performer's ceremonial labor from the performance ground up to heaven. Jesus and Mary lived and traveled in the Yoeme homeland. Some Yoemem visit with saints and Catholic personae during dreams. Each pueblo in the Hiak Vatwe celebrates its respective patron saint days with elaborate festivities. While Catholic spaces such as heaven and hell have little or no spatial consideration in the physical landscape, the fusion of Yoeme-Catholicism is pervasive in that iconic Catholic persons can be thought of as more present in the *hiakim*, in the land around the traditional pueblos.

Similar to the sea ania/heaven comparison, the yo ania is interpreted by some Yoemem as demonic; the Yoeme poet Refugio Savala clearly promoted such a view. We can see Savala as a prominent example of how Yoeme identity is diverse and in flux. In his 1980 autobiography, Savala describes the use of witchcraft in relation to the yo ania and writes that "these stories prove the statement of the *o'owimsusuakame* [men of wisdom] who follow *seya aniya* [sea ania] and godliness and reject *yoaniya*, the infernal" (39). Savala clearly adopted a Christian ethic after he became a catechist and worked at translating the Bible into Yoeme. Savala was very knowledgeable about his culture and Yoeme history, and he personally understood the yo ania as an inappropriate way to gain power or talent. Savala exemplifies just one of the many ways that Yoemem fuse the Yoeme worldview with various degrees of Catholicism, not to mention the multiple Yoeme Christianities.

Contrasting the view that he presented in his autobiography, Savala offers a more positive reflection of the yo ania when speaking with Painter. Perhaps it was the intended anonymity that led Savala to connect the yo ania with God. As one of Painter's collaborators, Savala writes that pre-Christian Yoeme culture was all the yo ania and that "it was natural then. They went by that, and that is all; and it wasn't bad. The sermons of the priests told them that the *yo ania* and witchcraft was bad, and they began to fear it and think it was bad" (1986, 11).[6] Regardless of his later moralistic interpretations of yo ania visits, Savala makes it clear that the yo ania is still accessible. Seemingly contradicting his other stance, Savala told Painter that "it has happened lately. Some young boys have said that their parents have been in [the yo ania] without taking anything or becoming insane. It can work on the side of God" (1986, 28). At times he clearly regards seeking and gaining powers from the yo ania as morally wrong.

Evers and Molina write that "others strongly resist this suggestion that the yo ania is somehow an 'evil realm,'" and they refer to respected Yoeme elder Don Jesús, who contradicts Savala's view. By their inclusion of Don Jesús, Evers and Molina disagree with Savala that "the *sea ania* has evolved as a source for good powers and the *yo ania* as a source for bad, even demonic, ones" (1987, 62). Evers and Molina's work with a distinguished deer singer from the Hiak Vatwe, Miki Maaso, also offers a clear example of how the yo ania helps Yoeme communities continue the practice of deer dancing and singing. In their article "The Elders' Truth: A Yaqui Sermon," Maaso, Molina, and Evers transcribe, translate, and annotate Miki Maaso's *yoo'ora lutu'uria*, or elders' truth. We know that Maaso's words speak directly about the maintenance of Yoeme culture, since Evers and Molina tell us that the yo lutu'uria is "knowledge about living in the Yaqui world that is considered central by virtue of being held in the memories of respected community elders" (1993, 226).

Maaso's sermon is appropriate for our study of Yoeme spatiality because he not only shows the interconnectedness of the various aniam, but also demonstrates that he himself gained the knowledge and ability for deer singing from the yo ania. Maaso learned the elders' truth not by being taught it by other Yoemem but as a gift from the respected home of the Surem.

To me, this was not told.
Like, the way you are talking now,
like this, nobody said it to me, and like this nobody said
it to me nicely, the two or three truths.
How could I have learned it,
and how I could have known it?
Didn't say it to me,
but I
heard them, at least I heard the sound like you.
But nobody said to me, "sing it like this, and in this way."
Because then the elders' truth
then, in that time, it was cherished.
It was respected, this, that is lying here
where we are sitting,
the carpet was respected. . . .

If someone picks up our rasper, lays hands on it,
if he is one who does not have the big heart
in the dream world he will see this,
our poor truth here.
Like this it was said,
"no, father,
no, young man,
don't touch this,
that is lying here."
"You might not sleep," would say,
"because this is the enchanted
enchanted world."
Like this truth sits.

Like this they valued it,

this is the enchanted world. . . .

Nobody taught me.

I just, on the blowing wind, I . . .

I caught it

and put it together in my head.

And maybe God says this,

and from the wilderness world,

the enchanted world, and maybe the . . .

maybe that, like that, the enchanted home says, maybe,

maybe, it gave me this,

and then I

I, the wind. . . .

What they heard, what they have sung, what they have heard,

what they have heard in the beginning, that truth

stayed in my head and in my five senses.

Like that I knew it.

Not like this,

the way that I am saying it

to you, nobody said it to me. (Maaso, Molina, and Evers 1993, 237–41)

In these words, by circumlocutory talking about the most respected of worlds, Miki Maaso identifies himself as one who learned from the "enchanted" world, the yo ania. He candidly tells how one may learn the elders' truth from the wind, from the wilderness world, and from God, keeping that knowledge in the five senses. As such, he is making claims regarding an embodied epistemology. Speaking in this manner, Maaso also demonstrates that the respected places in Yoeme culture are not separate realms but existing spaces that appear within each other sometimes, much like the beginning verse of the first deer song sung at pahkom: "Flower-covered fawn went out, enchanted, from each enchanted flower, wilderness world, he went out" (Evers and Molina 1987, 88). These places are home to the ancestral Surem, or in some cases to the "chupiarim," as Don Jesús called them. Sometimes when humans do something so disgusting or so inhumane, they halfway change into small amphibious animals and live in the wilderness. Yoemem call them chupiarim and tell of them living in the huya ania and sometimes the yo ania.

In his sermon, one thing stands out most evidently: the spaces of Yoeme cosmology and landscape provide people with ways of enduring, by being talked about in stories and deer songs, by being re-created in deer dances, and by giving some Yoemem the talent and power to continue re-membering all of the appearing, materializing, and indeed blooming worlds of Yoeme culture. These worlds are not "spiritual": they involve the body and the heart. The dream world, the wilderness world, and the enchanted world offer some knowledge, some "truth" that is not teachable, not said, but it stays in the head and in the "five senses." These ways of knowing, these epistemologies, are at once emplaced, place specific, embodied, and performed. In Yoeme words, and worlds or "aniam," we sense the clearest example of how any interpretation of Yoeme worldview must be centrally concerned with Yoeme ritual action, oral performance, and place-making.

Ignacio Sombra leads me and Felipe to a hill in Torim Pueblo called Avas Kaure, Cottonwood Mountain. Walking up the hill, we follow a path that has been forged by many Yoemem over many years. On top of the hill stands a pahko rama of mesquite and carrizo. Along the sides of the santo heka are benches for musicians and the ceremonial participants. Ignacio tells us that this is where Yoemem from the surrounding pueblos come to celebrate Holy Cross Day every May 3. Contrasting the Catholic calendrical cycle that places the end of Lent on Easter, Felipe tells me that the Holy Cross feast is the last day of Lent for the Yoeme. Traveling to this hill by the river, Yoemem come for a pahko and mass. On the north end of the santo heka is a stone cross atop a concrete altar. From the top of the hill we see the Hiak Vatwe, Yoeme River, to the east and mountains in the background. The gentle breeze is cool up here, and the shade from the pahko rama provides us with a sanctuary from the heat.

While not understanding most of Ignacio's words and depending on Felipe for translation, I hear the words *yo ania*. I immediately look at Felipe, who says to me, "Ignacio says this is the *yo ania*." I think, "This? This is the *yo ania*? I am standing in the *yo ania*?" I push for more. I ask Felipe to clarify what Ignacio is saying. Felipe says that Ignacio is about to tell a story, which means that I will have to wait for more answers, since Felipe always waits for Yoeme elders to finish talking before translating their words to me. Ignacio speaks at length, pointing to one side of the *pahko heka*, then the other. He gestures to the edge of the hill and then moves his hand in the air, like a snake's movement, across the center of the *santo heka*. His eyes get big as he pantomimes a person getting up to kill the snake. He switches to another character and mimes a person stopping the other from harming the snake. A strong gust of wind blows by, and Ignacio's voice fades into the sound of the wind, and he smiles at Felipe and me. Even before Felipe begins talking, I seem to understand much of what has just been said. Communication is so much more than spoken language. I knew what he was saying by how he moved his body, the way he acted out the scenes with his whole being.

Felipe tells me that several years back they were having a Holy Cross ceremony here when a large translucent snake crawled from the side of the *santo heka* and crossed the middle of the area, in front of the musicians. He says that a man stood up to kill the snake, but an elder stopped him. An elder musician at the ceremony explained that it would have been impossible to kill the snake because it was the *yo ania*.

"What do you mean, 'It was the *yo ania*'?" I say. "Don't you mean it was from the *yo ania*? I thought that the *yo ania* was a place."

Felipe says, "This is what Ignacio says: the snake was air; it just looked like a snake." Before I can ask any more questions, Ignacio starts off down the hill. Felipe tells me that we can ask more about the *yo ania* later.

Attempting to gain clarification of how Yoemem understand the *yo ania* as real and present in their current lives, I ask Ignacio Sombra if I might record his story about the Holy Cross hill, Avas Kaure, where we visited earlier that day. Sombra agrees to be recorded and speaks at length about the hill, the snake, and the *yo ania*. His talk, provided in part below, is the most detailed discussion of a specific *yo ania* location that I have encountered either in ethnographic accounts or in archival research. While Sombra makes it clear that he himself *has never seen the yo ania, he continually uses terminology usually found in a lutu'uria, or formal expression of truth. Ignacio Sombra's use of tea and ka tea is a linguistic indicator that what is being said is "the truth." By doing so, Sombra gives listeners an understanding of those fundamental ways in which Yoemem conceive of truthful living. As in Evers and Molina's work with Miki Maaso, we see that Sombra provides information about living in the Yoeme world that respected community elders consider vital.*

DAVID SHORTER: Perhaps we can talk here about Avas Kaure, the
    Holy Cross hill, the snake, and the yo ania?
GUILLERMO AMARILLAS:
    This is for the elders who lived here in the beginning.
    The little animal [the snake] is seen there during the
        ceremonies,
    and not only in the ceremonies.
    Whoever goes there, many of them say it is the yo' hoara, the
        enchanted home.
    If you are lucky there, you will see it.
    My father [Ignacio Sombra] will make it more truth to you.
IGNACIO SOMBRA:
    Like that it is said, kompae, we are recent people.
    In the beginning the people,
    where it is first known, Torim, where they call it "Avas Kaure,"
    since they have known about it
    the people of long ago
    like that they have talked about it,
    and we have just heard about the talk,
    and like that it goes to us.
    Like that we understand it.

    Many say, "Why do they call it Avas Kaure?"
    Like that, they don't know about it
    and they don't know it.
    Many say that he lives there
    the one who worked in the yo ania.

Not just now but a long time ago, the ones of long ago,
they said they knew about it like that.
The story keeps being born, over and over.
They say it does not have an end.

The little animal that is seen there really does not bother
    anybody.
Nobody does it hurt.
But once in a great while it catches a day
and it is seen there.
So like that the talk goes about it.
They too don't hurt him.
Like that they knew about and talked about it.
That little animal, when they are going to talk about him,
on the day before the vesper.
Like when they say it is the vigil of the flags, people are
    gathering there.
And that little animal is sitting in the bottom
or he had not come out.
In the late afternoon, after the sun went down,
after Ave Maria.
They say that he was going by the people there,
but he did not bother anybody.
He was seen just going through there.
So the men were talking to it.
So the man said to the snake, "Go ahead and go. Don't bother
    us anymore.
We are going to be busy here."
So they gave him permission, and he went into the hole.
This is the way people who were there saw it.
So this is it.
This is the way you will know it.
I have not seen it
and I have not seen it with my eyes.

FELIPE MOLINA: And the ones who want power, they go there?

IGNACIO SOMBRA:

They say that.

That is what they say about these people.

But in the beginning, the elders who lived there,

the fathers and the mothers did not just know things.

Whoever is not afraid of the enchanted homes

and who know about it can sell themselves and enter there.

They will talk to him in the night world.

Three times in a row you will go there.

It will come to him.

Whatever he wants.

Potam Pueblo, October 30, 1995.
Translated by Felipe S. Molina.

After asking the question that night in Potam, Sombra's son, Guillermo Amaril-
las, dedicated our conversation to "the elders who lived here in the beginning"
and told me that his father would "make it more true" for me.

From the beginning we, as listeners, are placed in relation to the ancestors and told about how the yo ania is there during the rituals *and* outside of the rituals. By telling the story and by hearing the story, performers and audiences are involved in the process of oral tradition and its actual ability to make truth. Sombra's talk is centrally concerned with community and knowledge. In particular, Sombra shows how a collective knowledge of community is defined in relation to specific places and the stories of those places.

Listening to the tape of that evening and reading Sombra's translated words, I can always find more depth and meaning in every line. Sombra speaks to us about the relationship between land and identity, saying that if people ask why the hill is called Avas Kaure, then "like that, they don't know about it and they don't know it." In these words, Sombra reveals that by knowing the name and stories of a place, one knows that place. Those who don't know of it don't know it. Sombra then connects the telling of these stories to the maintenance of identity by saying that "we have just heard about the talk, and like that it goes to us. Like that we understand it." Sombra's discussion of Avas Kaure strongly suggests that, for many Yoeme, identity relies on the performative process of storytelling. Moreover, the physical and cosmological spaces in Yoeme religious worldviews provide a shared cultural landscape for collective remembering.

Telling stories of places that open up ways of thinking about selves and community identities, we have returned to the beginning of the chapter, where Paula Valle imagines Jesus forming Yoeme lands with cornmeal. She tells us of the Yoeme land on which Jesus and Mary lived, a land that houses both Yoemem and their ancestors, the Surem. This same land of rivers and hills, even pillars, provides a means by which to learn deer singing, dancing, and the religious arts. With Ignacio Sombra's story of the yo ania experience at Avas Kaure, these two performed texts inscribe a local relationship between Yoemem and their land, a religious authentication of territorial sovereignty and their continued presence. Relationships were formed, are forming, will form. Yoemem construct worldviews from Catholicism, indigenous relationships, places, and people. These spatial acts of religious discourse fundamentally shape the ways Yoeme identities endure. In Sombra's words, "The story keeps being born, over and over. They say it does not have an end."

Ethnographic Dialogue 1

Ethnographies take many forms. The process of learning and translating another's culture is complex and yet basic to our human condition. At its intersubjective center is conversation between people. I have chosen select fragments from my field recordings in order to raise questions about the spaces between data, authoritative interpretation, ethnographic analysis, and the narrative form. The ethnographic dialogues that follow each standard chapter are translations of interviews with Yoeme research collaborators. Regardless of whether the interlocutors desired their names to be published, I have listed each only as a "respondent" rather than create pseudonyms. Due to some of the information conveyed in these conversations, not providing a name is the socially responsible choice. The dialogues individually textualize the content of adjoining chapters. Collectively, they bring more Yoeme voices into the conversation about Yoeme ethnography.

DAVID SHORTER: I know that the word *aniam* means "worlds." I know that there is *yo ania, sea ania, huya ania, tenku ania, tuka ania, nao ania,* and *kawi ania*. Are there others you can think of?

RESPONDENT: Well, yes, because you are missing *vaa ania*. It is the sea.

DS: *Vawe* means "the sea."

R: *Vaa* or *vawe*, all of the seas. And *teeka ania*.

DS: What is *teeka*?

R: It is the universe, not just the planet.

DS: It is space?

R: Yes, space. Teka, Sea, Ania, Huya Ania, Vawe Ania — and what more? I do not remember the others, but I am going to think about it today and will tell you and the others tomorrow.

DS: Are there legends about whirlwinds?

R: Yes, one can know when rain is coming by watching them.

DS: In ancient times, they say that the Yoemem made sand paintings. Do you think that's true?

R: No.

DS: There is a book in Spanish that says that after death the majority of Yoemem think that the souls are going to go to a place like heaven. But aren't there also people who say that after death a soul goes to live in the yo ania?

R: Yes.

DS: Which do you think is true?

R: Here, for the Yoemem, when a person dies, he always arrives at a house of enchantment, or yo ania. He does not go to the grave. The spirit body arrives at the house of the Surem, or enchantment, and the soul or spirit, it is thinking, because it made a promise when he was walking in the communities.

DS: You are using two very popular words, which are *alma* and *espiritu*, and both are Spanish words.

R: Yes.

DS: What do you think the words were before the Europeans came? Would you say *seatakaa*?

R: Yes. It is the soul. It is like the seatakaa. It is the same as spirit. To us, the Yoemem, we understand the soul and spirit to be *seatakaam*.

DS: Seatakaa is also an energy, a power?

R: So it is.

DS: I have spoken with Felipe Molina about this also, and Felipe says that there are people in the two communities, the Hiak Vatwe, and also on the other side, who sometimes speak about things, particularly like the yo ania and the transparent animals or illusions, and even now they speak of these things like they are evil, like they are devilish, like it is bad. And of course there are many types of people among the Yoeme pueblos, there are people that are more Catholic and those less Catholic, and there are people who try to do things the old way. Do you think that it is more popular among the majority of Yoemem here in Potam to think of the yo ania as something bad, or perverse, or evil? Or perhaps as simply an ancient thing? Or is it good? Is it part of the everyday culture? What do you think?

R: Perhaps our great-grandparents used yo ania for the good of the town. They used it to play the beat of the drum, in the celebrations of the holy eternity, in the celebrations of Saint John the Baptist in the town of Vicam. Therefore these people, our ancestors, used it to play games as well, because from the yo ania they returned with a stone or they promised their soul to the turkey or the crocodile. But these days I imagine that people only remember those ancestors who used it for negative purposes. And so now they think it is bad. But others say yo ania is good.

DS: It is thought of as both.

R: Both.

DS: Friend, if you do not want to answer any of these questions, please just say so. Some people find these subjects very personal. I understand. That said, there are approximately seven *aniam* that I know of: yo ania, huya ania, sea ania, tenku ania. That makes four. What am I forgetting?

R: Tuku.

DS: Right, tuku. I have many questions about the worlds, but right now I have a question about this, a world that I only have read about one time in all the books. It's called *nao*.

R: Nao ania

DS: What is nao ania? Is it only for witches?

R: Yes, witches do it. Nao ania. They do not say things like this unless it is true. This is a verified thing. It is a pot.

DS: What do you mean by "things like this"?

R: It is a verified thing. It is certain, reality. It is a small pot, and it has all the venomous animals designed on it.

DS: Venomous?

R: Those that have venom. And additionally, in there, they have some hair from Mexicans, Yaquis, Mayos, from everyone. And they have small pieces of clothing. Witches practice this in the center of a cross on the ground. They put the pot there, and the man or woman, they take off all of their clothes. Naked. Completely naked. Naked as God brought him into this world. And then the person goes dancing around the pot. These people don't do it to kill or enchant a person. Rather, they do it to bring sickness much like respiratory sickness with fevers. They do not use plants, like beans, wheat, corn, and natural things to cause pain, not just like any witch. No, they don't enchant them like that. This person contracts something like an illness from an epidemic. With this pot in the center of the cross, a light like mercury is emitted upward, brighter than a light bulb. As if there were a battery in the pot. This light goes up as by the art of magic. It goes up to twenty or thirty meters high and goes up there a little while and ends like a tube going upward as if—how can I explain this to you? Ah! The air, the artificial smoke does not leave. It scatters on the floor when the light lowers like little clouds. Well, up in the air the light takes its leave, like smoke. It dissipates and returns to the ground.

DS: Why do you use the name *ania* for this? Because I think that ania is like a world, a state of being, somewhere one could inhabit.

R: Yes.

DS: Ania is "to be."

R: Yes.

DS: But this is a pillar of light. So by *nao ania* are you referring to the sort of person who is using it, like the space they are in?

R: *Ania* means to say that it is possible to be used all over the universe. Like the yo ania, like the huya ania. The huya ania is not only in the Yoeme communities. It is global, at the level of the entire world.

DS: Yes, I understand.

R: And for these worlds, we attach *ania*. We put *ania* in the word and then the name becomes *yo ania, huya ania,* and *kawi ania.*

DS: What is *kawi*?

R: *Kawi ania* is "hills." Or just *kaw ania.*

DS: *Kaw ania* is different than *huya ania*?

R: *Huya ania* is not *kaw ania.*

DS: Because a hill is higher?

R: Yes. *Huya* refers to the bushes, the plants, like the mesquites, wamochiles, cactus, or whatever. And kawa ania is the pure mountain ranges. The Sierra Madre, they are kaw ania.

DS: *Tenku* is for dreams?

R: Yes, tenku ania.

DS: Dreams.

R: The person says *tenku ania* when meaning what they saw in their dreams. They could just say, "I dreamed," but when saying *ania* they mean those dreams when it is not in the tribe. You are dreaming of a place that you don't recognize. One says, "I had a dream, but I cannot remember or do not know what part of the world I was in. But I do know that dream." When they are mentioning this, saying that it was over there in tenku ania, they are saying that it is true.

For example, right now we are in your apartment in San Carlos. If I had a dream in which I awoke knowing I was in an apartment in San Carlos and then came here later to see this place, I would say that in the dream I was in the tenku ania.

DS: And are there usage differences? For example, we are talking, and I want to say, "Oh, we are talking tonight, at night." This "night" is only a night? But tuka ania is different, yes?

R: Yes.

DS: It is the possibility of something more at night, yes?

R: Yes, I know this. Tuka ania is specifically that. Tuka ania needs you to see it with your mind, for example, to dream it. Or like a clairvoyant, you are seeing through the night, without knowing whether anything is true. But it is.

DS: Ah, yes.

R: Imagine that you are seeing what is above over there, miles away. You are thinking, "Ah, well, there is a stone, there are two, three, four stones, or there is a stick through that area." You may not even know what you are seeing exactly, but you might go there someday and see it perfectly as it was in your vision. "Ahh, [revelatory sigh] I am there, I have already seen this, and I already know what was here, therefore I was in tuka ania that night I saw this." It is as if you went to a clairvoyant to see things. But you can do this only at night.

DS: Yes.

R: This is not about thinking. This is about doing it. You do not think of the yo ania. It arrives without you thinking of it. It is something sensory that arrives and makes you imagine. Or it makes you see different things than normal. If we are going to do this tonight, we would say we are becoming it. And the aniam, well, they materialize. This is how things are.

DS: I want to go back to an earlier question, because I want to understand. *Nao* translates as "corn cob?"

R: Yes, ear of corn.

DS: Nao is a corncob?

R: Yes.

DS: Because it is a thing in the pot.

R: Yes.

DS: And is it possible, when we are talking of the *choni*, that it belongs to the world of tuka ania, the night world?

R: Well, I have not seen a choni. But the people who have seen them say that it is like a pygmy, since it has dark skin, as if they were from Africa. They are about three feet tall with long enough hair to touch the ground. People who have seen them say that they are kept in these small drawers. And when they are in these drawers, they are like little calves or like a suckling pig. They say these are Apache beings and not from our tribe. I don't know. It might be a Cherokee thing or Apache. I don't know.

DS: You've heard that chonim are Apache?

R: Chonim are from Apaches. They have a code, these choni keepers. And like an oratory, when spoken they turn into a little boy. Like an invocation, no?

DS: Do you think that anyone in Potam has seen them?

R: Yes, there are chonim.

DS: But you have not seen them?

R: No, I have not.

DS: And the chonim also like *hiak viva*, Yoeme tobacco?

R: They say that they like this and needles.

DS: Needles?

R: Needles or anything make of steel. To give them food you have to get them needles, or steel, or *tetahaum*.

DS: Tetahaum?

R: In Spanish, they are called *chichicayotes*, these little squash. But they are really bitter. They say that chonim eat these

things. I don't know if they are people or animals. I am
unable to say. But my father and mother have seen them,
and they have told me that they definitely do exist. And
there are two or three people in Potam who do have
chonim.

DS: In 1945, there was an anthropologist in Vicam, and while
there he talked with men and women from the tribe who
said they believed in reincarnation. Do you think that is
a more ancient way of thinking? What do you personally
think about this?

R: Well, I will prove to you what I say about this: reincarnation
has existed from the holy time until right now, but two or
three people, perhaps fewer than ten people, can vaguely
recognize what their previous life was. Yes, they remember
it, but not with clarity, and they are not able to exactly
say, "I am reincarnated, and I was this particular person."
Sometimes they can tell you something about the past
of a house or a piece of land. I know a person here in
Potam, and I was there when he said, "I saw when they
built that church. Listen to me." [The church in Potam was
constructed in 1922. This collaborator, at the time of this
2003 interview, was fifty-one years old.] Well, how could he
have seen it when he was my age, even younger than me?
How could he have seen them construct that church?" I
said, "Yes?" to see what he was going to say, in order to hear
what he was telling me. So I said to him, "Good. Okay. So
right now, tell me how they built the church. How did they
form it? And who was the first person that ordered them
to build the church? Where did they first begin? Where
did they make the adobe bricks? Who worked on it?" Then
he said that the bricks were made from that far side of the
church, and then another thing, and who ordered it built,
and then all the workers. Some of the people that were
working on the church were my relatives. "Aye carumba!"

I said. Well, that happened with that friend. And so I just left it at that. I never questioned him again. I didn't say anything. Then, before my father died, at the end of a week, on a Friday in the afternoon, we were in the house talking, drinking coffee. And I said to my father, "Listen to this. That man told me that he knows when they built the church, and he said that his family worked there. I don't know if he dreamed it or if other people told him what he knows, but he says that he saw it with his own eyes when they were building it." "Ahhh, yes," my father said to me. "Well, I am very old, but even I am not able to remember the building of that church." But my father proceeded to tell me that the adobe bricks were made behind the church, and he told me the names of people that he had heard worked on the church, and there was agreement between the stories. My father added that they had a dance out in the fields that he had personally seen. I told him, "You liar!" And he said, "I saw what was going on there. Things. There. No one told me anything. I cannot explain it either. I don't know if I dreamed it, or if I really saw it. But I know that no one gave me this information." Then, another time, I was speaking with some other people, and they told me that he is reincarnated, in another body, and that from returning and returning he has seatakaa. But what happens is that he does not remember if he dreamed it, but he knows that no one told him where they constructed those adobes. He does remember that he had dreamed or had seen it.

DS: In other books, they say that Yoemem have sayings that very small children, very young ones, can sometimes know things of their past lives, things not possible for them to know. Or they will have a mark on their body exactly where their great-great-grandfather had a mark or something like that. Have you any knowledge of these things here?

R: No. From what I know, no. This confuses me also, and this other man talked with me about these things. But, well, I still have my doubts. Perhaps he is deceiving me. Maybe his father's father told my father's father something about the construction of the church. We have always been a people with an excessive vocabulary of deception, saying to other people something is true, so and so is true. But they are not speaking the truth. They are speaking with lies. But there is no test, like a real fact of reincarnation that you can say you know. For me, no one is going to tell me these things because these things did happen here. At that time, those men did live here, and I can verify it with my own psychology. Like hypnosis, I can verify what people say as lies or not. Right now, there is not a person that can tell me I can submit to a study so that they can analyze my mind to see if I was incarnated with my relatives in my past.

DS: Right now, in Potam, the majority of Potam residents believe in heaven?

R: Yes.

DS: In hell?

R: Yes.

DS: In purgatory?

R: Listen, purgatory is the same as hell. It is the same.

DS: Okay.

R: Yes, they believe in these things.

DS: Is there a mass at the church every Sunday?

R: Yes, in the Yoeme language.

2 Putting Worlds into Words

> During a hard day's work, our grandparents would worry and
> wonder about their homeland, which was still in the hands of
> the enemy, about their Yaqui brothers who were deported to
> places from which they would never return, and about those true
> Yoemem still holding out in the mountains of Bacatete. After such
> a day, our grandparents would sit outdoors on warm evenings in
> Tucson and on ranches in the surrounding area, resting before the
> battle that would recover their land. Then any event — a shooting
> star, a streak of bad luck, a newborn child — would start off an
> evening of "Do you remember . . . ?" as they recounted *etehoim*
> [stories] and talked of things that happened before the wars. Their
> children, our parents, would gather outside along the fringes of
> the group to listen to stories . . . of laughter, pain, and hope, all the
> voices from long ago.
> HERMINIA VALENZUELA, Yoeme writer and teacher

Herminia Valenzuela emphasizes a basic human process
of remembering.[1] She describes how this remembering allows for the
"voices from long ago" to continue to speak to her parents and consequently to Valenzuela herself, her children, and her children's children.
She is acutely aware of the connection between people's actions and
words and their continued relationships with their relatives and their
land. Many Yoemem create a future by sharing these memories, since
their acts of speech teach children to become storytellers and keepers of
the memories. Generations pass, and Yoemem still listen to etehoim from

before the war and even perhaps from before, when Yoemem formed the eight pueblos. Valenzuela says, in a distinctly Yoeme way, that nights of storytelling create memory and thus identity.

Jan Vansina's work explores the relationship between oral tradition and culture, arguing that narrative histories secure cultural continuity in a present aimed for the future. In *Oral Tradition as History*, Vansina tells us that "no one in oral societies doubts that memories can be faithful repositories which contain the sum total of past human experience and explain the how and the why of present-day conditions. . . . Whether memory changes or not, culture is reproduced by remembrance put into words and deeds" (xi). Vansina confirms the conclusions that many others have come to on ethnographic and literary representations of American Indian religions: whether labeled "myths," "stories," or "histories," oral traditions communicate the essentials of belonging to a community.

If, as Vansina suggests, "memory carries culture from generation to generation" (1985, xi), not only through the words of a story, but through motivated deeds emerging from the story, then we should seek to comprehend the acts of social remembering: dancing, singing, praying, oration, naming — in effect, seeking to understand remembering in all ways that remembering happens. Whereas the previous chapter surveyed the basic topology of a Yoeme cosmos, in this chapter I survey a particular collection of Yoeme mythistory that is foundational to understanding the relationship between many Yoemem and their claims of aboriginal authority: the Testamento. A collection of stories, the Testamento tells of the world flood and subsequent founding of the eight pueblos by prophets (angels in some stories) and Yoemem. By walking in procession while "singing the boundaries," the stories tell us, Yoemem received their territory as a divine inheritance, and they established the original "holy dividing line," those geographic boundaries designating Yoeme lands.

Building on the previous chapter, I show how the Testamento works as a narrative map, a cartographic speech act, and a textual practice that define Yoeme aboriginal rights to their land. The telling of the story that documents a history of territorial belonging precedes the history of European contact. In order to understand the primary historical importance that many Yoeme place on the Testamento, I first describe its basic components and then explain how the Yoeme Testamento relates to a larger corpus of etehoim heard in Yoeme communities. I then demonstrate that any understanding of Yoeme history and religion must account for the perspectives expressed in the Testamento, even as the Testamento itself grows out of specific dialogues between anthropologists and their Yoeme research collaborators. I pay particularly close attention to the historical era in which much ethnographic "data" and theorizing was taking place among Yoemem. Focusing on this period enables me to show how Yoeme ethnography has clearly grown from and helped to develop a particularly successful historiographic strategy.

Searching for the Real Testamento

In the spring of 1992, the *Journal of the Southwest* published a watershed issue devoted to Yoeme ethnology: "Hiakim: The Yaqui Homeland." Three years in the making, "Hiakim" contains maps of Yoeme territory within Mexico, photographs of the Hiak Vatwe from both the 1940s and the 1980s, selections from Spicer's field notes regarding the Testamento that were previously thought "lost," a copy of the full Testamento translated into English with a biblical comparison, and Evers and Molina's essay "The Holy Dividing Line: Inscription and Resistance in Yaqui Culture." Evers and Molina discuss the Testamento's possible origins, its use and function, its possible audiences, its circulation, how various Yoemem understand it, and why it remains central to understanding Yoeme history. I rehearse below some of what they accomplish, though without the eloquence and measure that Evers and Molina bring to their collaborative essays. I do not duplicate their line-for-line theological analysis or explore the differences between the versions of the Testamento available. I do pay close attention, however, to the form and function of the Testamento, since the following chapters deal directly with the Testamento and the Yoeme perspectives available therein. Specifically, I take up an issue to which Evers and Molina only allude: the framing of the Testamento as part of a larger process of performative historiography.

The Testamento is a collection of four narratives describing Yoeme relationships with the land, as those relationships were reconstituted after a world flood. The first part tells how this flood destroyed almost all the living creatures on earth: "everything in which there was a spirit of life under the heavens" (Leyva 1992, 93). Lasting for forty days and nights of flooding in which "all spirit of life ended," the waters receded, leaving a man by the name of Llaitowui with thirteen other men and eleven women on the Hill of Parvas, called Mataehale today. On the Hill of Jonas, a man by the name of Aitey survived with eleven other men and one woman, named Enac Dolores (although she would later turn into a statue of stone). Six others survived on Tosal Kawui, three more on Hill Goljota, and a man and a woman on Mount Sinai, Vakula and Domicilia, as well as birds, donkeys, and little dogs, seven of each. All of these hills and others I do not include here exist in the Yoeme homeland. I have driven throughout the Yoeme territory with elders who enjoy bringing my attention to "that one over there, from the flood."

In the Testamento's history, two angels came at dawn to announce the coming of another: "he who sets right the entire road of God." Such a small detail standardizes prophecy as efficacious, since the Angel Graviel comes and brings with him a rainbow, signifying the end of world floods. "God" then speaks and tells the Yoeme survivors that they should beware of "false prophets" who will say, "I am God." God warns them, "If you believe, they will raise false testimony, brothers against brothers and fathers against sons. They will kill one another. And the false prophets will give you the sign to deceive you and at the time foretold it will come" (Leyva 1992, 95).

This prophetic part of the Testamento has a certain resonance for those who remember the bloodshed in the mid-1990s when factionalism between "progressive" and "traditional" Yoemem threatened the safety and stability of the entire tribe.[2] Families turned against each other over a series of disputes over how to respond to crippling debt and a promise of bailout from the Mexican government. Since the bailout required selling land for an aqueduct to nourish tourist towns, the Testamento's prophecy of tribal deception seemed fulfilled during the same historic moment that Yoemem and their anthropologists heralded the importance of the "Rahum land myths" and the compilation of these oral traditions into a testament, or document, of land rights.

> *Arriving in Potam today was a feat I didn't think was going to be accomplished. After weeks of reading about violence in the northern territory of Zona Yaqui, I was not sure that Felipe would think such a trip was safe enough for us. He photocopied the articles from the Hermosillo and Tucson newspapers that, though offering conflicting details, seemed to agree that a Yoeme man was killed up near Guaymas. According to the reports, a group of Yoemem decided to sell a portion of the northernmost territory to Mexicans. A Yoeme man, now labeled a "traditionalist," didn't think that such a deal could take place without the approval of the governors of all eight pueblos. The "traditionalist," as the Mexican reporters call him, was run over by a truck, supposedly driven by the group of Yoemem who wanted the money that such an exchange would provide the tribe. Already, in my first day here, I can see how some people understand the violent actions that I read about in the newspapers.*

> *After dinner tonight Guillermo begins talking about the reports. Guillermo, his father, Ignacio, Felipe, and I sit around the table under the rama. Guillermo's wife and daughters sit by the kitchen fire, rocking babies to sleep, listening to our talk, and occasionally speaking in low tones to each other. The mood becomes very solemn as Guillermo discusses the tribe's difficulties in recent years. A faction of Yoemem from among several pueblos have decided that they will work outside the traditional lines of government (the eight governors) in order to secure more funds for children's education programs and for a type of sentinel police force. These "progressives," frustrated by continuing poverty and other tribal problems, want to start a new "traditional authority" of younger, more aggressive men. I immediately note the political strategy of the "progressives" calling themselves "traditional." The faction, according to Guillermo, is pitting neighbors against neighbors.*

> *At his mention of vecinos, I suddenly realize that for the last hour or so, we've been speaking in low tones (or at least lower than usual), while Guillermo*

peers every once in a while over his cane fence. My field of perception widens to try and hear anyone nearby. It dawns on me that the pueblo that I leave and return to is always changing. Last time I was here, no Yoeme had died recently at the hands of other Yoemem. Last time I was here, Guillermo seemed less concerned about which neighbors I visited and who might be sitting within earshot of his campo. So I, too, start listening closer to the darkness around us. Dogs are barking, and I hear children playing, although it is 10 p.m. A man rides by on a rickety bicycle, with a young lady sitting on his handlebars. Roosters are settling onto roofs and in trees; somewhere a Mexican radio station plays a Spanish version of an old Blondie song ("the tide is high . . ."). As if I had somehow physically left the conversation, I am pulled back at the speed of sound. I hear Guillermo mention the word testamento.

I look toward Felipe for an update on what's been discussed, and I see that his eyes are wide as he responds to Guillermo in the affirmative, heewi. *I get Felipe's attention by staring at him, and he smiles, almost laughingly, at me. (He probably thinks I was sleeping! I'll have to defend myself tomorrow, more for my sake than his.) Felipe explains that I did not really miss much, just that Guillermo was relating the death two weeks ago to the Testamento. According to Guillermo, many people understand the recent violence in the Río Yaqui as fulfillment of the prophecy in the Testamento, that the first elders were told that brother would kill brother over the holy dividing line. I don't quite remember that part, so I'll have to look it up when I get back home.*

Guillermo asks me for a piece of paper, so I reach over to my backpack and pull out a pen and my legal pad. He draws a rough sketch of the Yoeme homeland as decreed by Cárdenas. By now I'm very familiar with the shape of what he is drawing. I look over at Ignacio and realize he has remained quiet the entire conversation. He sits up to supervise his son's drawing efforts. Felipe and I move our chairs closer. Guillermo then draws a line parallel to the northern boundary but perhaps an inch below it, and he shades in the space between the two lines. He tells us that this is the area the young progressives are trying to sell. Ignacio slowly shakes his head disapprovingly or perhaps with fatigue, and he spits. I tell Guillermo, reciting tribal politics through tribal organization, "But they will not be able to do it. The eight governors will not allow that." Guillermo responds as he often does, a polite affirmative followed by a correction: "Yes, we have eight governors, and six of them agree that we should not sell the land. But these exchanges are taking place with Mexican lawyers in Mexican cities by a group of individuals claiming to be traditional Yoeme authorities." To lighten the mood, I offhandedly comment, "I wish I were a lawyer. Then I could really help." We all chuckle. Guillermo hands me back my pen, and I ask for the map, too. He gives it to me and asks for a cigarette. I hand out the obligatory last smokes of the day and pass around the lighter. We all move our chairs away from the table, and Felipe begins the customary end-of-the-day thank-you to the family. Afterward I grab my backpack and head out the gate to the truck. As I walk around to the driver's side, I see a man hunched down by a neighboring fence, his face shielded by the brim of his baseball cap. I think to myself, "Older men tend to wear cowboy hats." He doesn't acknowledge my presence, just spits. I throw my pack in the truck and head back to the rama, more suspicious than ever before. Up to now, I came down here and feared for my life just because I did not know what to expect from such remote travels and dealings with Mexican federales. Now I am beginning to fear for the lives of my friends who live here. What do others in the pueblo think about my hosts, with their visitors from "el otro lado"?

The second part of the Testamento begins with a formalized recounting of the Yoeme chain of authority, a narrative pattern still included today in important speeches and religious presentations.[3] The last groups mentioned are the Bow Leader Society and the Kohtumbre, the former responsible for protection of land and the latter responsible for all Lenten ceremonies. Since this second part of the Testamento is for many Yoemem the most important in defining land rights, and since it will be referred to throughout this study, I present the actual "singing of the boundaries" in its entirety:

God the Father ordered our poor
earth inheritance, the elders, the ones who were told to give it to us,
here the prophets arrived.
Well, lords, fathers, like this
when the year reached 1414–1417, here
our Dividing Line began, the inheritance we were given,

on January 6th, on the 6th, they went out to the south,

from the mountain there with little peaks,

that mountain, Mojonea, which is sitting in the ocean,

already, also, the little angel children and

our elders went out all together

toward Takalaim, they say,

already the prophets took to the road,

they started the line, Isiderio Sinsai,

Andres Cosme, Andres Quizo, Rabbi Kauwuamea,

these prophets, like that already, said this

to the people and to the little angel children,

the holy dividing line, before

the arrival of the Spaniards, in the years 1414–1417,

through the natives, Andres Cosme, Isiderio Sinsai,

and Andres Quizo and Rabbi Caumea, in order to

start the holy dawn song and they accompanied

the doctrine and commandments of God, in order to leave

a place, that is Takalai, and he said to them: "Go

forward singing hymns" and upon arriving at

Kokoraqui, said to them: "In the course of some years will come

some wicked men from Getsemanix, that is Nueva España, those men,

the image of Isiper, are

invaders and enemies of our life and they do not respect

others and they will keep these properties.

They will ask you: 'Whose land is this

kingdom?'"

This is what those prophets predicted.

Well, they talked with them like this

again at Kokorakipo they spoke with the people

to begin this holy dividing line,

the prophets Andres [Cosme] and Andres Quizo said to them,

upon arriving at Kokoraqui and

showed them the holy doctrine and commandments

of God and they said to them: "Look, the kingdoms, they will say

1. Translated as "forked" in Yoeme, Takalaim remains the northwest corner landmark of the aboriginal Yoeme homelands.

> to you, in order to deceive you." If they
> ignore you, tell them and don't believe them. If one of you
> says, "Well, then, take up the false
> testimony about this Holy Line,
> brothers against brothers, fathers against sons,
> they will kill one another."
> Like this they spoke with them,
> the ones who gave us our inheritance, the line,
> like this you will know it. (Leyva 1992, 98–99)

In addition to a concern for dates, names, and places, we also see a restatement of the internal division. Most important is the procession across the land, the physical movement of bodies singing and making a place theirs. From Mojonia to Takalaim, from Takalaim to Kokoraqui, the people demarcated their inheritance knowing that they would someday defend this claim against the "invader" from New Spain.

The third part of the Testamento includes the founding of the eight pueblos and names the founding fathers of each pueblo. Additionally, each of the pueblos is mentioned in relationship with a patron saint.

Although Ruth Warner Giddings came across a version of the Testamento without this section, Spicer's research coincides with Evers and Molina's description of this part as a conclusion (Evers and Molina 1992, 22).

Since there are different copies of the Testamento in the various Yoeme communities, Evers and Molina were able to view several versions of the document and inquire about an occasionally added fourth section, a personal commentary. The Yoeme elders who spoke to Evers and Molina explained that the Testamento is performed at times and read aloud at other times. Occasionally groups of Yoeme elders from all eight pueblos will meet, as in the writing of the original document, and they will make a copy and add a collective commentary for a Yoeme community that is without its own copy. Additionally, because it is clearly permissible, "and even necessary, for other Yaquis to 'unfix' it as it is read and discussed orally," the Testamento offers the current Yoeme communities a chance for dialogue with the past (Evers and Molina 1992, 23). Already the lines of distinction between oral and written are perforated and blurry: the Testamento is a document that remains open, a written form dependent on oral performance, a performance that affects the written record now and then.

Evers and Molina avoid giving a specific date or even an era for the Testamento's oral or textual beginning, but they clearly understand the Testamento as being created for the purposes of resistance that the Yoeme recognized as necessary from their first contact with the Spanish. They suggest as its antecedent the earliest known European account of the Yoemem, which describes an elder drawing a line across the ground and threatening death to any Spaniard who crossed it (Hu-DeHart 1981, 15). Evers and Molina write, "At some point, perhaps long after the Yaqui elder drew that line on the earth, other Yaquis wrote a narrative on paper as a way of reinscribing the same boundary" (1992, 4). Referring to this inscriptive act of control in 1533 (see chapter 3 below), Evers and Molina link the Testamento to boundary maintenance against intruders. Yet they go further by showing how the Testamento entails not just physical or geographic boundaries but cultural ones as well: "The 'Testamento' is one result of Yaqui efforts to continue to define their own culture through a narrative with the European history and Christian religion that followed Nuño Beltrán de Guzmán to the Yaqui homeland" (1992, 5). Evers and Molina insightfully note of the Testamento:

> Don Alfonso's "Testamento" suggests, then, one way Yaquis have actively interpreted the European history and the Christian mythology offered them by Jesuits and other later missionaries in light of their own cultural traditions. The "Testamento" indicates that through this process, Yaquis managed to separate the Spanish conquistadors from their Christian gods and to appropriate those gods as their own. Yaqui interpreters have in this way attempted a bold reversal to protect their homeland. They have turned the authority of the gods they appropriated from the Spaniards back on the waves of Euro-Mexican colonists who have followed in the long wake of the Conquest. (1992, 5)

Evers and Molina clearly demonstrate how the Testamento shapes the dialogues in the contexts of autonomy and land rights. The hills that saved the Yoemem from the flood are mentioned by name; the designation of the Dividing Line uses actual names of places around the homeland; the boundaries are sung around the eight pueblos still inhabited by the majority of Yoemem; and the unbaptized, immortal Surem live within the hills and wilderness that surround the eight pueblos. Evers and Molina describe the relationship between the stories and the places as legitimating: "A storied homeland establishes authority. Stories invested in the land return to invest authority" (1992, 41). After driving by the hills, being in processions that circle plazas, cemeteries, and ritual spaces, and hearing the faint sound of ancestral partying coming from the hills, I understand part of why my collaborators tell these stories. Understanding the colonial history of these lands helps me understand another part.

Spicer and others have considered the Testamento as mostly a nineteenth-century development, functioning to support Yoeme land claims against Mexican encroachers. Spicer's analysis of the Testamento, or "Rahum land myths" as he called them, is thus mostly focused on the period after 1820 (1980, 164–70). Even Evers and Molina spend a large part of their analysis focused on when the Testamento came to be known, all the while concentrating on the written form. Although they claim the Testamento "provides another case for ongoing inquiry into the complex relations between oral and textual practices," the authors do not give much attention to the Testamento as an oral performance (1992, 5). For example, when they come close to making sense of Don Alfonso's own interpretation of the Testamento as an oral narrative, they immediately turn to the written text. Note the quick turn from Don Alfonso's claim for oral performativity to Evers and Molina asking about writing: "Don Alfonso believed that the 'Testamento' was created by 'the ones who were left' when the great flood subsided. To us at least he did not say that 'the ones who were left' wrote it down. He said, 'They talked like this, they made this.' When was the Testamento first written down? Was it written in Yaqui or Spanish or some combination? Did the 'Testamento' or any parts of it exist in written form before Juan Valenzuela set down his version?" (1992, 28). While the questions about native literacy are important, I cannot help but think that we are being forced again into a search for written texts at the expense of learning more about what oral tradition has to tell us. Moreover, the distinction between oral and written narrows the question of "the beginning" by understanding literacy as the sine qua non of historical thinking. Much of Evers and Molina's essay struggles to find an original date of the Testamento's printing. In the section above, we see that even when Don Alfonso takes them to the beginning, they redirect their focus to the *written* beginning. He says, "They talked like this, they made it," and they immediately follow with the question of when the Testamento was first written down. Don Alfonso's statement deserves more attention because it emphasizes not a scholarly historicity but verbal documentation.

In an attempt to include all possible interpretations of the Testamento's origination, we must seriously consider Yoeme explanations. Yoeme elder Don Alfonso Florez Leyva was vital to Evers and Molina's text, since he gave them a copy of his Testamento, and he spoke at length regarding its use in Yoeme communities. Don Alfonso was aware of the copying and transmitting of the Testamento in the 1950s, especially during a meeting in which representatives from all eight pueblos gathered to settle the boundary of Yoeme lands. Each representative allegedly received copies of the Testamento from one very big book that was in the possession of one of the participants. Don Alfonso did not know where the book came from, and he suggested that it may have disintegrated or fallen apart afterward. He was, however, "very clear" to Evers and Molina that this "big book" was the direct antecedent of the Testamento copy given to all eight representatives and that the Testamento was written long before the 1950s:

> When the flood, yes,
> the water went down
> the ones who were left
> they talked like this
> they made this (1992, 4, 12).

We could turn to the Testamento narration itself to see when the flood water "went down" to determine the earliest possible date when the Testamento, in some form, could have existed. The Testamento begins:

> This happened, that on the 7th day of February
> the waters went over the earth in the year 614
> during the life of Yaitohui, the 7th day of the same month to the 17th
> of February, on that [day] there was a rain over the
> earth.

And the next section begins:

> And the month of July on the 17th the waters
> were subsiding until the 1st day of October
> the tops of the mountains were revealed and on the
> 1st day of November the waters receded over
> the earth. (1992, 93–94)

From Don Alfonso's perspective, then, the Testamento may have existed as early as November 1, 614, which is when the waters subsided enough

for Yoemem to begin walking the earth and reconstituting their homeland. To question whether such a date is empirically verifiable may be
as important as questioning whether a world flood, prophesies, or talking trees are ontologically possible. We define truth not solely through
known facts but also through the application of multiple types of knowledge. All of these events (flood, procession, prophecy) are part of a
historical frame (the Testamento) that helps many southern Yoemem
understand their own culture, their own history, and their own relation to
their homeland. In Don Alfonso's actual statement, we might understand
"they talked like this, they made this" as talking and making a body of
stories. Such an interpretation follows Don Alfonso's response to Evers
and Molina's question about the Testamento's name:

> They call it a Testamento because
> the elders in the beginning
> the ones who walked about
> like this worked on it
> like this they have taken care of it
> they listened to themselves, yes,
> they listened to themselves with one word. (1992, 24–25)

Locating the Testamento's emergence with the "elders in the beginning"
who "walked about like this," Don Alfonso suggests that those Yoemem
who sang the boundaries after the flood were the first to listen to themselves and agree (*senu nookpo*, with one word) on the Testamento.[4] And
since the act of listening is undeniably an auditory act, we could infer
that when the Testamento began (soon after the flood?) it was in oral
form, an aspect that continues today alongside the written text's shape.
No distinction can be made regarding Yoeme orality and literacy. We
know that this oral tradition is deep in Yoeme culture. When an expedition from the Texas Technological College ventured to the Hiak Vatwe
in 1934, one of the fieldworkers learned about this history from an old
man: "Williams learned by talking with the old man that the Yaquis had
long kept an oral 'history' of the tribe, handed down by word of mouth.
It seemed that the Yaquis traditionally had semi-official rememberers to

whom was entrusted the task of keeping alive the historical traditions, grievances, and wrongs suffered by the tribe. This consciousness of the past no doubt contributed much to the maintenance of the integrity and independence of the Yaquis and caused the tribe to be different from the other indigenous groups in Mexico" (Holden 1972, 13).

Yoemem hardly have the market cornered on native historicism, but Holden rightfully links the oral performance of history with sovereignty movements. That Holden thought "history" needed quotation marks and that he uses "rememberers" to substitute for "historians" provides evidence of the alternate or secondary status of local intellect, regardless of well-intentioned ethnographers. It would be another five years before Alfonso Ortiz (1977) declared "Some Concerns Central to the Writing of 'Indian' History," which outlined for many historians of that generation why Indian history was to be heard and not read.

So why adopt writing at all? Answering this question unravels a common binary in native studies, that of oral/literate classification. To begin unraveling, we must first distinguish between the Testamento as a written document containing three stories and as an oral tradition (perhaps three different ones) that precede Yoeme notational writing in the early 1600s. Most copies examined by Evers and Molina derive from the mid-1900s, although they note the possibility of it being written down after Jesuit schools were introduced in the pueblos during the 1620s. Almost as an aside, however, Molina includes in a personal commentary that Yoeme words exist for writing and paper. I consider Molina's observation important when thinking about the possibility of pre-European Yoeme notational systems: "The Yoeme words *hiohte*/writing and *hiosia*/paper make some of us wonder if some sort of writing system existed in the ancient past, but nothing is really known about this. *Hiosa noka*/talking paper is what we call reading. I think that more research could be done on this subject" (1992, 35).

As with many other native communities that worked with missionaries, the Yoemem seemingly began their practice of notational writing after missionaries settled within the eight pueblos in 1617. Some of the Catholic prayers and the Mass for the Dead had been written down in

Yoeme, Spanish, and Latin as early as 1620 (Spicer 1980, 326). While working on "The Holy Dividing Line," Evers and Molina unexpectedly discovered one of these early examples of Yoeme literacy. Given to them by Don Alfonso, the handwritten document names the first eight Yoeme lay priests and lists them as catechists for the first Jesuit missionary who lived with the Yoemem. Titled "Primer Matros Yaquis del Año 1619," the original document suggests that vernacular literacy was initially rooted in religious processes and civil governance (1992, 30). Perhaps the earliest written antecedent to the Testamento's third section, this document lists all eight communities and important religious figures in each pueblo. Evers and Molina were given, then, strong evidence for a tradition of literacy in the very first years of Yoeme-Jesuit relations; they were also able to link the primary sample of notational writing to the central focus of their study, the Testamento. The existence of such examples might suggest a Yoeme desire to begin making history by writing on paper.

As with most modernist binaries, literate/oral is born out of and engenders value judgments. Why assume that written histories were better somehow than oral histories? Spicer was wise to note the importance of Jesuit instruction for the history of literacy in Yoeme pueblos, but he may have projected his own values on writing upon Yoeme ethnography. Undeniably the beginning of Catholic inscriptions by Yoeme hands, these early acts of inscription, according to Spicer, took on a life of their own:

> These written documents had a special virtue and prestige, and in addition had the immense and sacred authority of the missionaries' sanction. The written traditions were unchanging, always employing the same words that had become familiar to Yaqui ears — words like itom buan bwiapo (in this weeping land), bahi liosem (the Three Gods), Itom Ae (Our Mother), and Itom Yauchiwa (Our Supreme Leader). These written words were constantly repeated, accompanying ritual activities taught by the Jesuits. The church rituals changed after the departure of the Jesuits, but the written words remained the same, and thus the process which the Jesuits had begun continued and intensified as more Yaquis came to use the written word. (1992, 30)

Basing his argument on the theory that the written word is more stable ("unchanging") than oral traditions, Spicer claimed that Yoeme peoples pitted prior life worlds like the *yo ania* against the "sacred written word" (1992, 30). Since he thought the Yoeme divided their world into Church and wilderness, *iglesia* vs. *huya*, Spicer interpreted the Yoeme as understanding Jesus, Mary, and the saints as connected with the written word and the pahko'olam and the deer as belonging to the woods. This dichotomy led Spicer to devalue the non-Christian rites, since the Yoemem were attempting to create a collective Catholic identity that rivaled that of the surrounding Sonoran Mexicans. He writes that "the dominance of the written word over oral tradition nevertheless affected in some degree nearly every Yaqui's evaluation of the church versus the pahko activities, and this produced some tendency to give a lower rating to the pahko-connected rites" (1980, 326). This statement is significant because it provides a, if not the, fundamental key to understanding Spicer's interpretive frame.

Spicer's ideas may now be articulated in two directions. First, he provides no documentation that Yoeme catechists themselves understood the written word as qualitatively better than their long-lasting and continuing oral traditions. Had the written word truly seemed of higher value to the members of all eight pueblos, a claim that would be impossible to prove, surely we would be able to find at least a few more examples of Yoeme writing. Nor does he offer any contemporary Yoeme views on writing's primacy. Also, Spicer is attempting to describe a process that took place between the 1600s and the nineteenth century. After three hundred years, the Yoeme people in Sonora seem no closer to abandoning their pahko'ola and deer rituals than they were at Jesuit contact. Spicer's description of a Yoeme spatialized dichotomy (pueblo vs. wilderness) is only somewhat correct. "Pueblo" and "wilderness" are two distinct realms, but they are part of an overlapping and interrelated multitude of realms of being. Spicer's interpretation also ignores Yoeme stories that include prophets in the wilderness and Yoeme *pahkom* in the villages, as well as Yoeme oral tradition that places Jesus and Mary in the mountains and pueblos before the eight churches existed (Giddings 1959, 106–15).

Yoemem were making notations on paper at least as early as the 1600s, suggesting that they were neither strictly oral nor solely literate and that they wrote for themselves as well as for others. These are not novel discoveries. Reviewing similar issues as they have arisen in other ethnographic inquiries, James Fentress and Chris Wickham (1992, 97) note that few, if any, cultures can be accurately labeled oral or literate: "Oral vs. literate is an unhelpful distinction, especially as it has been too often used by the literate to deny both rationality and legitimacy to oral culture. A better distinction is one found in all societies: that between stable and formal structures of narration and more informal ones." Fentress and Wickham are correct on this point only if we make a formal vs. informal distinction between Yoeme written materials. Whereas the Testamento has evolved into a formal narrative structure, one now hears less frequently in the communities the sort of mythology encountered in Giddings's *Yaqui Myths and Legends*. Whether due to intentional change at the time of Jesuit instruction or slow cultural change, Yoeme stories of boundary maintenance have become the most popularly heard. It could also be that these stories dominate the conversations with outsiders. In the ethnographic evidence available, we definitely see that formalized storytelling occurs less frequently than before. Conscious of the effects that saying such things has, my experience is that both formalized and informal storytelling occurs less frequently now than before I began my fieldwork in 1992.

Las Guásimas Pueblo, May 27, 1994. Our entrance into the pueblo is accompanied by much the same local response as on previous occasions. We are met with a few nods of "hello" and stares by the people on the main road into Las Guásimas. This time one of the neighbors' dogs chases us, barking, until I step out of the truck and throw on my cowboy hat. We enter the Florez campo, closing the gate behind us and tipping our hats at the house cross. Doña Juana comes out of her house and places a towel over her head, a makeshift rebozo, as I've seen her wear before. After touching hands with Felipe and me, Juana fetches two chairs and places them near the patio area of her house. She then gets us two cups of coffee and begins preparing our welcome plate of beans and tortillas. *Within ten or so minutes of Felipe and her talking in Yoeme, other family members come from wherever they were around the pueblo. Men come from the fishing boats, kids from the schools and dirt soccer fields, some neighbor women stop by to say hello. (Did they see us drive in? Did people tell them? Is there a communication network that works that quickly?) As each person enters the patio, we rise to touch hands and say, "Lios em Chania." After another twenty minutes of Felipe and those gathered discussing the health of family members and weather in Tucson, the sun begins to set and the temperature quickly drops ten or more degrees.*

Although this is only my third trip here, I can already tell that these are my favorite moments of fieldwork: my belly full, surrounded by elders speaking in Yoeme in their yard or campo, me not really understanding much and thus left to just wonder about where I am, the lives of the people around me, their living conditions, and their hospitality. In these private spaces, I feel less examined myself. At these times, I am thankfully not at the church or near the tiendas where people feel compelled to stare at me. (Is it my glasses? My clothes? What are the factors of my difference?) As the conversations move deeper into the night, the subjects tend to shift as well. What starts as weather and health slowly becomes tribal affairs and gossip about relatives. In the last two trips, someone would ask about me, and Felipe would explain that I am a student at an American university who is interested in religion or that I work with native people up north. The previous two times I was here, these answers would lead to conversations about Yoeme religion, ritual, and etehoim. On our previous trip to Potam, I was even invited to record a conversation about the yo ania. Tonight I am asked directly about what I think of my trips to the pueblos. I respond that I really enjoy coming down here, that everyone is very nice, that I appreciate the food, and that I really like seeing the ceremonies. Everyone nods. "Yes, the ceremonies are good, lots of people, lots of food." In Spanish, one of the men begins to explain the ceremonies that will take place the next day: a series of processions and the Running of the Old Man.

As the man talks, I am struck by the sound of children laughing inside the house. It dawns on me that the last time I was here, almost a year ago exactly, we were sitting around talking about the ceremonies and the children were sitting nearby and on the laps of the adults. As I am half-listening to the man,

I am thinking back to the previous year and the sense of importance that the children seemed to give to us adults talking about rituals and myths. Usually the kids at this household watch my every move and stay up as late as I do. (Are they waiting for gifts? Waiting for my attention?) I remember really enjoying the year before when the coffee flowed until midnight and the stories about land and legend continued through almost a whole pack of cigarettes. Tonight I am struggling to make out the individual words of the speaker over the sound of laughter and the staticky Spanish voice of Woody Woodpecker on the other side of the house door. Television! That's what's new! I can see the familiar flickering of bluish-grey light through the carrizo and mud-thatched walls. The light reminds me of caged lights used to mesmerize and shock flying bugs around picnics. No children surround us this time. Only adults are here this evening. Last year, the Florez family didn't have a television. I see the electrical cord run into the house through the cane wall from the outside. My ethnographic sense of change kicks in, and I immediately feel a sense of loss. Then I feel bad that I do. How presumptuous of me to make ethical judgments on someone else's access to technology. And then I realize that the topic of conversation among the adults has changed again.

Seeing the Testamento through the Trees

While the Testamento is clearly important to many Yoeme people, its compilation as a single text raises questions about its continued role in Yoeme oral tradition. As shown, the Testamento is a formal narration, encompassing spatial codes and linguistic mechanisms that help Yoeme people transfer their social identity as a land-based group to following generations. But the Testamento is not the only myth that uses spatial codes to historicize Yoeme land rights. To some effect, it replaces other stories of pre-Jesuit worldview, but only to a certain population. Some Yoemem surely appreciate the use of biblical personae and events within indigenous claims to sovereignty. In the remaining pages of this chapter, I explore the relationship between the Testamento and other oral traditions, paying particular attention to how certain myths develop from anthropological dialogues. The development and promotion of a certain mythology cannot be separated from the historical context of who was seeking to tell which stories about the Yoemem and their colonial resistance.

In contrast to Evers and Molina's treatment in their "Holy Dividing Line" article, an ethnographic inquiry into community knowledge of the Testamento reveals a picture much more focused on individual parts of the narrative or on different myths entirely. Evers and Molina suggest that the Testamento is well known, since a meeting of representatives in the late 1950s included a recitation and copying of the text for all pueblos (1992, 11). They review the ethnographic sources to determine how other ethnographers may have encountered the Testamento previously. They note that Spicer encountered a set of stories in Rahum Pueblo (the Rahum land myths) that would later become the Testamento. Evers and Molina give a couple pages of attention to a version encountered by Spicer in Rahum in 1942. While working under Spicer's direction, Ruth Warner Giddings wrote in her master's thesis that one tribal historian, Juan Valenzuela, knew the material and wrote it out for them.[5] Evers and Molina also discover a third version given to John Dedrick in Rahum in the early 1960s, apparently a text made from the 1951 "original copy" at the meeting of the pueblos there in Rahum.

We can see that the common coordinate in all of these versions is Rahum Pueblo. But the 1951 meeting in Rahum brought together only representatives from the eight pueblos, leaving open the question of how well the rest of the community members know the Testamento. In 1992 and 1993 an Arizona State University graduate student, Jim Mahoney, went to the pueblos to answer that question. While in Potam, the governor told him that a copy exists but did not indicate whether it was in his possession (Mahoney 1993). In Rahum, Mahoney was told that not all pueblos had a physical Testamento, but that one copy definitely exists in Guadalupe Pueblo, near Phoenix, Arizona (25). In Lomas de Bakom, a ceremonial leader told Mahoney that copies no longer existed in Ko'oko'im or Bakom, but that "all the Yoemem know about the Testamento and know what the words say" (32). In New Pascua, Arizona, Mahoney again heard that everyone knew about the Testamento. Mahoney heard the legend of the invisible pillar: "The old people say that there is a pillar, a big cement pillar. They say it's invisible most of the time. But it marks the borders of Yoeme land, and it's invisible to Yoemen who come across the lines, but when Yorim come up to the boundaries, the pillar appears, to show them they are crossing Yoeme land. If they try to get close to the pillar it seems to be farther on down [the holy dividing line]" (43). A pillar that appears and disappears? I cannot help but think of my journey to meet José Kukut at high noon by the rock formation called The Pillars. Like pots of gold under rainbows, the stories tempt you to keep up the search. But wait! Mahoney was not searching for a magical pillar: he was looking for the Testamento. It is telling that when Mahoney asks for the Testamento (or information about it), he receives a story with the trope of elusive searches. These diversions remind me of my own search for Testamento stories in the larger ethnographic literature on Yoeme culture and history. I searched various texts and archival files for information on the Testamento, but continually found other stories that seemed to be more widespread or more popular than the Testamento. Even Mahoney's search among the pueblos in 1992 suggests that as a written form the Testamento is not in every pueblo or that people are not talking about it. Another possibility is that the Testamento is defined not by a document but by a quest. The search for proof, the desire to obtain, to document — are these not the pillars of objective science? What exactly is appearing and disappearing?

After reviewing the sources that Evers and Molina read for evidence of the Testamento, I found that their sources often tell us more about other myths. For example, after Spicer asked Juan Valenzuela for Yoeme myths, his 1942 field notes show that he was told on March 11 about the singing of the boundaries. Yet earlier, on March 2, he was first told about the "talking stick."[6] In 1947 Spicer was working on a rough draft of "Processes of Yaqui Myth-Making," and he wrote that "there are a highly specialized set of myths *so far encountered in only one Sonora village* which is characterized by an account of a group of angels and prophets who, singing Christian hymns, defined the boundary by going around it in a body."[7] And in 1972, when Alfonso Ortiz wrote to Spicer asking for references to the best versions of the origin myth for the Yoemem and Mayo, Spicer replied, "There really isn't any such myth." He continues: "What exists are flood myths (*not very well or widely known among Yaquis* except in the Genesis biblical form), the talking stick myth in many forms and *the most widely known of all the basic myths*, the myth of the singing and making sacred of the tribal boundary, the myth of the Prophets and the Founding of the Eight Pueblos, and some others about origins of fire, etc."[8] In one case, his field notes with Juan Valenzuela, we see the Testamento being mentioned in part but as a continuation of a conversation that started with the talking stick story. In his own notes Spicer writes that only one town really knows the land myths. And in his letter to Ortiz he mentions the land myths but only after mentioning the talking stick, which is the "most widely known." Even in his book *Potam: A Yaqui Village in Sonora*, Spicer minimizes the collective value of the Rahum myths and the "prophetic talking stick" by stressing that these events are "either not accepted by other specialists [outside Rahum] as real events or are treated as non-historical in the sense that their time of occurrence cannot [be] fixed" (24–25). And in his book *The Yaquis: A Cultural History*, Spicer discusses the Rahum land myths as well as the talking tree, but sympathetically notes that the latter predates the former and is "widely known in the 20th century" (172). All of which is to say that while Spicer and Evers and Molina portray the Testamento as the "new mythology," the ethnographic evidence suggests that it is only part of a larger body of myths. We cannot find it as a "text." The Testamento is not ready-made and awaiting discovery. If anything, it is literally documented in the anthropological research.

In most cases when the Testamento is mentioned in the ethnological literature on the Yoeme, its popular currency is doubted, or it is mentioned in relationship with the talking tree. For example, Evers and Molina comment on Thomas McGuire's inability to learn anything about the Rahum myths in Potam when he was completing his fieldwork on Yoeme identity in 1975 and 1976 (1992, 7). Even after specifically asking for an example of Yoeme mythology, he was given the story of the talking tree, surrounded by an attentive group of children (McGuire 1986,

53).[9] When Ralph Beals worked in the Hiak Vatwe in the early 1930s, he was able to identify several "Cáhita myths," though he didn't label them as either Mayo or Yoeme in his retelling of them. And while he found a flood myth as part of a larger "Making of the World" myth, this version bears only some minimal resemblance to the Rahum land myths: Cristo Adan left a plan for the towns and a patron saint for each one, and he warned against selling any land to others. Then, as an example of what wise men talked about in "night sessions," Beals was given a version of the talking stick (1945, 216–18).

The Testamento is one of many stories that ethnographers have encountered in their work with the Yoeme. To be sure, except for the two or three most recent publications, the Testamento is never mentioned. We do not find examples of the Testamento, Rahum land myths, or establishing the eight pueblos in some of the most cited literature on the Yoeme: *Yaqui Women* (Kelley 1978), *An Autobiography of a Yaqui Poet* (Savala 1980), *The Tall Candle* (Moisés, Kelley, and Holden 1971), *Studies of the Yaqui Indians of Sonora, Mexico* (Holden et al. 1936), *A Yaqui Easter Sermon* (Painter, Savala, and Alvarez 1955), "The Elders' Truth: A Yaqui Sermon" (Maaso, Molina, and Evers 1993), and *Yaqui Deer Songs/ Maso Bwikam* (Evers and Molina 1987). The largest collection of Yoeme worldviews and ceremonies, Muriel Thayer Painter's 1986 *With Good Heart*, has several references to a flood but none that closely fit the Testamento description. For example, one person relates that there was a flood that killed everyone on earth and that preceded Jesus coming to the Hiak Vatwe and re-creating humans (10), and another collaborator mentions the flood as the division between the baptized ones and the ancestral immortals who decided not to jump on Noah's boat (11). So while Spicer claimed that the Yoeme were one of the "enduring peoples" of the world because of their synthetic and evolving Rahum land myths, we are struck by the absence of such land myths. How do we make sense of the myths' importance to Evers and Molina, Spicer, and Mahoney, but their relative absence from so many other texts? The question, to borrow from Evers and Molina, "provides another case for ongoing inquiry into the complex relations between oral and textual practices" (1992, 5).

The Testamento must be understood as only one of the various ways in which Yoeme people historicize their homeland and their aboriginal relationship with the hiakim. Let's consider two books that deal extensively with non-Testamento mythology: Ruth Warner Giddings's 1959 *Yaqui Myths and Legends* and Mini Valenzuela's 1977 *Yoeme: Lore of the Arizona Yaqui People*. Neither makes a clear distinction between stories from the southern and northern pueblos, since the informants for both books tend to be first-generation Yoeme Americans or binational residents. In both, however, the authors give focused attention to the great quantity of stories and legends told by Yoeme people. Giddings's research took place in 1942 in Potam Pueblo and around Tucson, mostly under the direction of Spicer or with his collaborators. She makes occasional notes of comparison with other tribal stories from around the Southwest, but avoids any cross-cultural analysis or any synchronic interpretation. Valenzuela's stories mostly come from her relatives, a respected family in Yoeme communities. Both authors list their sources and give titles to the individual stories, though it remains unclear whether the myths are actually referred to by those titles within the communities.

Although Giddings's text is cited often in ethnographies of the Yoeme, no one seems to have used her collection of stories to glean possible precontact worldviews. Although Giddings includes the story of a universal flood collected from Juan Valenzuela, this is the only example of Testamento material in more than sixty myths. The first story she presents is Lucas Chavez's rendition of the talking stick myth (25–27). And later in the text she includes a story about Chief Omteme, who used the information from the talking stick to better understand his first meeting with the Spanish (65–66).

Other precontact references in Giddings's text that have received little attention are the ones about powerful other-than-human persons. According to some of her collaborators, two very important pre-Christian Yoeme figures were Yuku and Suawaka. Yuku had one eye and was the god of thunder and lightning (32, 148). His wife, Namu, created rain with her tears. Their son-in-law, Suawaka, would watch for monstrous snakes from up above and send shooting stars down to kill them (138).

Sometimes Suawaka would come down to earth, and Yuku would get mad and shoot bolts of lightning at him. According to these myths, there were also gods or kings of snow, fire, and clouds (35, 159).[10] While several stories feature these beings, what remains the most constant feature is the mention of specific places in the Yoeme homeland. Most of the tales directly name the location in which the events occur. In this way, the Testamento is part of a more general process of locating events and powerful people from the past within the land of residence. Instead of "a land far, far away," Giddings's storytellers usually begin with "right here, at that hill called . . ."

Valenzuela's book *Yoeme* features more stories than Giddings's *Yaqui Myths and Legends* and a more diverse collection of community lore. Valenzuela's sources were born between 1898 and 1921, both in Arizona and Sonora. While Valenzuela does not attempt to relate any of her collected stories to tales in other tribes (a comparative exercise that Giddings attempts in only brief, uneven, and inconclusive fashion), her collection provides a more personal approach to the storytelling, since Valenzuela is working with her own family members. We can find a couple of similarities between these two texts. First, in Valenzuela's text we learn more about Suawaka and Yuku. Yuku's wife, Namu, is a rain cloud; her tears form the rain (56–57). We learn that Suawaka is thought to look like a fat, naked dwarf, only a foot high. The twanging of his bow makes thunder; the arrows are lightning bolts (22). Second, Valenzuela's book also contains many stories where specific place-names are invoked. Yoemem continue to use these place-names in the Hiak Vatwe. Third, as in Giddings's text, the talking tree story is at the beginning of Valenzuela's collection. I suggest that the story's placement speaks to cultural value, chronological considerations, or both. Valenzuela's text is a more comprehensive and detailed version of Giddings's book, with one exception: Valenzuela does not offer any versions of any form of the Testamento. Again, we are faced with an exhaustive text that aims to include a wide range of Yoeme stories but does not mention the flood, the prophets, or the forming of the eight pueblos. As we read across texts, Spicer's assessment of the Testamento as not being widespread gains validity.

Giddings's and Valenzuela's books show that Yoemem sustain a large body of mythology that includes stories of pre-Christian origin. Among these, most ethnographers have encountered the story of the singing tree or talking stick. We find in an examination of the available texts that only Spicer, Evers, Mahoney, and Molina have focused on the Testamento. Evidently the Testamento is only one of the many stories of precontact Yoeme life. Yet it has been a central concern for those authors interested in Yoeme processes of historicizing their rightful ownership of land. The Testamento is a mythopoetic document, a response to human needs and actions, originating in written form among certain Yoeme people who understood the writing down of the myths as a means to a political end.

Ethnographic concerns shape the information collected. In this particular case, anthropologists were romancing histories of resistance. We can hardly separate their research programs from the post–civil rights era focus on advocacy as well as the highly popular treks through native Mexico that so many U.S. scholars undertook.[11] Spicer was working with Yoeme communities, both north and south of the border, in the mid to late twentieth century. Giddings worked in the field under Spicer's direction. Evers and Molina, as well as Mahoney, were working in the late twentieth century with Yoeme collaborators, expecting their friends to effect change or at least awareness of their plight. One could say that the bulk of Yoeme focused scholarship was produced in post-1960s America, during a moment of particular attention to American Indian welfare. This group of scholars sought to understand a specific notion of Yoeme ethnicity: belonging to and owning a land base. The needs of the Yoeme communities and the interests of the ethnographers coincided to produce a concentration on one segment of Yoeme oral tradition: the Rahum land myths, or the Testamento. Perhaps the ethnographers here were simply taking the leads of their cultural insiders, or perhaps the Yoeme people were taking the leads of the ethnologists. No doubt both processes were taking place.[12] To bring this chapter to a close, let's consider the historical phase of Testamento research. Specifically, by understanding Spicer's and others' desire to help with Yoeme land claims, we see how the Testamento is authored by and authorizes a Yoeme agency that strategically engages the production of history.

The Mexican Revolution came to a close in the first decade of the twentieth century; so did the outright, brutal persecution of Yoeme people in Sonora. However, when most Yoemem returned to their homeland in 1911, they found not abandoned villages and towns but their previous pueblos now filled with Mexicans and some North Americans. As Spicer notes in his history of this occupation, "In 1908–1909 fliers were distributed in central California towns such as Visalia and Merced urging people to go to the Yaqui Valley and buy parcels of the 'most fertile land on earth' at $25 an acre" (1980, 259). By 1910, in the vicinity of two previously Yoeme towns — Cocorit and Bacum — land had been parceled out freely to Mexican soldiers and sold to investors from the United States. Indeed, one of the most dramatic results of this history of Americans taking advantage of Mexican colonialism is the development of large waterfront properties on an ancestral landmark, Takalaim (also called Tetakawi), in San Carlos, Mexico. Understandably, when the Yoemem returned, they saw that their aboriginal homeland had been invaded, and regaining it became a central goal for the next thirty years.

Between 1910 and 1940 the Hiak Vatwe became important to Mexican national politics as Yoemem first started taking back villages and home sites by force. From this period many Mexicans came away with the impression that Yoemem were brutal, warlike, and a threat to the postrevolution peace process. If you read the Mexican ethnologies of Yoeme culture from this period, Yoemem are consistently the "fiercest fighters" of the new world: their brutality is in their blood. From the point of view of Yoemem, reestablishing all eight pueblos would lead to a return to Yoeme governance and sovereignty. Battles over land grew more and more violent up to 1927, when a group of Yoemem decided that they should discuss matters personally with General Alvaro Obregón, the previous and perhaps soon-to-be reelected president of Mexico. By intercepting his train, however, Yoeme intentions were understood by Mexican leaders as hostile and worthy of retaliation. The result was

2. Once a strong and wide river, the Hiak Vatwe continues to flow, here bending around south of Potam Pueblo.

military occupation of all eight pueblos, forced deportation of Yoeme leaders, and even aerial bombardment with American-made weaponry (Spicer 1980, 262). For the next ten years Yoemem in the eight pueblos were subjected to continuous Mexican supervision. To this day heavily manned and armed guard stations remain at the entrance to the pueblos, ostensibly part of a U.S.-backed "War on Drugs," just the latest version of the military's presence across the Yoeme homelands. When military leaders started selling Yoeme lands to Mexicans in the early twentieth century, Yoemem were forced to begin working for these Mexican land-holders in order to feed their families. And in 1935, the Mexican govern-ment formed the Yaqui Irrigation Commission to develop a means to divert the Hiak Vatwe to Mexican cities and farms, away from its historic path. With the completion of the Angostura Dam in 1941, 250 miles upstream from Cocorit, water was directed away from three pueblos: Belem, Huirivis, and Rahum.

By the time President Lázaro Cárdenas instituted his pro-Yoeme reforms in 1937, a fundamental change had taken place in the homelands: Yoeme people were now dependent on Mexican banks and irrigation commissions, as well as on dealings with non-Yoeme landowners. In his essay "Culture Change in Northwest Mexico," Charles Erasmus writes that General Miguel Guerrero Verdugo, the chief of the Mexican Army of Occupation, had been working since 1927 to "bring all Yaqui land revenues under his direct control" (1967, 26). General Guerrero established his own rules of governance in the region, permitting Mexican cattle ranchers and woodcutters access to Yoeme lands while collecting portions of the rental fees. Additionally, the formation of the Ejidal credit societies during this time led to a lasting change in Yoeme landownership. By 1959 there were forty-six credit societies that still function today. Erasmus (1967, 27) offers the most succinct description:

> The lands of each credit society are worked as a block, using modern farm machinery. Profits on the wheat or cotton crops go principally to pay the original costs of land clearing, the rental of farm machinery, and to reimburse the bank for the daily payment to each member of the eight pesos for each day worked during the farming cycle. The remaining profits, which are divided among members according to the number of days worked, are so small that the daily assistance payment virtually constitutes a wage, and it is below the lawful minimum wage scale for the area.

Erasmus's 1967 description still holds true, with the exception of the daily wage: my collaborators always complain about the difficulty of feeding children or paying for medicines. The credit system provides many means for corruption on all levels: from the credit banks, which can hold Yoeme land as collateral or for society debt, to the society leaders, who receive a higher wage and are in a position to siphon monies or harvests from other members. However, the main concern of the Yoeme people with whom I have spoken is that the land itself becomes the means of exchange with the banks. In order to support themselves and accumulate collective wealth for such things as education programs and ceremonial performances, most Yoemem in the homelands are repeatedly forced to borrow money to use their fields, the profits of which are distributed so thinly that they are in constant debt. Essentially, they are working their own land but only earning enough for the most basic level of sustenance, always in fear of losing that land to the banks. So although Cárdenas decreed a Zona Yaqui, a tribal reserve much smaller than that originated by the "singing of the boundaries," community members struggle for complete control over their hiakim, or homeland. Whether explicit or implicit, ethnographies of indigenous communities, even at the turn of the millennium, are so often ethnographies of debt peonage.

Spicer saw the effects of these material changes when attempting to understand why the Rahum land myths had become so important to many Yoemem in the mid-twentieth century. Since Spicer was working in the eight pueblos in 1941–42, 1947, and 1970, his analysis of Yoeme identity in terms of mythology would obviously be heavily influenced by the social changes taking place at those times. His research, which clearly influenced what subsequent students of Yoeme ethnography considered, took place as Yoeme people were fighting for and redeveloping their own control of the eight pueblos. To do this, Yoemem were actively bringing together a history of landownership that gave them aboriginal rights and "divine" sanction for their work. That the Yoemem at that time concentrated on the "singing of the boundaries," the principal story of the eight pueblo formation, demonstrates how many Yoemem view their own historiography as authoritative, literally authorizing the story of Yoeme land rights.

Articulating Yoeme identity in terms of both oral and written performativity, I wanted to recognize the Testamento as a written and performed script that validates a particular history while emerging as a result of historical encounters and struggles. I do not want to privilege the oral stories as a traditional strategy that exceeds literacy. Rather, by examining the relationship between the Testamento and the larger body of Yoeme myths, what emerges is an opportunity to reflect on a cultural process that the Yoeme share with other indigenous groups. By creating not just stories of the past but religious histories that map a specific cultural place in the world, indigenous communities often rely on symbols and myths that are usually not considered official histories. However, if we take steps to understand non-Western historical methods, we are confronted with nonwritten religious worldviews. By tracing the convergence of Yoeme colonial history and the varying results of previous ethnographic inquiry of Yoeme myth, this chapter has isolated the land myths as one means by which to understand the relationship between history and myth. In doing this work, we also come closer to understanding folklore's role in social formation. As Russell McCutcheon (1998) eloquently writes, "Systems of social significance encoded within narratives of the epic past and the anticipated future, coordinated within behavioral and institutional systems of cognitive and social control, characterize our responses to the various incongruities and disruptions that come with historical existence" (71). For many Yoemem, then, the Testamento is simultaneously a claim for land directed to outsiders and one part of a religious view of the world, where culturally defined ways of sharing history create and perhaps define the continuity and continuance of an "enduring" identity.

Ethnographic Dialogue 2

DAVID SHORTER: Like I said earlier today, I know that there simply isn't a single Yoeme perspective. There are many opinions and many perspectives within the tribe. And I also know that there are many people who, because of their devotion to Catholicism, do not like to talk about certain things like this. This is a list of words about people who have power. And it is possible that there are more, and I want to know if there are more. But also, specifically, I want to understand the relations among these because it is possible that a single category is the same as another or that there are distinct differences between them.

RESPONDENT: Okay.

DS: The first word is moreakame.

R: Ah, yes.

DS: The second is suakame (pronounced as su-á-kame).

R: Suakáme (correcting me, su-a-káme).

DS: The third is hechicero.

R: Hechicero, yes.

DS: And we can compare these categories to that of brujos. And later we can talk about seatakaa. Do you have any thoughts about these?

R: Well, kompae, the word suakame means to say that a person is very intelligent, a person who can solve a problem that others are unable to solve with the brains that God gave him. We could say that someone who is suakame has more knowledge than others. This is what suakame means in the Yoeme dialect.

DS: Okay, so there are suakamem among the tribe now?

R: There are two or three people, or there may be more still. People that speak of things that break us, the problems that we have in our tribe, the negative treatment by the government, from the people who aren't of our race, the suakamem analyze these kinds of situations with the knowledge or with the facility to understand things as they are and solve them on their own.

DS: Is it inherited from parents through birth?

R: No. It is independent. It is legitimate.

DS: Is it possible to gain it or obtain it? Or is it something that one simply is, a way of being?

R: It is what you have in your mentality. If a person has something like the gift to explain a situation with facility, or solve a problem or to help other people see things as they really are, to explain them to the whole community, to tell them the truth and show them what are lies and make them see reality. Those are the words made by a Yoeme suakame.

DS: I understand. And moreakame?

R: Moreakame is a story in our tribe that continues like a legend across all of the pueblos at the level of the eight towns. A moreakame is a person who has the gift to be able to cause pain to another person in this manner, as if he were hypnotizing them, or it could be an extrasensory thing that enables one person to dominate another person.

DS: In order to dominate?

R: Yes, it is like this. This is moreakame.

DS: You think it has negative connotations?

R: Yes.

DS: It is not a word that you are going to hear very often?

R: Well, in the village, the majority of people say there are not many moreak, or moreakame. But in reality, it is not verified and analyzed to say "this person has a gift for causing harm to a person." It is like a criticism in that one moment he is in his own house or chatting with a friend, and at this moment something can happen to him. Immediately people will begin to criticize: "This other man has it to cause harm to them! He is the one who did this thing to you!"

DS: And are there also people who have seatakaa?

R: So it is. Seatakaa is a gift that a person has. I don't know if the same happens with Mexicans, whites, Chinese, Japanese, or whatever people of another tribe or people of another race. But people who have seatakaa will be walking into the village on their way to their house, and they will think, "What will be going on in my house?" or "What is happening today, right now while I'm away?" or "What is going on at this other place?" And seatakaa goes as if it were a dimension of telepathy like this toward that house. Or from the other point of view, they hear a commotion; they hear the person walking toward them, just as if they heard how that person is walking, with the same paces. This is what seatakaa means.

DS: And is it true that they can know when a child has seatakaa, because they have a look to their hair?

R: Eh, yes. In the village, we Yoemem have the saying that a person with seatakaa, or a person that could have a gift of doing things, they have two cowlicks [indicating circular patterns on the back of his head]. Also, they say that those people or those children can plant and grow things that will grow well. Why? Because he has the double cowlicks on the head. The hairs have, like, two different growth patterns.

DS: Do you also think that presently in the tribe there are categories of people other than these three (moreakame, suakame, and a person that has seatakaa) that could be signified by the Spanish word hechicero?

R: The one that has the closest relationship to a hechicero is the moreakame, since they have the gift to cause harm to another. But the hechicero can also cure certain people, sometimes the person that they harmed themselves. You could call this person a hechicero or curandero.

DS: Is it possible to be a good brujo, or is a hechicero a good brujo?

R: Well, there are two types of curers or witches, no? One works black magic and the other white magic. The people who work black magic have a gift or power to harm others. And likewise, they can remove what they have done. But let's take the white magic people. These people work like spiritualists. White magic is indebted to the ancient curers that have died in years past, and the present-day curers and spiritualists invoke these deceased people in order to heal the patient they have in their house. But these people already know perfectly well who it was that harmed a certain person. The curer, though, cannot retaliate and harm that other person because they are not authorized to cause harm to others.

DS: Hmmmm.

R: They work with the Virgin de Guadalupe, with the images of other saints and all the virgins and saints, Jesus Christ, and other images. And the person that works black magic, he doesn't have saints, he doesn't have these things that can be of God. Why? Because he is against God, doing harm to his fellow man. And at the same time, he can remove their pain. Even if he caused it, he removes it from them. But the brujo or the one of white magic is not authorized spiritually, morally, or physically. He is not authorized to harm another person or to say which witch did harm. Yes, he would say to you something like, like hieroglyphics, like in signs, that someone did you harm. "You were in this place" or "with certain people. I cannot give you a real name, but I give you this proof," like a riddle for you to figure out who contracted the harm and negativity. This is what he does, he who works with white magic.

DS: Let's say a person is having a pain in their arm that they think is caused by another person's thoughts. What do you call that?

R: Black magic.

DS: Black magic. And could a person go to a practitioner of white magic or a curandera for a consultation and to be cured?

R: Yes, so it is. This is what those with white magic have. They take you and first they touch the parts that hurt to see how it feels. Then they ask how you have felt lately, when you began to feel the pain, and if you are sure you want to start a quarrel with another person who caused the pain. Then they have to ask for help from all the saints and all the spiritual doctors who have cured like them in the past. They ask them for a favor. That help is needed to solve a bad problem of one person caused by another.

DS: In Potam, presently, are you sure there are people who have these abilities?

R: Yes, there are.

DS: Are there witches?

R: There are witches.

DS: With black magic?

R: With black magic and white magic.

DS: Are there hechiceros?

R: It is the same thing

DS: And curanderos?

R: It is the same, because they know how to do things and witch well. And they are also able to cure.

DS: And in Potam, are there people that have suakame?

R: Yes, there are two or three people.

DS: And moreakame?

R: Yes.

DS: Are there others who have power?

R: Well, there are people who are able to give the evil eye to children or even adults. But they say that it is not their fault alone. Now I don't know if this is because they are not conscious that they are giving it, or if they simply want to touch the child or if they really like it, or if the other person is really ugly, or if they simply are angry. In any of these conditions, one can transmit the evil eye as if through extrasensory power to a child or an adult. But the sender does not know what he is doing. So a person like a curandero rubs it with an egg and draws it from them knowing that someone put the evil eye on them. And it hurts a lot when they have the evil eye. It burns a lot like cockleburs. Later the eye begins to swell, and it needs the curer to rub it with an egg and say the prayers that cure them of this pain. They have this oratory ritual that makes the bad leave the person.

DS: Is there a relation between these people and a pahko'ola?

R: Pahko'ola? No, they don't have any relation.

DS: Almost eight or nine years ago, two elder Yoemem told me that moreakamem did not have normal families. For example, it is possible that they are bisexual or that one man could be married to two women, or married to a man and a woman. They said that I could tell who was a moreakame by seeing that their families were different. Have you heard something like this?

R: Yes, but not in those ways.

DS: Okay.

R: We have a different version here in Potam than they do in the larger eight pueblos. He that has moreak, a moreakame, knows that he cannot have many women. He can have only one, no more. Why? Because the moreakame is said to have a morea, a choni, a cigar, an earthworm, or another class of animals. And these animals, they say, are very dangerous, as much as men and women. No matter whether they are men or women, no matter what type of animal they have, they have a type of witchery. So if they say, "I can do what I want to," the morea won't allow it. It will kill them or cause the owners to kill themselves.

DS: Ahh.

R: It is as if a son were very jealous of his mother or of his father. The mother would not marry another man. Why? Because the child would want to accuse him of taking his mom who still loves his father. And the same with the father, saying, "I am going to tell my mother that you are messing around, that you are doing damage, doing bad." And if the mother or father is questioned in this way, gossip begins. Therefore the man, at the moment he has been talked about, knows that he has faulted morally and that it is not the fault of the little animals, those little people, the Surem. You have my permission to do what you want with all of this when you get to the other side. This has not been heard before, not in the Yoeme dialect. You will not hear this from Spanish speakers. So it is.

DS: Have you ever heard of children who can move or break things from afar?

R: Yes.

DS: Do you think this is a sign of these moreakame?

R: Not exactly. This child was my son. He died at two years old. When he was made angry, he toppled things off the table, off the cot, the chairs, or glasses or plates on the table, or whatever object, he knocked them down. But I don't know if . . . Thank God that I did not get mad by seeing what he broke. Or perhaps like you are saying today, that maybe with time he could have developed his senses about these things. Perhaps at some point he could have caused harm to other people. Because in my tribe, they say that these people do not have fathers or mothers. That they do not have a family, that they do not have brothers or sisters. If they get angry, it does not matter that they are mad at their mother. They are capable of enchanting her until she dies. This is how they tell the story. Someone could come to you and say this is not verifiable truth. It is, as of right now, a legend. It is like a legend because we all know it, but we cannot say it clearly or declare, "I know that you are a moreakame" or "I know that you are a witch!" We don't say this because we do not have proof with which to accuse them. Or perhaps we desire things to be good. Or because we have heard other people say something or have criticized a certain person that we take a hold of those words and then judge them without knowing them. This is how it is.

DS: When a person has seen the yo ania, are they said to have seatakaa?

R: Yes, this is true. But these people are also very protective.

DS: Oh, yeah?

R: There are two or three people that have been in these mountains, these houses of enchantment, and they don't really tell you what is inside. They leave it as a story. Like saying, "I will tell you this quaint little made-up story. And if it compels you to do what I did, then you will see what is behind those rocks, behind that mountain." But they don't give you more than that until you've actually gone there. But they don't tell them, "You know what? All that is inside there, you can have all of it!" They don't tell them anything. What they do say is, "Look inside the door. There are animals, and these animals will want to eat you and they'll attack you." But if you do not have fear of these animals, and without questioning their intentions, if you walk inside there, with your thoughts and with what your heart wants while walking, the doors are going to open for you and you will walk until you are inside. This is what they say.

DS: Ah. In the legends where there are people that can make hiak viva (cigarettes made with Yoeme tobacco that can be made to fly through the air, hit people, and cause harm), is it a hechicero or moreakame?

R: Moreakame, hechicero, brujo, it is the same family. It is the same family. It is one category. I have seen the flying cigarette. I do not know where it came from, who sent it, or who was the owner of that viva. I don't know. But, yes, I did see it. It is a cigar made from hiak viva and rolled with a cornhusk, almost as if it were a plane with little needles that make it stick. But one has it like a normal cigar. But it has the end burning, flying ten to fifteen meters high, lit like someone was running with a cigar in their hand. And it is heard from afar, and so you can run to see it and see the little ashes falling from it, just like the ash from a cigar. I saw exactly this.

DS: Only one time?

R: Several times. But I don't know where they come from, nor do I know who was the owner of this viva. But I do know I saw it. I arrived to see people bringing buckets of water because of the falling embers. Then we saw what it was and what it was made of, what it contained, the materials of this cigar. As I explain it, I don't know if it moved telepathically, if someone was moving it, or if it was given its own life, or what. This is all I can explain.

DS: And you have never seen a choni?

R: Only the noise. Just the noise. The noise of the choni is like a little whistle [makes an airy whistling sound].

DS: It is a high pitch?

R: Yes, very high. And when he walks above the house, it is as if he were a cat walking above, as if he were really heavy. And when he jumps, poom! It sounds as if it were really heavy and it weighs as if, like they say, because I have not seen what it looks like or what size it is. But they say that it is a small child, of thirty inches, with long hair and dark skin. He is like the size of a newborn child. And upon arriving at the owner's house, it is put in a small box that they say has a lock and is lined with pig's hair. Some say these are the scalps of Apaches, but who knows? I don't know if that part is certain. God knows. I cannot say if they are Apache because I have not seen them. So things are.

DS: But to hear it, to hear you, it is significant to me what you think. Are there chonim in Potam right now?

R: Probably.

DS: Probably?

R: Probably.

DS: There are legends that say that in the past it was possible for some people to remove their skin and walk the streets without their bodies.

R: No, this is a lie. I have never heard of this type of legend.

DS: You have never heard of moreakamem or a person of black magic that could?

R: Walk so?

DS: Yeah, walk invisibly?

R: No.

DS: Ok. What is a chupiari?

R: A chupiari is a person that does a particular type of sexual thing, a harm or danger, in their family, with their sons, with their daughters, or with their sisters or brothers or close family member or with people who are compadres or a person that loves one very much. They say "chupiari uu vato'i" (even the baptized can become these animals).

DS: Uu vato'i?

R: Yes, any person. Chupia means that one is condemned in Spanish. One is condemned as if one were chained for eternity to a certain animal. And this animal makes himself visible when that person dies. When they die, the person that is condemned, the Yoemem say when they see the

whirlwinds or winds or rains. Or here at Takalaim [a large
mountain in San Carlos, Mexico], in the afternoon we
can hear a noise alongside the sea like an explosion, like a
bomb. Boom! That's when the Yoemem say in Yoeme, "One
has arrived at their destiny." Now, Takalaim, this is the
house of those that are condemned. They are condemned
and required to stay there.

DS: So, after a chupia dies, they live in Takalaim?

R: Yes, in Takalaim. But we also have this story that these
people are being fattened up for our father Yuku and
Suawaka. They are simply being given time to fatten them
up. And when they are fat enough, they are eaten. And this
is where the legend ends. Anything more is not verified. It
is not scientifically verified, not even by Yoemem. It is like a
legend, like a story. How can I say this to you, a story of this
kind? What is it called? Mythology. So it passes, this passes
like a legend or mythology passes. So it is how it passes
with these things. But this is how you hear these things,
in a town or in a tribe. And not just in the Yoeme tribe. I
imagine that in all the tribes. Because the Mayos also have
a similar way of talking about someone that has done bad.
There is no proof, no place for someone to sign their name
and say, "Yes, this person died and I saw that he converted
to a snake or another animal and that it left his house." No,
this is what is missing. And this is what we would have to
do to corroborate it. It is like the conversation you and
I have had about the Jesuits. If they, the Jesuits, had the
ability to come to the tribe and talk with us, we'd ask them,
"Where are the Yoeme names?" As a Yoeme, I like knowing
the name of a person. I can investigate his lineage all the
way up until today. It is like when you look up what you
want to know on your Internet. I would do the same with
families of hundreds of years back. Who was this family?
Where were they from? Then I would go there asking until

I found where that family lived now. Perhaps they would have a piece of paper, a document that you could read. But what if he couldn't write? How could he give another sign to other people? It does not exist.

DS: Yes.

R: It is not verified. A Jesuit cannot, an archaeologist cannot say, "I did verify what the Jesuits did with the Yoemem." Why? Because it is not verified. On the other hand, what you and I are doing, I give you my name and in the future you will give to the people all over the world what I say to you, and if they do not believe you, I am at your disposal to whatever types of people to tell them what I am telling you, that they are real things, that they are certain and true things. One can say, "Oh, David Shorter, investigator, archaeologist of the Yoeme studies, who gave you this information?" Or perhaps you can invite me to a conference. I will gladly go and explain the same thing I am telling you. Why? Because it is a reality. It is the story of my town, of my life, of my people. I do not have a reason to go around deceiving people, even more so to you.

DS: Thank you.

3 Listening to the Tree and Hearing History

In what remains the most comprehensive ethnohistory of the Yoemem, *The Yaquis: A Cultural History*, Edward H. Spicer begins with contact stories from the sixteenth century. He does not include any Yoeme stories of life before the Spaniards arrived. This is a common problem in Native American histories: an exclusive reliance on documents written by European explorers, traders, or travelers. Such reliance can imply that the relevant past begins with Europeans arriving on the American continents.[1]

Not until Spicer's wife, Rosamond, found a collection of field notes in 1992 could we understand that Spicer was also interested in native Yoeme cosmology in terms of its historical insights. This "lost file" is essential to new interpretations of the Yoeme experience, since it offers pathways to writings by Yoemem, rather than simply about them. In his "Preliminary Report on Potam," Spicer records three precontact stories given to him in 1942 by Juan Valenzuela: a story of a talking tree, another of a flood, and one of Yoemem singing their boundaries. Although Spicer calls for legitimation from other documents, he places primary importance on researching these stories for what they say about an era undocumented by other ethnographers and historians. He seems to appreciate how these myths function within historiography.

To imagine such myths as history, Spicer makes a crucial distinction between a story and the internal interpretation of the story. He writes, "They all, along with other material which must be associated with them, should be studied internally and in conjunction with whatever there is in the historical records in order to get them placed in their proper relation to the rest of Yaqui cultural history" (1992, 116). Note the process: these stories should be "studied internally," alongside other Yoeme oral histories, and contrasted with the "historical records," which are external, documented by different terms. In a closed context of Yoeme historical production and consumption, Spicer does not argue that these stories need support, validity, or documentation. However, as non-Yoeme voyeurs, academics need some kind of written proof. For example, Spicer dates the origin of the talking tree story as pre-Jesuit, but writes:

> This interpretation needs all sorts of further support. It needs an inquiry into documentary sources; it needs the support of more mythical material of the same type; it needs comparative study of this material with other more standard and generally known mythology of the Yaquis. The material seems to me extremely significant and is widely worthy of all the study that can be given it. In it we have a beautiful example of myth-making in the process, and it will result in giving us also a keen insight into the most significant period of Yaqui history, next to that of the period of conversion by the Jesuits. (1992, 119)

Referring to the interpretations as "materials," Spicer demonstrates his interest in including Yoeme interpretations of their stories as part of their own historical process. Instead of setting myth against history, Spicer believed that "myth-making" — the relationship between stories and their tellers — sheds light on "history." He therefore foregrounds a current ethnohistorical method: asking not whether a tree can talk, but what it means for Yoemem to tell stories about a talking tree.

In order to feature Yoeme narratives of the talking tree, I survey the ethnographic literature on Yoeme myth and history and bring the versions together that can be found in the published documents. The result is a chorus of sorts, a bringing together of Yoeme speakers from various times and places to offer their individual stories of a collective Yoeme past. Performing such a mediumship helps explain how the tree, much like the Testamento, provides Yoeme communities with a strategic historical consciousness. Several scholars of Yoeme culture (Spicer, Hu-

DeHart, Evers and Molina, Sands) have collected the talking tree stories, and I will compare thirteen versions, closely analyzing two exemplary renditions. This chapter and the next show how Yoemem have made sense of Spanish and Jesuit culture contact and how they make sense today of their own historic and collective identity.

Driving toward Vicam Pueblo, Felipe tells me that the hill to our left is Omteme Kawi, or Angry Mountain. He tells me that the talking tree stood on this mountain in the vatnaataka, or beginning times. As we pull off the road to take pictures of the mountain, my mind rehearses the many stories I have heard or read about the tree and the world in which this tree spoke. The vatnaataka was the time of the Surem, the little people, maybe three feet tall, some of whom would later become the Yoemem. These Surem had no need for language because they communicated telepathically among themselves and with all living beings: plants, rocks, animals, even trees. Considered wise and immortal, these proto-Yoemem lived peaceful lives until a tree began to hum an unintelligible language. Some say the tree was singing. I look over at Felipe, who has been driving the last leg of our trip, and he notices that I am excited. Here is the spot where it all started: a strange sound from a tree, a young female transla-tor, prophesies of missionaries, cities, telephones, and airplanes. Only some Yoemem community members know all of the prophecies due to the revelatory impact. When asked specifically about why prophecies are described in parts and to only certain people, elders told me that listeners must be ready in order to understand correctly. One collaborator likened it to explaining the ways of the world to children, only telling them about death or sex when they have the capability to handle the information. In many ways, the talking tree story is about death and reproduction because it deals directly with mortality and how Yoemem come to exist as they are. The talking tree stories explain the transformation from small, immortal, psychic people to taller, mortal, speak-ing Yoemem. The story explains why the tribe would always be separated yet cohesive. And the tree was here.

But the hill seems so ordinary. Perhaps I was expecting something more spectacular, like a mountain of cosmic proportions. In fact, the hill is covered with radio transmitters, satellite dishes, and antennae of different heights.

3. Antennae emit humming noises atop Omteme Kawi.

*Sensing my surprise, Felipe tells me that the antennae on top emit a hum-
ming noise, much like the singing tree. I search Felipe's face for some sign of
comedy or a hint of how seriously to take his comment. Is Felipe intending
such irony, or am I simply struggling to make the connection? I ask Felipe,
"Weren't people upset when they built those transmitters and antennae on
top of this important mountain? Didn't people protest?" Shifting his normal
half-smiling facial expression to serious reflection, Felipe responds, "No, but
the tree told us about it. The tree sang to the Surem and told them about the
technology and changes that would be coming." I sit in silence, running my
fingers over the soft, felt underside of my camera strap.*

*I catch myself wanting to find some sense of community resistance to change,
to learn that the Yoemem living around Vicam fought some war of position
against the powers of transnational late-capitalist transnationalism. But Felipe
seems to be suggesting Yoeme compliance with progress and technology. The
analogy to colonization is tempting. Had the tree always calmed their experience of the new? After we sit awhile in mutual contemplation of the view, Felipe
adds that if a prophecy tells you the Jesuits are coming, you understand their
presence and welcome the revelatory disclosure. If a tree tells you that people
will communicate without being next to each other, what a perfect place for*

this technology, right where the tree first had problems communicating with the people standing there. The hum of the transmitters is no longer a conquering force but an echo of a long endurance.

I am still contemplating the talking tree. I wonder how telling stories of the tree creates a historical consciousness. To be sure, hearing different versions of the story has convinced me that we have much to learn about Yoeme perspectives on the Conquest or, as they call it, the "bringing of Christianity," the Konkista. Narrating the creation of their pueblos and communities, the tree gives Yoemem a way to make sense of their relationships with their ancestors, relatives, descendants, and outsiders. The tree continues to predict Yoeme endurance.

The Sounds of Prophecy and the Surem Divided

In their definitive 1987 study, *Yaqui Deer Songs/Maso Bwikam: A Native American Poetry*, Larry Evers and Felipe Molina locate the beginning of Yoeme identity in terms of the talking tree story. They describe many aspects of Yoeme culture and specifically focus on the verbal art of singing deer songs. To lay the groundwork for explaining a Yoeme world, they explain the talking tree in their chapter "Where It Comes Out." After recounting Luciano Velasquez's version of the story, Evers and Molina stress the importance of the myth:

> The separation described in this story is definitive. From the time of the talking tree there have been two kinds of Yaquis. On the one side are the Vato'im, Baptized Ones, those who accepted the seventeenth-century Spanish Catholicism offered them by Jesuit missionaries and absorbed it into their lives. On the other side are those who refused baptism, the Surem, the enchanted people, those who went away to preserve the Yaquis' aboriginal relation to the world. The relation between these two parts of the Yaqui world is complex and reciprocal, and it bears directly on our understanding of deer songs (1987, 38).

Although we will return to Velasquez's version, I use Evers and Molina's reaction to his story to support my introductory claim that the

Table 1. Talking Tree Constituents

VERSION	STORYTELLER	SOURCE	DATE RECORDED
I	Unnamed	Beals 1945: 223	1932
II	Unnamed	Spicer 1984: 240	1936–37
III	Rosalio Moisés	Moisés, Kelley, Holden 1971: xxiv–xxv	1934–55
IV	Lucas Chavez	Spicer 1988: 138	1936–37
V	Lucas Chavez	Giddings 1959: 25–27	Spring, 1942
VI	Informant 52	Painter 1986: 9–10	1948–75
VII	Anselmo Valencia	Kaczkurkin 1977: 6	1950–77
VIII	Luciano Velasquez	Evers and Molina 1987: 37–38	August 1982
IX	Javier Choqui	Ruíz Ruíz and Aguilar 1994: 31	1987
X	Don Esteban Jiménez	Ruíz Ruíz and Aguilar 1994: 17–19	1987
XI	Jesús Ramirez Valenzuela	Ruíz Ruíz and Aguilar 1994: 21–23	1987
XII	Unnamed	Erickson 2003: 470–471	1997

KEY
A = Female Translator(s)
B = Baptism
C = "Conquest"
D = God
E = Spaniards

singing tree is seminal, cosmogonic, and central to Yoeme oral tradition, ritual performance, and historical consciousness. As Kathleen Sands keenly concludes after her analysis of the tree stories, "What can be firmly stated is that the myth ties directly to the baptized/unbaptized concept that is essential to Yaqui self-definition, and that the various adaptations and changes in the myth over the years have real connections to the historical and cultural changes in Yaqui society over the last four centuries" (1983, 374). Kirstin Erickson rightfully emphasizes that these tree stories concern "the very inception of Yaqui identity" (2003, 467). And although Spicer and Hu-DeHart vary in their assess-

PLACE RECORDED	RECORDER	A	B	C	D	E	F	G	H	I	J
Pascua; Vicam, Sonora	Beals	×	×	×	×	×					×
Pascua, AZ	Spicer	×	×	×				×	×	×	×
Torim, Sonora, or Lubbock, TX	Kelley or Holden	×	×		×		×			×	×
Pascua, AZ	Spicer	×	×	×	×						
Pascua or Barrio Libre	Giddings	×	×	×	×		×				×
Pascua, AZ	Painter	×	×			×	×				×
Pascua, AZ	Kaczkurkin	×		×	×	×		×			×
Kompwertam, Sonora	Molina	×	×	×		×	×		×	×	×
Potam, Sonora	Ruíz Ruíz and Aguilar										×
Torim, Sonora	Ruíz Ruíz and Aguilar	×	×		×	×	×	×			×
Loma de Guamúchil	Ruíz Ruíz and Aguilar	×	×			×					×
Potam, Sonora	Erickson	×		×	×		×	×			

F = Sickness/Death/Mortality
G = Civil Life
H = Technologies

I = Help from the Ocean
J = Tree Precedes Disunity

ment of the talking tree's pertinence to their histories as I show in the next chapter, I bring together here the works of Yoeme historians and academic scholars in order to understand not only the tree's central role in Yoeme worldview but also how the strategy of singing trees wrestles Yoeme agency from Eurocentric histories of the Americas.

A survey of recorded and published versions of the talking tree stories reveals various interpretations, but also we see convergences and points of agreement.[2] As we track these stories and locate their parallels and parities, we can begin to develop a sense of how the tree myth has grown and branched while still developing from a unitary narrative trunk. In the following correlation of thirteen tree stories, I show that the myth always focuses on a prophecy, unintelligible at first, that reflects on how Yoemem prepared for European contact. The invariance on this theme, precontact disunity, displaces a common interpretation of Indian and non-Indian relations, that of first contacts as historical "ruptures." Competing with and complicating historical tropes of colonial loss and victimization, the talking tree story helps establish cultural continuity. Some Yoemem use the prophecy of the Spanish arrival to make sense of colonialism before the Jesuits arrived. Some of the storytellers draw on the Yoeme notion of the Konkista ("the bringing of Christianity") as a reference to what happens before the Spaniards. Locating the beginning of social disruption in precontact times, Yoemem provide a context where commonplace notions of "Conquest" fail to make sense of indigenous realities. The talking tree offers a retelling of colonization, missionization, and culture contact, with Yoeme agency at the center of history. For some Yoeme, the talking tree story continues to show how the Conquest began with internally generated disagreement, not with Spanish intrusion.[3]

Among the variations (see page 132) I am most struck by the differences in descriptions of the tree and the tree's interpreter. In terms of location, the only concurrence is that versions 7 and 12 place the tree on Omteme Kawi. Version 2 places it in the "middle of Suri country." In version 8, Luciano Velasquez of Kompwertam, Sonora, tells Molina that it could have been at Omteme Kawi or another possible option. He relates that "a tree was heard talking on a small hill called Tosai Bwia, White Earth. Some say it was heard at Omteme Kawi, but we say it was at Tosai Bwia." Velasquez says that the tree was "an old dead mesquite tree," and five Yoeme storytellers agree that it was either a "stick" or a "pole" (versions 3, 4, 10, and 11 and Valenzuela). Version 7 states that the tree was a Palo Verde, while versions 2 and 5 suggest a monolithic "pole" or "huge thick stick from ground to sky."

The contrasting interpretations of the tree's voice lead to the different names of the myth itself: talking tree, singing tree, talking stick, enchanted stick, and so on. Evers and Molina stress the importance of sound and language when writing about the tree: "They may be part of what we call myth, history, vision, or dream, but time and again in Yaqui stories the people must understand sound from beyond the limits of everyday language of their communities in order to continue. In this sense there are no creators in Yaqui tradition, only translators. All beginnings are translations" (1987, 36). Molina and Evers are supported by my survey, since we see that every story recognizes this struggle to interpret the tree. Velasquez tells us, "It made strange humming sounds. Nobody could understand the sounds" (Evers and Molina 1987, 37). In other versions, the tree hums strangely (8) or buzzes like bees (5). For some, it talks (6, 10) or makes noises in a strange language (7). The tree vibrates (1 and 2) or goes "tap tap tap" like a telegraph (3).[4] Regardless of what the tree does, almost every story tells us that the tree is communicating and, for the first time, that the Surem do not understand.

In order for the Surem to make sense of the tree, they must rely on an interpreter. In most stories the Surem receive help from a woman, but her name and role vary. She is either a wise old woman or perhaps the "mother of the sea," named a variant of "Yomu'muli" (2, 3, 4, 5, 7, 8), or she is a queen (1), but her royal status is not explained. In version 5, "Yomumuli" is the mother of "all the Indians."[5] "Yomumule" is simply "an old woman" in version 4, and "Yomumuli" is a "young girl" in versions 6 and 7. The "young girl" interpreter is not named in versions 1, 3, 9, 10, and 12. In story 3 her father is named "Mapoli," or poppy flower. Velasquez also described a male figure who was named, but whose daughters were not. Velasquez told Felipe Molina:

> These wise men [Surem] knew of one other wise man who lived near a little mountain called Asum Kawi, Grandmothers' Mountain. This man's name was Yomomoli, and he had twin daughters. The wise men visited him and requested that his two daughters interpret the talking tree. Yomomoli told them that the girls didn't have a good vocabulary, so they would be incapable of doing such a task. The men insisted. Finally they convinced Yomomoli to take the girls to the talking tree. But Yomomoli did one thing first. He took his twin daughters to the ocean. There they talked to a fish, so that they might better understand

the talking tree. At Tosai Bwia the girls stood on either side of the tree, and they began to interpret. The tree predicted Christianity and baptism, wars, famine, floods, drought, new inventions, even drug problems, and so on. After the tree had given all the information, it stopped making the sounds. (Evers and Molina 1987, 38)

Velasquez's naming of the man in effect gives more attention to the man's role in the story. Further, we can see in version 8 that the female translators are characterized as not having a good vocabulary and must request assistance from their gilled helpers.

Due to the respect that Yoemem and others have granted to Juan Valenzuela as a tribal historian and interpreter of Yoeme culture, I pay particularly close attention to his rendition of the "Talking Stick and the Surem," as titled by its recorder, Edward Spicer. Because this is one of Spicer's earliest recorded versions, we should pay attention to how the story's specifics buttress Spicer's larger body of scholarship. In the previous pages I provided my own analysis; these are not exactly the most appropriate ways to read important stories (if they should be read at all). In light of these concerns, I present Juan Valenzuela's version in its entirety:

There was a time when the people of the Yaqui River knew nothing about baptism. This was some time before the Conquest by the Spaniards and marks the beginning of the real Conquest in the Yaqui country.

There was a stick at Vicam. It was of mesquite, and it was very thick. It spoke sometimes with a voice that was very unpleasant. People came to listen to it, but there were none who could understand what it said. The old people of Vicam tried and so did the older people of the other eight pueblos. There were many wise men in those days, but there were none who knew what the stick was saying.

There was a man named Mapooli, who lived in the west of the Yaqui country. He lived a little way toward the sea from the present place of Mapooli on the Southern Pacific Railroad. He had a daughter named Mapooli [sic]. The old people of the eight pueblos came to him and told him that they would like him to listen to the stick and say whether or not he could understand it. He said that he would have to get ready. So he took his daughter and went down to the sea. Here he caught a fish and had some conversation with it, telling it what the pueblo wise men had asked him to do. The fish asked him why he had to do this, and he said that the *mayoria* [majority, or group of elders] had ordered it. Then the fish said he would help him with what knowledge he had. So Mapooli went to Vicam with his daughter, and they found all the people of the eight pueblos gathered there. The stick was speaking in its very terrible voice every half hour. Finally it began to talk again. Mapooli was there with his daughter, and she translated what the stick was saying. It said: "There is a thing called baptism. All those who are baptized will die." This is all it said. Mapooli told the people. There was an angel in the sky above whose spirit had been talking.

Immediately all the people in each of the pueblos were divided into two different groups. Every pueblo, wherever you went on the Yaqui River, had one group of people who wanted to be baptized and one group who did not. The people got great piles of wood and took them to Vicam. There, one group planned to burn the talking stick. There was a great fight all up and down the river, the people who wanted to be baptized fighting with the people who did not want to be. They fought hard. Eventually the people burned the talking stick, but those who wanted to be baptized were baptized. Those who would not be baptized became enchanted. Everywhere on the Yaqui River they were enchanted, like the Mesa Encantada near Roosevelt Dam in Arizona.

These people who became enchanted remained here but no one knows where they are exactly because they cannot be seen. Sometimes a person hears a drum or a violin, and it is probable that this is the music of the enchanted people. Sometimes when a *pascola* musician is a very good musician it is said that he learned his music from the enchanted people. They, like the Yaquis, are the descendants of the Surem, who were the small people who lived everywhere in the Yaqui country in the ancient times before the talking stick was in Vicam and before the beginning of the Conquest which started with the talking stick.

Spicer provides this version of the talking stick in his "Preliminary Report of Potam," or his "lost file" (1992, 127–28). Since this version told to him by Juan Valenzuela differs in many ways from most other versions, I will detail the points of departure as well as resemblances to other interpretations.[6]

In terms of historical periodization, Valenzuela clearly dates the earliest events as pre-Christian in the first sentence. This historical designation is in every version. Even in the one story that does not say before Christianity, version 3, the storyteller says that the tree talked before the Spaniards arrived. By consistently placing the story before Jesuit contact, these Yoeme speakers present Yoeme agency in their choosing or not choosing baptism. Hence the most important comment in terms of understanding Yoeme historical consciousness is in the second sentence: Valenzuela states that the "real" Conquest happened before Spanish encounters.

For Valenzuela the tree is more like a single stick, and he doesn't mention the location of the tree, as others do, on Omteme Kawi or Tosai Bwia. While he says that the voice is "very unpleasant," Valenzuela doesn't mention the telepathic Surem, or proto-Yoemem, who would have found undecipherable communication strange and possibly unpleasant because they didn't need to speak to communicate with other Surem and other-than-human persons.[7] After fifteen years in a Yoeme community, Muriel Thayer Painter was able to learn that the telepathic Surem "were little people, about three feet high, who were never sick." Painter's informants told her that the Surem lived in "a unitary world in which man and animals, insects, flowers, indeed, the whole world of nature and man, had a common psychic life" (1986, 4). Or as Beals records in 1945, "At the time all spoke one language, but only Queen Yomomúli could understand the pole" (223). Since this tree's utterances were the beginning of disunity in other versions, Valenzuela may be suggesting that Conquest begins with the inability to communicate.

While the strong role of women as culture bearers in Yoeme worldview has always been central to their collective identity, Valenzuela chooses to feature the presence of "wise men." Although both Valenzuela and Valesquez (version 8) name only the male character, they agree with the other storytellers that the actual translator was female.[8] In fact, in six versions (3, 5, 6, 7, 8, and 12), either the father figure must defer to his daughter(s) or the teller specifically mentions that none of the "men" could translate the noises from the tree. The female translator is often called Sea Hamut (Flower Woman), a woman with special powers, and she is sometimes a great hunter, a queen, or a wise old woman. She is sometimes, as in Valenzuela's version, sought in the west where she lives or visits the ocean before meeting the tree (3, 8, 12). As Erickson notes, Kathleen Sands writes that many southwestern native peoples associated movement from the west with new and unwanted things: slave raiding ships, Spanish travelers, and so on (Erickson 2003, 472; Sands 1983, 363–64). We also know from the work of Muriel Thayer Painter that the special powers of the seahamut are often connected with powers from the ocean (1986, 5–9, 11, 12, 102).

Wanting to get away from the children and pueblo, Guillermo and I take a drive into a neighboring Mexican city for a bite to eat. Traveling with him through cities across Sonora is always an interesting experience, since I can see how neighboring communities react to my Yoeme companions. Since I'm not from Mexico, I often find myself on a learning curve about Indigenous-Mexican race relations. Last year when walking down a sidewalk near the market in Obregón, a Mexican man intentionally bumped into Guillermo and instead of saying, "Excuse me," he offered a definitive "Pinche Indio" or "Fucking Indian." Just last week, when telling a food server in another city that I was in the area working with the Yoemem, he responded matter-of-factly, "There aren't any real Yaquis anymore. Just those lazy fake Indians down by the river." I think about these moments while walking into a beachfront tourist bar in San Carlos, wearing my tennis shoes, jeans, shirt, and glasses. I can see the waitress look at Guillermo's homemade sandals, his dirty cotton pants, and cowboy hat. She leads us to our seats, gives us a few moments, and comes back to take our order: "What can I get you?" she asks me. I order nachos. She writes that down on a small pad of paper and then asks me, "And for him?" Not immediately recognizing the dynamic, I ask Guillermo what he wants to eat. He says in Spanish, "I'll have a hamburger." She jots something down and says to me, "Does he want fries?" Guillermo answers, "Yes, and coffee." She writes down something and tells me that she will be right back, not once looking at or directly addressing Guillermo. I look at him, and he looks at me, both of us half-smiling at the situation.

After eating, we drive around the boat harbor of San Carlos. Heading north, we see the large mountain of Takalaim. Known as Tetakawi by most of the locals and tourists, Takalaim is the northernmost peak of the Sierra Madre Occidental mountain range, and it towers over both the town of San Carlos and the Sonora Bay. The mountain, the bay, and the beaches contribute to a south-of-the border paradise for retirees and partygoers across northern Sonora and the southwestern United States. Only 250 miles south of Arizona, a well-maintained highway connects San Carlos to the large state universities of Arizona and to Mazatlan, Guadalajara, and Mexico City. As Guillermo and I drive around the marina to the base of Takalaim, we are conscious that this tourist destination is built on historically Yoeme homelands. Takalaim is not solely considered the most northwestern point of aboriginal Yoeme territory; the mountain plays a major role in traditional and contemporary Yoeme worldview.

I park on a small path that runs across the base of the mountain, and we get out to walk. The sun is setting, and we turn to watch the spectacular scene of fishing boats off the coast, backlit by the golden orange sinking into the silver ocean. "I've always wanted to come to Takalaim," I say to Guillermo. "Felipe and I talk a lot about this mountain, since I ask him a lot of questions about what happens after death according to traditional Yoeme worldviews."

Guillermo watches the seascape quietly as the sky darkens. After a minute or two, he replies, "Here I have heard the sounds of the music, the little fiesta, and the laughs and voices of our ancestors."

"Surem?" I ask.

"Yes, Surem."

I know this is an opportunity unequaled in Yoeme ethnographic research: a collaborator willing to admit firsthand experience of Surem. "And? How was that encounter?"

Guillermo points at the slope off the northern side of the mountain, about halfway up from the base: "We were coming back from fishing. We spent some time working, and we came up through here and right around there, from there we heard the sounds. The tampaleo, the violins, the rattles, faintly but actual."

"You mean 'actual' like how you hear my voice right now? As real as I am speaking?"

"Well, not as close, but of course real."

"And did you stop by and visit with them, the Surem?"

Guillermo chuckles. "No, kompae, we walked faster! We moved like chickens walk away from the cook's fire!" *He mimics the movement of men holding supplies under their arms, walking quickly, like chickens.*

We both laugh, looking around at what is now in just five to ten minutes a different environment. The sky is dark blue, almost black far to the east. The contours of the land are less discernible with less ambient light; the green of the mesquite and cacti blend into a dense forest around us. I look to see if I can still perceive the path to the car. Yes, but barely. The huya ania is joining the tuka ania around our talking about the yo ania. I look back at Guillermo, this tall, strong man, and tell him, "I am surprised that you were afraid, kompae."

He takes off his hat and says, "Yes, well, these things are serious.

"I know a man," *he continues,* "who has been inside there." *We both look back to where Guillermo motioned before.* "A neighbor there in Potam. A good friend. I do not want to tell you his name because I want to ask him first. But I do think he will talk with you. I will talk with him first. And you will record him with your machine, and he will tell you, perhaps, what he saw. He told me. He went inside and passed hours with them, having a pahko all night in there. He told me much. I don't know if he told me everything. He has gained some knowledge, kompae. This is true. And he went in right over there."

I listen attentively, and then respond slowly to emphasize my sincerity: "I would very much like to meet him. Ask him if I can come talk with him." Guillermo replies, "Of course I will talk with him. Next time you come back, *we'll go see him."* Guillermo takes some steps in the direction of the car, and I feel he is wrapping up our conversation.

"But I have to ask you, kompae," I add, *"before we leave here tonight: I thought Takalaim was where, after death, people went who committed incest in their lives. Did your friend join those deceased people for a pahko? Did you and your friends hear music coming from those ones living in the mountain? Or are those people with the Surem in there?"*

Guillermo looks back at me and without missing a beat replies, "No, kompae. It is different. In this one place are two. The Surem are under the earth, and their houses open up here and there, in mountains, like caves. You will see the openings. And Takalaim is a place where people go after death. They stay there. They are bound here. You could not go there. We feel sorry for those deceased. These are not the same places, but they are both here in Takalaim. I suppose it is difficult to understand."

"No," I add, *"not when I think about it like you do."*

We begin trying to find our way back to the car, although now the path is barely visible. We are both straining our eyes to use the faint reflection of light from the ground. "Watch out for snakes!" Guillermo calls out.

After walking in silence for a few minutes, we reach the car. We shake the loose dirt from the bottom of our shoes and get inside. I put the car in neutral and let off the brake, allowing us to roll backward toward the paved road at the base of the mountain. Shifting into drive, we move forward and roll down our windows to feel the ocean air. We pass a new subdivision of houses being built at the base of Takalaim. "Big houses." I point out.

"Yes," Guillermo replies. *"Many Americans are moving to San Carlos."*

"Yeah, the land is more affordable here than on the coasts in the United States. But I am sure they do not know who lives in Takalaim already."

Guillermo just looks at the nice houses surrounded by tall brick walls. I venture a little more. "Kompae, do you think it is dangerous for them to live there on that mountain?"

Guillermo seems not to have a sure answer, but says a bit more thoughtfully, "Well, I am not surprised. This is what happens."

Tree stories differ, each telling a new history. As should be expected, some versions cast pre-Catholic ways as backward or pagan. For example,

4. Each year brings more housing developments up the face of Takalaim.

either the woman who helped her people is considered a great person, or she is the carrier of bad news and is somehow associated with that badness. According to some storytellers, some Surem accuse her of making up the whole translation (1, 2, 5, and 6).[9] In Valenzuela's version, the Surem continue to live within the earth, a component we see in all thirteen of the published versions. Most tellers mention specific place-names and add that the Surem visit Yoemem and others during ceremonies or at other times, often in the form of ants. The gaining of talents from the Surem is consistent across most accounts; however, for some, including some of Painter's collaborators, such a power is portrayed as evil (1986, 4–11). Another critical difference within the stories is that, although four storytellers clearly designate the tree as predating God or religion, three people say that either God or an angel was speaking through the tree.[10] The power to communicate, then, is transferred by the speaker from nature (trees and fish) to the heavens (angels or God). As is the case with myths, we see the storyteller's level of Christian sensibility or the speaker's desire to tell the recorder something presumed important to the audience.[11] These differences make the conventional narrative structure that much more evident. The conformity and homogeneous aspects of these thirteen versions clearly lie in the failure to communicate, community division leading to community cohesion, and the prophetic nature of the myth.

All of the accounts revolve around a prophecy. Valenzuela's is the only version that I have found in which the only thing the tree mentions is baptism. While baptism is one of the invariables in all of the stories, never, except here, does the tree *only* foretell baptism. Usually the tree also sings of trains, telephones, cars, death, agricultural changes, the United States, and even nuclear bombs. I have even heard versions that foretell a time when humans and their extraterrestrial ancestors will reunite. Often, when the talking tree story is referenced, Yoeme speakers use shorthand to refer to "the prophecies" or "as we were once foretold." This space for interpretation, more clearly in myths of prophecy, supports Jan Vansina's claim that oral traditions are essentially histories told to secure cultural continuity in a present aimed at the future (1985, xi). We cannot underestimate the importance of these prophecies if we are to understand contemporary Yoeme culture in Potam or how many Yoeme think of their own history. As Evers and Molina declare,

> The focus of the story is not so much on what the talking stick sounded like as it is on what the young woman is able to hear. In the vibrations of the talking stick the young woman hears a message that marks a boundary between an ancient Yaqui way of living and a way of living that takes account of the new world created by the European presence, a boundary between myth and history, immortality and death, a boundary between the language of the wilderness and the language of the town. It marks, then, not so much a creation as a re-creation, a time "when the earth was becoming new here." (1987, 37, quoting Don Jesús)

In light of their comments, Evers and Molina help us comprehend the fundamental split that occurs after the Surem hear the translated prophecies. Some Yoemem say that the decision to split into two groups occurs after much heartfelt deliberation. In Valenzuela's version, Yoemem respond hostilely, wanting to burn the tree, and they fight with each other (see also versions 3 and 11). In other versions, instead of coming together for a fight, the Surem come together for a big pahko, "religious fiesta," where the deer and other animals come and join the dance (Evers and Molina 1987, 38). All versions agree that some Surem wanted the changes and others did not.

Valenzuela emphasizes this most important theme in all versions: there would be two groups from now on, the baptized and the unbaptized. Part of the tribe separates in every rendition of the story. Some of the Surem go underground; some move to the sea or bodies of water. Note that Valenzuela and all the other storytellers place this bifurcation before Jesuit contact, thereby affirming Yoeme agency in their own, internally produced societal transformation. Valenzuela states clearly in the last line that the "real" conquest began with the singing tree, in effect agreeing with seven other storytellers. Valenzuela and others thereby effectively displace the idea of an original cultural rupture due to European contact.

We may have problems imagining such a moment: a tree, a stick, whatever it is, we cannot even see it very clearly. Is it singing, humming, talking, tapping, or vibrating? We have difficulty hearing it exactly. But we know that, in a unitary world, a voice appears. This voice marks the first time that a people cannot understand something or someone. In a unitary world, the Surem hear the voice of differentiation, the essential example of otherness. And then, amid this confusion, a powerful woman interprets the coming of otherness: gods, baptism, crosses, Jesus, Jesuits, Spaniards, mortality. And for the first time, they must consider dying. They must consider living as Yoemem *and* Surem, not solely as Surem. The world is unitary, and the tree introduces the language of cultural pluralism. In a very real way, identity will soon be internally contested. The people will separate and move away from each other, and yet they will remain collectively one people. The stories of the tree claim that the Yoemem had already come to understand otherness before the Spanish had arrived. The tree had already prepared the way for Yoeme-Jesuit relations. In Valenzuela's words, the conquest was internal. In Spicer's field notes we can hear Valenzuela stressing this point: "Most people say that the coming of the Spaniards was 'the Conquista' but actually it was not. The Conquista took place long before that,"[12] "when the eight pueblos were first established and the first conquest took place."[13] The conquest, for many Yoemem, began with a tree, its prophecy, and the people no longer living in a unitary world.[14] The European explorers and the Jesuit missionaries, then, are the secondary actors in Yoeme histories of the Konkista.

As a historical tactic, the talking tree prophecy evidently has much to offer our wider studies of indigenous identity, especially when those identities are similarly contested in the name of sovereignty as are Yoeme communities throughout the 1800s. Spicer suggests that the talking tree myth fully developed as an oral tradition in the early nineteenth century, at a time when Mexican encroachment was particularly fierce (1980, 172–73).[15] Clearly, indigenous people use oral tradition effectively to maintain social cohesion and health, particularly during times of cultural conflict, both external and internal. Since the earliest written evidence of this story comes from the 1900s, we are not able to trace how many generations of Yoemem have been talking about vibrating trees. Yet the Surem/Yoemem physical split offers an intrinsic representation of contact with the Europeans where Yoemem demonstrate their own agency to decide how and why such relations should begin. Erickson (2003) eloquently and accurately notes that the relationship formed by this split can be seen as a model for their present-day transnational and diasporic community. By moving to the mountains and ocean, the Surem continue to avail themselves of Yoeme physical and cultural relations: the Surem remain living ancestors to the Yoemem. In this way, Yoeme ground their indigeneity in the landscape, providing their communities with aboriginal kinship solidarity. The story of the Surem living in the earth provides a distinctly Yoeme answer to James Clifford's question, "What does it mean, at the end of the twentieth century, to speak . . . of a native land?" (1988, 275). For some Yoemem, it means that they can link their identity to their aboriginal homeland, since the world of the Surem was already indigenous and unchanging.

Beyond these local struggles over land, the talking tree prophecy speaks to the intersections of historical research and subaltern studies. What happens when natives represent European contact as internally predetermined, when the Konkista comes before the conquest? What are Yoemem doing politically by saying they anticipated Spanish arrival and were prepared for the ensuing changes? In examining the various talking tree stories with their consistent patterns, I see a Yoeme historicity that does not subordinate religious events to the false construction of objectivity. Indeed, considering their reliance on prophecy, Yoemem consciously construct a nonlinear history of submergence and sustenance. We need no stretch of the imagination to conceive of a historiographic practice that decenters a primary Euro-colonial rupture. The conquest, the process of colonialism, started before Yoemem met the first intruder. Surem disagreed on the implications and personal satisfaction of a Christian axiology, engendered in moral beings working toward a postmortem salvation. Of course, academic histories tend to represent indigenous peoples as the responders, or worse, as objects of European historical action. That is, the natives were discovered, conquered, colonized. Other common historical tropes assert that native lives were ruptured, ruined, transformed. Subaltern scholars, indigenous intellectuals, and community historians across the indigenous Americas have been shattering or ignoring that master narrative of "the history of Europe" since early explorers and slave raider historians began writing it. Without suggesting that all colonized people experience history in the same manner, or that "subaltern" theories appropriately represent indigenous peoples across the Americas, I want to assert the talking tree as a native discursive practice. By historicizing the conquest as a matter of internal community disruption that was handled according to indigenous methods — the result of which is a strong link with the land and an enduring aboriginal life — Yoeme mythistory displaces European centrality. Moreover, since the Yoemem were awaiting the Spanish and their new technologies, the history of Europeans is subsumed by the Yoeme historic trajectory, one of the many "processes of self-determination to defy, erode, and sometimes supplant the prodigious power of imperial cultural knowledge" (Ashcroft, Griffiths, and Tiffin 1995, 1).

I was once told that, if a tree tells you the Jesuits are coming, you understand their presence. The prophetic story provides recognition, softens the newness, and eases the sense of rupture. The tree enables a reading of history that foregrounds tribal knowledge, agency, and control; essentially, the talking tree bears the fruit of power. Yoemem look back and forward, and they see themselves as practitioners of their history.

Twelve Versions of the "Talking Tree" Story

1. UNNAMED STORYTELLER, 1932
From Ralph L. Beals, The Contemporary
Culture of the Cáhita Indians, *223*

Before, there was a tribe from whom the Yaqui are descended. They knew nothing of God, but among them was a great pole, three spans in diameter, with one end in the earth, the other in heaven. It vibrated as though talking. At the time all spoke one language, but only Queen Yomomúli could understand the pole.

She interpreted that it spoke of a God who made the earth for human beings to live upon. The pole said that the time of conquest would come and all would have to be baptized.

Many people were angry; only a few said they would receive the benediction. The others said it was not true, that only Yomomúli wished it.

So Yomomúli burned down the stick with a powerful cigarette, rolled up the river under her arm like a carpet, and went away.

Those who had not wanted to receive benediction sank into the earth.

2. UNNAMED STORYTELLER, 1936–37
From Edward H. Spicer, Pascua:
A Yaqui village in Arizona, *240*

Yomu'muli was an old woman, some say simply a wise old Yaqui woman; others say that she was the mother of the sea to whom fishermen prayed. She lived in the Yaqui country a long time ago when the Suris lived there.

At this time there was a tree without branches, like a telephone pole, in the middle of the Suri country. This tree kept vibrating all the time.

The Suris knew that it was talking in some language, but they could not understand it.

Finally they decided to go to Jomu'muli and to get her to translate what it said. She came and listened to the talking tree for a long time. Then she translated all that it had said. All the Suris were standing around in a big crowd listening. Jomu'muli told them that the tree was saying many things.

It told about the making of the earth and how plants and animals and men, too, came to live on the earth. It said that sometime in the future many strange things would happen. People would talk to each other over long distances without shouting. They would fly through the air and they would travel over land faster than anything then known. Finally a god would come and show the people how to baptize themselves. When they were shown the secret of baptism, then everyone should be baptized because it was a good thing. When Jomu'muli said these things, there were some who believed her and some who did not. Some said that they would get ready for the things that were to come and others said that they would not. After a time Jomu'muli saw that what the talking stick was saying had caused trouble among the Suris. She decided to go away so that the trouble would end.

She made a cigarette out of the tree and went away to the north. No one knows what happened to her, but all that the talking stick said has come true. Some say that the people who didn't believe the talking stick went into the ground and remained Suris.

The others were baptized and they are the Yaquis.

3. ROSALIO MOISÉS, 1930s–1960s
From Rosalio Moisés, Jane Holden Kelley, and
William Curry Holden, The Tall Candle, *xxiv–xxv*

Long ago, the Surem lived along the Yaqui River on one of the now abandoned channels south of the modern river. These people were short statured like Filipinos. For thousands of years they did not know how to farm, but lived by hunting animals, gathering wild potatoes, fishing, and collecting shellfish and shrimp along the coast. They had no religion, no government.

One day in Surem country a dead mesquite tree or dry pole (palo seco) began to go tap-tap-tap like a telegraph set, but no one could understand what it was saying. They went to ask the wise man, Mapoli, who lived to the north near Guaymas Bay, if he could help them.

He said his daughter could tell them what it meant. She was a sirena who lived by the sea.

She told the Surem and her father that white men coming from the east would bring them seeds to plant and cows and horses, and that they would baptize all the children. The tapping tree told of many wonderful things that were to happen.

Many of the Surem were afraid. They fought among themselves.

Some, who moved away to the north to settle along the present course of the Yaqui River, became the Yaqui tribe. The other Surem have disappeared, and their river died. The Yaqui settled into the eight pueblos. These pueblo names are very, very old. Afterwards the Spaniards came and baptized everyone, and then the Yaquis had a religion.

4. LUCAS CHAVEZ [1936–37]
From Edward H. Spicer, People of Pascua, *138*

The Mexicans have many different beliefs, all kinds of beliefs and religions. They have so many different kinds that sometimes they call them cualqueristas [whatever-you-pleases]. But the Yaquis always have and have had only one belief. There are old stories about the only belief that they have had. The old men knew all these things. They couldn't read and some people say that they didn't know anything at all, but they actually knew everything that was going to happen. They knew about the conquest and they were waiting for it.

There was the old woman Yomumule who told them.

They wanted the conquest to come because they would be baptized.

So Yomumule took a river and rolled it up under her arm and all those Yaquis from whom we came went with her and the others went into the sea.

And those Yaquis who believed her were baptized and waited for the conquest. Then the Mexicans came and the trouble began.

5. LUCAS CHAVEZ, 1942
From Ruth Warner Giddings, Yaqui
Myths and Legends, 25–27

Long before the conquest of the Spaniards, when all of the land which is now Mexico was wild, this country was called Suré. It was thus called because it was populated by Surem, children of Yomumuli. All Indians, the Hueleves, the Opatas, the Pimas, the Papagos, the Seris, were created by her. At that time there were animals living on land and in water. Huge turtles lived in the permanent water of the river and the sea. This was before we had agriculture.

There was a huge thick stick which reached from the ground to the sky. The stick kept talking, making a humming noise like bees. The Yaquis has very wise men in those days of the Surem, as we do now, but none of the Indians nor the wise men could understand what the stick was saying.

Only Yomomuli could understand and she wanted to help her people whom she had created. She didn't particularly care what the stick was saying but she told what it said.

It was telling the Indians and the animals how to live. It told the animals which were to live by hunting, and which to live by eating the grass. It told how, someday, the Conquest would come, how Jesucristo would appear, as he was to appear to all people. She herself didn't like the laws very much.

Some of the laws were disagreeable to the Indians, and they did not like Yomumuli's interpretations of the truth as sent by Dios in the sky to the people on earth. Many people said that Yomumuli was just making all this up. According to her, the talking tree said that the people would soon have leaders, captains, and would be baptized. The people did not believe this. Yomumuli was angry that her people did not believe, though she herself felt as they did. It didn't matter to her what this stick was saying. She did not like it. But she knew that it was true. Since she did not like what was going to come to pass Yomumule decided to go away. She was angry and decided to take her river with her. "I am going north," she said. And she took this river, rolled it up, put it under her arm, and walked away on the clouds toward the north. The people did not like the prospect of this Conquest which was coming. So they either descended into the earth to live inside the hills or they went to live in the sea. They were very powerful people, these Surem. Yomumuli left a chief on each hill, and the hills were named for these men. These chiefs did not like the coming conquest either.

Only a few people liked what the stick predicted, and these waited. These men are the Yaquis. They grew to be taller than the Surem who had gone away. The Surem were little people, but very strong. They still live in the hills and the sea. They favor man and help him when they can. Some, in the sea, are like sirens and live on islands. Others are whales who come near to a boat to warn it when it is in danger. All of the Surem are wild pagans. If a Yaqui is lost in the monte, these little people help him by bringing him food and fire, and then they go away. Some say the Surem are very rich and have many cattle under the hills.

6. INFORMANT 52 [1948–1975]
From Muriel Thayer Painter, With Good Heart, *9–10*

[The yoania before the Talking Tree] was like a lost world. They were some place by themselves. They weren't civilized. And they just kept to themselves. They were alone in a corner, without having communication with anyone else like the Mexicans.

They ate wild things like spinach, and they would eat some kinds of lizard and rabbits. [Deer?] Maybe deer. They didn't wear clothes except something around the waist. They had seataka and ute'a [sic] because those came from the Suris. They didn't have morea (witchcraft). There were so few people and no one had any envy toward anyone else. Morea and all that came in when the Talking Tree spoke. And those that believed in the Talking Tree got together, and those that did not believe the Talking Tree went underground and became ants. The Talking Tree told them what to do and to get well organized and even asked them to get married and baptize their children.

[The Tree] started to talk when there was a bunch of people together, and these people got scared of it. So they gathered to see what the Talking Tree was talking about, but nobody could understand it. It went on for nights and days, and the people stayed around to see what would happen. It must have gone on for some time, because the people were starving because they had no food, because they were more interested in the tree.

Finally, this young girl who kept to herself, she didn't bother no men nor nobody. She lived in the woods. She told her father when he came home from hearing the Talking Tree if he could understand what the Tree said, and her father said no, he wished he could understand what the Talking Tree. Then the young girl said that she could understand the words that the Talking Tree was saying. So the father gladly took her over to the Talking Tree to know more about it. So they took her over and sat her under the Talking Tree. So the Talking Tree started talking. After the Tree stopped talking she translated what the Tree said to the people. And that is where they said [who is "they?"] Itom Achai whom we call God. It was God speaking.

[He] wanted the people to get baptized, get married right, and learn to make fiestas. Also it explained to them that all sorts of sickness would be coming to them and that there would be death.

And so a lot of the Suris believed what they were told, and a lot of them didn't believe, so they turned into ants.

7. ANSELMO VALENCIA, [1950S–1970S]
From Mini Valenzuela Kaczkurkin, Yoeme, *6*

It has been many centuries, in times long gone, that the Yaquis were not as they are now. They were Surems, a very little people that lived in el Cerro Surem in Sonora. The Surems were a peaceful, quiet people who couldn't stand noise and violence.

One day, the people noticed a tree that seemed to be making noises in a strange language. This tree was one big, ash-colored Palo Verde, which was growing in the middle of the region, on Omteme Kawi. While the villagers gathered around, the leaders attempted to communicate with the talking tree.

However, it was of no use, not even the most important leader could interpret the message.

During this time, a very young girl, Yomumuli, kept tugging at her father's hand and whispering that she could understand the tree. At first her father ignored her, then he became angry at her insistence. "All right, you will do it in front of the village, and then you will be punished publicly for your foolishness." So Yomumuli sat down close to the tree and translated word for word what the prophetic tree foretold for their future.

It warned of the coming of the white man with armor and new weapons; it told of the coming of much strife and bloodshed against these intruders and others, and much suffering for a long time among the Surems, but that they would eventually overcome their adversaries. It told of the coming of modern man's trains: "A road will be made of steel and an iron monster on it." It told of much much more to come, then it said, "There will be much suffering for years, much noise, and confusion. You must decide what to do. For those among you who cannot stand noise, you have a choice of leaving if you do not want to face such a future."

So, the Surems divided into two parties, and those who could not stand such a future walked away. Some say they walked into the sea and live there still. Others say they turned into black ants and live underground under the hills.

Those Surems who stayed eventually grew taller and changed into the Yaquis as they are now, and they were strong enough to fight off the Spaniards when the time came.

8. LUCIANO VELASQUEZ [1982]
From Larry Evers and Felipe S. Molina, Yaqui
Deer Songs/Maso Bwikam, 37–38

In the time before the Spanish conquest the Surem lived in the area that is now west of Ciudad Obregón. The river was Yo Vatwe, Enchanted River. In this region the Surem had their homes, and they lived on both banks. Their houses were called hukim. They were built of sticks and mud and were about four or five feet high. They hunted, fished, and farmed to stay alive.

Well, anyway, during those early times a tree was heard talking on a small hill called Tosai Bwia, White Earth. Some say it was heard at Omteme Kawi, but we say it was at Tosai Bwia. This tree was an old dead mesquite, and it made strange humming sounds.

Nobody could understand the sounds. That bothered the Surem.

All the intelligent men in the Surem land were notified and told to visit the tree. None of those intelligent men could figure it out. They all had to admit failure. They could not decide what the meaning of the tree was.

These wise men knew of one other wise man who lived near a little mountain called Asum Kawi, Grandmothers' Mountain. This man's name was Yomomoli, and he had twin daughters. The wise men visited him and requested that his two daughters interpret the talking tree. Yomomoli told them that the girls didn't have a good vocabulary, so they would be incapable of doing such a task. The men insisted. Finally they convinced Yomomoli to take the girls to the talking tree. But Yomomoli did one thing first. He took his twin daughters to the ocean. There they talked to a fish, so that they might better understand the talking tree. At Tosai Bwia the girls stood on either side of the tree, and they began to interpret.

The tree predicted Christianity and baptism, wars, famine, floods, drought, new inventions, even drug problems, and so on. After the tree had given all the information it stopped making the sounds.

The Surem were happy, but they didn't really like some of the things they heard, so they planned a big meeting. The meeting was held near a watering hole called Yo Va'am, Enchanted Waters. This is the region between Vicam and the modern town of Colonia Militar. There the Surem held both a meeting and a dance of enchantment. At this meeting some of the Surem decided to leave the Yaqui region, while others decided to stay and to see these new things. At this dance of enchantment, they say a real live deer came to dance for the Surem.

After the dance the Surem who were leaving cut up a portion of the Yo Vatwe, wrapped it up in a bamboo mat, and took it north to a land of many islands. Other Surem stayed around and went into the ocean and underground into the mountains. There in those places the Surem now exist as an enchanted people.

Those who stayed behind are now the modern Yaquis, and they are called the Baptized Ones.

9. JAVIER CHOQUI [1987]
From María Trinidad Ruíz Ruíz and Gerardo David Aguilar, "Tres Procesos de Lucha por la Sobrevivencia de la Tribu Yaqui: Testimonios," 31

The Surem who lived here before did not know of baptism. They were never familiar with it. They did not know anything. They lived like animals. They spoke only of ways to survive, about how they could help themselves, and about what they could grow. This is how our ancestors talked about it, our parents, our grandparents; they were the ones who told it to them. Before the elders visited one another they sat and chatted, but not like us. They took our cigarettes and talked while smoking. They talked about what was going to pass. This is how they spoke. No one told stories to them.

Some Surem didn't want the baptism. They didn't accept it. They said that they didn't want it. Other Surem desired that all the Surem would want it. And those who didn't want baptism weren't welcomed by the others. Then they told them that some priests would arrive to baptize those who had accepted. When the priests arrived, the Surem didn't leave either. They didn't go anywhere.

They stayed here in the land where they lived and continued living. And they walk here like us. They don't look like us. They also have their authorities like us.

That is what we have of our ancestors, the blessing of our ancestors. The priests told us. Those that did not want the baptism went into the earth. They disappeared because this is how they were left; we all have seen them. But no one likes this animal that walks below us because we do not know how it is working with us, how it lives with us. We don't know, but he also descends from our ancestors. And they are like that because they did not accept the blessing. And we come from those that did accept the blessing. This is why we believe in God and why we fully listen to him.

10. DON ESTEBAN JIMÉNEZ [1987]

From María Trinidad Ruíz Ruíz and Gerardo
David Aguilar, "Tres Procesos de Lucha por la
Sobrevivencia de la Tribu Yaqui: Testimonios," 17–19

The Surem were little beings that lived to be 500 years old, men as well as women. Up until 100 years old, they were still young. They only ate animals like rabbits, birds, and rats, and they ate them raw. They were not acquainted with fire; nor were there knives or rope. This is how they were. They lived on flat lands, in caves and in valleys, like foxes. At this time there were no horses nor mules nor cows, but big animals were everywhere.

They say that there was a wooden stick that spoke to them there, to the Surem. "People, what is the stick going to say?" a Surem said.

"I don't understand it," another said.

"Well, let's just go listen to it," they said, and they went. Twenty men went to where it was, the dry, wooden stick that was talking.

"Do you understand?" they asked each other.

"No!"

"Then lets go get a girl," the Surem said. "We will see if she understands what the wooden stick is saying."

And the twenty men went, and they said to her, "Over there is a stick that is talking, but we don't understand it."

And the girl said, "I am going there to see if I can understand it."

"We will take you," said the others, and they went with her to where the talking tree was. The girl knew what was happening in the earth, in the sea, and in the air, because that is what the stick told her. "I am going to listen to see if I understand it," the girl said. Then she added: "The wooden stick said the following, although I do not know if the Surem will believe what the wooden stick says."

"Good! Allow us to know what the stick says."

The girl said: "It says that they come from the sea, and they come from the three seas, further, from the edge of the sea, and from the other shore, some tall men bringing with them priests who are going to want to baptize. Also, they are going to build churches in the town in order to baptize."

"But we didn't want it!" said the Surem.

But they had to believe in them. They are going to baptize them; and they are going to give them knowledge to cook food with fire.

"But we didn't want it!" some said. But there was a small bunch of Surem who wanted to be baptized, and to these others they said: "We are not going to wait for them; you wait for them, if you want to wait."

Some went to the mountains. Others put themselves into the river. Others put themselves into the earth, and others put themselves into the sea carrying them with the Suré River. Those who put themselves into the earth are ants, others are bees, and others insects.

Like they said, those who came from Spain brought priests to baptize the eighty people who remained in agreement. They created the eight churches that are in the eight pueblos and left to the maestros the prayers, vespers, and vigils. This is how the Surem were left to continue their lives, with their children baptized. Over time they became taller, until they reached our height. They baptized the eighty Surem, who before would reach 500 years old. Over time, they did not reach the same age. While growing taller, they also lived shorter lives. The people who went to church constructed houses. The priests advised them to stop eating their meat raw, nor meat with blood. For this they gave them fire, beans, garbanzos, so that they would live. Moreover, they brought them horses and many other things.

11. JESÚS RAMIREZ VALENZUELA [1987]
From María Trinidad Ruíz Ruíz and Gerardo
David Aguilar, "Tres Procesos de Lucha por la
Sobrevivencia de la Tribu Yaqui: Testimonios," 21–23

The elders who existed in this world, those whom the young know very little, and those who were spoken of and spoke in those times, these elders were the Surem. They existed in this world, and they nourished themselves with sprouts, spinach, amaranth, and maguey. Their women made pots and plates. The men dedicated themselves to the collection of edible plants that they later traded, and also to gathering firewood. The Surem did not wear clothes, just the loincloths. They wore their hair long and they were of short stature.

Over where there is Pitahaya, that is where the Surem met. Where the upright stick is, that is where the Surem spoke.

They went over to the stick, but no one could understand it, nobody except a girl named Lot. She was the one who spoke to the Surem. Some of them agreed. Others did not like what the stick said to them, that they were going to be baptized.

Some Surem wanted to be baptized, others did not. More said that it was going to come to pass. To this the others threatened a revolution: "It is better that we fight, those who want baptism against those who do not want to be baptized." For a time, they pursued each other. In Pótam those who did not want to be baptized remained, but some of them went to make an arrowhead in a place called Vicam Pueblo. Here they fought for three days and three nights with only one arrow and arrow point. They were fighting with that one arrow: when they shot it, it returned. Their opponents realized that the one arrow was returning, and so they put a worm on the tip, and it broke the next time it was fired. With the arrow broken, they stopped the war. This battleground became known as Vicam Pueblo. The chief of the Surem, named Charad, died here.

Some of the Surem left, and they threw themselves into the sea, converting themselves into fish, and those that remained on the land were underground, and they converted themselves into ants. When they finished, they left the river where it is now.

We depend on them.

12. UNNAMED INFORMANT [1997]
From Kirstin C. Erickson, "'They Will Come from the Other Side of the Sea': Prophecy, Ethnogenesis, and Agency in Yaqui Narrative," 470–71

Yes. The Surem. This is a dicho [saying], nothing more. It is a dicho, that the Yaqui tribe, well concerning the issue of history, they are very backward. In the questions of archeology, the tribe is lacking, no? In the question of history. Very poor. In those times, they passed the story along (but just by word of mouth, words only) of the Surem. Well, about 5,000 years ago, those people lived here. . . . And that they were very, very wise, as well. They knew that the Spaniards were going to come here. Some went up into the sierra, and others fled underneath, underneath the earth, here. Hmm? And the Surem, well, they were very able in every respect. Before the Spaniards came.

Here at Omteme Mountain, there in that place, there appeared a wooden pole. A wood pole like that, tall. . . . It was like a telegraph, no? Like that.

But no one understood it. And they went for a wise man who lived out there. And there were other wise ones, and they went for them, too. . . . I believe that it became angry. It became angry because many people gathered. . . . They call it that, "angry," the Angry Mountain, Omteme. Kawi Omteme. They had to ask the question of all the animals, of all the birds who were there. They asked the question. . . .

And so some little birds came. Little birds like this. They came and said they knew where the wise one lived. It was a woman. "This one," they said, "lives out there. Near the sea. Near the sea, that is where she lives, Maapol. Hmm. . . . One who is called Maapol. And this one will know. She lives there," said the smallest bird. And so they went for the young woman, a Yaqui poetess. "That is fine." And they arrived out there. And she accepted. She told them, "Tomorrow, very early in the morning I will head over there. I've got to notify my papá and every-one." In achai [my father]. In achai. That is how they said the words "my father" at that time, "in achai." Hmm. . . . And they left and arrived. And then in the morning, at about one o'clock in the morning there, the young woman got up, no? She grabbed her bow and her arrows, made a lunch, . . . el agua [water] . . . and she wrapped it all up in a bundle. . . . Now the Yaqui poetess took to the road. And she didn't arrive that same day. Until the next day, at twelve o'clock. At midday she arrived. But with her came her entire troop. Along with her came mochomos [ants], scorpions, ants. Hmm? And then they arrived there. And the animals arrived along with her. They were her soldiers. Many people disappeared when they saw these animals coming. . . . And now in the afternoon, she began. She lit a cigarro [cigarette] of the macuchus [Yoeme tobacco]. And she began to smoke it. They lit their cigars, and they smoked, every one of them. And now she began to dream. She dreamed for a long time. Hmm.

"Well, gentlemen," she said, "now everything has come to me. It is nothing, this. Other people are going to come. They will come from the other side of the sea. People . . . like us. The same. It's just that they are from over there, and we are from here. But they are the same people. They have the same spirit, the same thoughts that we have. The same heart, the same eyes, the same nose. All of it. They are going to come here. And from here on, when these people arrive, there is going to be a change. A change, another way of life. They are going to bring a thing called religion. They shall bring an upright pole, crossed with another. [Informant makes the sign of the cross with his hand.] There is a person hanging there. And this is the way it will be. Now there will be no deaths. Everyone shall continue living. Hmm. And there is a person who dies for all the people. . . . And there is another Lord called God. He sent that one to save the world. . . . They will teach you that he died for us. They are going to bring many things. And they will bring a green ball like this, with some seeds in the center, that you are going to learn to plant. And they also are going to bring with them a little bundle that looks like a little nose, a seed, and this you will also plant. You are going to plant garbanzo. And other things. And some other seeds, to plant here. These people are going to come here. . . . You just need to prepare yourselves. You are going to need many things, bows. So that they don't grab you by surprise. Guard your territory here. Guard your territory. Mark your borders. Mark them. They are going to come."

She was with them for a while, "Now I am going back," she said, "I am going back." And she went out there, no? The poetess. Toward the south. And the poetess told the Yaquis to get their arrows, to raise their bows. [Informant explains that they stood in a line and shot arrows into the distance.] "Now it is marked. Now it is marked." And in fact, where the arrows landed, they surrounded it with some marks. "And now they are going to arrive here. . . .

And so the Surem who were there, they left. They wrapped up a piece of the Yaqui River, like this. [Informant makes a wrapping motion with his hands.] Each one grabbed a piece of the river. This was the river that used to flow over there. Over there it flowed, 5,000 years ago. Hmm. And so . . . New Spain was established. . . . And that is the way it happened. The Yaqui tribe has never left the Yaqui River. The government of Porfirio Díaz, and General Lorenzo Torres — they all wanted this land, the land of the Yaquis. . . . But they couldn't finish them off. Many fled to Tucson, over there. And to this day, they are there. They have their own reservation and are now recognized as a North American tribe. . . . And that is how it was.

Ethnographic Dialogue 3

DAVID SHORTER: Some authors say that supposedly there is an original copy of the Testamento from the Rahum meeting in 1954. They say this original was copied for each of the eight towns and that each pueblo governor has a copy. Do you think this is true? Do you know something of this matter?

RESPONDENT: Well, sometimes the older people, they use confidences, and they talk very confidentially. If you are not a member of the authority in this time, they do not let you know. Right now, already in these cases, they have drawn it, to tell it. Although, there is no, um, I cannot deceive you. I cannot tell you "yes" because I have not seen it. I am not sure. I would tell you something if it was true, and I would give you my word with my heart.

DS: Have you heard that there are pillars that you cannot see, but they are like a hallucination that marks the holy dividing line of Yoeme territory?

R: No.

DS: You have never heard of this? I don't know, but there was an author who says that they are there.

R: No.

DS: In the stories, and in the conversation, it is still possible in Potam and in other towns to hear about "the eight towns." But there aren't eight towns anymore, are there?

R: No. Right now there are five towns that are together: Potam, Vicam, Rahum, Wiivisim, and Torim.

DS: There isn't holy week in Pitaya?

R: Yes. At the church of Saint Peter.

DS: Are there holy weeks and festivities in Loma de Bacom?

R: Yes, there are.

DS: Loma de Bacom is now like one of the eight, though not originally. Is that like the other three?

R: Yes, of the original eight. They are members of the Yaqui tribe and property of the group of those eight towns. But right now it is as if they are separate. They don't think the same way as in the other towns.

DS: In one of the earlier anthropological books, it says that originally one of the eight towns was Abasurin. Have you heard of Abasurin?

R: If any of my ancestors had said this word to me, I do not remember. I do not believe it existed.

DS: In which year were the people who left for Arizona starting to come back to the villages in the *hiakim* to live? Is it before or after 1939?

R: Before and after. Some returned, and others stayed to live on the Tucson reservation over there.

DS: Ok, I think that it is very interesting to know more about the relations between the Yoeme tribe and the other indigenous groups in the sixteenth or seventeenth centuries. The history books say that the following were your neighbors before the Europeans arrived.

R: Okay.

DS: The Mayos? Obviously, yes.

R: Yes.

DS: Los Ambos?

R: Yes.

DS: Before and still?

R: And now.

DS: "Oparos" or "Uparos"?

R: What?

DS: U-P-A-R-O-S.

R: I know that they are not neighbors. They are a tribe, but they aren't neighbors.

DS: Not close to us now.

R: No, they aren't close to Potam.

DS: Ok, not before, still not close.

R: The one that is closest to Potam right now is the Ópatas.

DS: Close to here?

R: They are very close.

DS: Before European contact as well?

R: Yes, and also now.

DS: Apaches?

R: No, not Apache.

DS: Never?

R: Never.

DS: Nebomes?

R: Them neither.

DS: Tehueco?

R: Tehuecos . . . Tehueco isn't a tribe.

DS: It isn't a tribe?

R: It is a word from, I don't know, Aztec or something like that.

DS: Ocorones?

R: No.

DS: Ocorones? They are not close?

R: Well, they are not as close right now. These are alongside of the bay of Mexico.

DS: Huasavis?

R: Huasavis are neighbors, like eight or ten hours.

DS: Mochocabis?

R: Mochikawi? Yes, neighbors.

DS: Ajomes?

R: No.

DS: Are there others?

R: Well, the closest neighbor is the Tarahumara.

DS: How many hours?

R: Well, it depends on the road because it is a bad road, not a highway. You have to arrive by the mountain range.

DS: They live in the forests?

R: In the valleys and in the mountain ranges.

DS: Other tribes?

R: Guarajillos. Pimas. Seris. Tatauus.

DS: Tatauus?

R: In Nogales, in the Río Colorado San Luis.

DS: Where are the Guarajillos?

R: Here in Sonora, a little to the side of Alamos here toward the interior.

DS: Close to Alamos?

R: Yes, close to Alamos

DS: Do they have a culture similar to Yoeme?

R: They have everything, except they do not do Holy Week. They do not practice Lent. But they have the dance of Pascolas and of Matachinis.

DS: I have two masks that I bought in a museum supposedly from the Guarajillo. They seem to be a wolf and a horse.

R: Yes.

DS: Well, this is interesting. How about I describe something that I have read, and you correct what you want. There were two very important characters or persons before the Spanish, Yuku and Suawaka.

R: Yes.

DS: Yuku has one eye and is in charge of the rain.

R: Yes.

DS: Would you call him a god?

R: The god of lightning.

DS: Lightning. Yuku's wife was Namu, who would send the rains when crying. And Suawaka was the husband of the daughter of Yuku and Namu.

R: Yes.

DS: And Suawaka appears to be a snake and also in the stars.

R: Yes.

DS: Sometimes Suawaka comes to the earth and Yuku doesn't like it.

R: Yes, he doesn't like that he comes.

DS: And to get him to return, he causes huge thunderous storms?

R: Yes, so then he goes and comes around at another time.

DS: Supposedly during these very ancient times, there were others. There was the god of clouds, of hell, of many things. Have you heard something of these names?

R: Well, previously, there was Tulu, and as you probably know, the Yoemem worshipped the gods of the rain for the sowing of the seeds.

DS: Ah.

R: And they also worshipped Suawaka as if he were a god because he took people who had committed a mistake in the community, or a sin, and he changed them into animals. They tell a story in our tribe that certain people who committed bad things, when they die, on that day, there is a storm, and it makes a small hurricane with winds and rain. That is Suawaka coming with Yuku, and they come from their homes and convert the person into a snake. It is hard on the community to have that rain and wind. It is a bad omen. People will say, "That man will become a snake!" Why? Because he did something very bad to his sons or his grandsons or with his daughter-in-law. That's when Yuku and Suawaka enter the action.

DS: Ah, so that's when the two of them get involved.

R: Yes. To come for the soul, or for the animal, to take it away.

DS: And how does Suawaka appear?

R: He's a dwarf.

DS: Does everything sound right?

R: Yes, yes, it is fine.

DS: Well, the last question for this session is about the missionaries. In the seventeenth century, the Jesuits wrote that there was much that they could not understand. For example, they wrote that there were figures in the Yoeme houses, made of wood and stone, like statues.

R: Yes, statues of saints.

DS: But they are from before the Jesuits?

R: Yes. The tribe was not evangelized by the Jesuits because the tribe already had their gods and their saints.

DS: The Jesuits also say that the Yoemem, before the Jesuits, had something very similar to personal spirit, a personal protector.

R: Yes, they are the saints that I just talked about. I have to tell you that the day the Jesuits arrived in Sonora, the tribe already had their *pahko'ola* dances, *matachinis*, the deer dance, the processions, all in the Yoeme language. And quietly, the evangelists helped, but very little. The Yaquis, the Hiaquis, the Yoemem already had their separate culture. And like you often say, that the Yoeme language uses Latin words and speech. Well, these people who came to evangelize, they came from European countries, from Italy, too. One of those Jesuits was from Italy, and so you see some of those things in our culture. But if you don't know where these people came from, then you cannot know everything about where this tribe, this big family of ours, came from.

DS: We often think the Jesuits all came from Spain.

R: But I don't know if they are Italian or from somewhere else. They were Latino as well.

DS: Well, we know who they were and where they came from. One of the first Jesuits was from Italy, that's true. And then later, four more came eight years later. Most were from Spain.

R: Spaniards. But I ask you, was their language Latin or Spanish?

DS: They used both. The Jesuits knew both, and it was required that they learn the indigenous dialects; it was part of the law of the Society of Jesus. And from their writings I know some of the things they thought they knew: that there were wooden figures, that there were sand paintings, and that there were doctors in the tribe.

R: Curanderos.

DS: Curanderos, who suck elements away from the body, yes. What is strange is that many of these things are unfamiliar to Yoemem, but they are familiar to other tribes. Do you think it is more likely that the Jesuits were wrong or that these things are too ancient?

R: It is a mistake. It is not about things being too ancient. Because if it were ancient, the people here have been getting together and talking since, well, always. They have talked about the wooden saints. I don't know exactly how we came to practice Lent, the crucifixion of Jesus, and all this and more. I don't know perfectly who calculated with theory our beliefs or whether they simply invented them. I do not know who or how it was. But they did have stories that when the Jesuits arrived, we had the same relations. We had these stories, and they coincided with holy week. This is Yaqui tradition. Yoeme. Here is Yoeme.

DS: Yes.

R: More so, I do not know if the people took things voluntarily. I myself imagine that it happened mainly by tenku ania. They saw dimensionally what was happening, like in a dream, they did this, and this, then this and this. This is what I think they did before the Jesuits. But then a year later or so, the Jesuits arrived, and we already had seen it. But if you look at what the Jesuits say, well, I am going to tell you that it is not true.

DS: Good. That is all for that. For people who study
history, the history of Mexico, it is interesting to them to
understand the differences between conceptions before
and then after the explorations. And so I have some
questions about the use of certain words. For example, in
a book about the Yoeme in Arizona, *hiapsi* is used all the
time in reference to souls. Do you think that hiapsi and
soul are the same?

R: Yes, it is the same. Spirit, too.

DS: What is *mukia*? Is it just the body of the deceased?

R: Yes, it is the body after death.

DS: And *anima*?

R: It is the spirit, the heart, and soul.

DS: Spirit, hiapsi, and soul, all the same?

R: There are three and at the same time one.

DS: For you they are the same.

R: Yes, the same.

DS: In 1941, Professor Spicer was living in Potam. And in his
books about that time in Potam, he says that there was a
mythological conception that in the west was a land of the
dead or that the west was associated with death. Have you
heard of such a thing?

R: In Potam?

DS: The people that were being interviewed in 1941 said that in
the West there is a land of the dead. Have you heard of this?

R: No, no. This is a lie.

DS: Have you heard of a woman named Ana Maria and a giant
who marked the territory with the four arrows shot to the
edges of the Yoeme territory?

R: No.

DS: This is a question about what happened in earlier days.
There are two elders in Arizona who have told me that in
earlier times small animals were tied with these little red
ribbons in procession.

R: San Lázaro?

DS: Well, in these processions, they specifically mentioned a frog.

R: Oh, Saint Frog.

DS: Yes, but tied with red ribbons. And they would hold him up and then walk in a procession. They said the music for this was played on the drum. Have you heard this?

R: No, I have not heard of this.

DS: When you hear of it, do you think that it is true that the processions in Yoeme culture always run counterclockwise like in the *kontim*?

R: Yes. That makes sense.

4 Our History of Nuestros Triunfos

How might we reimagine the history of colonial contact? In this chapter, I compare Spicer and Evelyn Hu-DeHart's narratives of the same Spanish-Yoeme contact period and ask how those histories might be supplemented by more attention to Yoeme agency and historical consciousness. We will see that Spicer does not actually rely on the talking tree to help explain Yoeme motivation, although at critical points he does suggest Yoeme intelligence and strategy. For her part, Hu-DeHart provides the most comprehensive summation of the contact zone. However, because she does not consider the tribe's oral tradition as reliable documentation, she overlooks the significance of the talking tree story. As a result, her history underestimates Yoeme power and strategy during this crucial contact period. Spicer and Hu-DeHart's works differ in methodology and outcomes in very telling ways. My contribution to their narratives seeks to understand how talking tree stories provide insight into Yoeme agency during the early European contact period. My central goal is to balance non-Yoeme historical accounts with Yoeme "documentation" in the form of their internal modes of historiography: their oral traditions and particularly the talking tree story. The project thus moves us closer to understanding how Yoemem perform, narrate, and conceptualize their history in nonliterate forms. This process of reading backwards is only one component of the performative approach to native history, which would entail among other tasks the rereading of written histories to decenter the subjects that were written into the documents. We are, of course, trying to retrieve unclear and perhaps unattainable shadows, but as Florencia Mallon (2000, 204) aptly describes this work, "It is the process itself that keeps us honest."[1] In her twofold call for responsible research, this is the dusty archive considered concomitantly with the muddy fieldwork.

In the period from 1533 to 1617, the phase of Yoeme-Spanish interactions before Jesuit missionaries entered Yoeme territory, Yoemem were able to control much of their early colonial experiences. By weaving Yoeme oral tradition like that of the talking tree into the scholarly histories written by Hu-DeHart and Spicer, we can move toward understanding Yoeme history from a Yoeme point of view, what Raymond Folgelson calls "ethno-ethnohistory" (1974).[2] If we consider the talking tree as "documentation," then Yoeme history emerges, one that includes boundary maintenance, ally formation, and some decisive control of contact with Europeans and other native peoples. To view these aspects of culture contact, one does not have to accept that trees can talk; we must simply acknowledge that indigenous theories and methods of historical narration are substantial.

To discuss the events between 1533 and 1609, three Spanish expedition accounts are useful: those of Diego de Guzmán, Alvar Núñez Cabeza de Vaca, and Diego de Ibarra. While these explorers came to Yoeme lands for different reasons — Guzmán wanted slaves, Cabeza de Vaca was wandering home, Ibarra was looking for areas to start mining settlements — all three could be understood as tentacles of a Spanish order. Based on the earlier reports of Hernán Cortés, Spanish rulers accepted several consequential impressions: first, that the indigenous populations of New Spain were all conquerable as were the Aztecs; second, that in such conquests one might encounter all the wealth of the Seven Cities of Cíbola, the Kingdom of the Gran Quivara, and/or the Kingdom of the Amazons; and third, that the natives of New Spain needed Christian enlightenment and civility.[3] By examining these three Spaniards' written reports of the Yoemem we learn more than how these impressions were unrealistic; we also learn how the Yoemem controlled much of their own future. In the three cases that follow, the Yoemem present themselves, receive others, and control contact situations on their own terms. Understanding the Yoeme history visible in these accounts prepares us to consider the following era of Yoeme-Jesuit relations in which Yoemem combined Catholic and indigenous worldviews to reshape their rituals, symbols, and myths.

Drawing the Lines: The Yoeme-Spanish Contact Zone

The first known non-Yoeme written account of the Yoemem comes from a historian on the Spanish slave-raiding expedition led by Captain Diego de Guzmán.[4] On October 4, 1533, the expedition arrived in northwestern Mexico, at the Yaqui River, which Guzmán then renamed to no effect "Río San Francisco." The expedition scouts came back to Guzmán with word that Yoemem were ahead, preparing for battle. According to the expedition historian, Guzmán divided his men into ranks of "one-and-a-half leagues" deep and started marching toward the Yoemem. They saw "an old man more distinguished than the others, because he wore a black robe like a scapulary, studded with pearls, and surrounded by dogs, birds, and deer and many other things. And as it was morning, and the sunlight fell on him, he blazed like silver. He carried his bow and arrows, and a wooden staff with a very elaborate handle, and was in control of the people" (quoted in Hu-DeHart 1981, 15).[5] Using his staff, the Yoeme leader then drew a line on the ground, kissed the line, and threatened death to any who dared to cross his mark. The expedition historian notes in his journal that Captain Guzmán then proclaimed his peaceful intentions and requested food. The Yoeme leader said he would oblige if the Spanish would allow themselves and their horses to be tied up. The historian writes that Guzmán would do nothing of the sort, and aiming their largest cannon at the Yoemem, "we shouted 'Santiago' as we fired it, and pounded on them" (Icazbalceta 1866, 302).[6] Perhaps Guzmán should have accepted the Yoeme conditions: after an undocumented period of fighting, the Yoemem forced Guzmán's expedition to retreat in severe defeat.

Based on that battle, many historians have framed their representations of the Yoemem in three distinct ways. First, by winning the fight Yoemem maintained aboriginal possession of the most fertile agricultural land in Sonora, Mexico. Second, they secured their reputation as, in the words of Guzmán's historian, "the fiercest fighters in the New World" (quoted in Evers and Molina 1992, 3). Third, since that line in the sand was the farthest north into Yoeme territory that these Spaniards traveled, Yoeme identity would originally be linked with physical acts of demarcating cultural and geographic boundaries. The image of this line drawing resonates throughout Yoeme historical accounts and the multiple ways in which Yoemem define otherness.

Shortly after meeting Felipe in 1993, I asked him if he would look over some of my college research papers that I had written on Yoeme history and world-view. Although he was very busy at the time, working with several linguists, ethnobotonists, and a children's deer singing group, he said he would look at them when he had the time. Back then I would see him only once or twice a month when I drove down from Tempe to work in the Arizona State Museum in Tucson. Mostly we would go to Marana Pueblo and meet, have lunch in town, or talk with elders from one of the other Yoeme communities. One of the privileges at that point of my life was being able to devote so much time to reading books, and I combined trips to the archives with opportunities to meet Felipe and discuss the archival materials. I would work in cold piles of yellowing paper from morning until lunch, meet Felipe to discuss what I had found, go back and work through the afternoon, and then meet Felipe again to discuss what was in the state's museum collections. He was hearing from me about what the museum held pertaining to his culture; I was learning how to think about those materials from his perspective. We did this for years while also taking trips to the pueblos in Mexico, joining my archival work with contemporary ethnography.

On one of my trips to Tucson I met Felipe at La Indita for lunch, and I was surprised to see him waiting with a folder of papers. They were my essays; he had read them and made notes all over them. Although he hadn't said anything previously, I had just assumed he wouldn't take the time with all he had to do. Plus, I had been warned by my professors that most community members simply don't have the luxury of time to sit around making the implicit explicit for outsiders. Now my three essays, all written for college courses, were covered in red ink: "wrong," "not true," "almost," and the like. But I was so grateful for his editorial comments that I didn't care that they were mostly negative.

Since each paper was written for a different professor, the introductory section of each included a short history of the tribe. These were mostly summaries of the "first contact," the Spanish era, the Jesuit era, the Mexican era, the diaspora, and resettlement. At that time there wasn't a casino era to write about. Over lunch we flipped through the first paper so that he could read the comments and discuss what he or his partner, Herminia Valenzuela, had to say about my writing. During the review of the first paper I noticed that he skipped over one of his comments in the margins that read, "Let's discuss!" It was written next to a paragraph about the first conflict with the Yoeme army in 1533. We looked at the second paper, and he had written the same comment next to a paragraph discussing the same encounter. In the third paper, again to the side of the paragraph about the Spanish "first contact," Felipe had drawn some exclamation marks in red ink.

By the time we finished reviewing the last paper, we had eaten our food and our plates had been cleared. As the waiter placed our coffee in front of us, Felipe said, "I want to talk with you about the Yoeme-Spanish battles." I remember the coffee tasting bitter and strong as I sat listening to him. "Perhaps it was the first thing written about the Yoeme by the Europeans. Perhaps not. But the story of that battle is repeated by every historian. Even newspapers articles start their articles about the Yoemem and their fighting capabilities against the Spanish. Now we have kids running around in gangs thinking that this warrior mentality is a good thing. They justify the shooting and violence by saying they are fighters by blood." Felipe sounded exasperated by the information he was conveying. I let a few seconds pass while I fully digested his message.

"Felipe," I said, "I want to be sure I understand what you are saying. Are you asking me to not write about that part of the tribe's history? Because I think that these are exactly the sort of histories that should be told, histories of resistance and strength. These are the rare moments in the history when the Indians are winning. It is one of the best things about Yoeme history; you beat the Spanish in four or five consecutive battles. And that story of the old man drawing a line on the ground? With all those animals around him in fighting formation? That's one of the best images of cultural contact that I've ever heard." *After being so happy that Felipe had critiqued my writing, I surprised myself by contesting one of his opinions. I wanted to assure him that I was receptive to different ideas. "So do you think the Spanish were lying or creating some romantic notion of what the Yoeme people were like?"*

"Oh, no," he said, "I like to imagine that encounter as much as you do. But all that language of being the 'fiercest fighters in the New World.' Who does that serve? Do we want our children proud of that quality instead of others?"

It clicked. I heard what he was saying. Something about his choice of words resonated for years. How do histories serve living people, particularly those historical images we think are inspiring? The braves, the chiefs, the warriors, the fighting Indians — they all struggle against someone. These are counterpositions, opposite of another fighter who might then elicit empathy or sympathy. Or perhaps we prefer the cloaked old man communicating with animals and standing alone in an epic ethnic and nationalist duel for access to "undiscovered lands" and the riches of gold supposedly lining the walls and paths of the pueblos.

"What is the solution, Felipe? I think these stories of colonial resistance are important so that we don't continue seeing all native people in America as powerless and conquered."

"I think it would be better if you at least stopped repeating the 'fiercest fighters' comment that the Spaniard may have written. Otherwise we'll keep having kids think they are still those fierce fighters, driving around and fighting with Mexicans and other groups as if they were living in another century." I agreed that I didn't want that to happen. I thanked him for reading my papers and asked him to thank Herminia for me. "Chiokoe Uttesia, Felipe. Your opinions mean a lot to me." Felipe smiled a bit humbly and said, "Well, I'm just one Yoeme talking."

While the details are limited in the written accounts of that first battle with Guzmán and his expedition, both Spicer and Hu-DeHart note that the Spanish were seriously routed. Spicer mentions that the Yoeme showed the greatest fighting ability of any natives of New Spain and moves on to describe Yoeme settlement patterns, population, food sources, and so on. Hu-DeHart, the committed archivist, contributes greater detail to this portrait of Guzmán's expedition. First, she writes that although the Spanish "chauvinistically" claimed victory, they were forced to retreat full of admiration and praise for the Yoeme fighters. She writes that out of the Spaniards' seventeen horses, only four survived the battle. Hu-DeHart then quotes the Spanish historian: "I have seen none fight better than they. . . . If it were not for the flatness of the field on which we fought, they would have inflicted even more damage to us, which was serious enough" (1981, 16).

Second, Hu-DeHart asserts that the Yoeme and Spaniards probably ended that battle with differing ideas of the outcome. She writes that after the fight, "that night" a Yoeme elder came to the Spanish camp and presented to Captain Guzmán a gift of three turquoise-studded maces.[7] For Hu-DeHart these were to "appease the foreigners and send them away" (1981, 16). However, she continues, these maces confirmed suspicions: Guzmán concluded that the Yoemem were hiding treasures in their villages. Then Hu-DeHart extracts a few brief comments from the anonymous Spanish scribe concerning some general observations about the Yoemem. For example, he wrote that the Yoemem had a very large population, mostly living in houses like the Mayo, though bigger. Also, he noted that the Yoemem did not make sacrifices or worship idols, but that they did worship the sun "like heathens." He said they hunted quite a bit and that their language sounded like German. These comments raise two important questions that Hu-DeHart does not explore: First, how would the ship's historian know Yoeme practices of "worship" from his very brief encounter with them? Second, if Hu-DeHart is correct about the "confirmed Spanish suspicions" of Yoeme treasures, then why did the Yoemem not encounter further serious acts of exploration until 1610? I use the word *serious* here as a means to discuss Spicer and Hu-DeHart's next point of difference.

Spicer moves quickly from the battle of 1533 to the next large battle of 1610, yet Hu-DeHart directs our attention to what she calls one of the "most bizarre and incredible adventures of the New World." On the other side of the continent in 1527, a group of Spanish explorers went awry, leaving only four survivors of the Pánfilo de Narváez expedition on the Florida coast. Alvar Núñez Cabeza de Vaca and his three fellow travelers trekked west, through Texas and Chihuahua, arriving in Sonora. The four were joined in Culiacán by "thousands of friendly Indians" who thought they were miracle workers (Hu-DeHart 1981, 16). Cabeza de Vaca moved southward into Yoeme territory, noting signs of Spanish presence. These notes, Hu-DeHart argues, provide us with the second written account, after Guzmán's historian, of the very early Yoeme-Spanish contact period.

Cabeza de Vaca's account offers us two additional observations about the Yoemem. First, we know by his conversations with Hiak Vatwe inhabitants that his visit followed earlier Spanish contact and that the Indians understood Guzmán's presence as otherworldly or, in his terms, "heavenly." Hu-DeHart writes that when visiting the Hiak Vatwe, Cabeza de Vaca noticed around a native's neck "a little buckle from a swordbelt, and in it was sewn a horseshoe nail." Reasoning that such an object must have originated in Europe, Cabeza de Vaca asked where the ornament was from. He was told that "men with beards had come from heaven to their homes and that they had horses, lances, and swords" (1981, 16). Whether the reference was to the sky, sun, Spain, or elsewhere, Cabeza de Vaca's report enables us to date his presence in Yoeme lands after earlier European contact, perhaps Guzmán's brief encounter in 1533. Additionally, we are led to believe that Guzmán and his expedition may have been considered as "not of this world" in a precontact Yoeme cosmology.[8]

The second issue that Cabeza de Vaca helps us understand about Yoeme people between 1533 and 1536 (the date he met up with fellow Spaniards south of Sonora) is that Yoemem had already begun rearranging their communities due perhaps to their earlier encounter with Guzmán. According to Cabeza de Vaca, once they reached the point "which Diego de Guzmán reached," there were clear signs that the Yoemem were preparing for the worst. Yoemem gave Cabeza de Vaca and his thousands of companions "over two thousand loads of maize," an indication of large food banks and generosity toward peaceful strangers. Cabeza de Vaca also noticed "many of the people had apparently deserted their homes and fields to flee to the mountains, in obvious fear of the white invaders and slave hunters" (Hu-DeHart 1981, 17). If Cabeza de Vaca's observations of stored food and community separation are correct, then at least two issues immediately come to mind. First, if they were afraid of white invaders, couldn't the generosity also be read as tribute? Second, we can see a connection between what was occurring on the Hiak Vatwe and the talking tree's prophecy of a pre-Christian diaspora, the transition from a singular community, a large group of one classification called the "Surem," to a group of pueblo-dwelling Yoemem and a group of proto-Yoeme ancestors who move to live in the hills, remaining as they were prior to hearing the tree's prophecy. This latter group, the Surem, was not interested in what was being offered, and so they escaped to a place in Yoeme landscape and stories where they could live undisturbed as before. This primal diaspora and the relationships that Yoemem maintain with the Surem are fundamental to many Yoeme worldviews. Most Yoemem on both sides of the U.S.–Mexico border continue to reference this dual community.

The last written contact story of the sixteenth century offered by Hu-DeHart but not by Spicer is that of Basque prospector Diego de Ibarra's nephew, Francisco, and his travel historian, Balthasar de Obregón. In the summer of 1565, returning from the Casas Grandes River in northwest Chihuahua, one of Francisco de Ibarra's followers suggested establishing a Spanish settlement along the rich Yaqui River. Approaching the region from the Gulf of California and cognizant of the Guzmán incident in 1533, Ibarra sent a messenger ahead of his group to assure the Yoemem of his peaceful intentions. According to Obregón, the messenger said that "the Yaquis were glad of the coming Christians. They promised a good reception for the general and his men."[9] Indeed, when Ibarra arrived in Yoeme lands, he was greeted by five hundred Yoemem in feathers, with conches, bows, arrows, seashells, and beads, offering gifts of "fish, game, and other foods which they had in their land."[10] Providing a rich and stereotypical description of what Hu-DeHart calls a "bountiful, sensuous pagan paradise," Obregón estimated the Yoeme population at around fifteen thousand. Two points should be highlighted about this encounter. First, this figure of fifteen thousand would coincide with the talking tree story in which half of the Yoemem stayed in the villages while the other half moved to the mountains.[11] Second, we know from Obregón's messenger that the Yoemem were expecting Christians. Whether or not the messenger suggested missionary intentions to prepare for a friendly reception, we see again how the talking tree story makes sense of Yoeme motivation. The tree story narrates Yoeme preparedness and direct engagement with their Others.

One final observation from Obregón's records should be noted here: the Yoemem did not want the Spanish to leave this time. In fact, according to Obregón, the Yoemem were so sad upon the departure of Ibarra's group that they begged them to stay and promised to feed them and take care of them for as long as they wished to stay. Ibarra was set on leaving, and so the Yoemem sent with him a group of two thousand Yoemem, still dressed in their farewell celebration clothing. Not until reaching the Mayo territory, just south of the Yoeme, did Ibarra understand Yoeme intentions. Entering Mayo villages, "with great determination and courage," the Yoemem "plundered, killed, and destroyed the fields and homes of their cowed enemies" (Hu-DeHart 1981, 19). After bringing the Yoemem and the Mayo to peace negotiations, Ibarra and Obregón learned that the Yoemem were on hostile terms with all their surrounding neighbors: Mayos, Uparos, Opatas, Apaches, and Nebomes.[12] Ibarra had made whatever promises were necessary in Yoeme territory to ensure safe prospecting; the Yoemem had used his men to present a more powerful fighting force to the Mayos. Without detracting from her larger narrative slant, Hu-DeHart concludes that the Yoemem "demonstrated a practical flexibility and tended to seize the initiative in establishing their relationship with alien groups interested in them" (1981, 20).

Other scholars of northwest Mexico report Yoeme battles with neighboring tribes.[13] These battles are important to remember because they refute the romantic misunderstanding that Native Americans were peaceful among themselves until European contact. These battles also qualify Kathleen Sands's view that "the attempted invasion of their land in 1535 [sic] by the Spaniard Guzmán is . . . their first recorded test as

Yoemem and marks the beginning of a struggle for tribal survival and identity" (1983, 365). However, if Yoemem were fighting neighbors before the Spanish arrival, then the various struggles — over resources, power, perhaps even identity and survival — predate European contact. The history of Indian-white relations must be seen in the context of preexisting and continually negotiated Indian-Indian relations and intertribal dynamics.

The Yoeme confrontation with Guzmán and his army seems to have been unique among primary Spanish/indigenous conflicts elsewhere in Mexico. This first-contact story suggests that multiple readings are required when representing the "conquest of Mexico." Ross Hassig begins Patricia de Fuentes's book, *The Conquistadors*, by writing in the foreword: "The Conquest of Mexico in 1521 was a major watershed in world history — the invasion, subjugation, and colonization of a 'New World' that had developed without influence from the Old." On the contrary, given Yoeme victory over Guzmán, we know that Mexico was not totally conquered, at least not in such a sweeping manner. Hassig's use of "watershed in world history" suggests that we in the world not only share a history but also agree on which events are "watersheds." Yoemem might understand a tree that hums prophecies as more of a watershed than winning battles against outsiders. Enrique Dussel (1995) complicates this notion of a shared "world history" by contrasting indigenous views of European culture with Hegel's view that Europe was the origin and goal of history (19–36). Dussel's larger project focuses on the conquest as "modern," and he devotes attention to multiple views of the same event: European invasion of indigenous lands across present-day Mexico. Dussel's work questions Eurocentric histories of Mexico's conquest period, suggesting that we have much work to do to understand the Conquest from indigenous standpoints. Other histories of native groups may indeed prove similar to those of the Yoemem, although we would need to recognize and compare these histories systematically. In this case, the talking tree stories explain how Yoemem chose to engage the world of New Spain with military and cultural strength.

Yoemem Prepare the Way for Jesuit Missionaries

Between 1607 and 1617, Yoeme territory was the site of much activity, since the Spanish were charged with preparing the way for the Jesuits' entrance into the Hiak Vatwe. When in 1591 the first Jesuits arrived in Sinaloa, just south of Sonora, Captain Diego Martínez de Hurdaide was given an army of twenty-five soldiers to clear the missionaries' way northward. Considered immensely successful in subduing the tribes south of the Yoeme, Hurdaide underestimated the well-known Yoeme ability to resist any forceful entries into their land. This section briefly describes Hurdaide's three attempts to conquer the Yoemem, and it explores some major differences between Spicer and Hu-DeHart's accounts of this important stage of Yoeme-Spanish relations. In particular, we still see Spicer's continuing focus on Yoeme agency in missionization (a version consistent with Yoeme stories of wanting baptism, as seen in the talking tree story) by contrasting his narrative with Hu-DeHart's interpretation that the Yoemem were tricked into allowing Jesuit entrance. A history by the people themselves (folklore) regards both community and individual logic and reason exactly where an archival history leaves only the writers' traces.

In her narration of Hurdaide's colonial movements in Sonora, Hu-DeHart posits that due to a series of unplanned events, Yoemem believed that they had no choice but to accept Jesuit missionaries into their pueblos. During the uprising of the Ocoronis of the Fuerte River just south of the Hiak Vatwe, an Ocoroni leader by the name of Juan Lautaro fled inland to the Yoemem for safety. According to Hu-DeHart, Lautaro's "charismatic leadership" persuaded the Yoemem that the Spanish posed a serious threat to their security and well-being. Fearing Yoeme resistance to his entrance, Hurdaide, who was living with Tehueco Indians, sent word to the Yoemem to renounce Lautaro. When the Yoemem chose not to respond, Hurdaide then sought some sort of peaceful arrangement by inviting Yoeme leaders to the bargaining table. In San Felipe, Hurdaide convinced the Yoeme leader, Aniabailutek (whose name means "the world ended by a flood of water") that peace could be maintained if they agreed on an exchange: for two Yoeme female captives, Aniabailutek would bring Hurdaide the Ocoroni "troublemakers" with the help of some Tehueco Indians that Hurdaide would provide. Basing her story solely on missionary accounts, Hu-DeHart writes that "unfortunately for Hurdaide, Anabailutei was unable to keep his word, for apparently he did not act with the consensus of his people" (1981, 26).[14] When Aniabailutek arrived back home, Yoemem jumped on the Tehuecos, taking their clothes and horses and then killing them. Confronted by rising Tehueco anger that their people had been used in a deadly trade-off, Hurdaide had now put the entire Spanish and Jesuit operation in danger. Hu-DeHart writes that with the Tehuecos ready to inflict revenge (she doesn't mention against whom — Spanish or Yoeme), Hurdaide felt obliged to take punitive action. While the events may have proceeded as such, Hu-DeHart assumes the worst about Yoeme actions by representing their leadership as ineffective.

By 1608 Hurdaide had increased his army to forty Spanish soldiers on horses with an auxiliary force of some two thousand Indians, mostly Mayo and Tehueco. Entering the Hiak Vatwe, Hurdaide's army met a surprisingly ready and waiting Yoeme front. Using poisonous arrows, Yoeme troops killed many of Hurdaide's men, forcing them to retreat to San Felipe. Hurdaide was able to recruit more troops (fifty mounted soldiers) from Culiacán and immediately returned. Once again, the Yoemem "humiliated" the Spaniards, forcing most of their would-be oppressors into the woods in all directions and leaving behind Hurdaide and his immediate envoy.[15] According to Hu-DeHart, Hurdaide and twenty-five others had no choice but to withdraw up a hill close to the Yaqui River. Without food or gunpowder, "they sucked on lead bullets to relieve the thirst caused by a scorching sun," while the Yoemem "deliberately cavorted before their eyes in the refreshingly cool water of the river" (1981, 27).[16] As a last ditch effort to escape, the captain sent their weakest horses galloping toward the Yoemem, drawing Yoeme attention away long enough for him to escape with his men on their faster horses.

Several issues stand out in Hu-DeHart's version of these battles.

Although she notes that the missionary account of these battles is not fair and balanced, Hu-DeHart does not convey Yoeme intelligence during these confrontations with Hurdaide. First, knowing the ways that Yoeme would position themselves as allies with neighboring tribes, Lautaro's role as a non-Yoeme leader of Yoemem indicates wise planning from the very beginning. By relying on him as the go-between, Yoemem could always use the "troublemaker" as the scapegoat. Hu-DeHart's statement that Anabailutei acted without Yoeme consent is unsupported by documented Yoeme political formation. Since representatives varied by need, to be representative meant going with a plan of action and tribal approval/support of whatever actions were taken with outsiders.[17] We have no way of telling whether the Yoeme ambush of the Tehuecos was premeditated before Anabailutei's visit with Hurdaide. That the Tehuecos would want revenge was surely a Yoeme intent, since they were ready for their appearance as part of the exchange for Lautaro, and they were waiting for the Mayo/Tehueco/Spanish force that followed. Finally, Hu-DeHart seems too easily persuaded by Spanish accounts that Hurdaide and his twenty-five men survived for any other reason than that the Yoemem wanted them to escape. She writes about their narrow escape from the hill: "Only by using his wits did Hurdaide save himself and his men from this hopeless situation" (1981, 27). From what we know about Yoeme fighting capabilities, the hill would have been no problem for Yoemem to traverse, especially in their own territory. Lastly, after outwitting all earlier Spanish armies, Yoemem would be unlikely to respond "as predicted and hoped" to weak horses without riders.

While my questions do not negate Hu-DeHart's ability to chronicle accurately the larger outcomes of Yoeme-Spanish encounters, they suggest an underlying tendency not to attribute Yoeme agency where Yoeme foresight and predetermination seem to be most clear: the early stages of missionization. For example, in her continuing narration of the events following Hurdaide's narrow escape, she claims that Hurdaide, "outwitting his adversaries, this time circulated alarming rumors throughout Sinaloa that the colonial government was planning an enormous military invasion of the Yaqui. Conveniently for Hurdaide, by coincidence a pearl-fishing boat was cruising the Sinaloa coast at this time, thereby confirming for the Yaquis the disquieting reports. To top off his scheme, Hurdaide embellished it with additional rumors of three squadrons already poised for the attack on the Hiak Vatwe. Finally, he let it be known widely that all the Indian nations desiring to settle old scores with Yaquis would be invited to join the invasion" (1981, 28). For Hu-DeHart and her Spanish sources, these rumors of a pending overwhelming assault, along with amazement at Hurdaide's "magical" escape from the last battle, were enough, "and Yaquis sued for peace." On 25 April 1610, 150 Yoeme representatives witnessed the formal signing of peace in San Felipe, receiving praise and gifts from the Jesuit fathers present. At the request of the Yoemem, the Jesuits then promised that missionaries would be sent to the Hiak Vatwe as soon as new person-nel were available.[18] In the seven years that followed, Yoemem made sporadic trips to San Felipe to confirm their desire for a future Jesuit mission in the Hiak Vatwe.

Hu-DeHart admits that her missionary sources offer little in the way of Yoeme motives for waging successful battles against the Spanish and then, surprisingly, asking for peace. Her own interpretation of Yoeme changes in sentiment was that the Yoemem perceived their earlier vic-tories to be "hollow" because they had no prisoners of war and that they grew apprehensive from listening to the Ocoroni visitors. She also reasons on behalf of the Yoemem, arguing that choosing peace was more pragmatic than dealing with "whole settlements of rapacious foreign intruders" or a "futile, protracted struggle" (1981, 28).[19] Hu-DeHart offers these interpretations without looking to Yoeme oral traditions. She did not consider the singing tree's prophecy that the Jesuits would bring positive changes to the Yoeme communities, although doing so clearly helps us understand Yoeme historical consciousness. Rather, she moves quickly to narrate the Jesuits' slow but steady move northward toward the Yoemem, describing a famine in Mayo lands and the revolts in Tepehuan country. Yoeme ethnohistory here seems part of a larger moment of colonization: European strength overpowers the helpless Indians across the discovered New World.

To be fair, Hu-DeHart's archival work remains the closest reading of Spanish sources available. She brings the various sixteenth- and seventeenth-century historians, explorers, Spaniards, and Jesuits into conversation with each other, enabling her readers to study the Yoeme-European contact phases as the various Spanish travelers wanted that past represented. She often notes that she only has Spanish sources and therefore her picture is "rather one-sided" (1981, 26). As I demonstrate below, however, we have reason to question how such written accounts screen Yoeme ingenuity and intelligence in this history.

This week I realized how uneven my knowledge of the Yoeme is, particularly in regard to the U.S. communities. While some aspects of the culture are by now quite familiar to me, others remain obscure. I have been attending this "Yaqui Language and Culture Class" at South Mountain Community College for about two months. Now that we're able to form sentences off the cuff, I'm sure that the other students think I'm fairly bizarre. Since I have been going to the pueblos in Mexico for seven years now, I have picked up much of the vocabulary related to the areas of my research. The other students, though, are from Guadalupe, Arizona, the Yoeme community farthest from the hiakim and most directly affected by the Phoenix metropolitan area. I began this class with the notion that, as the only non-Yoeme student, I would just keep my mouth shut and try not to embarrass myself. But I forgot that I'd be required to speak constantly in a language class. Additionally, it was the things I was saying that showed an inversion of the outsider and insider roles.

Last week, the teacher asked us to use a sentence with a noun, a verb, and a direct object. I went first. "Octavio choni vitchu" (Octavio sees a choni). Some people giggled while the teacher and assistant teacher (both older women) started laughing heartily. I had said that Octavio was looking at a small, some consider mythological, being that is three feet tall and lives on metal and a special type of tobacco. The reference was deeply Yoeme, from the sort of stories one gets late at night with elders or from anthropologists. One young lady asked, "What is so funny? It's just a 'star.'" "No," the teacher replied, "stars are 'chookim.' David said 'chonim,' which are small protectors that grow from scalps." The rest of the students looked at me with curiosity. This was the first time that I evidenced not just prior knowledge of the language but some level of understanding of a Yoeme worldview.

In class tonight, though, was a particularly odd exchange. We were talking about professions, repeating after the teacher's models: "Jorge is a sheep herder. Jorge bwalero." Then the class repeated "Jorge bwalero." The teacher continued: "Laura is a leader. Laura ya'ut." We repeated "Laura ya'ut." Then she asked for volunteers to make their own sentences. As usual, everyone dropped their heads to look at their papers. She waited a bit, pacing the front of the room. Then she called on me: "Davíd, hita teuwa'e" (Say something). I couldn't think of anything quickly. Every profession I could think of was a Spanish loan word: paneleo (baker), mineo (miner), traampa (hobo). Reaching for something quick and easy due to my research, I said, "Ignacio moreakame." One young man laughed, and the room was otherwise silent. I had said, "Ignacio is a powerful psychic," something I was studying in my research. I assumed it would be not only a correct answer but also a well-known word among the Yoemem in the room.

The main teacher looked at the assistant teacher and then said, "Okay, that's good. Anyone else?" But the students didn't know what I had said. One asked, "What did he say?" One teacher responded, "Ignacio is very smart." The young man who laughed a bit said, "Oh, I thought it meant 'homosexual.'" The students started talking among themselves, and the teachers again looked at each other, trying to figure out how to handle the situation. I was confused because I didn't understand what the problem was. Why wasn't my answer correct? Why didn't we just move to the next exercise? I spoke up again. "I'm sorry. I thought the word was common. In the pueblos, it just means that the person is a psychic, a person who knows things before they happen or who can tell what is going on in other places." The teacher's assistant, a woman in her late sixties, turned to the class and said, "Davíd is using a word that we don't use much here in Guadalupe. In the past, we used it more. You should have heard this word before. These people, moreakamem, are important in the community." Her tone was slightly scolding and was the perfect maneuver to get us focused together. The issue seemed resolved.

After class, a couple of Yoeme students in their twenties and thirties were standing outside the building's front door. As usual, I started to pass them to *go to my car. For the first time, one of them called out my name and asked me to come over. The young guy with her, the same guy who seemed to know the word* moreakame, *asked how I knew so much about "Yaqui culture." I told them that I had been traveling to the pueblos in Mexico for over five years and that because I mostly work with elders there, I have picked up some words in our interviews. The woman said that she had heard of the words* chonim *and* moreakame *from her uncle, who still spoke the language there in Guadalupe. The guy said, "Moreakame isn't used much up here because people started associated it with being gay or bisexual." I told him that I had heard from one collaborator that the word had nothing to do with sexuality. But I had also heard from two other collaborators that* moreakamem *were often bisexual. I was happy to have this conversation with these classmates. I asked, "So are you taking other classes besides the language class?" They both said yes. "We're both in Octaviana Trujillo and Antonia Compoy's class, Yaqui History and Culture." Happy to change the subject, I said, "Oh, good. I know Dr. Trujillo and like her a lot. But I do not know much about her class. Is she teaching any of Hu-DeHart's books on Yaqui history?" The guy replied, "We read her history of the Yaquis during the Revolution." The young woman added, "For the earlier history, we read Spicer." "Well," I said, "they both do a good job. The class sounds good. I'm glad Dr. Trujillo and Antonia Compoy have agreed to teach here in the community. If it weren't for this language class, I would have a hard time learning how to speak Yoeme." They both agreed, and the young woman said, "I am hoping to be able to speak to my grandfather, who mostly speaks Yoeme." The guy said he was going to be a ceremonial leader when he returned from the army. I asked if they wanted to grab a cup of coffee, but they both had families at home. We said our good-byes and started walking to our respective cars. I yelled out, "See you both next week! Aman ne tevote!"*

Spicer was reflecting on some of the same materials as Hu-DeHart: Ralph L. Beals, Bartolomé de las Casas, Gerard Decorme, Francisco Paso y Troncoso, Andrés Pérez de Ribas, and Carl O. Sauer. Although Spicer's work fails to consider many of Hu-DeHart's resources (Carlos Basauri, Miguel Othón de Mendizábal, George P. Hammond, and Agapito Rey), his cultural history of the Yoeme portrays Yoeme deliberation and power. In *The Yaquis* (1980), Spicer outlines and preemptively negates Hu-DeHart's historical account in her text published one year later. As if anticipating her interpretation of the European reports, Spicer summarizes the reasons that Hu-DeHart later gives for the Yoeme turn toward peace; then he writes: "No convincing evidence is presented to support this view" (15). Spicer demonstrates that Hu-DeHart's analysis is based on assumptions contrary to what is known about Yoemem. Yoeme leaders did not act as if they feared Europeans; rather, they were "deeply interested" in new things appearing on the horizon. They knew that they could obtain these things on their own terms if they could prove their strength and independence to the Spanish soldiers, which they did. Approaching San Felipe from a "position of conscious strength" (Spicer 1980, 15), the Yoemem asked for and received a constructive missionary program that, according to Yoeme accounts, was prophesied. In these ways they avoided a destructive military takeover of native economic and political programs. Spicer's argument echoes the many versions of the talking tree by pointing to new things, Yoeme preparation, and an aboriginal future when community division fundamentally supports claims of autochthony.

Spicer shows that the Yoemem went to the bargaining table a confi-dent people, with a working knowledge of what they could gain from such an accord. He supports his argument by providing his reader with two aspects of this period that Hu-DeHart does not acknowledge. Spicer reasonably assesses the plausibility that Yoemem were intimidated by a possible Spanish front led by Hurdaide. Closely reading the same sources as Hu-DeHart, Spicer shows that the last battle between Hurdaide and the Yoemem was enough to assert Yoeme dominance in the area for all to see. Hurdaide was "the military commander of the west coast region" of Mexico (Spicer 1980, 13). Over time, he organized the largest army ever assembled in northern New Spain, consisting of over four thousand warriors from the other tribes; forty-four of the fifty Spanish soldiers were on horses, in armor, with swords and lances, and deploying a can-non. Yet they still lost to a Yoeme army that was twice their number, according to the most famous of Spanish sources, Pérez de Ribas's 1645

Triunfos de Nuestra Santa Fé entre Gentes las mas Bárbaras y Fieras del Nuebo Orbe (1944, 71).[20] The Indian allies of the Spanish were so completely routed that they left their dead and wounded on the battlefield. While all Spaniards were wounded, none were killed, suggesting that if Yoemem had continued to use poisonous arrows, few of Hurdaide's soldiers would have survived.[21]

Although they are both reading Pérez de Ribas's *Historia*, Spicer takes seriously a vital detail that Hu-DeHart seems to mention as a conclusion to the various encounters: from 1610 to 1617, Yoemem had been visiting Sinaloa consistently, talking with Jesuits, and witnessing the changes taking place with Jesuit assistance. As seen elsewhere on the continent — in the fur trades and northeastern Atlantic conflicts — natives actively "worked" the contact zone.[22] Beginning with a Yoeme named Conibomeai (Crow Feather Kill), then with two female representatives, and then with a delegation of over four hundred in which all eighty Yoeme *rancherías* were represented, Yoemem visited the Jesuit missions of Sinaloa, Ocoronis, and Guasaves. Speaking in mutually intelligible tongues, the Yoemem were talking with the Tehuecos, Mochikawis, and Ajomes, unhurriedly observing, under peaceful conditions, how Jesuits and other tribes had transformed the land into new styles of farming tracts and how they developed governing organizations responsive to local ceremonial societies. Spicer justifiably writes that "it seems reasonable to regard this sort of preparation as of great importance in effecting the generally peaceful and even enthusiastic reception of the Jesuits who finally came four years after they were first requested by the Yaquis" (1980, 17).

Spicer also writes that Yoemem had begun moving from scattered communities to larger settlements before the Jesuits arrived (1980, 63). According to Pérez de Ribas, Yoemem from over eighty dispersed settlements joined eleven along the river (1999, 346, 350). Juan Valenzuela also describes these pre-Spanish moves toward the Hiak Vatwe banks. In Spicer's field notes from 1942, Valenzuela tells him that the real Conquest took place "when the division into eight pueblos was made . . . long before the Spanish." Later, he tells Spicer that no government ordered the Yoemem to establish the eight pueblos (Spicer field notes 1942, A-505-a). Spicer clearly interpreted Yoemem as actively managing their contact zones and using practical means to maintain sovereignty during the same period in which other tribes were suffering great losses.

Although Spicer offers a salient interpretation of Yoemem "suing" for peace with Hurdaide, another scholar's views are important to consider. In his essay "Prelude to Conquest: Yaqui Population, Subsistence, and Warfare during the Protohistoric Period," Thomas Sheridan brings together several views of this "extraordinary turn of events." Sheridan describes Hurdaide's view that because the Yoemem were impressed that so few Spanish died in their previous battle, the Yoemem "decided to be allies rather than enemies of the Europeans" (1981, 74). Sheridan also recounts the view of Jesuit historians Alegre and Decorme as agreeing with Hurdaide about Yoeme impressions. Then he notes the opinion of Spicer detailed above. Sheridan concludes his review of others' interpretations:

> All of these explanations are probably correct and certainly are not mutually exclusive. By 1610 the Yaquis must have realized that they could not defend their territory indefinitely against the combined forces of the Spaniards and their Cahita auxiliaries from the South. Furthermore, the new deities and rituals the missionaries offered must have seemed powerful and attractive during a time of great social upheaval. Yaquis had already experienced several epidemics of Old World diseases against which traditional curing practices were powerless. . . . The Europeans promised spiritual as well as material prosperity and the Yaquis, after a period of successful military resistance, quickly succumbed to Spanish temptations. Nevertheless, none of these explanations completely account for the Yaqui decision to accept missionization because none of them pay particular attention to the regional political and demographic dynamics of Southern Sonora prior to Spanish colonization. (74)

Sheridan moves to his theory that chronic warfare threatened intertribal relations and regional integrity, and thus the Spanish were "able to take advantage of this situation" (75). Sheridan provides his readers with a comprehensive analysis of the available documents regarding native populations, hunting practices, trading relationships, and warfare in the Hiak Vatwe. He combines a notion of religious pragmatism (though his essay fails to follow up on this issue) with a notion of practical desire for peace to make sense of Yoeme relations with Hurdaide. In his final analysis, Sheridan argues that Yoeme communities saw more benefits coming from peace than from continued warfare.

While recognizing the common historical trope of contact that the Yoemem must have been impressed by "Europeans and their belief systems" (74), I want to push this case a bit further. Feasibly, at the time, Yoemem had every reason to think that they would continue winning battles with the Spanish because they had won every previous fight. And if we assume, just for a moment, that parts of the Testamento in some form existed before 1610, then we might be closer to a Yoeme perspective on why asking for peace made sense. As an oral tradition, the other-worldly sanction of territorial sovereignty would justify military strategies of resistance and accommodation. An epistemological commitment to prophecies of community cohesion would lead to decisions based in confidence, not fear. To understand Yoeme history, we must work in conversation with distinctive Yoeme ways of thinking about, recording, and sharing history. The talking tree prophecy clearly provides a way of understanding new worlds and unprecedented change, a sensibility that recognizes indigenous intentionality.

Spicer's account of Yoeme encounters with the Jesuits and Hurdaide provides a contextual narrative of Yoemem setting and deciding on the conditions by which to enter a new era. In contrast, Hu-DeHart portrays the Yoemem as having learned a lesson from the intelligent Hurdaide: "But after the rather hollow victories over a determined and clever Captain Hurdaide, Yaqui pragmatism and flexibility prevailed, prompting them to choose peace over a futile, protracted struggle" (1981, 28). Hu-DeHart demonstrates her perception of Yoeme military resistance as "hollow." She portrays the Yoemem as being forced to bend to Hurdaide's cleverness and determination. Although Hu-DeHart notes that the Yoemem were pragmatic and flexible, her reliance on written documentation prevents her from balancing the details of European intelligence with descriptions of native strategies.

In the Shade of a Tree

When Yoemem recite the talking tree story, they tell us they expected the Jesuits, thus grafting the missionaries onto a Yoeme history. Spicer helps us make sense of this proactive desire for change and adaptation. Due to the prophecy, the Jesuits, and to a lesser extent the Spanish, had to choose a different approach to colonialism. Spicer shows how the Yoeme relationship contrasted sharply with the terms of other native-Spanish settlements. The ground on which the Yoeme people dealt with the Europeans, he writes, was not that of a conquered people, nor was it that of a tribe too lacking in policy or organization to resist infiltration: "The unique nature of these early Spanish-Yaqui relationships was an important determinant of the whole Yaqui future" (1980, 16). As Sheridan notes in his insightful comparison of Spicer and Hu-DeHart, Spicer "describes in detail how Yaqui political and religious life are intertwined" and "elicits a Yaqui model of society and then critically applies it to the non-Yaqui documentary record" (Sheridan 1988, 178, 183). I fully concur with his take on Hu-DeHart: "When she restricts herself to a straightforward narration of events, her two books provide an excellent complement to Spicer's more ambitious analysis. When she attempts to draw conclusions about Yaqui religion and political organization, on the other hand, she falls into the inescapable trap of the conventional narrative historian: a fatal dependence upon incomplete or misleading information" (184). Sheridan acknowledges the silences that exist in documentary records of indigenous contact zones. And although he doesn't attempt to bring Yoeme historical traditions into his analysis, he does critically reflect on the gaps in both Spicer's and Hu-DeHart's histories. This gap may be filled perhaps by Yoeme stories of their own past. By explaining the prophecy and how some Surem remained, Yoeme represent themselves as determined and clever: they resist the conquerors while pursuing the prefigured Konkista that the tree predicted. We have, then, a historical narrative or genealogy of surviving, yet changing, indigenism.

Yoeme history raises general questions about how we might reconsider contact relations and native historical traditions. Focusing on Yoeme agency in the early stages of European contact, it now seems unreasonable to rely on commonplace notions that Spanish power and military might have overpowered "primitive" political and military strategies. Indigenous peoples aggressively defined the terms by which they and outsiders would clash and coalesce. Yoemem created boundaries, drawing lines between themselves and the Spanish as well as other tribes. Yoeme boundaries were violently firm or strategically temporary according to extended pressure and Yoeme needs. Just as the Spanish were entering into new relations based on precontact concepts of "savages" and cities of gold, Yoeme myths show that Yoemem also acted according to preconstructed prophecy internal to tribal cosmology. Moreover, by seeking to understand Yoeme history in terms consistent with their own internal sensibilities, we critically reevaluate Western historiographical practices. How do nonliterate documentary methods succeed where written texts fail? As Kenneth Morrison discovered about Algonkian mission history, "The Jesuit sources provide rich details about actual face-to-face relations; the folklore remembers the central dynamics of those meetings" (1979, 74–75).

I do not claim that prophecy actually predicts genuine historical events, nor do I interrogate Yoeme truth claims. In this light, I offer a rereading of the Yoeme history where indigenous intentionality is central. That is not to say that I have written a history of any sort. If anything, I have simply used one possible evaluative standard, mythistoric sensibility, to compare two historical accounts, Spicer's and Hu-DeHart's. Mythistoric, as the hybrid conjunction of insiders and outsider's claims about the past, asks how to better understand "what has happened" within the context of a people's cosmology. Mythistory emphasizes the "my" belongingness and the facticity associated with both ontology and axiology: people make logical choices based on their ethical systems, regardless of whether or not such decisions are sensible to outsiders. In some cases, myth can substantially affect social practice in those societies that prioritize bidirectional historicism: stories of the past are always about the future. In their dealings with outsiders Yoemem consistently demonstrated foresight and the power to achieve their own goals of working with the missionaries without being under Spanish rule. Their orientations are both described by and modeled by the stories of talking trees and the oral traditions compiled into the Testamento. But to be sure, the histories under consideration here, Spicer's, Hu-DeHart's, and the numerous historical "documents" from which they are drawn, are not the sort of histories one hears on the pueblo. When telling me of their past, Yoemem never mention Pérez de Ribas or Hurdaide. We don't sit around the table talking about the three phases of Spanish exploration into the Hiak Vatwe. Still, I do not hesitate proposing how Yoeme mythistory would be enacted. The evidence of Yoeme historiographical thinking lies within the embodied acts of ritual and ceremony.

Ethnographic Dialogue 4

DAVID SHORTER: In order for people to understand the
contemporary situation among Yoeme people in the Hiak
Vatwe, I think that we are going to return to just after 1939,
when President Lázaro Cárdenas says, "The Yoeme people
have their land here, their Yaqui Zone." So, immediately
after 1939, was there work? Was there money? Was it
immediately the good life?

RESPONDENT: Well, Cárdenas made peace with the Yaqui
tribe, telling us, "I am going to speak with you all. I want
one thing for you, as president of the republic. I want to
offer you a territory where you can live in peace, and also I
want to give you the right to 50 percent of the water in the
dam," which today is the Alvaro Dam outside of Obregón.
And being the president of the republic, he signed a
presidential decree where he promised to help the tribe in
this way. It was 1937 when they made these agreements.

DS: Very soon after, Yoemem needed credit?

R: From 1950 to 1953 is when they began preparing the land
for agriculture, the Yaqui lands, the Yoeme lands for
cultivation, and they made irrigation canals, they cleaned
the lands. They did not level them, because at this time
there were not levelers. We borrowed money to do this
work. We borrowed money for the expensive leveling
machines in the 1980s and also the other products and
tools for better planting. We borrowed for years. Banco

BANRURAL raised its interest rates very high, so the
Yaquis, the Yoemem, we left owing something to the bank.
In those years, the banks offered machinery without saying
anything. But then, after all the fields were planted and
harvested, they would come back and say we owed them
more interest than what was agreed upon. We who are
left, the people that have a piece of land, are renting it to
the Mexicans, because we do not have credit to be able to
cultivate our lands. And it is very expensive to sow lands.
It takes money to even ask for credit or other financing.
But if we had someone to help us resolve our problems, to
give us credit or loans, we would be able to work our lands.
I am sure that at the level of the eight towns we can again
lift ourselves up, like the first days that Banco BANRURAL
offered credit to the Yoemem. And the Yoeme youth, they
do not have an opportunity to work of what was their
fathers', the little pieces that they have to sow, because they
do not have credit. There is no stable work. There are no
businesses. For this reason many Yoeme youth leave the
towns to work in the temporary factories or to work on
the land cutting tomatoes, to cut chilies, melon, squash,
watermelon, all sorts of products. These owners of the
businesses send the products out of the country to sell them
for more money. These products do not stay in Mexico.
These products are transported to other countries. And the
worst thing in the whole world that you can see, that I can
imagine, is that they are paying them 60 or 80 pesos daily
(approximately U.S.$6] for eight hours of work, from 8
a.m. until noon, and from 1 to 5 p.m. And the poor people
in the factories closer to the U.S. border are being paid 60
or 80 pesos as well, for ten hours of work. And if a Yoeme is
missing work, no matter the reason, they charge them 200
pesos [approximately $20] when they return to work.

DS: A person who did not understand the situation very well

would say, "But they have all the land. It is their land, their zone! Why are you all not rich? They can work the land."

R: We have a creditor or a financier that offers a credit so that we can work our own lands. Outsiders say that these bankers are trying to help us, much like the Banco BANRURAL of 1954 to 1980. But instead of helping the tribe, it is just falling into debt. The banks gave us a loan that came due in three cycles: October, December, and March. The Yoemem began to plant with that money thinking we could pay them back when the crops were sold. But in the middle of the planting cycle, the bank wanted its money back. Had the bank waited until after the time of sowing, yes, sir, it would have had its money. But the seed, the plant, has a definite time before one can sow it. If the planting time passes, the plant will grow, but it won't give produce. It does not produce, like planting it in its [proper] planting epoch/season. This was what the bank had with the Yoemem. And for this reason now the Yoemem cannot work their own lands, because there are people, poor people, humble like the Yoemem, like the Mexicans, like other tribes, whom instead of helping, the government does not guarantee anything. Always and all of the time, they want to keep the lands, not only of the tribe, no? I imagine this is a national problem. This is the problem that we cannot sow our lands.

DS: What can a young man do? Let's say he is a newlywed, and he wants to work. What are his options? There is work on the land, yes? For example, I know that you have some land.

R: Yes.

DS: And you have sons.

R: Yes.

DS: Could he decide to work on the land?

R: Yes, yes, he could. There isn't any problem if he had the know-how, the machinery, and sufficient money to work the lands. I could advise him. My son knows that if he had a little bit of money, I could say to him, "Look, benefit from it. There are my lands. Go sow them." But we don't have the money. If the gods give you good luck or an opportunity like I told you, maybe we could benefit so that the family would be a little better off.

DS: And if he wanted to work in the factories up north, is it necessary to work eight hours each day?

R: Ten hours. Ten hours is the scheduled minimum in the factories each day. From 4 a.m. and they return to Potam at 6 or 6:30 p.m.

DS: Do they have to pay for the bus?

R: No. The same maquiladora gives them these services.

DS: It is approximately 60 or 70 pesos each day?

R: Each day.

DS: And it's a factory for car parts?

R: Yes, metal parts for cars.

DS: A person working in the sea as a fisherman, how much do you think that he makes?

R: Well, the sea is a mystery. In the sea, sometimes you win double, and sometimes you don't win anything. Sometimes, when the sea gives you something, it gives you so that your whole family eats. But sometimes you do not bring back anything. You don't even get the price of gasoline for the engine, and you are completely defeated when you arrive at your home. Why? Because you did not find shrimp or crabs or other kinds of fish.

DS: And you said yesterday that there are two or three months when there isn't anything?

R: Yes.

DS: In summer?

R: Yes, in summer. Therefore, they go to the countryside. They are there right now. There are a lot of people that go to the countryside to cut tomatoes, to pack and bale other things. Why? Because in the bay or the sea, there is not enough to be able to maintain your family.

DS: In Potam, do you need to pay for your own electricity?

R: Yes.

DS: And it is approximately how much every month or two?

R: Every two months? Well, it depends how much electricity one uses, though it would be about 500 or 600 pesos ($45 to $55). If you do not have a refrigerator, or if you do not have fans, or if you do not have other things, it comes out to be a little less still. But if you have more things, the electricity goes up.

DS: And you said that they have to pay for health, for medicines and doctors. How much does a visit to the doctor cost?

R: The social insurance is currently charging 4,800 pesos [$439] per year.

DS: For your entire family?

R: Yes, for our family. But it does not cover children over the age of fifteen.

DS: Really?

R: As soon as they are sixteen, they will not accept the social insurance from the government. Then they charge you 10 to 20 dollars for a consultation.

DS: Just to be seen?

R: Yes, just to be seen.

DS: So you have to pay the 4,800 pesos and that covers your family until the child reaches sixteen, and you can go to any hospital in Sonora?

R: No, this is simply for the clinic in Potam. We are stuck going there. But if we want to go someplace where the doctors have a little more, we go to the hospital an hour away in the next city. We can go to the clinic here and get a prescription, and they have a limited amount of medicines and machines. So, in many cases, the person might need tests, X-rays, or ultrasounds. We cannot have these at the local clinic. So we have to go to Guaymas or Obregón, where we cannot use social insurance.

DS: You end up having to go to a hospital where you have no insurance?

R: Not only that, but when we get there, they say we must eat a piece of bread or drink some soda before we are tested. And we haven't eaten and have no money. And then the tests come back and say we need more tests, perhaps at another location. They say that health care is affordable for poor people, humble people, for people who work, a day laborer, a person who works in the countryside. But I have had my family there, and to admit one person, it costs more than buying social insurance. Because every moment, they are giving you prescriptions. "Oh, you know what, sir? You are lacking this syrup, these injections, and this serum. You are missing these vials." In our local clinic, we don't even have a machine that analyzes blood. The doctors do not care that we cannot do these things in our local clinics where our insurance pays. So what does one do? One has to begin borrowing money or selling what little property that's left. One goes to the Mexicans and says, "You know what? I need money. I cannot get out of this predicament." Often to just lend money, these people say to us, "Listen, do you believe I am a public beneficiary?" They try to humiliate the person, even if they are sick and asking for money. This is how our health is connected to the health of the land.

DS: Do you have to pay for your children's education?

R: Yes.

DS: The uniforms?

R: Everything.

DS: The books?

R: The books, too. Like with my daughter entering high school. She needs thirteen books, including mathematics, Spanish, natural sciences, geography, English dictionaries, Mexican dictionaries, biology, literature, more and more. There are thirteen units of work, and there are thirteen teachers in high school. They spend 34 to 45 minutes with each teacher. They start at seven in the morning and leave at 2 or 3 p.m., depending on their grade. The teachers leave at 4 p.m. And the children have to take their taquito or their parents have to give them a few cents so that they eat a torta, a sandwich, or a soda or a piece of bread. And besides the books and the lunch money and the uniform, just to register for school costs us 375 pesos. So then multiply that by how many children or grandchildren you have.

DS: How much do their outfits cost?

R: The school sells the uniforms for 400 pesos each.

DS: For each student?

R: Each student.

DS: Can you approximate for me how much it costs to eat for one week?

R: Well, we don't eat meat regularly. Without meat and things that are more expensive, I would say it would be beans, flour, lard, sugar, coffee, and pasta. We can no longer eat meat, or chicken, or fish, or other kinds of proteins. Just a little cheese. Right now we have ten people in my household. So we are only guaranteed breakfast and perhaps a little dinner. That takes two kilos of beans, and one kilo of beans costs 20 pesos, and a liter of oil costs 15 pesos, and the lard costs 15 pesos, and the pastas another 15 pesos. But the most important thing, coffee, costs 52 pesos. The sugar costs 9 to 12 pesos per kilo.

DS: What about flour?

R: Ah, well, we eat some tortillas in the morning and some in the afternoon, because we do not have the luxury of eating three times a day. Six kilos cost 6 pesos, so we need about 36 kilos per day.

DS: Do you use cornmeal or corn flour?

R: Yes, we use Maseca.

DS: How much does it cost?

R: The Maseca costs 7 pesos, which makes three batches of corn tortillas. And for all this food and math, be sure you multiply for seven days.

DS: Okay. And do you need to pay for water in your house?

R: Twenty pesos each month. This isn't exactly to a corporation, but more like a cooperative that works the pump. Unlike electricity that depends on usage, this is a flat fee of 20 pesos.

DS: In Potam, you have a piece of land, yes?

R: Yes. About nine hectare (about seventeen acres).

DS: It is your own? It belongs to your family?

R: Yes.

DS: And do you have people working on this land?

R: Yes.

DS: Mexicans?

R: Yes, Mexicans.

DS: And the Mexicans are paying you?

R: Rent is about $8,790 pesos [approximately $800].

DS: And what is growing?

R: Wheat and sometimes corn.

DS: And do you need to pay to water this land?

R: I am not planting; I am not going to pay. They are the ones who pay for the water to sow.

DS: Pesticides?

R: Yes, everything.

DS: And how much wheat or how much corn does it bring in each year?

R: Well, depending on the climate, sometimes a hectare of wheat yields six or seven tons.

DS: And for how much can they sell six or seven tons?

R: Right now, presently, they are getting about $1,680 ($153) per ton.

DS: How much goes to the Mexican and how much goes to you?

R: This is for the Mexicans only. No longer do they give us anything.

DS: But it is your land.

R: But they no longer give us anything. They are giving us nothing more than rent.

DS: So they pay you about $800, but earn themselves about $8,000?

R: Sometimes more, sometimes less.

DS: And is there a standardized policy for how they pay you your $800?

R: They keep the money at all times like a bank. Then we will go to them and say, "You know what? I need this because this or that is happening to me." They keep the money because we don't know when the children will get sick, or when we are unable to work ourselves, and then there are the ceremonies and pahkom, and the burial costs, and such. If one person dies, the burial can cost around $1,300. That is $500 more than our entire yearly payment for the land's rent.

DS: I see. And the reason that the Mexicans are working your land is because they have the machines and the staff and knowledge to do it easier than Yoemem?

R: Well, there are Yoemem that also work them for them to earn money. But sometimes they bring in people to work tractors, tillers, mixers, and irrigators. They bring these non-Yoemem to work the lands as well.

DS: Is it possible to have your land, that you own and rent it to Mexicans and also work on your land for those Mexicans, to gain money twice, one time for the rent and one time for the other work?

R: Yes. If I had money, I would sow my lands myself. Why? Because in this government, the Mexicans call the people sowing the land "pro-campo," and like a government subsidy, they help the agriculturists by giving them 960 pesos per hectare, not to the landowner, but to the land renter. So consider that right now the Mexicans are getting money to work the land and then the earnings of the produce.

DS: So why don't you get that money from the Mexican government and use it to sow your own land?

R: Because you receive that money after showing the government that you have previously earned money from selling the produce or seeds that you yourself raised. The money helps those who have a record of their previous sales. You have to show you are working the land to receive the assistance.

DS: Approximately what is the population of Potam? Six thousand?

R: Yes, counting the recently born.

DS: Approximately how many men of your age have land?

R: About half. The other half don't have anything. For example, my sons do not have anything. My piece of land supports my entire family.

DS: So how many families have pieces of land as you do?

R: Five hundred families.

DS: Are there more pieces of flat land to give?

R: Yes, there are many. The problem is that there is no water, or rather that we do not have canals to irrigate the lands. Right now there is enough water coming through the Alvaro dam to irrigate everything, but the government does not want to help the tribe, the Yoemem.

DS: Now the tribe is receiving 50 percent of the water?

R: No.

DS: But the government says that it is your right.

R: Yes, this is what they said, but it is not happening.

DS: And the tribe knows what is happening?

R: Yes.

DS: But you cannot do anything to receive more?

R: Well, no. So for this reason there are tribal officials contesting the government right now. They want the late 1930s agreements to be respected, including the boundary agreements. The language was not vague in those agreements. We have posts marking that territory; we see that it says 50 percent of the water from the dam. So why are the Mexicans controlling the pump? These matters were already settled; we know what is ours and where the boundaries are. With a little help, we can say, "This is ours!"

DS: Yes.

R: Half of this water belongs to us and half to them. We want to install a meter to see where the water is going. If more water is going to the Mexicans, they have to cut back so that they do not finish the water that is inside of the dam. But, as of now, we do not have proof.

DS: All of this is a particular type of business thinking. Is there a section of the tribal government that is managing these things? Do you rely on the traditional authority of the eight governors, one from each village?

R: Only the eight governments.

DS: There isn't an agency?

R: No, no. And for this reason right now the Mexicans who are renting make and unmake what they want to do over there. But if we had a person or someone or many that want to invest their money, then they could help us come out ahead. And if that were possible, then who knows? It could work. If someone said, "You know what? I am going to put the money in myself, and I will gain some of the profits with the Yoemem." We could expect some interest rates, but they could be better than the one the banks have on us now.

DS: So is the current problem based on high interest rates on outstanding loans or new loans?

R: There aren't any more new loans.

DS: Since when?

R: Since 1985.

DS: Are any Yoeme families working their own parcel of land?

R: Not one. Everything is rented.

DS: Everything Yoeme is rented?

R: Everything Yoeme is rented.

DS: And these Mexicans are living in the pueblos or coming into Yoeme territory each day?

R: They live in Obregón or in Guaymas or in Guasave or in Navojoa, in other parts, but they come to say, "How is my work doing?" or "How are my plants doing?" They only come to see their sowing and their crops once in a while.

DS: Are there many Yoeme women working outside of the homes?

R: Yes. For several years now, women have been working wherever men are working, in plants, factories, the countryside, everything. They work like men now. They do this to help men pay the bills of the family, to buy food, clothes, tennis shoes, sandals, and little things that the family is missing. But more than anything else, they help buy food.

DS: For the boys who are between twelve and fourteen, who are going to complete school, what do you think that they will do?

R: Well, right now, here in the community, there are young men who are certified as engineers, as secretaries, as bilingual teachers, but the government does not want to give them the opportunity to work. They already have their diplomas, already have their studies realized. Now what they lack is someplace to accommodate them so that they can work in their chosen vocation, to be what they want to be. You know how someone in school says, "I want to be an engineer." Right now there are people that are licensed engineers, they are biologists, and they go on cutting tomatoes for a factory. They are working on the land. Why?

DS: With all of this education.

R: With all of it. And why? Because the government, many Mexicans, they do not want to give them an opportunity to use their diploma for their work.

DS: Is it possible that a young person can have the education to be a bilingual teacher and still be working in a factory?

R: It is like this now.

DS: Okay, I want to go back for a moment. I understand that with the plants near here, near the pueblo, it is necessary to work ten hours each day for only 70 pesos. Why would a person move so far up north by the border to work, like in Mexicali, Tecate, or a border town? Because it is more money?

R: Yes, it is more money each day.

DS: Approximately how much?

R: Right now they are paying my oldest son 900 pesos for five days of work. So by earning 180 pesos each day (about $20), he is earning more than double what they make here near the pueblo.

DS: Do women earn as much as men at the factories, either near or far from here?

R: It is the same. She is a laborer from every angle. She is a laborer, and there the man is earning like the women.

DS: Can we use your house for an example of how much women contribute to the total income?

R: Sure. In my house are my two daughters, one daughter-in-law, and my wife. My other daughter moved in with her husband's family.

DS: Are any of them working outside the house?

R: No.

DS: And how many children are living with you?

R: Five.

DS: And you have one son who left to work by the border, but one son-in-law here at the house?

R: He is working by making charcoal.

DS: And you have another son who is about to finish high school?

R: He is working cutting squash. I believe that right now he is cutting melon.

DS: Do your son and son-in-law give some money to the family?

R: Yes. My son gives me the money, and I put it together with mine and buy the basics. Well, primarily what we secure is the beans and the coffee, and the flour, things we cannot go without. The other things, rice, tomato, onion, chili, and pasta, we get it from those who sell us the leftovers because they are very expensive fresh.

DS: Now, you have eleven people, and only six months ago you had your oldest son living here and your father was still living.

R: Yes.

DS: Do you think this number of household members is normal in Potam?

R: There are others who have even more.

DS: Yes, I know that there are other possibilities, but what is normal?

R: Well. We are a lot. But I want to be a family, near my daughters and sons. I say to them, "You know what? You have already gotten married. You already can make your life. Or you have already made your life. But how I love you. See how good this is, this time now, how the situation is?" I cannot let their hands go. I cannot stop helping them. And therefore I tell them that together with the good and the bad, that we go helping ourselves with what we are here. And with my son who went far away to work, well, I believe that he is not lacking food to eat. I hope he calls. That is why I carry my cellular phone daily, because he might call today. [Pauses to flip open phone and check for missed calls.] But here, between everyone, we help. Therefore, it is the norm of a family to be five children or with you and your women and three more children. With my children, I cannot tell them, "Get out of here." Why? Because they are my children. I love them and love seeing them. And for this reason I have them here in my house. But if they had to leave to work, like my oldest son, and go to Tucson or Guadalupe or Phoenix, I don't know where, but if they take these routes, have these ideas to go over there to work, I cannot disagree. It weighs on me that my children go so far away from me to help themselves, but I do have the manner of "You know what, son? Don't go. I have enough here. I can help you all, or let us go and everyone live together where there is work." Seeing the situation as it is, I can only wish them well and know that they look for their own future, their own life. If the gods loan them good luck or some person can over there, far from me wants to help them, as good as I would, for that I would be very grateful. And yes, yes, it hurts me to say this, but it doesn't matter.

DS: Well, when you think of these things, of the economies of living, of how it is so difficult, do you think that something in the tribe can be done differently?

R: Well, it is probably in the days of tomorrow, maybe, that a person emerges that wants to help us. I do not think that with eight hectares, with three hectares, with two hectares, and so on into the future, that I would have money to help this situation. I can only maintain this poor life. But I know how to work the land. Therefore, my idea is to plant, to get a little money. I want to plant vegetables. Vegetables, during the time of production, my family can eat something and then I can sell vegetables in the markets, and from my house, and I don't know, outside to other people that have restaurants. I could sell produce, no? And I could give them a just price, not to sell them like we are buying them now, for so much. Because right now all sorts of food, much like the basics, like produce, today everything is very expensive. And what they are paying us does not enable us to buy all the basics for the family's nourishment. Well, what more can one give? If one bank, or outside people, or an outside government, if one said, "Oh, we are going to help the Yoemem, the Yaquis, so that they can plant their own lands again." Or one could say, "I am going to give you all one more opportunity to see if you all do or do not want to work." But as it is, the government does not want Yoemem to work or to profit. They just want the lands. Like now, the knife wants a piece of our lands. This he will do today. And tomorrow he will want another piece more. And in a little while he will want another piece more. If we sell it piece by piece, well, the day of tomorrow will come, and we will not have anything. We will be left poorer than we are now, poorer than we are.

Reconsidering "Writing"
and the Proof of History

After eliminating all other criteria which have been put forward to
distinguish between barbarism and civilization, it is tempting to
retain this one at least: there are peoples with, or without, writing;
the former are able to store up their past achievements and move with
ever-increasing rapidity towards the goal that they have set themselves,
whereas the latter, being incapable of remembering the past beyond
the narrow margin on individual memory, seem bound to remain
imprisoned in a fluctuating history which will always lack both a
beginning and any lasting awareness of an aim.
CLAUDE LÉVI-STRAUSS, *Tristes Tropiques*

The difference between peoples with and peoples without writing is
accepted, but writing as the criterion of historicity or cultural value
is not taken into account; ethnocentrism will apparently be avoided
at the very moment when it will have already profoundly operated,
silently imposing its standard concepts of speech and writing.
JACQUES DERRIDA, *Of Grammatology*

The preceding chapters engaged different claims about how
writing practices have affected both historical and anthropological discursive practices. Underlying this discussion has been the suspicious
concern for power, both the power to claim authority, and the authoritative power of representation. Before moving to the second part of the
study, an examination of performed Yoeme literacies, I want to pause
to consider some historical antecedents of early twenty-first-century

ethnography. This section's epigraphs articulate two positions toward a civilizational theory of writing. As Lévi-Strauss suspected, writing often constitutes the dividing mark between pristine societies and those that have acquired literacy and thus, inevitably, the tools for domination and empire building. Derrida offers a strategy for deconstructing the oral/literate dichotomy. He situates literacy as one mode of communication among others, all of which reflect ideological and political conventions. I counter Lévi-Strauss's claim with Derrida's analysis in order to highlight the ways literacy has been used as an evaluative term to distinguish logic, civilization, and the defining factor of what constitutes history. I particularly want to differentiate Lévi-Strauss and Derrida as well as relate them to a diverse body of literature that challenges the historiographic authority of written texts over nonliterate communication.

Establishing how rituals are inscriptive and historiographic, this interchapter bridges the book in three ways. First, this theoretical interlude provides a means of assessing the ethnographic narratives thus far presented. The previous chapters demonstrate how Yoemem utilize both written and oral practices to share historically pivotal stories of the Testamento and the talking tree. I discussed how the dichotomy, oral/literate, fails to account for the continuation of oral practices after the adoption of literacy. Non-Yoeme authors rarely, if ever, consider Yoeme oral histories as documentation. At best, such performances register as informative in a general manner. Expanding accepted notions of writing and history, I consider briefly the ideological context of legal standards that affect native peoples everywhere, since judicial reliance on written documentation places primarily oral peoples at a serious disadvantage. I discuss the ways that dancing and processions might be considered nonliterate yet valid expressions of historical discourse. Looking at narrow definitions of writing and history, I sharpen the study's continued focus on the spatially inscriptive, nonliterate and literate, forms of Yoeme ethno-ethnohistorical discourse.

Claude Lévi-Strauss provides my first point of reflection, since his understanding of the literate and nonliterate dichotomy is central to his theory of cultural difference. In experiences made famous by his classic account *Tristes Tropiques* (1977), Lévi-Strauss traveled to the interior of Brazil where he encountered the Nambikwara. During an instance of exchange between himself and tribal members, Lévi-Strauss passed out pencils and paper as he has with previous tribes on this journey. He noted the irony of his own actions, since "the Nambikwara have no written language" (357). However, he noticed that a group of Nambikwara had busied themselves drawing wavy horizontal lines on the papers, and since he had never attempted to amuse Nambikwara with artistic drawing, Lévi-Strauss concluded that they were attempting to write. One member of the tribe, the leader, "grasped the purpose of writing." And this began what the anthropologist famously called a "Writing Lesson." Surrounded by other Nambikwara, the leader pulled out of a basket a piece of paper with scribbled lines and pretended to read a list of objects from the respective members that would be traded for Lévi-Strauss's items. Lévi-Strauss noted that the leader thus accomplished the act of amazing his group while also allying and equating himself with the white man.

Unable to sleep that night, Lévi-Strauss replayed the incident in his mind and concluded, "Writing had, on that occasion, made its appearance among the Nambikwara." It was not that they learned how to transcribe speech, but that they knew what it meant to do so: "It had been borrowed as a symbol, and for a sociological rather than an intellectual purpose, while its reality remained unknown. It had not been a question of acquiring knowledge, of remembering or understanding, but rather of increasing the authority and prestige of one individual — or function — at the expense of others. A native still living in the Stone Age had guessed that this great means towards understanding, even if he was unable to understand it, could be made to serve other purposes" (359). From this realization about the Nambikwara leader's use of writing, Lévi-Strauss then shifted the focus of his report away from Brazil and toward human culture. He went on to describe how writing becomes a defining factor of civilization. Writing can "be thought of as an artificial memory, the development of which ought to lead to a clearer awareness of the past, and hence to a greater ability to organize both the present and the future" (360). Writing brings with it the building of empires, the integration of political systems, the classification of individuals and their distribution among various classes. This line of thinking enabled Lévi-Strauss to conclude that a primary function of writing is to facilitate the enslavement of other people. Although he admitted some exceptions to this rule from his understanding of pre-Colombian America and ancient Africa, Lévi-Strauss hypothesized that writing is "indispensable" to establishing enduring dominions. He returned from the field understanding writing as a simultaneously empowering and corrupting achievement. The shift from oral to literate cultures alters forever their traditional ways of knowing and being.

The idea that writing systems were absent in Native American cultures and that this lack indicates a less civilized and less-human being was a centerpiece of Spanish debates regarding colonizing the Americas. In the early sixteenth century, as Thomas Berger (1991) notes, Spanish conquistadors and government officials justified their treatment of the Aztecs and Incas on the grounds that the Spanish were a superior race: "To the European conquerors, the Indians had no story to tell; indeed, insofar as they were without a written language, they had to depend on Europeans to give an account of their history and beliefs. The persistence of Latin American disregard for Indian rights stems from these early encounters" (13–14). Berger observes that the equation of a "written language" with civilization was explicit during the 1550 debate at Valladolid.

Temporarily suspending further explorations of the New World, King Charles V of Spain summoned a meeting of scholars to pose the question of how to justify the Conquest in terms of justice, reason, and divine right. He brought together a renowned advocate of Indian rights, Bartolomé de Las Casas, and Spain's premier philosopher, Juan Ginés de Sepúlveda. Citing Aristotle's view that some races were inferior to others and born for slavery, Sepúlveda argued that the Indians were developmentally retarded. His proof for this diagnosis was their practice of cannibalism. Las Casas countered that such acts proved a devotion to their gods and therefore demonstrated reverence and religiosity. Sepúlveda then claimed that the Indians lacked civilization because they lacked European technologies and that they "not only possess no science" but "also lack letters and preserve no monument of their history except certain vague and obscure reminiscences of some things in certain paintings. Neither do they have written laws, but barbaric institutions and customs." In his presentation to the audience Sepúlveda argued that the Spanish had a divine mission of bringing to these "little men" the gifts of "writing, books, culture, excellent laws, and the Christian religion" (quoted in Berger 1991, 21). In response, Las Casas provided firsthand accounts of Indian architecture, economy, and religion — but to no avail.[1] King Charles's meetings never reached a formal conclusion, and the expeditions to the "New World" continued, as did the dichotomy between civilized and noncivilized people, with writing as a crucial dividing mark.

Many scholars have highlighted the effects of this conceptual dichotomy of literate and nonliterate cultures, linking the stereotype of the nonwriting subject to the concomitant processes of colonization and the writing of history. Linda Tuhiwai Smith (1999) notes how nonwriting societies are often viewed as incapable of critical thinking, objectivity, and complex thought (28–29). Terry Goldie (1995) articulates a similar view, but further shows how this Othering process, characterizing nonliterate cultures as having different epistemes, leads to a common description of these people as mystical or having oracular power (236). Thomas Patterson shows how the colonizer's understanding of writing as the basis for authentic civilization plays out in functionalist, evolutionary, anthropological descriptions of culture (2000, 49–53). Specifically, he draws on the works of Stanley Diamond (1974) and Gledhill, Bender, and Larsen (1988) to demonstrate how commonplace notions of state, nation, law, and economy are each reliant on the existence of notational writing. These scholars agree that writing is a constitutive element of civilization.

Eric Wolf's 1982 "Europe and the People without History" succinctly characterizes the basic stereotype of nonwriting cultures. Without the ability to write, native communities are assumed to be incapable of proper historical thinking and historical representation. Michel de Certeau's 1988 book, *The Writing of History*, unpacks the process by which "history" has come to mean "writing" and how that conflation is therefore linked to reason, logic, and the scientific method. In a similar move, Jon Stratton describes how historians' reliance on written sources leads to the exclusion of native perspectives on historical events. Stratton also notes that salvage anthropology was born out of the desire to do for the natives what they were purportedly incapable of doing themselves: inscribing their traditions and teaching others about cultures and their pasts (1990, 241–42). Thus it comes as no surprise to hear "postcolonial" scholars such as Dipesh Chakrabarty pressing for the decentering of Europe in historiography (1995), or José Rabasa (1993, 2000) construing alternative histories of Latin American imperialism and demonstrating how the teaching of writing in colonial contexts violently produces the subaltern subject. Gayatri Spivak (1988, 1996) asks how we are to reread and rewrite the histories of colonialisms and find the voices of silenced subalterns. Tejaswini Niranjana uses Spivak's work to center subaltern studies directly on rescuing and restoring the unwritten voice back into colonial histories (1992). These scholars join Homi Bhabha (1985) in articulating historicism as a technology of colonial power.[2]

Articulations of writing within contexts of imperial and economic domination continue to frame examinations of indigenous rights and sovereignty. In 1973, over four hundred years after Las Casas and Sepúlveda debated in Valladolid, the Supreme Court of British Columbia denied aboriginal title to the Nisga'a tribe. Chief Justice H. W. Davey concluded that "they were undoubtedly at the time of settlement a very primitive people with few institutions of civilized society, and none at all of our notions of private property." Writing on the case, Thomas Berger sees the court's decision as resting upon a central divide between native and non-native concepts of proof. "They could not accept that people without a written language can, nevertheless, have an elaborate legal system of their own. And, as for their aboriginal title, how could the court acknowledge it? It was ill defined; it was not recorded in a system of title deeds and land registration; it was not a form of private property but property held communally by the tribe or clan" (Berger 1981, 150). The

Nisga'a took their case to the Supreme Court of Canada, where fourteen months later the tribe lost again, four to three. Perhaps an indication that times were changing, the dissenting opinion of Mr. Justice Emmet Hall went on to become the basis of Canada's 1982 guarantee of aboriginal rights. Hall's argument was directly aimed at Mr. Chief Justice Davey's previous assessment of Indian culture as relying on the same standards as were used by European colonizers centuries earlier.[3]

In his account of the Mashpee's 1976 land claim, James Clifford demonstrates the difficulties that indigenous peoples face in the Western legal system. Clifford documents the stories of tribal members, the research provided to the courts by academic historians and anthropologists, and the complicated notions of "tribe," "culture," and the particular histories of intercultural dynamics in Cape Cod. After relating to his readers the court's decision against the Mashpee Indians, Clifford discerns the logic of such decisions. He explains how the lack of archival evidence for tribal continuity proved fatal to their claim: "The Mashpee trial was a contest between oral and literate forms of knowledge. In the end the written archive had more value than the evidence or oral tradition, the memories of witnesses, and the intersubjective practice of fieldwork. In the courtroom how could one give value to an undocumented 'tribal' life largely invisible (or unheard) in the surviving record?" (1988, 339). Ultimately, as with the Nisga'a, the Mashpee were facing a structural prejudice embedded in the legal system and, as Clifford points out, in the writing of history. In a literalist epistemology, proof relies on evidence and evidence on knowledge, which in turn must be documented in writing. Clifford argues that although natives' pasts have been mostly unwritten, or miswritten, this documentation or lack of it becomes the basis for legal decisions of major importance. The courts use the same measure of proof as conventional historians and "history feeds on what finds its way into a limited textual record. . . . Even the most imaginative history is tied to standards of textual proof" (1988, 340).

One need not search too far to find similar battles being fought by other indigenous peoples (Brandt 1996; Slagle 1990). Almost every issue of *Cultural Survival Quarterly* provides details of such struggles around the world. But how does one reverse long-established ways of thinking about documentation and the supposed validity of written sources? If indigenous cultural continuity and identity center on myth and ritual, it becomes crucial to bring nonwritten "evidence" to bear in court cases. One way to address these issues is to seriously query what we consider to be "writing."

No scholar has disrupted notions of writing more radically than Jacques Derrida. Responding to Plato, Socrates, Nietzsche, Freud, Heidegger, and Saussure, Derrida's *Of Grammatology* (1974) provides a science of writing that assumes "that historicity itself is tied to the possibility of writing; to the possibility of writing in general, beyond those particular forms of writing in the name of which we have long spoken of peoples without writing and without history" (27). Derrida's main concern is to deconstruct the evolutionary (and teleological) concept of writing as secondary to orality, showing the complicity between Western epistemology and alphabetic writing. Using terms that change and sometimes double back on themselves, i.e., "trace," "reserve," and "difference," Derrida develops a concept of arche-writing. As the possible play of differences, arche-writing can be found in any sort of "marking," whether by hieroglyphics, pictures, voice, music, sculpture, fashion, or a line drawn in the sand. Derrida expands "writing" to include any move to differentiate, contrast, or communicate. Derrida shows that Lévi-Strauss, like Rousseau, was caught between the binary of writing and speech, valuing one over the other. Showing that writing and speech are both subcategories of arche-writing, Derrida demonstrates that the Nambikwara were always writing, always engaged in marking differences.

Derrida's sense of arche-writing provides a means to reevaluate the entire field of semiotics. Although many scholars have challenged Derrida's work, I am most drawn to Walter Mignolo's application of Derrida's concept of nonnotational writing to redefine what we consider a graphic sign.[4] In *The Darker Side of the Renaissance*, Mignolo develops a theoretical definition of writing largely based on the work of David Diringer. Mignolo writes:

Semiotically, a graphic sign is, then, a physical sign made with the purpose of establishing a semiotic interaction. Consequently, a human interaction is a semiotic one if there is a community and a body of common knowledge according to which (a) a person can produce a graphic sign with the purpose of conveying a message (to somebody else or to him- or herself); (b) a person perceives the graphic sign and interprets it as a sign produced with the purpose of conveying a message; and (c) that person attributes a given meaning to the graphic sign. Notice that in this theoretical definition of writing, the links between speech and writing are not necessary because writing is not conceived of as the representation of speech. (1995, 78)

This move away from the dichotomy, writing/speech, enables Mignolo to examine all forms of communication and self-representation that may be evidenced from the colonial period. Applying poststructural theory to semiotics helps Mignolo reevaluate native writing practices across Latin America.[5] He argues that unlike those who analyze "colonial discourse," he would prefer to label his field of study "colonial semiosis," since it would indicate a change in our understanding of both the colonizing and colonized peoples' hermeneutical constructions of the New World. Specifically, Mignolo wants to reorient colonial studies not just to what is being communicated within the colonial encounter but also to how those indigenous communities themselves understand communication and its relationship to knowledge. Like Enrique Dussel (1995), Michelle Cliff (1985), and Rodolfo Kusch (1963), Mignolo is seeking what might be labeled an ethnohermeneutic or an ethnophilosophy.

My discussion of Yoeme religious practices contributes to this recent academic attentiveness to the ways that primarily oral peoples practice historiography or autoethnography. In the next chapters, we see that Yoeme deer dancing and procession inscribe modes of thinking about history. Yoemem emplace their stories of past relations with others and their expressions of cultural and territorial boundaries. I join Mignolo and others in developing a scholarly method that appreciates the specific cultural values of literal and nonliteral historical discourse. Resultant scholarship would need to proceed from the premise that, as Clifford articulates it, "all human groups write — if they articulate, classify, possess an 'oral-literature,' or inscribe their world in ritual acts. They repeatedly textualize meanings" (Clifford and Marcus 1986, 117–18).

I reference Clifford because he characterizes the wide range of activities that demarcate meaning and its negotiation, including the inscription of place in ritual acts. Although Mignolo is seeking to move away from the writing/speech dichotomy, he never examines non-Western examples that are not material or notational; he never examines ritual or cultural performances as writing. While it is an invaluable study of nonliterate hermeneutics as found in maps, pictographs, speech genres, Andean *quipu*, calendars, and rugs, Mignolo's work leaves me wanting to take full advantage of his idea of colonial semiosis by critically seeking the ways that bodily movement and religious rites inscribe and decipher meaning. As in Derrida's theory, Mignolo's project seeks to dissolve the oral/literate dichotomy in order to ask more nuanced questions regarding the specific contrasts between indigenous and European historical practices during the early colonial period.

Similarly interested in reading literate and nonliterate technologies historically, Brian Street (1984) focused on the socially constructed and constructing aspects of literacies. Street proposed we approach the study of communication technologies within an "ideological" model of literacy. In contrast to the "autonomous" model, which argues that cultures will naturally switch from oral to writing technologies, the ideological model of literacy suggests approaching writing systems as simply one form of communication, which does not wholly replace previous technologies. Street surveys multiple cases where writing practices are considered less reliable and incapable of ensuring accurate meaning. Street's ideological model maintains that writing practices share all the supposed deficiencies of oral practices: they are unreliable, unfixed, and subjective. Indeed, both literate and nonliterate forms of communication often are born from, and reflect, preliterate ideologies. The adoption of writing by a culture often signals a moment in which issues of authority and ownership are at climactic contestation.

The Yoeme practice of learning writing under Jesuit direction imme-diately comes to mind. The revival of the Testamento was linked to non-Yoeme encroachment as well as to increased anthropological interest in native resistance movements. Street argues that discursive practices reflect specific social contexts. Historicizing the use of literate forms of communication provides clues to past cultural values and pragmat-ics. All contemporary cultures such as the Yoeme "write" because they demarcate difference in expressive forms, but they do so in culturally specific projects.

Street's approach raises questions that are relevant to my methodol-ogy. What do nonliterate forms express about the reasoning for their continued use, especially in light of nonliterate options for documenta-tion? How do these nonliterate inscriptions relate to possible literate expressions within the culture? Do the two forms contribute to the other's success? Are some forms explicitly directed toward outsiders? Are certain contents (ancestral definitions of territorial boundaries) more effectively shared in nonliterate forms that embody the spatialized dynamics of the signified event or historic moment (processions around the church cemetery)? As will be shown, Yoemem express historical discourse in ways that most effectively sustain community *lutu'uria*, defined as "ritually performed knowledge."

To study ritual as a performed historical text moves us beyond the boundaries of a single disciplinary approach. Textual notions of inscrip-tion need to be complemented by performative approaches.[6] In the introduction to *Exceptional Spaces: Essays in Performance and History*, Della Pollock speaks about the relationship between embodied acts and the production of history: "Drawing on distinct and overlapping resources, performance studies have not only demonstrated the impact of performance on history but also generated the working premise of this book, which is that combining performance and historical methodolo-gies will yield substantial new insights into the structure and function of many forms of cultural production" (1998, 2). Crossing disciplinary boundaries between the social sciences and the humanities, Pollock calls on researchers interested in history to consider the epistemological strength of embodied, nonliterate expressions. Pollock points toward my next chapter, which examines Yoeme rituals for what they have to say about Yoeme history and the ways that history is read and performed. My discussion reevaluates earlier ethnographic accounts of Yoeme rituals as religiously unimportant "art" forms. On the contrary, these rituals will begin to appear historiographic and autoethnographic. As we shall see, Muriel Thayer Painter and Edward Spicer share the view that Yoeme deer dancing continues primarily as entertainment. Pollock characterizes this view and points to its blind spots: "At once bolstered and burdened by history, performance as both a genre of practice and an analytical trope resists narrow identification with either entertainment or high art industries. It floods the chambers of significance, on the one hand, and preciosity, on the other, to which it is commonly dismissed. Relieved of their respective isolation within discourses of history, performance proves powerful; history proves affective, sensual, and generative" (1998, 2). Pollock supports our return to the Yoeme performances and our continued examination of nonliterate inscriptions. I turn to the deer and *pahko'ola* dances as a way to discern more about the shaping of Yoeme Catholicism in the early years of Jesuit collaboration. Performed texts, the deer and pahko'ola dances, express local theories of a collective past in the method that they choose for documenting and sharing those theories. This interpretation grounds Pollock's argument that "insofar as performance is thus aligned with historicity against history, it is especially capable of disseminating cultural knowledge — of dispersing meaning in time and across difference" (26). Focusing here on indigenous methods and theories of history (historicity), and not the academically sanctioned result of literate histories (history), Pollock reminds us that as we expand our categories of what gets to count as "writing" and "history," we must be willing to consider what such histories might look, sound, or feel like.

Paying particular attention to the inscriptive and spatial ways Yoemem communicate historical and ethnographic discourse, the following two chapters provide clues to the above questions. In doing so, my research provides supporting evidence that the dichotomy of literate/oral and the categories of "writing" and "history" often fail when applied uncritically to native groups who, like the Yoemem, write historical discourse through performances while also utilizing written documents and records. In contrast to the view of writing as a definitive civilizational break, the Yoeme experience suggests a more complex transformative continuity. As with their measured adoption of Catholicism, most Yoemem use writing practices such as the Testamento and the Books of the Dead to refine and strengthen a long history of asserting a cohesive, enduring, and aboriginal identity.

5 Hunting for History in Potam Pueblo

Holy Saturday, 15 April 1995. I go to Old Pascua to watch the pahko. *Felipe is singing with his brother, Steven, and nephews, Adam and Steve Jr. They sit in a row on their flower mats to the right of the dance area. At Old Pascua Pueblo, the pahko takes place in a* santo heka *already constructed on the south side of the ceremonial square. A fence extends halfway across the santo heka, and a rope separates the performing space from the onlookers. I find myself behind a crowd of thirty or forty people watching the* pahko'olam *dance. The musicians then take a break. While people are applauding the dancers, Felipe and his fellow deer singers stand up to stretch their legs. Felipe sees me and waves. He points to the benches away from the santo heka. We sit, smoking cigarettes and talking about my trip down and my studies. Felipe gets up to return to singing. He tells me to follow him, and when we get to the rope separating the performers and their family members from the spectators, Felipe raises the rope, steps under, and then holds the rope for me. I sit next to Herminia Valenzuela and Felipe's mother, Paula Valle. I attempt my newly learned Yoeme greeting, "Lios em chaniavu," and they politely smile and respond in Yoeme.*

I receive more attention this evening than I ever have before at Yoeme ceremonies. Throughout the night, pahko'olam crack jokes and give me a "You know what I mean?" look. Since this is my fourth year visiting the Old Pascua ceremonies and my third year visiting the Hiak Vatwe, we seem to have built a type of social familiarity. Soon I come to feel like a batboy, fetching water or a cigarette lighter for the dancers. People from the crowd ask, "Who are you related to?" "Are you a student?" "Do you know what they are saying?" "Do you know why they are doing that?" When Herminia and Felipe's mother leave, other Yoemem take their seats next to me. The man on my left tells me that he arranged the flowers hanging from the ceiling and that he has been working in the kitchen all night. The woman on my right asks me if I knew that the pahko'olam were dancing the rosaries. I notice an elderly Yoeme lady holding herself tightly within her rebozo as the chilly air spins around the santo heka. I get up and give her my coat. I then leave the dance area, passing the fariseos (ceremonial guards) who are wrapped in blankets, sleeping next to the small fires that will be kept burning all night. I walk to my truck and lean against the front grill.

Away from the crowd I can see the stars and the mountains to the north of Tucson. I still hear the music, but I also hear children playing, although it is after midnight. I see low-riders cruising the streets of Old Pascua. I see some Anglo bikers pull up and dismount their Harley Davidsons. They join the others around the dance area, all watching the pahko'olam shuffling their feet to the music. Walking past a couple of men smoking cigarettes, I remember that Larry Evers wrote about a night like this in the book Yaqui Deer Songs. By the fire and the resting fariseos, I wonder whether the pahko'olam are really dancing a rosary and whether Yoeme men usually cook for the pahkom. I wonder what it means to sit inside the rope. Why do some Yoemem in the roped area give me dirty looks? I wonder where I am going to sleep tonight. I look back to see the pahko'olam handing out cigarettes to the crowd. I check my watch. It's almost 1 a.m., definitely too early to think of sleep. I walk back to the santo heka, but instead of going under the rope, I stand behind the bikers. One of the Yoeme ladies who was sitting inside the santo heka earlier brings me a cup of coffee. I offer my thanks informally with a gentle "Chiokoe" (Thank you) and take the cup. Noticing the exchange, a couple of the bikers turn around and ask me if these Yaquis will be dancing for a long time. I say, "Yeah, probably forever."

Watching the people who are watching the performers, I think of the work involved in continuing the rituals. The men and women in the kitchens, the people cutting the confetti, the children sleeping in the church as angels, the masked "big head" performers sleeping outside beside the fire — everyone comes together every night during holy week. Every year they repeat the ritual, and every year it is new again.

5. A public art piece alongside the highway in Sonora.

6. A grain mill sign in north-central Obregon.

Throughout the northern state of Sonora, Mexico, one cannot go far without encountering the image of a deer dancer: on large signs, as car window decals, as statues along the highway, on public announcement flyers, even on prepackaged grocery items such as salsa, milk, and bread.

For many Mexican citizens, these images do little more than associate a Sonoran heritage with the indigenous populations that "once lived there." For many Yoemem in both Mexico and the United States, the deer dancer image speaks to issues of cultural continuity, tribal sovereignty, and ritual sacrifice. Earlier scholars of Yoeme ethnohistory noted that the deer dances and their associated pahko'ola dances contain a particularly clear example of pre-Jesuit Yoeme ritual, since the ceremonies make relatively few references to Christian symbols. All of the ethnographic literature as well as my fieldwork among the Yoemem suggest that deer dancing is associated with hunting, a means of securing appropriate relations with the animal and plant world, especially the deer.

In the Yoeme homelands, deer hunts are rare. My tribal collaborators emphasize the difficulty in successfully hunting deer, the danger

7. The maaso (Salome Jicoamea Esquer) and pahko'ola (Mateo Cocmea) perform along-side the Hiak Vatwe in 2004.

of offending deer through inappropriate behavior, and the labor-intensive preparation of the deer carcass for ceremonial and household use. Although everyone freely admits that they enjoy it when an uncle or godparent makes a gift of venison to their families, these occurrences are lessening in frequency. In Potam Pueblo, with a population of approximately five thousand individuals, deer have been hunted only on a few occasions per year. And when discussing those hunts, tribal collaborators never mention a deer dance associated with the expedition. Yet the performative rite of deer dancing takes place every year for the Lenten *semana santa* (Holy Week) ceremonies, for the *lutu pahko* (death anniversary ceremony) of a person's funerary rites, during almost every pueblo *fiesta*, and as part of many cultural exhibitions throughout the Americas. So why do Yoemem continue to hold rituals for almost nonexistent hunts? Why does the dancing continue after deer hunting no longer sustains Yoeme culture?

Answering these questions about deer dancing will inevitably feed a broader investigation into Yoeme ethnohistory. I describe below how deer dancing still provides sustenance for Yoeme communities. Sustenance here is not supplied through hides and meat, but in indigenous identity maintenance. My study then involves the combined foci of performance and religion in a particularly congruous way, since Yoemem never perform the deer dance in a purely secular manner. And whether for themselves or others, the dancing makes cosmology, history, and collective identity present and real.

This chapter also reconsiders the use of the label *conversion*, which is the act of turning one thing into something else. Yet the word does not differentiate in terms of the degree, extent, or length of change or why the change takes place. Deer dancing tells a specific history of religious differentiation and traces a distinctly Yoeme way of understanding Catholic personalities and ethics.

I quickly learned while doing fieldwork in Yoeme communities that in order to understand their worldviews, I first had to grasp the significance of Yoeme relationships with deer. Yoeme deer dancing recalls how Yoemem made sense of Catholicism during Jesuit contact and how they continue making sense of their other-than-human relations with the living world around them even now. Drawing on the discussion of the various *aniam* (realms or worlds of being), I interpret deer dancing ceremonies as Yoeme representations of knowledge and truth. After characterizing some Yoeme attitudes on deer hunting as recorded in the ethnographic literature, I describe one particular deer dance form, *maaso me'ewa* (running the deer), and then demonstrate how this performative act assists in providing an ethnohistorical explanation of Yoeme-Catholicism and of larger questions of religious change and continuity.

As in many indigenous communities, Yoeme worldviews cannot be easily divided into separate spheres of religious and nonreligious activities. Thus my use of the word *religious* relies on a very broad but useful definition of the term provided by Sam Gill: "Those images, actions, and symbols that both express and define the extent and character of the world, especially those that provide the cosmic framework in which human life finds meaning and the terms of its fulfillment. We will also consider as religious those actions, processes, and symbols through which life is lived in order that it may be meaningful and purposive" (Gill 1982, 11). Gill's definition reframes the role of deer dancing as a principal component of the hunting ritual. Yoemem assert that the ritual fulfils an ethical requirement and establishes a dialogue with their nonhuman kin. Previously represented by ethnologists as "profane" entertainment, the deer dance provides a lens on indigenous Catholic syncretism. Specifically, my research into deer dancing demonstrates that historical claims of conversion not only fail to tell the whole story of native agency in colonial zones but also overlook the role of indigenous performance in historically narrating a consistent and practical precolonial ritual logic.

Both Jesuit documents and Yoeme oral traditions show that the Yoemem were eager to learn new technologies during the seventeenth and early eighteenth centuries. According to the singing tree myth, Yoemem had already received prophetic knowledge that such changes were coming. Still, many ethnographers fail to acknowledge that Yoeme religiosity continues to be grounded in an aboriginal ritual logic. On the surface, many Yoeme rites seem to indicate that they had converted to Catholicism. Prominent scholars of Yoeme culture such as Edward Spicer, Muriel Thayer Painter, and Ralph Beals have tended to accept preconceived categories of sacred or profane, Christian or pagan, pre- or postcontact. These are of course dichotomous terms that fail to characterize Yoeme religious thought and action accurately. Persuaded that Yoeme dances were simply folk art, scholars have seldom understood the ways deer dancing asserts Yoeme truth claims regarding history and identity. My own approach argues that the deer dancing ritual offers a model for understanding how Yoemem grafted the Catholic figure of Jesus onto older views of ritual sacrifice and hunting. This study then joins the work of others such as William Merrill, Kenneth Morrison, and Vicente Rafael to investigate the maintenance of aboriginal worldviews during periods of social assimilation.

Deer Hunting as a Mode of Sustenance

In earlier times Yoeme society depended greatly on hunting: rabbits, peccary, badgers, raccoons, and iguanas, but most important, deer. The

Coues whitetails (*Odocoileus virginianus couesi*) were the largest animals living in the Yoeme homeland, and they provided the people with hides, food, and religious utensils used for healing. Yoeme hunters pursued deer with arrows and snares, occasionally with fire drives, and later with rifles. According to contemporary Yoeme collaborators, other animals in the wilderness, such as rabbits, bees, and vultures, helped the deer avoid hunters and, conversely, sometimes seemed to have helped the hunters to trap them. Yoeme hunting groups consisted of at least four men who bathed themselves with sage and their weapons with chili pods on the morning of the hunt. They stalked the deer wearing deer masks and skin, often relying on their dogs for assistance. The men held an arrow in one hand and a bow in the other, simulating the deer's foreleg movements, enabling them to approach the deer very closely. Being so close not only provided the hunters with better opportunity to kill the deer, but also, according to several sources, helped them learn deer language and deer ways. The leader of the hunt was always a man who knew deer language and who possessed *seatakaa*, translated as "flower body" and sometimes "flower gift" or "flower power." Communication laid the groundwork for a direct relationship between the hunter and the deer.

Indicative of their kinship obligations, Yoemem linguistically refer to the deer as *saila maaso*, which translates as "little brother deer." When addressing or referring to the governing deer or leader of the deer, as they do when asking him for permission to hunt and kill him, Yoemem use the term *malichi* (fawn). To ask for such permission, deer dances were performed the night before the hunts, celebrating the relationships between humans and all of the other-than-human persons in the wilderness (*huya ania*), particularly deer.[1]

Yoemem still describe a number of practices and behaviors associated with appropriate deer-human relations. For example, I have heard that only Yoemem who receive positive dreams from the governing deer or deer leader should attempt to hunt, and even then hunters must always ask the deer for permission before leaving the pueblo on a hunting trip. While hunting, the men must always think good thoughts, concentrate and yet not think too much. One should never think sexual thoughts about women, even wives, during the hunt, or else the deer may become jealous. Yoemem should not kill for sport and should never look a dying deer in the eyes. Nor should a hunter blow on his food when eating.[2] Failure to meet these and other obligations could lead to misfortune and the failure of the hunt. Yoeme elders tell many stories of deer blowing tiny thorns into the hunters' eyes or bodies; of bullets turning around in midair and striking the hunter; of deer hiding from the hunters; and of hunters never having successful hunts or having mysterious pains in their arms or legs.

Although only a selected group of men continue to hunt, the form of these pre–deer hunt ceremonies can be gleaned to a certain extent from oral and performative traditions. Deer dancing can still be seen in contemporary Yoeme communities at death anniversaries, during the Blessing of the Palms celebrations as part of the passion play of Jesus, and for the respective pueblos' saints' day festivities. In the Yoeme language, these dance events are called *pahkom* (singular *pahko*, ceremony). Just as in the actual hunting parties, deer dancing requires at least four people: one dancer and three singers. Sitting on the ground in a line, one singer plays the water drum and the other two play raspers while singing the deer songs. The deer songs express the perspective of the deer, plant, flower, or animal friends in the wilderness. Thus they always describe the deer's special realm; that is, the *sea ania*, or flower world. In these rituals the dancer enters the area, sometimes called "flower patio," as a young deer. The first song is often considered the cleansing or purifying song. As the dances continue throughout the night, the deer dancer is referred to as an adolescent deer and then as an adult. In the morning the final songs will refer to him either as an old-man deer or as a newborn. As is the case in the actual hunting practices, the deer dancer wears the head of a deer on top of his head, and in each hand he holds gourd rattles, enabling him to convey more effectively the deer's actions as they are described in the accompanying songs. The deer dancer is preceded into the ceremonial space by *pahko'olam* (old men of the fiesta, also known as *pascolas*), who bless the entire space, including attendees, and who entertain the people by becoming animals from the wilderness who taunt, mimic, befriend, and sometimes hunt the deer dancer. The deer dancer must dance the meaning of the deer songs, showing everyone the beauty of the flower world, and he must grow old and allow himself to be the focus of verbal attacks. He is pursued and sometimes killed by the pahko'olam, thereby demonstrating the sacrificial nature of all existence so that life may continue. Thus the unifying symbol throughout the ceremony is the Yoeme notion of sacrifice: the flower, or *seewa*.

Any discussion of Yoeme ritual must necessarily include references to Yoeme worldviews. Most, if not all, Yoeme ceremonial performers understand their world as dimensionally composed of overlapping, yet distinct, worlds or realms, called aniam. The ethnographic literature suggests that Yoemem perceive of approximately ten aniam, referred to, respectively, as *tenku ania*, "dream world"; *tuka ania*, "night world"; *huya ania*, "wilderness world"; *yo ania*, "enchanted world"; *kawi ania*, "mountain world"; *vawe ania*, "world under the water"; *nao ania*, "corn-cob world"; *teeka ania*, "from the sky up through the universe," and the *sea ania*, "flower world." Yoemem might reference a number of aniam or, indeed, all aniam, since the dances might have been held at night ("night world"), the dancers' abilities might have come from dreams ("dream world"), and the songs might be substantiating sea life or animals in the sky ("world under the water" "from the sky up through the universe"). Each of these worlds provides a home for powerful beings, and Yoemem relate deer dancing to three worlds specifically — yo ania, in that the deer emerges from an enchanted home; huya ania, in that the deer goes into the wilderness world; and sea ania, in that the deer dances for us in the flower world.

In terms of Yoeme worldviews, the sea ania is of primary importance, since most community members in the southern pueblos understand flowers, *seewam*, as the actualization of sacrifice and of the nurturing acts of giving. The most nurturing aspects of nature are found in the sea ania: streams, lakes, clouds, rain. The deer lives in the sea ania, and when he is killed he is said to be laid "atop a bed of flowers." As noted above, hunters must have seatakaa, or flower power, to hunt deer successfully. In their extensive study of deer songs, Larry Evers and Felipe Molina write that the most common words found in the songs are Yoeme terms for flowers. Flowers adorn the deer dancer's antlers and skirt, as well as the necklaces and hair of the pahko'olam. For Molina, a respected scholar and deer singer, the main purpose of the songs is to bring the deer's voice from the sea ania to the ceremony. He notes that "almost every piece of regalia and every instrument used in deer dancing and deer singing may be called *seewa* or *sea* as well" (Evers and Molina 1987, 52).

The deer dance always entails the dancing of the *pahko'ola* (singular of *pahko'olam*, also known as *pascola*). Wearing black masks, pahko'olam lead the deer dancer into the performance area where they will spend the evening dancing with him, clowning around with each other, and entertaining the guests. When not dancing with the deer, pahko'olam wear their masks backward or hang them from the left side of the head, since the devil is said to come from the left. Common mask designs include the elongated goat-face style with ears and horns and, more recently, canines. Mask makers often paint small insects or desert animals on the cheeks or foreheads of masks. Typical Yoeme pahko'ola masks feature a band of small triangles pointing inward around the outside circumference and are thought to represent goat's teeth, sunrays, or mountains. Many masks have crosslike patterns that some people relate to Christianity, although Edward Spicer interpreted them as a pre-Jesuit symbol for the sun (1958, 434–36; 1961, 31). I have also heard from various collaborators that these particular cross shapes were precontact sand painting symbols for the sun. Both the elongated and face-shaped masks have either goat hair or horsehair dangling over the eyes and from the chin. The ethnographic literature strongly links pahko'olam with goats and with the most ancient and respected realm, the yo ania. Their precolonial beginnings are referenced by their oft-used title "old men of the fiesta," with "old" referring to their respected or ancient quality, not their ages. Since they are also sometimes called "sons of the devil," it bears repeating that a minority of Christian Yoemem tend to relate the yo ania to concepts of evil and the devil. When attending an all-night pahko, the banter and antics of the pahko'olam help elevate the moods and energy of the crowd. The dancers are charged with passing out cigarettes to the audience members, and more often than not they create quite a stir by teasing the deer dancer, musicians, the female societies to their right, and even the spectators.[3]

The ethnographic literature contains numerous descriptions of both the pahko'olam and the deer dances.[4] One rarely finds a newspaper story or journal article about Yoeme culture that does not include an account of these dancers, the music accompanying their motions, and their actual dance choreography. In the United States, these descriptions often portray the deer and pahko'ola dances as a southwestern native art form or, more simply, "folk art." Such categorizations do apply, since the dances, as with other tribal public performances, assert a sense of belonging to a specific region (if not the epitome of regional "locality"). But deer dancing as an art form also expresses a specific indigeneity, coming from a particular place. The combination of the aboriginal figures of the pahko'olam and the deer with the Catholic features of the crosses, saints, and Jesus portrays Yoemem as border crossers on both cosmological and geopolitical levels. The dances transfer cultural roots that are religiously hybrid. Although the dances are tribally specific, they present a history analogous to those of other borderlands native groups. Deer dancing expresses precontact religious worldviews, a syncretic borderlands fusion with Spanish Catholicism, and a unique Indio "heritage" within Sonora regionalism.

Not always appreciated for their multiple values, deer and pahko'ola dances are popular attractions for non-Yoeme neighbors. If someone knows anything about Yoeme culture, they are familiar with these rituals. Because of the detailed descriptions elsewhere regarding the deer and pahko'olam, I have avoided repeating that material here. I have sought to provide a baseline understanding of these ceremonial performers on which I expand below. Still, the basic description of deer and pahko'ola dancing demonstrates a continuing relationship to the community's long-standing relations with deer, other animals, and the various aniam. Nowhere is this relationship more evident than in the particular series of deer songs and dances called *maaso me'ewa* (killing the deer), often called *maaso nehhawa* (running the deer), since the deer leaves the dance area and runs among the spectators.

Maaso Me'ewa: Killing Deer for Entertainment?

September 1994. Jim Mahoney, Felipe Molina, and I traveled to the first "Mexico–U.S.A. Border Indigenous People Meeting" in Tecate, Baja California, Mexico. Over three hundred people from a dozen indigenous tribes assembled at the Tecate Cultural Center. After Rigoberta Menchú spoke to the crowd, people broke into smaller groups to discuss border-crossing issues with the press. Felipe Molina and I were listening to a press conference held by a leader from Chiapas, when he heard from one of the Yoeme men from Hiak Vatwe that several of the attendees were going to perform some of their respective tribal dances after dinner behind the cultural center.

That night, the crickets' chirping was louder than I have ever heard. I remember feeling out of place: I was one of the only two or three people at the conference whose primary language was English. The night was just perfect for a long-sleeve shirt. People began pulling chairs outside toward a roped-off clearing. The tuning of violin strings and the plucking of the harp slowly joined the crickets' songs. The Yoeme deer dancer stepped into the performance area. I had watched deer dances in the context of the Easter ceremony, and so I was surprised by the people who had brought cameras and recording devices. Recording devices of any type are generally banned from all ceremonies that are held in the pueblos. Although I had forgotten my camera, Jim was recording the whole evening.

The tampaleo *(the musician who plays a flute and drum at the same time during a* pahko*) tuned his drum, tightening the skin over a small bed of coals. The violin and harp found a pattern in each other's melodies, and the masked* pahko'olam *followed the* moro *(the manager of the* pahko'olam*) into the dance area. The* pahko'olam *had red tassels in their hair, blankets around their waists, and shells and abalone around their necks. At first their masks hung to the side of their faces. The deer singers were on their mats, the violinist and the harpist opposite, and the* tampaleo *was on the adjoining side of the harp. The* pahko'olam *entered, purifying and blessing the area; at such times they howled and barked, the language of the* huya ania*. When not dancing, the individual* pahko'olam *smoked or teased the crowd. They called out comments to the deer singers. Then the* tampaleo *sounded out twelve beats, and* the deer singers started sliding their raspers. The tampaleo's flute and drum joined the others. Low voices of the crowd were still audible over the music until the pahko'olam started banging their sena'asom (hand clappers). One pahko'ola began a short dance and then stopped. The other pahko'olam joined him in patting out the dirt around them with their feet, flicking rocks out of the area with their toes. Focused as I was on these unfolding actions, I hadn't noticed the deer dancer enter the dance area. He wore a stuffed deer head over a white head wrap, and a skirt, a scarf around the abdomen, a belt of hooves around his waist, a necklace made from colored beads and abalone shells, and leg rattles. He held two large gourds made into rattles.

Saila Maaso (Little Brother Deer or Younger Brother Deer) began looking around the area, at the crowd, at the singers. His eyes seemed to follow his nose, smelling and then seeing the source of different scents. He pranced lightly around this world. He looked around the flower world, his home "beneath the dawn." Moving slowly around the dance area, Saila Maaso peered into the eyes of the spectators. It became impossible to distinguish the sounds of the crickets, the voices of the pahko'olam and crowd, and the music from the performers. On this cool evening in Mexico, the crowd gathered around in awe of this deer's beauty. Suddenly, Saila Maaso shook the gourds so sharply that I was shaken, as were most of the crowd. Everyone's eyes looked for the origin of the new noise. Someone's camera flashed.

People started throwing coins on the dance area, and the pahko'olam used their toes to grab the coins while not missing a beat. The music had reached a steady pace, and after five or ten minutes, the pahko'olam got down on their knees and started pantomiming coyotes, howling and sniffing each other and the ground where the deer had just danced. At each howl, Maaso looked up to locate the distance between himself and the noises. The coyotes approached, at times stopping to urinate or to sniff each other's rear ends. The deer stopped rolling his gourds and stared at the approaching coyotes. The crowd froze as one of the coyotes ran toward Saila Maaso and leaped. The deer turned quickly and kicked at him, making the crowd draw closer around the ropes.

Prancing away, Maaso turned to face his attackers, bent down, and charged at the closest coyote. The coyotes bent low to avoid the counterattack. Saila Maaso stomped his foot, then jumped at least two feet into the air. He landed,

confidently staring straight at the approaching and howling coyotes. The chil-
dren around the area opened their eyes even wider, looking at their parents
to see if it would be okay for our Brother Deer. The rhythm of Maaso's gourds
was in sync with the water drum and the various rattles. The tempo increased
as the coyotes closed around the deer. Faster and faster, the rhythm sped. Then
the coyotes charged at the deer, jumping and pulling Saila Maaso down to
the ground. Everyone gasped. Except for his lower half, the deer was hidden
by the surrounding coyotes' bodies, all competing for his head. Licking their
lips and attacking each other in victory, the coyotes removed Maaso's head
and fought for possession, each taking the head and eating part. Their feasting
sounds were horrific.

Then, transformed, the coyotes stood upright as pahko'olam. As in the
bwe taewaim ("big days," or the week of Easter), and the rest of the year,
they would surely dance again until morning. The dancing and joking would
continue with occasional breaks to smoke or to heckle the spectators around
the santo heka. During the breaks from dancing, if the pahko'olam came
close to the singers and the drummer, the deer stopped them with a light push
or tug. At the end of the dancing, the eldest pahko'ola addressed the crowd,
and together all of the pahko'olam danced in formation toward the harp and
the violin player. The crowd applauded, and the moro lifted the ropes for the
pahko'olam leaving the performance area.

While the Yoemem shared this dance with the indigenous people at
the conference, the same story, danced by the same characters, is often
"requested" by spectators at civic performances across northern Mexico
and the southwestern United States. The dance, or maaso me'ewa, is
popular because of the highly dramatic hunt and death of the deer and
because it suits certain images of the heroic hunter. Additionally, Evers
and Molina suggest that the fixed set of deer songs that accompany
this play and the pahko'olam's burlesques come together "to provide
an expression of the very core of the ritual of the deer dance that is as
powerful as any we know" (1987, 137). Although the maaso me'ewa dance
is seen most often at lutu pahkom, I was not surprised that the Yoeme
participants chose to perform this set of songs at an international con-

ference regarding indigenous rights. After watching Mayo dances and Tarahumara foot races, I realized that the groups were demonstrating how they knew themselves. The performance of "the very core" of the deer dancing ritual within this public and pantribal context brings to mind a long history of native peoples who traveled, performing their culture for outsiders. Such events raise questions of performers' intents, nonnatives' interpretations, and the perceptions and receptions of the other native observers. Does the combination of performances from multiple tribes lead to their being interpreted as "folk art," as opposed to rituals, ethnography, or even history?

In *The Yaquis: A Cultural History* (1980), Edward Spicer provocatively argues that enduring peoples share a "language of action." His reading of that language, however, was often, and understandably, seen through the lens of modernist dichotomies. *The Yaquis*, the culmination of Spicer's forty years of research on Yoeme identity, insightfully stresses the importance of ritual activity as a central factor in maintaining identity in spite of transnational and interethnic factors. On the other hand, he misrepresents Yoeme understandings of ritual and identity by characterizing Yoeme religion as a belief system that emerges from natural-supernatural dimensionality. Spicer also decontextualizes Yoeme ritual performance by maintaining a functionalist distinction between "sacred" and "profane" ritual activities (Morrison 1992b, 207–9; Carsten 1993, 43–45; Shorter 2002, 91–92; 2003, 199). Judging from his published work, Spicer's focus on pahko'olam and deer dancing as "arts" prevented him from understanding these activities as effective ritual actions. As far as he was concerned, the deer dance could no longer function as a religious activity if deer hunting no longer took place regularly. However, to consider deer dancing solely as a nonreligious (that is, profane) activity would be to miss an essential aspect of Yoeme "endurance."

Unfortunately, Spicer's functionalist approach and assertions have been influential, and they have led the anthropologist Robert Redfield, for example, to state that "one ceremonial institution, the deer-dancer, having no meaning except the old connection with hunting, is becoming simply secular entertainment, and thus, inadequately supported

by functional value, tends to disappear altogether" (Spicer 1984, xiv).[5]
Spicer later acknowledged that the initial acts of cultural revival for the
immigrant Yoemem in Arizona were, in fact, the deer dances and the
Masses for the dead (1988, 259). Yet he never reconsidered his serious
claim that pahkom were fading in importance:

> We have seen that the deer-dancer, while still a participant in cer-
> emony, is surrounded by secular attitudes. His appearance depends
> on conditions dictated by personal considerations. A *fiestero* may feel
> that he does not want to spend the money necessary for the food for
> the dancer and his musicians, or the deer-dancer himself may not care
> to dance. Nothing will happen to anyone if the latter does not appear.
> He is not an essential in the ceremonial pattern. The deer-dancer's
> activities are, furthermore, gradually being disassociated from those
> of the *pascolas*. As this happens, his connection with those aspects of
> the culture which are supernaturally sanctioned — the church orga-
> nizations — becomes very tenuous. He is gradually becoming simply
> an entertainer. (Spicer 1984, 298–99)

As far as Redfield and Spicer were concerned, the function of deer hunting had undoubtedly diminished as a primary cultural activity of Yoeme
life. Spicer, however, did not always appreciate how these deer dances
had been and remained central to sustaining Yoeme religious identity.[6]
Although he was aware of the importance of the dances to collective
ethnic symbolism, his functionalist (and Eliadian) view of ritual led him
to portray deer dancing as having become entertainment.

Another ethnographer of Yoeme worldviews, Muriel Thayer Painter,
has much to offer on the meaning of pahko'ola and deer dancing, although
she, like her teacher Spicer, understands the dancers as primarily entertaining. Painter's book *With Good Heart* (1986) offers a rich compilation
of Yoeme interpretations and interviews that derive from almost forty
years of collaboration with Arizona Yoemem. Painter devotes a chapter,
"The Native Dancers," to the lore, practices, regalia, and powers associated with pahko'ola and deer dancing. She makes insightful if slightly
survivalist comments about those two dance groups, noting that they

are "a profoundly important part in the life of Pascua," and she observes that "it is in discussing these two groups with informants, watching and listening to them at fiestas, that one gets a glimpse, however fragmentary, of the world before the padres made their contributions to Yaqui culture" (1986, 241). Painter's chapter offers over fifty pages of Yoeme voices, telling her about what dancing pahko'ola and deer mean. Although informants are continually quoted, Painter's interpretations frame the discussion and usually both introduce and conclude her extended quotes. Her interpretation of the events tends to override Yoeme interpretations of their own culture. Despite her collaboration with Yoemem, Painter, like Spicer, assumes that Yoeme religiosity is essentially a belief system that makes oppositional distinctions between pre-Christian and Christian-Yoeme views. Moreover, one can see in her text that her collaborators' statements do not always support Painter's conclusions.[7]

Painter's interpretation of these performances is evident in her concluding remarks on the respective dancers. Her views are in line with Spicer's comprehension of the pahko'olam as being fundamentally "profane" clowns who dance in order to retain the crowd's interest in them (Spicer 1980, 94).[8] Yet Painter wavers on her own ability to make such claims. Of the pahko'ola, she states that "it is true that he has been given a function in the ceremonies, although primarily as an entertainer and ceremonial host" (1986, 271). She then ends her section on the pahko'ola by almost defending the previous statement with an interpretive disclaimer: "It is difficult to obtain a precise statement as to the deeper meanings and derivation of the pascola role" (1986, 272). Painter supplies the reader with many Yoeme views of pahko'ola dancing (1986, 282–305), but in her own interpretative framework surrounding those "insider" voices, she implies that pahko'olam are important to Yoeme ritual only as clowns.

Painter points to ritual efficacy without fully appreciating the importance of a performative approach for an understanding of contemporary Native American cultures when she says that "it is only with the deer that the pascolas can re-create the ancient world, remembered in dance, mimetic dramatization, and in the words of the ancient deer songs." In her assessment of Yoeme dancing, she concludes that "there appears to be no way to determine how important in earlier days the deer songs and dances were merely as entertainment. They have been continued after the ritual function has fallen into disuse" (1986, 299). Painter here rehearses a crucial problem in the study of Native American ritual activity. Her approach precludes the possibility of discovering how Yoemem value religious entertainment by suggesting that pahko'ola dancing should no longer be conceived as efficacious ritual performance.

The effect of such thinking, as Sam Gill warns, "is to distract us from understanding the full religious importance of clowns" (1982, 95). As Gill was addressing the interpretation of clowns, ceremonial hosts, and masked dancers who use humor in indigenous ceremonies, his comments are directly relevant to pahko'olam and offer an alternative to the analyses of Spicer and Painter. Whereas the latter authors viewed pahko'olam as having evolved into entertainers within deer dances, Gill argues that most clowns balance the evocation of fear with that of humor. The uses made of the cross by pahko'ola dancers, their often vulgar actions, their dancing with, and their sometimes killing of, the deer, and their ability to make us laugh and to instill fear with threats of public embarrassment support Gill's claim that clowning embodies a mastery of symbolic inversion. "As a consequence," he writes, "ritual clowns commonly have the powers to heal, to bring luck in hunting and war, and to assure fertility in plants, animals, and human beings" (Gill 1982, 96). The contrast is clear, and Painter's and Spicer's readers would be left to assume that Yoemem may have originally danced pahko'ola for real, life-changing reasons, but "that was then," and now they perform merely to provide a humorous spectacle. An approach closer aligned to Gill's would illustrate not only the humor and art of the pahko'olam but also their power and ritual accomplishments.

Dancing a Place

Like most indigenous rituals, the Yoeme deer dance is centrally concerned with space, both physical and cosmological. Since the deer dancer embodies the first deer, the deer songs place Yoeme listeners in direct relation with their collective past. For many if not most Yoemem, deer songs are definitive of their social collectivity, surviving some 450 years of colonial encounters to express group identity. The poetics of the deer dance, indeed, the pain of the pursuit and sacrificial joy, are the poetics of Yoeme memories.

Today the deer dance can occupy a seemingly profane space of entertainment offered to tourists of indigenous culture in circuslike environs. But deer and pahko'ola dancing offer instances of public memory, moments of religious history writ with and on bodies. Yoeme ritual performances are occasions to share memories and establish a collective sensibility, linking the memory of the aged with that of the young. Yoemem combine Catholicism and indigenous Yoeme knowledge to maintain a singing and flowering worldview. By dissolving the hermeneutic dichotomy between Catholic sacrality and profane native arts, a Yoeme form of history emerges. This form of historicizing is a collaborative product of Yoemem and Spanish, Yoemem and Mexicans, Yoemem and their anthropological interlocutors, and particularly of Yoeme and their Jesuit guests centuries earlier. For example, during the deer dance, pahko'olam inscribe crosses on the ground while invoking as saints the names of animals important to aboriginal life. These inscriptions demarcate the performance space as well as the place of sharing collective identity. They provide a context by which to better understand Yoeme concepts of ritual theory and epistemology, since the symbol of the cross becomes desymbolized and embodied with agency.

Pahko'ola behavior is a purposeful means of establishing, transmitting, and reinforcing the ultimate values of Yoeme culture, while appearing to make light of them. The moro (ritual leader) will lead the pahko'olam into the pahko santo heka (ritual dance area) because, as Molina tells us, "they are not humans at this time." In these ways pahko'olam are different beings: they become "over there," in a place of otherness. Molina adds that the pahko'olam created a space for the pahko to begin:

When they had finished dancing to the tampaleo, they started to bless the ground. They stood toward the east, home of the Texans, and they asked for help from *santo mocho'okoli* (holy horned toad). Each *pahko'ola* marked a cross on the ground with the bamboo reed with which the *moro* had led him into the ramada. Then they stood toward the north and said: "Bless the people to the north, the Navajos, and help me, my *santo vovok* (holy frog), because they are people like us," and they marked another cross on the ground. Still they stood toward the west and said, "Bless the *Hua Yoemem* (Papagos) and help me, my *santo wikui* (holy lizard)," and they marked another cross on the ground. Finally they stood toward the south and said: "To the south, land of the Mexicans, bless them and help me, my *santo vehori* (holy tree lizard)," and they marked the last cross on the ground. The head *pahko'ola* said: "My holy crosses, we have marked you on the ground so that you can protect us from all evil that might harm us." . . . Now that the ground had been blessed and purified, the *pahko* was ready to begin. The deer dancer would arrive shortly, and the people were ready to enjoy and be blessed by the *pahko*. (Evers and Molina 1987, 83–84)

Pahko'olam spatializing the pahko santo enable us to understand ritual performance as actual transformation, as opposed to "simply secular entertainment." The pahko'olam ask the "holy" animals to bless the neighboring people, the men bless the ground in the four directions with crosses, and this act of inscription protects the pahko'olam from evil.[9] Since the pahko'olam address the crosses, the crosses in the ground are clearly not representational but rather actual embodiments with their own flowering concerns. The dancers also bless the ground with these crosses, who then have the ability to return the blessing. Ironically, the inscribers of the crosses are already ontologically "over there," yet they are creating a boundary where the "over there" is safe. In these ways they are deliberately working effectively with otherness. The pahko'olam create forms that exercise intentionality and power. The entire pahko then blesses the people in attendance. This is not just an entertaining folk dance. These dances highlight the power of ritual, the importance of spatializing, the community of beings in a Yoeme cosmos, and the religious significance of entertainment.

In this one ceremonial act, the hybrid and syncretic character of Yoeme worldviews comes into view. As seen in references to the devil, the beings of a Christian hierarchy inform appropriate Yoeme actions and morals. Such a view is further clarified by the pahko'olam wishing to be protected "from all evil." I cannot help thinking that as clowns they are mocking these references as they also address them as powerful. Similarly, I continue to ask how holy frogs, lizards, and horned toads are to be understood? Clearly, the hierarchy of beings moves across species more fluidly than in an orthodox Roman Catholic cosmology. Moreover, the fact that the dancers address the crosses directly and understand them as having agency to bless and protect suggests a nonsymbolic notion of ritual inscription. The crosses do not refer to a signified power or deity. Rather, their ontological status demonstrates a Yoeme theory of ritual that is evident in the saying of prayers over meals (where one blesses the food rather than asks for blessings), cross greetings (where one greets the cross when arriving at plazas), and throughout the deer and pahko'ola dances described in this text. The pahko'olam write on the ground to make a place different from other places, a place where the various aniam are available, where history can be re-membered, identity developed, and flower shared. The embodied dancing and singing create a powerful relationship between the performance space and all who come to the pahko.

Yoeme worldviews, for many, cannot be easily condensed into either a sacred-profane dichotomy or a Catholic description of heaven, hell, and the human saints. While each village church is a place for Mass and religious processions, the mountains and the wilderness world still provide the community with transformative power. The deer dance takes, and makes, place wherever performed. The pahko'olam create a safe space, and yet they are associated with the devil (by some) and the little desert friends of the deer (by most). The aniam are present to the performers and audience. And, as I show below, Yoeme concepts of knowledge and truth are often bound more to these songs and dances than to the Bible or scholarly histories.

Deer Dancing as Mission History

Indigenous ceremonial performances offer historical narratives that often run counter to tropes of conversion. Anthropologists have frequently sought to explain native people's conversions with concepts like assimilation, acculturation, syncretism, or fusion. William Taylor describes how three main processes — "pagan" resistance, syncretism, or Christian transformation — have been hypothesized regarding Indian religious change in Mesoamerica, although his claim is applicable for other regions as well (Taylor 1996, 51–62). Due to what Ashis Nandy (1983) considers the implicit metaphor of conquest, many scholars, including Nandy, work from the position that there was a "shared culture" of colonialism. According to Taylor, this scholarship acknowledges the accommodation and appropriation, not just the submission, linking the colonized and colonizer (6).[10] Or, as is evident in William Merrill's ethnographic study of Rarámuri worldviews, newer religious forms are often adopted to some extent, though not at the expense of a core of indigenous cosmology (Merrill 1988, 79–84). At the very least, culture change is a conversation toward both collective and competing goals. When writing about acculturation and assimilation, scholars choose to posit syncretism and hybridity over models of either simple resistance or transformation. By doing so, people see their own agency in the emergence of new cultural forms as well as in the continuation of endemic logic. Theories that posit syncretism over models of resistance and transformation demonstrate the intersubjective character of transculturation and highlight the dialectical process of culture change (Pratt 1992).

Taylor demonstrates multiple ways in which various scholars of colonial New Spain have pursued syncretic models. He notes that according to J. Jorge Klor de Alva (1982) and Miguel León-Portilla (1990), the majority of native groups borrowed just enough Christian symbolism to appear converted (Taylor 1996, 53). Taylor also notes that William Madsen (1957) spoke of two kinds of syncretism: one in which symbols or god figures were added without deep change taking place, and another in which emotions and beliefs actually experienced change. The recognition of these two forms of change was instructive for Madsen in his work among the Maya. As a result, he came to the conclusion that this native group did not change its core religious values during missionary instruction. As with the Yoemem, the Maya were relatively isolated for almost a century with only a few Jesuits working in their territory. Although Taylor finds Madsen's differentiation between deep and surface change instructive, he has also criticized Madsen for not giving credit to the parish priests and Jesuits for their roles as insightful and accommodating interpreters of the Catholic faith (55–57).

Taylor explains that like Madsen, Nancy Farriss, who also worked with the Maya, retained the language of syncretism, while adding to that notion a sense of layered convergence (Farriss 1984, 57). Farriss tones down the difference between deep and shallow change, but demonstrates how the Yucatec Maya merged their indigenous worldviews with Catholic deities and saints forming a "creative synthesis." Farriss joins Madsen in representing the Maya as moving toward a Christian identity without "conversion." Farriss argues that the three main factors that enabled this situation to emerge were the lack of Spanish encroachment deep into Maya territory during the first century of Jesuit relations, the small numbers of Jesuits present, and their sense of necessary indigenous molding of doctrine. Although the missionary conditions expressed by Farriss and Madsen were much different than what natives encountered in southern and central Mexico, the Yucatan experiences are important here, since their geohistorical contexts are similar to the Yoeme example.

Because both Madsen and Farriss downplay the internal native agency and logic that clearly must inform any reading of "conversion," I will return to the Yoemem by way of more promising scholarship. I wish to specifically mention the works of Inga Clendinnen, Elizabeth Wilder Weismann, and Kenneth Morrison, who interpret cultural change as reflecting a coherent indigenous sensibility and intelligence. Clendinnen (1987, 154–60) finds that some colonial native groups in central Mexico appropriated only those aspects of Catholicism that seemed appropriate within their preexisting religious logic — for example, the adoption of saints as other-than-human intercessors, or Mary as a powerful feminine embodiment of fertility. Weismann (1985) reaches a similar conclusion in her study of central Mexican indigenous art, asserting that the Indians adopted those Christian practices that were familiar to, or even strengthened by, precontact religious ideas. For both authors, Catholic drama in ceremonies and myth provided local tribes with additional means of expressing and thus of continuing non-European worldviews. While both authors seem attached to uncritical notions of "the sacred" and "deities," Taylor rightfully considers Clendinnen's and Weismann's works to be exemplary studies, as they focus on religious change under colonialism without utilizing common concepts of substitution, imposition, and loss. Taylor gives credit to these two authors for opening "the possibility that Indians innovated in order to maintain the familiar" (1996, 61). Native responses to colonial missions appear as, in William K. Powers's words, "logical transformations based on earlier cultural context" (1987, 124).

As an ethnohistorian of native colonial encounters and their effects on indigenous religiosity, Kenneth Morrison provides an eloquent description of and direct assault on the widespread use of "conversion" in both colonial and mission histories. Describing the intersection of seventeenth-century and early eighteenth-century eastern Algonkian and French-Catholic cosmologies, Morrison demonstrates that religious change need not mean conversion:

> The main problem with conversion is that it stipulates a particular and singular outcome to religious encounter. To describe eastern Algonkian religious change as conversion is to fail to understand that change itself is a process, and particularly a process of discerning, negotiating, making, and adapting religious meaning. The category conversion is intimately related to the pervasive view that Native American history proceeds in terms of victimization and cultural decline, and in terms of non-Indian views of a universal, progressive, and Christian history. Algonkians were not simply victims, however, and they did not lose their cultures as a result of contact with Europeans or Christianity.

Morrison's work calls for more nuanced interpretations of cultural exchanges and transformations. He holds that religious change did occur in the seventeenth and early eighteenth centuries, but he is also correct to doubt the usefulness of the label "conversion" in that context. Morrison's conviction is persuasive:

> Conversion claims that Native Americans came to agree with pervasive and aggressive critiques of their cultures and life-ways. Conversion denies that either pre- or post-contact Native American cultures had or have systematic and rational integrity. Conversion contends that Native Americans themselves perceived the superior truth claims of Christianity as a series of over-arching theological and cultural propositions about the nature of reality. Conversion claims that Native Americans repudiated their religious traditions, and thus their way of perceiving, thinking, valuing, and acting. Conversion concludes that Native Americans turned away from ancient truth, and moved towards a system which offered them a morally better, and intellectually more effective, way of understanding the world. Conversion stipulates that Christianity proclaims a new truth by which Native Americans could understand an unprecedented, post-contact world. In all these ways, conversion is a problematic category, and one that fails utterly to understand the distinctive and integral character of Native American life both before and after contact. (2002, 33–34)

Morrison challenges us to engage more carefully with the epistemological systems from which natives were reasoning and the values on which they relied to decide which cultural changes were practical. Tropes of religious conversion assume that European cultures were superior, that precivilized natives lacked practical ways of being in the world, that Christianity provided an undeniable "truth," and that precontact religiosity was abandoned. Morrison justifies, then, an abandonment of the term *conversion* in those cases of culture contact that fail to evidence a consummate exchange of values.

Put another way, if, as Vicente Rafael writes (1993, xvii), conversion entails "the act of winning someone's voluntary submission" and the "restructuring of his or her desires as well," then it seems more appropriate to say that the Yoemem never converted to Catholicism in the seventeenth century. From the documentation — using previous ethnographic accounts as well as Yoeme ritual and myth as evidence — Yoemem adopted (as one would adopt a child) Catholic personae and associated relations into their still-visible and still-sensible religious worldviews.

Of course, deer dancing and pahko'olam are just a few embodied claims by which to counter the comments of one historian of Yoeme missionization, who stated: "Jesuits proceeded to stamp out what they considered to be heathen customs" (Hu-DeHart 1981, 32). Spicer, on the other hand, describes the conditions that placed Yoeme in control of their "directed cultural change." Yoemem in the seventeenth century had been inspecting Jesuit missions south of their own territory for years before inviting the Jesuits into their homeland in 1616. One year later, Father Andrés Pérez de Ribas arrived with another missionary, Tomás Basilio, and four Zaque Indian converts who spoke a mutually intelligible language to Yoeme. As was Jesuit custom at the time, no military escort was requested nor was one provided for their stay in Yoeme territory. Although Pérez de Ribas left after a year for a higher position in the Society of Jesus, four other missionaries replaced him. Spicer highlights the fact that in the next century of Jesuit presence, no more than six missionaries at a time were living within the Yoeme villages. This low ratio of Jesuits to Yoemem offers critical evidentiary support for a more complex portrait of Yoeme-Jesuit encounter.

In order to understand Yoeme religious change in the seventeenth century, the dynamics of Jesuit instruction are relevant. If, as many historians describe, the approximate Yoeme population in the mid-1600s was thirty thousand, then there were at least five thousand Yoemem per Jesuit. Since this period also entailed the process of consolidating the more than eighty Yoeme *rancherías* into eight pueblos, there were clearly some pueblos without constant Jesuit presence. The Jesuits managed their project by developing a program to train *temastianes* (sacristans). These locals were the first to learn the Catholic prayers and would assist in communicating the Jesuit message to the other community members. According to Spicer, the villagers would only see the Jesuits at Sunday Mass or at the large collective ceremonies (1961, 440). Thus the primary work of translating Catholicism to the people fell on the temastianes, of which there were never more than twenty (1980, 21). Spicer was of the opinion that this mediation process on the part of a small group of Yoemem, still residing with kin groups in the villages, remains the important factor in order to understand how Yoemem actively adopted some new religious forms but not necessarily their meanings (1961, 33).

From Spicer's point of view, the ratio of Yoemem to Jesuits, the role of the temastianes, and the absence of any non-Jesuit Spanish in Yoeme communities for over a century enabled Yoemem to pick and choose what parts of Catholicism made sense within precontact worldviews (1958, 434–38; 1980, 20–21, 60, 62). The cross provides a telling example of this. Looking back over two hundred years, Spicer writes that Yoemem somehow seemed very receptive to the cross. But, despite Jesuit intentions, Yoemem referred to the cross as "our mother," and placing her in a dress with ornamentation, they celebrated her at their spring festival (1958, 434–36; 1961, 31). Spicer suggests that the cross may have been used before Jesuit contact in 1617, because when Pérez de Ribas first arrived, he was greeted by a large gathering of Yoemem, each of whom held small crosses (Spicer 1961, 31).[11] Moreover, from watching the interplay between references to the church and the huya ania, or wilderness world, Spicer labels the religious change one of "oppositional integration," where the Yoemem were offered "alternatives" to their existing religion (1961, 29–30; 1980, 70).

Continuing Spicer's line of reasoning, the contemporary deer and pahko'ola dances demonstrate how Yoeme ceremonial integration attests to a critical and practical response to Jesuit alternatives. These rituals and their embodiments within the larger ceremonial calendar demonstrate the Yoeme adoption of Catholic alternatives into a still visibly indigenous religious logic. In these contemporary performances, Yoemem teach everyone present about Yoeme reception and materialization of Catholicism. After weeks of preparing for Easter, and slowly dramatizing the passion of Mary and Jesus in Lent, the narrative climaxes in the defeat of evil and the triumph of Jesus.[12]

Spatially, the deer and pahko'olam are at the center of that ritual. When the villagers and spectators leave the church and plaza, they follow the deer and pahko'olam back toward the everyday, toward their homes, and toward the huya ania. This movement is one of return and also of sustenance. Yoeme identity is sustained through the embodiment of Yoeme relations to Jesus, Mary, deer, and other living beings. Such relations are aptly defined by the Yoeme concepts of flower, or seewa.

In the most comprehensive analysis of flower symbolism in Yoeme culture, Morrison demonstrates how their understanding of flowers as reciprocating sacrifice provides Yoemem with an indigenous theory of ritual power, by which they integrated Catholic cosmology and Christian ceremonial performances into their worldviews. In his essay "Sharing the Flower: A Non-Supernaturalist Theory of Grace," Morrison argues against a wide and deep disciplinary current of Eliadian influence in the study of religion.[13] Working specifically outside of sacred-profane and natural-supernatural binaries, Morrison shows the pervasiveness of flower symbolism not only in relation to Yoeme concepts of the deer and pahko'ola but also concerning ideas about God, Mary, Jesus, the saints, and ceremonial labor. He explores how Yoemem understood Christian dimensionality within preexisting terms of ritual sacrifice and shared responsibility among all cosmic beings. Since most of the previous ethnographers of Yoeme culture dichotomized Yoeme ritual into foreign notions of sacred-profane, supernatural, worship, or belief, Morrison's examination of flowers brings us closer to understanding Yoeme Catholic identity. His analysis of the flower as a nonsupernaturalistic theory of grace exemplifies the way Yoeme ritual, regardless of its Catholic characteristics, proceeds from a commitment to other-than-human kinship. Morrison's explanation of Yoeme ritual theory helps us think about deer dancing and its continuation, within a ceremonial calendar that seemingly emphasizes Christian devotion more than a hunting culture.

Yoemem explain their concepts of Christianity through their stories of Jesus living in the Hiak Vatwe and their portrayals of his life and death during the Easter ceremonies. For Jesus to come to earth as a man, God enlisted the help of the sun, moon, stars, and planets, providing a Yoeme ethic of cosmic sharing and reliance on others. His birth came about only because Mary found a flower in the river while collecting water, and she placed it in her bosom in order to walk home and share the flower's beauty with Joseph. In stories of Jesus as a man, Yoemem describe him as walking in the huya ania, out in the wilderness, healing people among the flowers. Although he was hot, thirsty, and tired, he had the self-discipline to keep walking and helping people. When he became frustrated with the world and wanted to kill everyone, his mother told him that he could only do so if he returned the breast milk that he had taken from her as a child. In this way she taught him that humanity relies on giving. And when he was about to be killed by the soldiers, Mary left for the wilderness and transformed herself into a tree so that an unknowing Joseph would cut her down and make her into a cross. Some Yoeme say that she opened up her arms in the shape of a cross and that her sacrifice for him enabled them both to ascend to heaven. And when Jesus was nailed to the cross, the blood that flowed from his wounds hit the ground and sprouted into flowers. For all of these reasons, Yoemem sometimes refer to Jesus as "flower person." They relate to him and Mary in terms of ethical behavior and sacrificial reciprocity.

Jesus' giving of himself for others is also evident in the Easter ceremonies in which Yoemem portray Jesus during the first weeks of Lent as a baby without a home, then as a young man, and then during Holy Week as an old man. Toward the end of the "big week," the old man is literally chased around the pueblos and surrounding wilderness by the soldiers and by masked "big head" monsters who seek his death. In the large Lenten processions increasing and intensifying throughout Lent from weekly to daily, and then in the last few days occurring both day and night, Yoemem carry statues of the saints and the Marys (Mary Magdalene, the Virgin Mary, and Our Lady of Guadalupe) while the fariseos and masked men follow in pursuit of Jesus embodied by the old man.[14] The soldiers, out to find Jesus, finally catch him in a garden constructed of willow branches called Gethsemane. They bring him on horseback around the church plaza so that others can mock him and tease him, and they tie him to a post and whip him. The soldiers replace the old man's role by a large, almost life-sized cross from which hangs the corpus of Jesus, covered with a white cloth. When they finish acting out the nailing of Jesus to the cross, they lift it and the figure, still covered with a white cloth, and the flowers that were wrapped in its folds fall to the ground beneath where Jesus now hangs. The fariseos and masked others, who are clearly happy at the "crucifixion," move him inside the church and lay the corpus on a bed of flowers. During the night the body of Jesus disappears from under the big noses of the masked guards. On the morning of Holy Saturday, the fariseos and other masked ones use a series of processional formations and intensifying staccato rhythms to rush the church repeatedly. As protectors of the church and the saints inside, *anhelitom* ("little angels," children dressed as beautiful angels) whip these "evil" aggressors with willow twigs and chase them out of the church. After the last assault, the black curtain — which had cut off the front quarter from the rest of the church — is thrown wide open to reveal all the anhelitom and saints. Christ has risen, the tomb is empty, and the anhelitom chase the defeated aggressors out of the church for the last time. One of the ceremonial societies of Mary, called *matachinim*, play their music and dance flowers for her, holding flower wands and wearing flower hats. The pahko'olam dance first in the church, then, moving outside the front doors, they dance around the "flower patio." Because the deer is dancing and flowers are everywhere, we know that the performers are successfully presenting sea ania, the beautiful world of sacrifice and communion. The deer is dancing the sea ania present, and the onlookers throw confetti flowers at the attacking soldiers. For what seems like hours, multicolored flowers drifting on the wind shower down on the community. After the whole community defeats evil, fireworks shoot into the sky, heralding Saint Michael's return to heaven because he has collected everyone's flowers that they shared through their ceremonial labor during the previous months.

My understanding of the Yoeme dramatization of this battle between good and evil reflects an approach to reading indigenous rituals as ethnographic. Particularly, I am led to agree with Richard Trexler that "missionary theatre of Mexico *was* ethnography" (1987, 594, his emphasis). In contrast to Trexler's focus on the clergy's role as the ethnographic authors, I prefer to think diachronically about native authorship and communicative intentions, both internally and externally.

It might be assumed from this description of Holy Saturday that Yoemem simply added the precontact deer and pahko'ola dances to the Catholic ceremonial calendar, or deer dancing might be interpreted as a metaphor for the life and divine role of Jesus Christ, as the Jesuits taught the Yoemem about them. I have described deer dancing rituals and the Yoeme performance of Christ's passion in ways that suggest comparison: the hunt, the sacrifice, the worlds or aniam involved in the ceremonies, the shared components of flower, and so forth. While the comparisons seem evident, the causal relationship between Yoeme views of Jesus and deer must also be borne in mind.

Deer dancing as a prehunting ritual demonstrates Yoeme-deer reciprocity and an acknowledgment of their mutual sacrifice. Deer dancing as a contemporary mode of collective-identity formation demonstrates community survival in the face of persecution. These hunting rituals bring together a very large complex of indigenous Yoeme religious views, including the deer songs as other-than-human language, the aniam as real and present geographical transformation, the interplay with pahko'olam as kinship relations, and, of course, flower symbolism as cosmic and communitarian give-and-take. Seen in this larger frame, Yoeme-deer relations provide a preexistent logic by which Jesuit stories of Jesus, as well as a history of colonial dynamics with the Mexican government, can be understood. My research thus supports the claims of Evers and Molina, who note that any parallels drawn between deer and the "Lamb of God" are basically non-Yoeme interpretations (1987, 129). I would add that the parallel confuses the poetics with the politics of representation. To say that Yoeme communities perform the killing of the deer as a native passion play suggests that an axiological shift, a missionary success story, took place in Yoeme communities. To contend, however, that Yoemem understand Christian consciousness because they already understood human-animal relations as being powerful, familial, and epistemologically grounding enables us to recognize an indigenous logic that was neither turned into something else nor "converted."

Organic Historicism in Potam Pueblo

At the beginning of this chapter I asked why Yoemem continue to perform deer-hunting ceremonies when their sustenance activities minimally include deer hunts. I believe that deer and pahko'olam survive because they nourish Yoeme senses of self through grounded, embodied ritual action. These performances document a particular history of syncretic traditionalism through both Catholic references and aboriginal ritual logic. Studying such performances as efficacious community autoethnohistory enables us to better understand how previous interpretations reflect modernist anthropological impulses. In relation to Yoemem in particular, by understanding Jesus in terms of a deer figure and not vice versa, it becomes possible to see how the concept of "conversion" fails to represent Yoeme history adequately.

This Yoeme case study might call for further research on how aboriginal hunting practices and modes of sustenance have informed both ethical views on social relationships and indigenous responses to Christian notions of grace, the supernatural, divinity, worship, religion, and so forth. Hunting might represent what it means to be human. Perhaps other native communities also continue their hunting ceremonies in some form because, like the deer and pahko'ola dances, these rituals signify collective identity, the basic ideas of traditional cosmology, and an internal means of ritualistically "writing" one's place in the landscape.[15]

Edward Spicer and Muriel Thayer Painter both interpret the deer and pahko'olam dancing as entertaining, constituting profane activities within the larger sacred, Catholic ceremonial system of the Yoeme. In order to achieve a more contextual understanding of Yoeme ritual activity, I have shown some of the problems that result from categorizing culture within modernist binaries. I have also wanted to show the complexity of notions of conversion within native mission histories. I developed these contentions after asking how Yoeme ritual was communicating knowledge of collective history and thus ethnic identity.

We must heed Renato Rosaldo's warning, "Rituals do not always encapsulate deep cultural wisdom" (1993, 20). In my observations of many rituals both in the Yoeme communities and elsewhere, I concur with his observation: "Although certain rituals both reflect and create ultimate values, others simply bring people together and deliver a set of platitudes that enable them to go on with their lives. Rituals serve as vehicles for processes that occur both before and after the period of their performances" (20). Rosaldo cautions against confusing a ritual event for a definitively essential, cultural core. In the Yoeme case, it bears repeating that the "killing of the deer" dance that I described is only one set of deer songs, among many others. As I describe in the next chapter, deer and pahko'olam rituals are part of a larger corpus of meaningful religious actions. And, of course, the range of expressed Yoeme religiosity is wide enough to include agnostics, devout Protestants, and a multitude of Catholicisms, with each individual relating to pahkom differently. In every Yoeme pueblo, I have noticed Yoeme men and women of all ages who are seemingly apathetic to the dances, but these people are always a minority.

On the other hand, Rosaldo's comment does assume that sometimes rituals do "reflect and create ultimate values." Such is the case with deer dancing most, if not all, of the time. In both southern and northern communities, Yoemem speak of deer dancing as central to tribal identity. As Evers and Molina describe, when forced to prove the northern Yoemem were an indigenous tribe to the U.S. Senate Select Committee on Indian Affairs in September 1977, Yoeme leader Anselmo Valencia provided the following evidence: (1) Yoeme had lived within U.S. territory before the Treaty of Guadalupe; (2) the majority of community members were actually born in the United States; (3) many Yoemem serve in the armed forces; and (4) a distinct language and culture exist as demonstrated through deer and pahko'ola dancing. Commenting on this last contention, or what they call "the heart of Mr. Valencia's successful argument," Evers and Molina write that "the continuation of the deer dance and deer singing through four centuries of attempted conquest is, in Mr. Valencia's judgment, one of the primary evidences that Yaquis remain Yaquis" (1987, 19–20).

In an article entitled "'Like This It Stays in Your Hands': Collaboration and Ethnopoetics," Molina wrote that he has come to know the elders' truth as the "knowledge about living in the Yaqui world that, by virtue of being in the memories of respected community members, is considered to be central" (Molina and Evers 1998, 26–27). Molina draws on Spicer's description of *lutu'uria* as belonging to those who demonstrate the "highest of all human qualities," since they spend their entire lives committing themselves to the fulfillment of Yoeme religious obligations (Spicer 1980, 85). Molina then specifies that such obligations are nothing less than Yoeme ceremonial participation. Clearly, lutu'uria is knowledge that is socially constructed. Molina further explains: "There is then a sense in which the *pahko* becomes the kind of 'proving ground.' ... Subsequent performances during the ceremonies in the towns will be the occasion for this knowledge to be recognized and validated" (27). Molina directs our attention to a type of knowledge that might be recognizable in other indigenous cultures, social knowledge. His description of the ritual performance of knowledge also supports my claim here that we need to move toward non-Western theories of knowing and truth, or what Nancy Hartsock has called "standpoint epistemology" (1984, 231–34; 1987, 204–6). Providing a community-based definition of knowledge and a social method of verification, Molina's description of lutu'uria demonstrates how deer and pahko'ola rituals provide Yoeme communities with a veritable historicism.

Although the inscription process takes (and makes) place through nonliterate acts, pahko'olam differentiate Catholic and Yoeme personae, dimensions, and ways of knowing. Effectively, these acts are performed ethnographies of a certain Yoeme life-world that many community members consciously engage as their tribal identity. If these histories and interpretations of Yoeme culture lack Western historical notions of "documentation" or anthropologically verifiable "data," then the rituals are fulfilling at least one purpose: "The *pahko* is a place where an opposition between knowledge gained in the towns and knowledge gained in the mountains is negotiated" (Molina and Evers 1998, 27). Since the time of Jesuit contact, and probably before, Yoemem have been sustaining community knowledge through the negotiation of ritual.

Ethnographic Dialogue 5

DAVID SHORTER: I have a lot of questions about the processions and the hunting of the deer. Do men in Potam or the Yoeme towns still hunt deer?

RESPONDENT: Yes, they hunt the deer, but not just for the sake of killing, nor to sell it or to trade it. Instead they do it to nourish their families or when the community wants a head for a festival or the hooves of the deer to use in Holy Week. They use him for the belts, for the [masked "big nose" society]. That is why we kill the deer in the tribe.

DS: What do you think? How many deer are taken each year?

R: Killed?

DS: Yes, by Yoeme hands.

R: Well, not many, not many at all. Yoemem don't kill deer just to kill them. It is as I just finished explaining. But when we need the hooves, yes, we will kill some, probably around fifty or sixty.

DS: Each?

R: Well, I know that they kill around 160 to make belts, and the meat is distributed in the town to your brother and your uncles or to your family members, and they give part as a gift to the governor. But the meat is never sold or traded. They do not sell it outside of the tribe to the Mexicans or anyone who cannot kill a deer inside the tribe. This is strictly prohibited.

DS: Do you think that the hunts still have at least four men, like in ancient times?

R: The most important thing is that one must be prepared to hunt the deer. The deer is very superstitious. He can smell a person from more than one hundred or two hundred meters. He can hide or go away to the other side of the mountain so that you can't kill him. In order for that not to happen, a Yoeme hunter uses this material they call "mariola," "chili tepin," or "yawaron."

DS: As a salve or perfume?

R: As a body salve. The Yoemem hunters take off the spines and make them into oil. These are things the deer eats. Dandelion is the deer's favorite food.

DS: Is it true that the lead deer hunter must have seatakaa in order for the deer to allow himself to be killed?

R: Well, that could be true, but this is not a Yoeme thing. The entire world has seatakaa. They are very reserved people, the people that have seatakaa. But, yes, these people have the facility to kill a deer or to successfully hunt whichever type of animal they want.

DS: There was a book published in the 1930s that said for the Yoeme there were deer and then there was a deer leader, like a boss deer.

R: Well, look, this is a question. I am very sure that it is all over the world, not only here in the tribe. It is in the whole world that each group of deer has this animal. It is like he puts himself on vigil. He is a watchman. He is going to watch out. The deer is the most superstitious animal in the whole world. I have seen them come down to a brook at night or to eat plants. If there are two or three deer, they do not all come together at the same time. They are taking care; they arrive two first, then one. Or one will walk ten paces and then stop as if tending the parameter of this space. Then the other deer will walk. They are looking after each other, ten by ten or fifteen paces, until they arrive at the water. And they do not drink the water at the same time. One only, one first is allowed to drink water and then the other. I think that with other animals, they will just arrive at the water together and drink, slurp slurp slurp, and everyone is drinking, but not the deer. One deer drinks while the other is watching out.

DS: It is as if one is saying, "Go ahead, I can watch."

R: Yes! That is how it is. Or "I will take care of you."

DS: Okay, I understand.

R: This is how the deer is.

DS: It is said that a person should never look in the eyes of a dying deer.

R: Yes, because I believe that in the eyes, it is as if there were little spines that can come out of them, and they can hurt the vision of the person who is watching. And for this reason it is not recommended to look a dying deer in the eyes.

DS: Have you heard something, I think that is a little funny, when I was working here in the first few years, there was a man who knew a little about the tribe, and he said to me, "David, when you are in the pueblos, do not blow on your food or hot drinks."

R: Blowing?

DS: Because the Yoeme do not blow on foods, he said. But then I read that a person that was hunting deer was not supposed to blow on his food. Is this true? Is this a saying or a proverb?

R: Well, it is a saying, and it is true. In terms of food in general, there are Yoeme people who can cure, and one should not blow on their remedies because it can remove the power of the remedy and even the power of the curer. And food is respected. Why? Because all food is sacrifice. Because one has to sacrifice to obtain food, and the food is sacrificing as well. To blow on food is like opposing it, pushing its essence away. But today you see the children and even older people blowing on hot food to cool it down, right? But, in actuality, it is not recommended.

DS: Is it normal that in each *lutu pahko* they kill a deer?

R: No, not exactly. At the lutu pahko, they only kill a deer for someone who was in a position like a governor, a captain, a commander. But you wouldn't do that for a corporal, or a horseman, because they have different positions. You cannot kill the deer in front of the Son of God. If you want to kill a deer, you have to ask the authorities to be sure the Child of God is not going to be at the ramada. If you request a deer, it is possible to get permission.

DS: Then they can have a deer?

R: They have to have a deer.

DS: Do you want to have a whole deer for your father's lutu pahko next year?

R: Yes. Yoemem tell legends that each Yoeme person, when born, they are born with a deer. Well, it doesn't matter where, here, in Obregón, or in hospital in Guaymas, to be born a Yoeme, in the mountain they are making a deer. So when a person dies, they have to either kill or mimic the killing of that deer so that the spirit of that person is not agitated or lingering in this world.

DS: At the end of pahko'ola dancing, after the last song, the elder pahko'ola tells a story or makes an oration. What is it called?

R: Canary. *Canary* means to say something like this. This is what they say, this, the *canario*, the final canario. There is another canario when it begins also. This canary says: [performs the canary in Yoeme]. This last one is the same, but they say it when they have finished their work. In Spanish it would be: "Ladies and gentleman, we are here in this ramada with the intent to complete the promise that we made with you all from the day before yesterday that you all went home with this petition, with this favor that we have requested. Today we are here in this ramada to complete what we have compacted, but before anything, that God, although he has done many things for our good, for the good and for the bad, that hopefully one of the things will affect your body, your soul, and your spirit, that all are in good health today on this most grand day, from the smallest to the largest. And also the people that are from the Catholic Church groups and all the groups and all the personnel of the pre-church groups that they also have the same health that we desire from everything that we encounter here. And also we want God's pardon if we say things or if at any given moment bad words leave our mouths. We ask for pardons from the entire family, the entire town, and we ask that God will pardon us in case we come to commit these failings." This is what they say in Yaqui dialect.

DS: Ah, it is a lot. And the pahko'olam also say in an oration while marking the ground with crosses, "Saint Lizard," "Saint Horny Toad," "Saint Frog," etc. Why do they name these animals? Why not other animals? Why the small ones, the ones that live close to the land?

R: They use these names. Why? Because they say that they bring the rattlesnake tangled in the feet. You know the butterfly cocoons around their ankles and calves and how they rattle? For that reason a pahko'ola cannot speak during the ceremony after saying the canario. After performing the first canary, the pahko'olam turn into, well, they do not belong to good. Therefore, they only pronounce animals. And so these animals help them dance so that they will not tire during the night. They help to pass the night, as they must. They are like saints. They are patron saints, and they help them. Like Saint Frog, who we invoked to bring rain. We put Saint Frog on a little platform and tied his arms and legs to the corners so that he stayed in the middle. And they adorned him with flowers. He was on his altar. We then walked in a *konti* procession with the deer and pahko'olam.

DS: My understanding is that this is a very old ceremony, yes?

R: Yes, it is very old.

DS: It is not presently done?

R: No, this is considered ancient.

DS: How old? Ten years? One hundred years?

R: Probably not since the 1940s. I have not seen it recently.

DS: Why is it not common now? Because people don't want to do ancient things?

R: No, it is not the ancientness. I think because people do not remember the whole process. They don't know all the prayers exactly or how to invoke the god of rain to bring rain down. Now that there are no rains, if they knew the prayers, I believe they would do it. But they do not know these orations, these prayers.

DS: Do you think it was a very similar konti procession, as with the military societies, a procession circling around the church?

R: Ah, no, no. Or it is the same konti, but they do it instead at the river, or at the canals, or they pass by the mountain, not by the church. They did it in the *huya*, something like this. No, in the mountain.

DS: When the pahko'olam use these animal saints, it is comical. But it also seems very serious because the animals are important for rain as in the case of the frog. Additionally, it is interesting that the pahko'olam are like animals while invoking animals.

R: Yes, we are invoking them. These are orations and prayers and songs, and we want all types of animals to have nourishment to sustain this life.

DS: And can these animals and pahko'olam make the dance space safe?

R: Yes, and the dance makes everyone safe.

DS: Do you think that all the Yoeme presently think that?

R: Yes, everyone.

6
Yoeme Place-Making: Acts of Loving and Giving

This final chapter grounds the previous discussions on myth, ritual, and history through an examination of place-making. I look at the activities in the home and in the pueblo that demonstrate the manner in which Yoeme community life is inseparably known and affirmed through social reciprocity: funerary practices and ceremonial processions. In both of these rites, Yoemem create, maintain, and transform their spatial relations with other Yoemem, both living and deceased, with powerful cosmological beings, and with non-Yoemem. Acts of boundary marking define these rites, since identity formation requires borders between cultural realms, whether they be cosmic (humans and their ancestors and other beings), social (community organizations), or geographic (landmarks and physical demarcations). Yoemem verify the syncretic character of this collective identity by paying attention to place-making and the boundaries constructed within and around these places.

In funerary rituals, ongoing relations with ancestors cross the boundaries between the living and the deceased. The *animam miika* rituals (feeding departed souls) highlight the dimensional relationships between town life, church authorities, and the *aniam*. These ceremonies also further complicate the literate/nonliterate binary discussed in chapter 3, since at the center of animam miika events are books of the dead, which contain the names of those who have passed. Sunday *kontim* (processions) bring together pueblo residents and the departed as they circle the church grounds. In kontim, Yoemem embody their grounded relations with Catholic figures within mythistorical movements. In caring for their deceased relatives and walking in kontim, Yoeme communities emplace precontact and Catholic mythology within their pueblos in ways that highlight cosmological, civic, and ethnic boundaries.

A word on my use of *place* and *space* is in order. Throughout this chapter I remain focused on concepts of place, more so than space. Distinctions between place and space have been debated since the days of the ancient Greek philosophers. Rather than rehearse the contours of that debate here, I have come to agree with those cultural geographers who understand space as unmediated and places as those spaces acted upon and shaped by activity.[1] Another way of saying this would be to say that "place" is a socially constructed site. Since the Yoeme language has no word for space, but does for place (*bwia*), I utilize *place* as the root word of *place-making* in describing Yoeme spatial processes of defining themselves and their social worlds.

As with many other aspects of precontact Yoeme life, little to no ethnographic data exists for understanding funerary practices and concepts of an afterworld. In general, these topics have received no more than a few pages of description in each of the five or six works that describe Yoeme culture.[2] Filtering the published sources for information on Yoeme perspectives on and rituals for the departed does yield an assortment of details that can be pieced together. Although none of the writers reflect on practices before the twentieth century, with the exception of one sentence by Pérez de Ribas (noted below), we are still able to discern how Yoemem ritually map social relations and boundaries through their caring for deceased community members. I focus below on those ceremonies that might be considered funerary: the burial, the *lutu pahko* (death anniversary), and the animam miika rituals every October and November. I draw from my time in Potam and contribute contemporary ethnographic specificity in order to demonstrate how the rituals contribute to local Yoeme place-making processes.

The Death and Burial Rites

Previously the most detailed descriptions of Yoeme funerary practices came from the 1930s, which is when communities along the Hiak Vatwe allowed Ralph Beals, William Curry Holden's expedition, Alfonso

Fabila, and Edward Spicer to live within them and observe pueblo life.[3] Considering how mortuary practices, like fashions in dress, belongings, and behavior, reflect social status as well as cultural conceptions of death, previous scholars of Yoeme history surprisingly have not detailed the full process of Yoeme death rites. In the details of these activities, many Yoemem clearly care deeply for their deceased relatives to the extent that collective Yoeme identity in Potam, and perhaps in other pueblos, includes those proto-Yoeme Surem who still inhabit the earth, the living community members, and those who have died. The embodied acts of Yoeme place-making are sensually clear in the audible and olfactory senses. Yoemem note presence and absence, literally, by the ringing of bells and explosion of skyrockets, the serving of delicious food, and the acts of listening to, not writing, the names of the deceased.

Sitting among family members or working the field, at any point of the day or night, Potam residents are acutely aware of sounds. An ethnographer here must almost immediately attune himself or herself to a different way of processing noise. One learns to keep track of which dogs are barking protectively and whether those barks are followed by different dogs closer or farther away. The direction will tell you if someone is coming toward your house. Bread and vegetables can be purchased in the morning by listening for the man on the bicycle riding slowly through the village saying in a monotone, just audible enough to hear but not enough to wake people, "Pan. Pan. Naranjas. Cebollas. Papas. Pan. Pan. Pan." The sound of the soccer ball bouncing tells you the children are out of school. In several houses I have watched as the elders stop to listen to the birds' songs. Often the tweets and chirps lead someone to announce that guests will be arriving from far away. I don't want to mysticize these moments or keep them from view: my point is that my Yoeme collaborators seem to be listening to more than I am accustomed. And in this audioscape, day or night, the heart drops just a bit when one hears a bottle rocket.

Skyrockets are sent up immediately when a person dies or when the body of a deceased person is returned home. Although previous ethnographers wrote that the skyrockets were carrying the deceased's souls to heaven, my Yoeme friends explained them differently.[4] First, a skyrocket is lit to welcome the deceased person. The second is to announce to the village that the body is now at the house. The third bottle rocket tells neighbors and friends that they can come to the house of the deceased. Someone from the family will then walk to the church and tell the lay priest (*maehto*) that there has been a death in the family. After the skyrockets, then, someone rings the church bells to announce the news to the community. If a man has passed, they strike the largest of the three bells. The medium and smallest bells are run to announce the passing of a woman or a child, respectively. The first people expected to join the family of the deceased are the maehto and the *kantooram* (hymn singers). After they sing the prayer of salvation, an elder from the family who knows the language will officially proclaim, "We are now going to watch over the deceased." I have been told that this must be in the Yoeme language and stated directly to the maehto and singers. As a performance, the statement makes a place: the family members establish a guardianship and a protective relationship. The boundaries between the living and the dead seem here to be particularly thin, both temporally and spatially.

If the deceased is an adult, the family elder will go to get the five pairs of godparents and the one pair of birth godparents, collectively called *vato'o yo'owam*. During this time the family members are cleaning and dressing the body. In earlier times the body would be prepared with an herbal salve, which would help sustain the body without deterioration. In contemporary times, the family usually has twenty-four hours before burying the body. The bodies are given some mark of their position in society: a small part of their regalia is placed on their body. In the case of a *pahko'ola*, a mask is placed on top of his head and a note beside him states, "He is a pahko'ola." All bodies receive a Yoeme-styled rosary as well. Dressed nicely and presented on white sheets, the bodies are then ready by 4 a.m. to hear the good-byes from their relatives, neighbors, and community members. People come to say good-bye in "their last dwelling place."

When a child dies, after the body is home, the parents must go tell the godparents the sad news. The godparents are also asked to come take care of the body. Often the child's body is then taken to the godfather or godmother's house (they are not married to each other by Yoeme custom). The godfather calls for a celebration with pahko'olam, *matachinim*, kantooram, and maehtom, with the godparents supplying everything. The godparents also make little paper flowers in the shape of angels, which they will place with a rosary in the grave with the child's body. Generally the mood is tempered by an often-stated notion that when children die they immediately return to "La Gloria," a common Yoeme notion of heaven. The burial procession for children, also within twenty-four hours, leaves directly from one of their godparents' houses.

Whether for adults or children, the idea of a soul leaving the body and floating directly to heaven is not immediately recognizable either in the ethnological literature or in the community.[5] Yoemem use the word *hiapsi* to refer to the hearts of living people and the souls of the deceased. One will also hear *mukia* for the individual's postmortem body. *Anima* is the common word for spirit or soul. *Anima* is also the name of families' books of the dead, which I describe in detail in this chapter. In one publication, Beals writes that the animam hover for three to eight days (1943, 54). Two years later he writes that the spirits only remain around the pueblo for three days (1945, 75). Savala states that spirit leaves the body immediately at death (1980, 92). Most sources and my collaborators agree that the spirit lingers until the *novena*, nine days later.[6] Painter also writes that a category of souls, *chupia*, or those who erred ceremonially, may linger much longer than nine days (1986, 88). Some Yoemem still have the maehtom and kantooram sprinkle water around the places where the deceased spent most of his or her time, and some families use incense to "clean" the house. Similarly, the godparents sprinkle water in the grave at the cemetery.

Turning to these burial practices, we get a clearer picture of how the deceased are cared for in spatially important ways. Twenty-four hours after a person's death, or around noon the following day, the godparents come to the house of the deceased and lead the gathered groups in a circle of touching hands that normally accompanies joint ventures

8. The church and mostly wooden crosses marking the gravesites in Rahum Pueblo.

between families and godparents.[7] Then they direct everyone in a procession to the graveyard. Spicer describes the importance of these actions as spatial and embodied recognitions of the societal order (1980, 95, 195). Human action validates the house cross as signifying the Great Cross of the pueblo church (Spicer 1980, 66). The formation of a procession that originates at the house and moves through the village to the church creates a collective recognition that Yoeme community is a collaborative construction of households, church groups (like the godparents and kantooram), and the aniam surrounding the town. This separate but united social organization is then danced by deer and pahko'olam at the novena. On the burial day the body is carried in a procession to the cemetery just in front of the church. Although one could easily imagine a group of people walking unorganized toward a location, the fact that Yoemem here walk in formation demonstrates a comforting order to the world in a time of grief. Reaching the cemetery, close to the door of the main church, the body is buried in a shallow grave as close as possible to the nearest relative. Sometimes in simple wooden boxes or in more expensive coffins, and sometimes simply wrapped in cloth, the body is laid with the feet toward the church. Often a cross of palm or reed is placed in the grave. Many people place a second set of clothes in the grave for the next life. And although some elders remember burying the deceased on top of other family members, and although some people still prefer that manner of burial, my particular collaborators preferred not to but did not sound judgmental about the practice. After the burial, the whole group of godparents, family, friends, and the church groups walk toward the large plaza cross, "The Cross of Forgiveness," and the family thanks everyone. The group is reminded to come to the novena at the family's house.

Nine days later, usually after work or around 4 p.m., the family has prepared the house patio area to receive the guests. Everyone comes together to give the deceased a farewell blessing for his or her journey. On the house patio, the matachini society dances and the maehto and the kantooram sing on the church side of the house cross. The pahko'ola and the coyotes dance on the ania side of the patio, the division marked by the house cross. Whether for adults in their own homes or for children in their godparent's house, family members construct a particular spatial arrangement for the activities that have begun already — the visits by church groups — and those coming nine days later for the novena. In these houses family members construct an altar next to and centered by the patio cross, facing the *ramada*. A small crucifix veiled in black and sometimes holy figures are placed with the book of the dead atop the altar. Each family has a book of the dead, or *animam*, which is the same word used for "soul" or "spirit," but not to be confused with *aniam*, which are the worlds, states of being, or realms of relations, i.e., *huya ania, yo ania,* and *sea ania.* The house cross provides a clear visual divide then between two distinct spaces, since the church groups, kantooram, and maehto will sit on the church side of the house cross and begin singing hymns from the Catholic Mass for the dead. The pahko'olam, deer, and sometimes the coyote society (wiko'i ya'ura) will come to perform on the opposing side of the space. By literally connecting or bridging these two spaces, the altar provides a shared space for a photo of the deceased, the books of the dead, and images of religious figures in the forms of crucifixes and *santos.*

9. The house cross in the foreground is in line with the altar cross in the pahko rama (ceremonial ramada); both crosses bridge the church side on the left with the aniam side on the right.

Physically presenting a post-Jesuit aesthetic that reveals demarcated separation, the house cross thus centers the division between a side for the church groups and a side for the dancers who will arrive later. These demarcations resonate historically, ceremonially, governmentally, and cosmically: we see them everywhere. The church/aniam divide is physically constructed in the *campo* and will shape the activities of the *pahko* and church blessings. Hosted by the parents and often with assistance from godparents — a church-sanctioned ceremonial kin group — the church and nonchurch groups side by side offer complementary blessings of the deceased. In dying, as in living, the individual contributes to and draws from the combined powers of pre- and post-Jesuit dimensions. The skyrockets cross the division between land and sky, suggesting ethereal pronouncements of someone's passing. That the pahko'ola receives a church-validated note in addition to his ceremonial regalia suggests that the pueblo division between church and huya ania is recognized in the afterworld.[8] In general, such dressings demonstrate the primary importance of religious labor. Noting that children go straight to "heaven" demonstrates that some Yoemem understand souls as going from earth to an atmospheric afterworld, which, upward from the pueblo, corresponds to a Christian notion of heaven.

> *Arriving in Potam this afternoon, Felipe drove us directly to the church plaza. Usually we come straight to my kompae's house to meet the family. Felipe said that we should first visit my komae, who had recently passed away. At the church, we got out of the Jeep and walked to the Great Cross, where we removed our hats, genuflected, and crossed ourselves. We then began searching for her grave. The Potam cemetery (approximately thirty yards square) is filled with small painted crosses, all the same hue of light blue. Since the graves are shallow, each has a mound of hardened mud, creating an elongated dome shape. There are no boundaries marked between the graves, and so we have to step carefully in the ten inches or less of space between the mounds. At times, I have to pause and balance myself so as not to step too close to a cross, some soiled plastic flowers, or the weathered remains of a crepe-paper wreath. Some of the small crosses have names written in black ink or paint on one of their horizontal arms, but most do not. I figured my komae would not have had one of the large concrete tombstones, since her family always seems to be struggling for money. Felipe was leading us this afternoon, and I saw him stop at one cross and motion to me that he had found her. He removed his hat, and when I reached her small mound, I removed mine. I looked down and saw the hand-painted cross with her name, Antonia Flores Buitemea, 3 Junio 1929.*
>
> *I didn't know what to do with myself or my thoughts. I personally don't associate these mounds of dirt with where the deceased now reside. Since Felipe was in repose, I figured I should stay there and stare downward, too. I stood there thinking it was sad she wasn't around anymore. She was always so nice to me, even in my first trips. She had only one leg, and one of her hands was deformed. She was bedridden but seemed to micromanage the entire family from that one spot. Since my first trips entailed a lot of me just sitting around while everyone went about their business, I often sat with her in the cool darkness of her mud-thatched cane room, an oscillating fan rotating back and forth across us. I would ask her questions in Spanish, and she would answer so sweetly, her voice light and scratchy. Then she would yell as loud as a siren*

for someone to bring us some food or something, and one of her adult children would move swiftly to meet her request.

Often, since I didn't want to be too nosy during my first visits and because she seemed to lose energy quickly, I would just sit in silence with her. She would point to things or animals and say their names in Yoeme. I would try to repeat what she said, and she would repeat it to be sure. There were small exchanges with much silence in between, as I pointed to the puppy lying in the sun, the rooster picking through the ashes, or the large clay water pot dripping slow drops into the earth: ili chu'u, totoi o'owia, va'achia. At her gravesite, I thought about these things, and I grew happy that I had known her. I thought of all the things she had seen in her life and how I probably wouldn't have ever been invited back had she not approved.

I caught myself expressing my gratitude in my thoughts to her, but I didn't actually think of her there. I have never visited cemeteries regularly because I never lived where my family was buried. When I left New Mexico to attend college, I moved away from the graves of my ancestors. I hadn't thought that I was lacking a space for communication with my deceased loved ones. I found myself today in one of those moments of cultural difference: What does it mean to walk by the graves of your departed ancestors every day? Would it change how I thought of my community if every death required such a production, particularly if I lived in a household with three generations of family members? Weekly skyrockets, bells ringing, ten godparents, church groups, dancers, processions to the cemetery, a party nine days later, a year of mourning, a celebration to end the year of mourning, a month of the departed returning every October, the constant living while engaged with dying: how do we begin to understand ourselves as always in active, responsible relationships with the dead among us? As I sit here in my home away from home, I am beginning to realize that we're not just sharing time together as I "do fieldwork" but that I'm also starting to build relationships with their departed loved ones. As I come to help with the animam miika ceremonies, I am feeding the dead, too. As I walk in the processions, I'm bodily asserting myself into a collective reconstitution of a distinctly Yoeme social order and ethic.

We crossed ourselves at the foot of my komae's gravesite and put our hats back on as we walked toward the Jeep. An old Yoeme man sitting by the door

of the church tipped his hat to us, and we offered our respective Lios em
chania's *back to him. We got into the Jeep and drove to my kompae's house.
With the joy we have come to expect at these arrivals, the family told us that
it was good to see us as we walked around the yard touching hands. I didn't
see Ignacio, Guillermo's father and Antonia's husband, and I asked where
he was. "He is lying in his room." I asked if I could see him, and Guillermo
showed Felipe and me into their house. Fully dressed and covered in several
blankets, Ignacio rolled over slightly to offer his hand. He looked frailer than
I had ever seen him, although he did manage a smile for us. Walking outside,
we looked at Guillermo, and he responded in Yoeme that his father was still
mourning and that he spent much of his days in bed. We all fell silent, and
I felt heartbroken. This was my first visit here without the oldest wife and
mother of the family being alive. Changing the mood, Guillermo remarked that
he knew we were coming because a little bird had told him so a couple days
beforehand. I responded that his mother always heard similar messages from
birds about our arrivals. He responded that we should go later to visit her in
the cemetery. Felipe told him that we had just come from there, and Guillermo
looked simultaneously a bit sad and a bit happy. I'm sure he was missing her
but touched that we would pay her a visit first thing upon arriving.*

Crosses outnumber other forms of grave memorials in the eight
pueblos, although a variety of memorials surround the churches. In
the Potam churchyard, for example, stand both wooden and concrete
crosses, grave curbs, *cerquitas* (enclosures for candles or flowers), pot
holders, *relicaritas* (larger structures that enclose statues), and even a
couple of large mausoleums (though built over the grave). A cemetery
near a neighboring village features large concrete structures of Chinese
design, reflecting a time when a group of Chinese moved into the village while the Yoeme community was forced to the hills during their
battles with the Mexicans. In Pitahaya, a village closer to the ocean,
Beals noted that graves were decorated with designs in shells made by
brothers of the deceased (1945, 81). The cemetery is filled with only
wooden crosses in Wiivisim, a community with almost no Mexican
residents. Walking through the churchyard cemetery at Potam, a pueblo

surrounded by nearby Mexican ranches and having a relatively high population of Mexican and mixed-blood families, the wide range of grave marker styles tells a story of social plurality in terms of race and class. Some Yoeme families have had the desire and ability to memorialize their departed with concrete gravestones or adobe head slates with engraved names and dates. Mexican families purchase most of these types. The dates engraved on these headstones or enclosures suggest that their use increased in the last thirty years. Some of these may have been built on top of older graves. Still, Yoemem in Potam continue to use the wooden crosses.[9]

In *Silent Cities: The Evolution of the American Cemetery*, Kenneth Jackson and Camilo José Vergara (1989) examine a full range of graveyards and burial markers throughout the United States. They demonstrate the historical changes in grave commemoration and what such transformations say about societal shifts in attitudes toward death and the role of cemeteries. They also read the language of grave markers for what they can tell us about ethnic status. Whereas the American cemetery was generally visited less within the past century, and in many cases reflected changing cultural aesthetics like Revivalism and Minimalism, the cemeteries in Hispanic communities continued to be visited and cared for; their graves remained prominently marked by crosses (Jackson and Vergara 1989, 58, 74–82, 91). Mexican Americans continued to place flowers and candles on gravesites, even after the Housing and Urban Development Department reported in 1970 that cemeteries served a "transitory and unimportant" purpose (107, 109). For Jackson and Vergara, important ideological differences between Mexican minorities and the general U.S. population are reflected by these graveyard varieties. Higher economic status tends to support the reliance on visual technologies like video cameras and photography, leading to a more transportable and faithful means of remembering loved ones. Wealthier people tend to move or travel more often and further away, resulting in distances from their relatives' graves. And the higher average age of death that accompanies wealthier societies leads to a diminished sense of premature loss of life (120). Mexican American cemetery activity, on the other hand, suggests that mortality is a more orienting organizer of life (118) and that the departed can recognize the language, thought, and action of a cemetery visitor (107). Jackson and Vergara also argue that Hispanic efforts at commemoration signify a claim to their adopted land (59). In their final analysis, they note that cemeteries are more prominent when they are part of "an intuitive belief that the dead persist," that the departed do not vanish, that they communicate with the living, and that some life force resides in the place of burial (121).

Although Jackson and Vergara focus on American cemeteries, their use of graves as indicators of social values is relevant to the study of Yoeme death rituals. Their work supports the contention that cemeteries are distinct and positive expressions of religious ideology on the land.[10] As a spatial expression of death, a cemetery "tells us a great deal about the living people who created them" (Francaviglia 1971, 509). Jackson and Vergara's focus on ethnic groups' differing attitudes toward burials validates Richard Meyer's claim that the manner in which ethnic groups make cemeteries — the sites, customary practices, and material objects — provides "a most powerful and eloquent voice for the expression of values and world view inherent in their self-conscious awareness of their own special identity" (1993, 1). Contributing to folklore, cultural history, religious studies, archeology, architecture, ethnic studies, and landscape studies, works like Jackson and Vergara's book enhance necro-geography's important role in the ethnological sciences.[11] As I am able to see in Potam and other Yoeme communities, cemeteries literally ground the dynamic features of contemporary culture in a particular manner distinct to a people's history on the land. Because Jackson and Vergara interpret cemeteries as reflecting historical shifts in class, multiethnic demography, and worldview, they affirm the possibility that mortuary spaces and the human actions therein exhibit historical consciousness in both public and private terms.

Jackson, Vergara, and those authors I have brought into conversation here reflect the second wave of "death awareness" in academia that mostly sought to supplement the research of Emile Durkheim, Arnold Van Gennep, and Robert Hertz fifty years earlier.[12] While Van Gennep (1909) offers still-valuable interpretations of ritual as the natural process of social classification and categorical thinking, I appropriate "second-wave" writers due to their concern for multidirectional influences among local histories, culturally distinct actions, and the cosmological and physical places shaping and shaped by these histories and actions. These concerns I relate to Yoeme performance.

The Lutu Pahko, Animam Miika, and Books of the Dead

Yoemem actively maintain community in the one-year postmortem ceremony called the *lutu pahko*, or sorrow ritual. Beals briefly notes that the death anniversary is celebrated with a feast one year after the death, and if the individual was married with children, then pahko'olam and the deer will dance (Beals 1943, 55; Beals 1945, 75, 77). Both Beals and Savala note that the lutu pahko removed the mourning and ceremonial restraints from individuals (Beals 1943, 55; Beals 1945, 78; Savala 1980, 175).[13] Organized by family members, the ceremony lasts two to four days, finances and work schedules permitting. For weeks preceding that ceremony, family members are inviting the performers and erecting a large ramada of mesquite posts, cane walls, and roof. The ramada includes four distinct stall-like spaces for the altar, the kantooram, deer, and pahko'olam, and a small *vakot cari* (snake house) for the pahko'olam to keep their performance accessories. The family begins preparing enough *wakavaki* (customary beef and vegetable stew) and tortillas to feed upward of fifty people for two days. Arrangements must be made to provide sleeping areas for the out-of-town guests. The maehtom arrive at the house and help the godparents build an altar, atop of which they arrange a cross and black tablecloth. The parents of the deceased place the family's animam (books of the dead) and sometimes the animam of their relatives' families on the altar. On one side of the patio space in front of the altar, cane mats are placed on the ground for the maehto and kantooram. The other side of the space is open for the pahko'olam, coyotes, and deer.

Upon arriving at the house, the deceased's relatives and godparents receive black cords (*luutum*) that they tie around their necks. Yoemem draw the ceremony's name from these luutum: *lutu pahko* translates as "cord ceremony." Until the next day, when the cords are cut and burned in clay bowls at the base of the house cross, those with cords should remain ever mindful of the deceased and not think negative thoughts. Soon after the first group of people arrives, the family members and godparents are joined in the patio by kantooram, pahko'olam, deer, and sometimes coyote for a big meal, usually of flour tortillas and wakavaki, and an all-night pahko. Prayers and songs are sung from the church side of the ramada, and the other groups play music and dance all night in intervals. While most of the guests are enjoying the dances, there will come a point in the evening when all of the godparents (usually ten) are invited to sit at a large table in or near the house, away from the sheltered dance area, or *pahko rama*. Everyone is fed a large meal, and each couple is also given a pail of stew and a pail of *atole* (Mexican bread pudding) The eldest of the deceased's family will formally thank them for being godparents and being supportive of the family during their year of mourning. This person usually says a few words about the life of the departed so that the group can recognize the contributions he or she made to the family, the neighborhood, and the tribe. Attesting to the importance of this ritual, Spicer wrote that not hosting a Lenten pahko in one's house is acceptable, but it would be "unthinkable" not to have lutu pahko (1980, 85). The production of these ceremonies is no small feat, considering how much work and how many people are necessary to build ramadas, cook, prepare spaces, transport people from various villages, sing, pray, perform, and, of course, do all the cleaning and watching over children that such events require. At a lutu pahko ceremony that I filmed in January 2006, three dozen men and women prepared for weeks, and the guests and performers numbered over a hundred. At that time a Yoeme acquaintance in Potam told me that the village holds two or three lutu pahkom every month.

With the exception of Beals's one comment that food is prepared for the deceased souls, there are few references in the scholarship or at the actual ceremonies attesting to the presence of departed spirits at the lutu pahko. The ceremony appears to be focused primarily on the welfare of the living. As we saw in the previous mortuary rites, individual well-being and collective welfare are sustained through the joined duties of parents with godparents, church groups with Christian powers, residents of the particular village and their families with friends from neighboring villages, and nonchurch dancers with relatives outside the village like the deer or Surem. Spatially, the transformation of the house yard into ritual ground, divided between church and nonchurch societies, reflects and reaffirms the distinctly hybrid religious identity particular to the Yoemem. The cutting and burning of the black cords releases the living from mourning, but these acts also call the individuals back to their societal obligations and commence the celebration with food, family, friends, and the religious societies, all inside the house patio and ramada. By placing the books of the dead on the altar, the family members bring their memories of their ancestors to the lutu pahko, acknowledging their place in front of the cross, on the plane that defines yet bridges the two interrelated sides of Yoeme Catholicism. On one hand, we could say that the lutu pahko is the last funerary ritual for a person, but many Yoemem participate in an annual remembering of all departed souls come October.

Translated as the "offerings to the souls," annual animam miika ceremonies complete the set of formal, patterned practices of caring for deceased family members. Although the physical offering of food does not take place until the first week of November, *animam miika* refers to the presence of souls weeks before the actual table is set for the meal. The family members who have passed away return to the pueblo during the entire month of October (Fabila 1940, 187; Spicer 1980, 347). According to Spicer, the animam watch everything that people do. They are not a malevolent presence at this time, but they are elders. Hence a person must be careful of his or her behavior during October. In everything that living Yoemem do, they should show respect (Spicer 1954, 123). During this month, community members may be seen spending more time than usual at gravesites, repacking the dirt, repainting the crosses, setting out candles by the graves, or just sitting alone or with friends. This is my

10. The animam miika table is filled with items enjoyed by the deceased. The family's book of the dead is wrapped in a scarf front and center.

favorite time to be in Potam. These four weeks lead to an increase in stories and memories of a deceased family member. October is a time for fond recollections of when the individual was living and for more appropriate behavior, but not because the animam will report on what they see. Rather, the animam should be honored by their relatives' and friends' hard work and *tu'i hiapsim*, or "good hearts" (Spicer 1980, 326). The month ends in several evenings of hanging out with the dead. The cemeteries in the pueblos take on the mixed air of macabre and romance. Flowers and candles adorn all the graves while people play music and sit and have a drink with their departed loved ones.

On November 1, All Saints' Day, family members wrap crepe paper around the patio cross, and they may crown the cross with a paper or plastic wreath that will be taken to the cemetery the next day. Although there are variations, most households in the eight pueblos construct tables from mesquite, cane, and plywood, which are positioned directly against and in front of the house cross. These tables tend to be more than five feet tall, and they are covered with a clean tablecloth. Many Yoemem place flowers, candles, and a glass or bowl of water on the table. But soon they add many more items, primarily food, that their departed family members enjoyed while living. Some families include cigarettes, prepackaged candy, or soda — whatever they believe will make the animam happy. According to Savala, the souls can inhale the foods through their smells (1980, 198). Many Yoemem generally understand the animam as partaking of the food. I was once told that the meals nourish the animam for their long trip back to heaven, but Spicer may offer a more representative explanation when he writes that the offerings are made "so that the spirits will return to their land with good will toward the villagers until their next visit" (1980, 347).

I would be amiss not to point out once again the individual and collective labor involved in these "productions." Living in the pueblos, one is reminded at every meal of the lack of money to buy meat. They also lack money for covered shoes, eyeglasses, basic medical care, insulin for diabetics, books for the students. Traveling from the United States, I see a lot of need. But then you see the amount of human energy committed to the building of a dance ramada, the groups of women showing up with their own bags of flour or Maseca to spend hours making tortillas for the lutu pahko, or perhaps you see the family cooking all day and running to the markets at the last minute to set the perfect animam miika table. I have found myself on these errands to buy crepe paper, a wreath for the gravesite, or cigarettes for the departed. I have gone to the huya ania to get the best-looking mesquite limbs for a table, sweated throughout the afternoon to dig the holes for the table's legs, and then made sure the tabletop was perfectly level and the correct width to best show the flower embroidery on the tablecloth. And in these times I find myself counting the hours of labor and the expenses for the food and decorations. I see people struggling to make enough to feed their families, yet here they are cooking all day to put food on a plate on a tall table for the deceased. In contrast to houses made of cane and the poverty in the pueblos stand these abundant tables from which they feed their dead. Such celebrations are focal points of community commitment to their departed. The disparity between what is spent on the living to live and what is spent on the dead to live with respect is all the proof I need to truly know that these are not merely symbolic gestures of gratitude or ancestor worship. These are the acts of loving and giving that sustain kinship and endurance.

Most Yoemem set these animam miika tables in the afternoons or evenings when family members can stop by the store on their way home from work to buy candles or other food items for their visiting animam. If a household prepares a table, then the maehto and kantooram will visit the table, conducting a vigil service and reading the names from the family's book of the dead. The church group may socialize if they do not have to rush to the next house, but they are customarily offered food and drink to enjoy immediately or to take home to their families. At the end of the day, small flickers of candlelight can be seen throughout the cemetery, the neighborhoods, and on the community's edge bordering the desert. These lone, susceptible flames pay recognition to those who passed away outside of the village, traveling or running away, Christian or not, Yoeme or not (Painter 1986, 312).

The next day, All Souls' Day, families gather at the graves of their loved ones. With water buckets, tools, wreaths, flowers, candles, and other decorative items, they manicure the graves, markers, and surrounding area. Sometimes graves are partially unearthed and repacked to a smooth, elongated dome shape. The cross at the head of the grave might be made more stable. Fresh and plastic flowers are arranged in containers or simply laid on top of the low mounds. Commonly, toward evening family members use candles of all types to line the entire circumference of the grave or to place in an aesthetically pleasing order at the corners or along the top by the headstone. Chanting "Responses for the Dead," the maehto and kantooram walk from grave to grave. An occasional skyrocket may be heard. Soon the graveyard is filled with hundreds of people, even more candles, and the wonderful cacophony of songs, prayers, laughs, gossip, and stories. In this cemetery space Yoemem publicly and privately demonstrate their understanding that the deceased continue to be respected, active community members.[14]

What seems consistent from the earliest descriptions to the most recent is that Yoemem generally consider ancestors as able to return to the villages, that people generally have warm and intimate feelings toward animam, and that they understand animam as associated with the places of their burials (Pérez de Ribas 1999, 367; Spicer 1954, 123, 124; Spicer 1980, 328). Such views of death and the afterlife suggest that Yoeme relations with the dearly departed are spatially distinguished. Animam do not seem to be restricted to heaven or by inactive "sleep" until a later date, i.e., the tribulation or Second Coming. Associated with their burial places and able to inhabit the pueblo, animam continue to constitute notions of "local" pueblo life and collective identity. This place-conscious view of the deceased is noted by Spicer when he writes that the deceased are considered together in a spiritual world or "their land," but that this world's nature and conceptualization are not important to Yoemem.[15] The important issue is that households are understood as including nonliving members and that animam come to town (1980, 328, 347; 1984, 83). Spicer's description of conflicting Yoeme views of the afterworld is supported by the many contradictions he and Painter recorded regarding heaven, hell, and purgatory (Painter 1986, 89, 90–91; Spicer 1980, 67, 327, 328). However, the ethnographic sources agree that animam are more physically present to the community but are considered complementary to Christian dimensions.

The final aspect of the animam miika ceremonies that I want to describe is these other animam, the books of the dead. The term animam, as I have noted, refers to the spirits of the deceased as well as the books of the dead. I have confirmed Spicer's interpretation that no household was without a book of the dead, attesting to their widespread value in Yoeme communities (1984, 84). These books are clearly a primary reference for Yoeme interaction with the departed relatives. The books are small, often notebooks with either hard or soft covers. Many families keep the books wrapped in white cloth or silk scarves. They are not intentionally hidden or kept secret; they are objects of pride for some. As Spicer noted, "Keeping these and having them sung over as frequently as possible is an important feature of family life" (1954, 124). Better understanding the role that these books play in Yoeme ceremonies demonstrates how the departed souls have a place in contemporary pueblo life and how that place develops through a specific history of tribal literacy.

Only the maehto enters the names of the deceased family members. In addition to their Christian names, the maehto adds any ceremonial title or military office that the person held or attained, i.e., captain, general, or war chief. From the books that Spicer saw in Pascua Pueblo in the 1930s, frequently more than two hundred names of adults and almost as many children's names were written in each (1984, 84, 117). That number coincides with the books I saw. The names are divided into three groups: men, women, and children. The maehto also adds "special drawings" that have religious meaning. In the books I have seen, the writing is very neat and appears formal. Some sections of the book include prayers in Spanish, and other sections begin with short verses in Latin. The lists of names are followed by blank spaces in which names can be added later.

From ethnographic reports in multiple villages, scholars portray an active and constant relationship between the animam and the people. Yoemem place these books central to Lenten household fiestas and the Holy Cross ceremony in May (Painter 1986, 399–400, 517). Beals observed that in the 1930s Yoemem in Potam took the books to church every Sunday where prayers were said for them (1945, 81). One of my collaborators, in his fifties, said he has never known this to be the case. Spicer wrote that the books were taken to any ceremony where an altar was set up and where maehtom and kantooram gathered, since singing while the books were on an altar demonstrated the living's respect for departed community members. I have not seen that movement of books either. The sung-over animam (books) will in return help the living when they become animam (departed). I have not heard of the books as animated or empowered. They are not like crosses drawn on the ground that can bless the dancers. They seem to be more a site, like a gravesite, where presence is possible because communication and address provide access. Demarcations draw forth memories, and when embodied through a performative act like an oral reading or a procession, a relationship is affirmed as living and potent.

As a component of ceremonial place-making, the books of the dead signify borders between cosmological and civic dimensions. As noted in the previous descriptions of funerary practices, the books of the dead are placed on household altars and tables for animam miika. On the patio altar, the books sit on the raised platform that faces the divided spaces of church and nonchurch groups. Along with a cross, the books on the altars are above the ground where kantooram sit on mats and where the pahko'olam dance. As such, the books link the two spaces, dividing and crossing the border between church and nonchurch performances. The animam, both as "books" and "souls," receive the blessings of both parts of the one religious tradition. The books help mark distinct spaces within the ceremonies for the departed.

In many ways, the books of the dead exemplify place and boundary making in Yoeme ritual activity. Reflecting the distinct history of Jesuit presence in and then absence from the pueblos, the animam as books cross the categorical boundary between literate and nonliterate peoples. The uses of these books in funerary, household, and Lenten ceremonies show a local spatialization of Jesuit teachings within the Yoeme landscape and cosmography, since they are physically and ideologically central to the church and ania division/fusion. The reading of the names inside the books invokes the departed loved ones, their resting place near the church, and their visits to the pueblo each October. Animam miika performers make the written oral again. Additionally, when considered as core to post-Jesuit religious identity and the resulting set of activities for the caring of the deceased, the animam signify a means by which to discern otherness. Spicer grants that not all Yoemem in the 1800s would have had knowledge of the complex interactions and symbolism between the living and deceased Yoemem, yet he figures that no Mexican or other non-Yoemem were even slightly aware of them. I am struck by the way Spicer frames Yoeme religiosity as a means by which ethnic identity is asserted. Differing in opinion, I would say that ethnicity is the last thing on their minds when hearing the names of their loved ones. I've been there for those readings, and I'm convinced by the labor of the participants that one has the names read to demonstrate loyalty to a tradition that may provide some, particularly the young, with a sense of kinship solidarity. As with Surem stories, the animam remind Yoemem of the constantly present promise of relations forward and backward in time, above and beneath the earthly realm of human life and suffering.

Yoeme relations with their departed were indeed, in Spicer's words, "a source of sense of common identity among Yaquis. As such [they were] a basis for non-identification with Yoris [Mexicans] and others" (Spicer 1980, 309). Remaining true to his era's focus on resistance to cultural assimilation, Spicer saw how Yoemem perceived Mexicans as lacking in true Catholic devotion. Comparing the two groups' actions for All Souls' Day and animam miika, Yoemem could see that the Mexicans did not understand the souls as returning for an entire month, nor did they prepare elaborate meals for the deceased, keep books of the dead, or host the maehtom and kantooram for a household recitation of all the departed family members. Spicer related Yoeme views of Mexican Catholic ceremonials as "slipshod and shortened" (1943; 1980, 157, 326–27).

I do not doubt that many Yoeme notions of ethnic difference were and are expressed in terms of religious performance, but I would say the focus is internal rather than external. Through embodied ritual acts and oral history, countless Yoemem understand grounded cohesion in spite of spatial division between the immortal Surem and the mortal Yoemem. The mythically granted and designated homeland provides continued orientation to church as well as ania dimensionality. The historical kismet of temporary and controlled Jesuit instruction leads to community reliance on lay priests' writings and interpretations of Christianity and the Catholic cosmos. These three factors contributed to Yoemem understanding their collective identity as distinctly emplaced, composed of the living and deceased, and continued through ceremonial labor.

March 31, 2000. We left Tucson this morning at 3:45 a.m., and so before driving into Potam, Felipe and I decided to rest a bit under a large cottonwood tree outside of the village. After about an hour of sleeping in the shade and the cool breezes from the fields of wheat, we drove up to Guillermo's house around 2:30 p.m. There, over coffee, we discussed the trip and mutual friends and families. After an hour we heard the drum from across the plaza announcing the beginning of the konti. Guillermo, Felipe, and I walked to the church to see the people slowly coming from around the village. Standing in the slight shade of the church's bell tower to avoid the scorching heat, we saw the masked fariseos gathering between the church cross and the church doors. Godparents escorted little boy and girl angels between the two sides of the cemetery and into the front of the church. Because Wiivisim Pueblo was joining the Potam Easter ceremonies this year, the number of participants was larger than in the previous year. There were two crucifixes to carry accordingly.

Shortly after 4 p.m., an elder member of the kohtumre ya'ura (Lenten Society) approached us. After we tipped our hats, the man spoke a few sentences and Felipe and Guillermo each said a few words, all in the Yoeme language. The man left, and I asked Felipe why he had come over. Guillermo asked if I was strong, and I gave Felipe a confused look, not understanding the question's relevance. Felipe half-smiled and told me that "we" had just agreed to lead the konti by helping to carry the large crucifix and the statue of San Juan. I was floored. After years of trying to blend into the crowds, I was going to have to lead a large procession around the church plaza through the Stations of the Cross. And I would have to do it while lifting a heavy statue for over an hour. I understood Guillermo's question now: Did I want the cross, which is so heavy that it is carried in a cloth sling around the neck of the holder? Or did I want the San Juan duty, which requires four men to hold a statue level while walking quickly in unison? I volunteered to carry San Juan.

We removed our cowboy hats as we entered the church and walked to where San Juan stood next to the other male figures. As the kantooram, flag bearers, and the women's group started ordering themselves, Felipe and I tried to figure out how to hold our hats in one hand and hold the saint up high with the other, while keeping the platform's back half level with the front half, which was going to be carried by two men of differing heights. Since I was a good foot taller than the other three, I had to hold the post away from my shoulders, unable to rest the post near my neck, as I had seen before was the norm, particularly when we would stop at the Stations. Still inside the unlit church, I was already drawing attention. I resolved at that moment to remain focused during the konti on carrying San Juan with good heart, but I knew I was about to be visible to

YOEME PLACE-MAKING | 275

the community as never before, because I had never before been asked to be a godfather and participate in those pueblo-wide ceremonies either.

Surrounded by the soldiers in black and the masked big heads, the church groups began walking out of the church toward the first Station of the Cross. The flag bearers and candleholders led, followed by a man with an incense holder. San Pedro was carried by one man, as was San Paulo behind him. Felipe, the two other men, and I were next with San Juan. As we moved through the plaza center, I felt the spectators' stares, but I focused on simply carrying San Juan well. Guillermo followed with the large, six-foot-tall Potam crucifix. Behind him another man carried the Wiivisim cross. Maehtos, kantooram, angels, and flag bearers from the respective pueblos surrounded each cross. Surrounding these people was a massive crowd of konti procession participants of all ages. Trailing, but with increasing speed, were twenty-eight masked fariseos in two files. Along with the flag captains, kabos, and sergeants, the masked men were in pursuit of Jesus.

Felipe and I carried San Juan for the first four Stations. Then we walked alongside our relief walkers for three and carried him for the last seven Stations. We slightly dipped the saints as a genuflection toward the mesquite crosses that mark the stations. As the procession moved around the plaza, the dust billowed from the shuffling feet, coating our bodies. We literally became grounded, as a group, in our collective singing and walking the boundaries of the church area. Keeping the saints and Marys away from the pursuing army, we emplaced the story of Jesus and his struggles toward the cross. As I listened to the Latin and Spanish coming from the maehto and kantooram, I looked to my left and right and saw the masked fariseos, who kept anyone from leaving the procession with their threats of whipping or worse. At one of the last stations I remember looking back and seeing the other masked ones catching up to us. A protective urgency came over me and the others; we picked up the pace of the konti in order to outrun the men who were hunting Jesus. I actually felt fear when I saw the masked men approaching. I thought of the deer's animal friends in the monte, helping him escape the hunters. I thought of Yoemem in the seventeenth century, inheriting a Christian mythology that they blended with indigenous worldviews. I thought of the Yoemem in the following centuries who had to run through the desert from Mexican soldiers in

11. Two men walk across Potam Pueblo plaza, the intersection of church, cemetery, and the paths of the kontim in the foreground.

order to protect their cultural inheritance. I thought of Yoemem immigrants running through the desert across la frontera al otro lado.

When we returned to the church, my shirt stuck to my body and my arms were tired. But we had to wait for all the groups to return before setting down San Juan. I was relieved to be done and out of the dust. Yet the dust was in me and on me. I had withstood my own fears of the unwanted attention during the konti, and I felt a sense of achievement for contributing my physical labor to the pueblo's hard work. The man who approached us earlier came again as we were slapping the dust off our hats and pants. He asked if I could carry the pueblo crucifix on the last Friday of Lent, two weeks away. Guillermo translated the question for me and relayed back to the gentleman that I might not be back on that date. Two hours after we left, the three of us walked back to the campo for squash soup and refried beans. Our bodies were a bit sore and dirty. We were very hungry. We smiled a lot that night as we joked about each other's performance — our struggles with the weight, our too-slow or too-fast pace, our fears of being whipped by the fariseos or of being outrun by the masked men. As I was about to fall asleep, I longed for a shower and hoped I would be back for the last Friday of Lent.

Konti Processions as Acts of Possession

As with the various ceremonies for the deceased, Sunday kontim exemplify an expressive form of Yoeme worldview that extends beyond the temporal bounds of the Lenten season. Perhaps because these processions do not directly involve pahko'ola or deer dances, they have not received significant scholarly attention. Another similarity to funerary rituals is the way Sunday kontim reflect Yoeme locality in the embodiment of boundary and land maintenance. In these mythically grounded processions, Yoemem move across the land, inscribing their distinct place and history in the earth, nonliterately mapping their geographic, cosmological, and civic relations.

The Yoeme word *konti* (*kontim* is plural) can be translated as "a circular procession," though it has come to mean simply "procession." Spicer and Painter recognize konti as a surrounding, taking over, or taking possession (Spicer 1980, 99; Painter 1986, 117). When I asked Felipe Molina if "possession" could be said in Yoeme as "konti," he responded that the link between kontim and possessions holds symbolically. As I understand him, just as a procession (konti) may surround (konte) a particular place, that area might be said to be under the control of those surrounding it. In household fiesta kontim, for example, the church group proceeds in a line around the patio space, literally making place for their effective ritual labor. In Lenten kontim, fariseos take over crosses, households, holy figures, and the church plaza. Since Lenten kontim are performances of the Way of the Cross, and since they have been studied extensively as the localization of the passion of Jesus within the syncretic Holy Week ceremonies, I will limit my scope to Sunday kontim.[16]

In their general form, processions cannot be clearly characterized as pre- or postcontact activities. According to Bruce Smith (1999), processions as acts of possession were a regular feature in England from as early as the fifteenth century. Called Rogationtide, Gang-Days, or "beating the bounds," parish members walked and prayed in processions along the boundaries of the parish, proclaiming "the church, the fields and woods, the houses and streets as *their* place in the world" (1999, 32, original emphasis). Although the Rogationtide seems related to kontim, no direct connection has been traced.[17] Beals (1945, 202) accepts Pérez de Ribas's claim that Jesuits directed the first outside processions in pueblos neighboring the Yoeme; further, he applies this claim cross-culturally to the Yoemem. As with almost all of Beals's interpretations, this one too seems contrary to contemporary local practices and interpretations.

The earliest explorers described precontact Aztecan processions (Braden 1966, 72). Spicer also remarks (1980, 61) that pre-Christian processions were present in tribal communities that neighbored the Yoemem. Painter quotes two Yoemem who state what I have heard consistently in my fieldwork: that in the Hiak Vatwe, animals were decorated with ribbons and carried around in processions accompanied by drumming (1986, 122). Yoeme friends have told me that processions were a part of their aboriginal ceremonial activity, entailing frogs or other small ground-burrowing creatures that could help bring the rains. However, they claimed not to know much more about their form or meaning. If Beals was right that aboriginal Yoeme ritual proceeded counterclockwise, then he was right in one sense — kontim do follow an indigenous directional logic (1943, 65; 1945, 189; Spicer 1980, 175).

Every Sunday morning after Mass is read by the church maehto, the eldest captains of the military society lead the other military society members, governors, fiesta sponsors, the church-based groups, and then the *kia pueplom* (just people), community members without current ceremonial obligations, through the front doors of the church. According to Spicer's observations in Potam, the most important function of the military society was leading the Sunday kontim, carrying an image of the Virgin of Guadalupe (the society's patroness), holding their bows, and wearing their customary fox skin headdresses (1980, 210). Behind them the governors stiffly hold their canes of office upright in front of themselves. Before the procession reaches the first of the four crosses surrounding the church cemetery, a *fiestero* captain waves a flag three times at the cross in a ritual salute. After the image bearers, military captains, and village participants arrive, they perform devotions of prayer and song to the cross. Repeating this stop at the other three crosses, the procession circles the cemetery on the west side of the church and proceeds inside through the front doors (Spicer 1954, 140; 1980, 173–75; 1997, 77–78). As an example of the group's size, Spicer confirmed decades ago what we might find in contemporary times: that the Sunday kontim could have between seventy and eighty formal participants and twenty-five or more kia pueplom (1954, 141). Although these numbers might not be representative of the other eight pueblos, I concur with Spicer that in Potam at least, the Sunday konti was the "fundamental ceremonial activity in pueblo life" (1954, 139). To better understand his comment, we need to consider the significance of the four crosses, the leading role of the military society, and the ritual effect of collective movement in a procession.

Interpretations of the four crosses will undoubtedly vary among those asked, but Spicer gives us a sense that the four konti crosses generally symbolize territorial boundaries. Crosses as designs predated Spanish arrival in Mexico (Braden 1966, 61–62; Pérez de Ribas 1999, 346). Spicer notes that the four tall crosses of the Sunday kontim previously symbolized Matthew, Mark, Luke, and John, and he speculates that the crosses and a weekly procession honoring them were likely missionary introductions (1980, 174). Yet as we find throughout Yoeme culture, the meanings of the konti crosses now reflect the distinctive blend of Yoeme myth and history. According to Spicer, the crosses have come to represent the "four corners of the world," "of the Christian world," "of the Yoeme world," and, more specifically, "of the four corners of Yoeme territory" (1954, 139; 1980, 173, 310; 1997, 78; Crumrine and Spicer 1997, 535, 544). The view that Yoeme lands have four boundaries is supported in stories of a giant Yoeme bowman who, at the direction of a woman named Ana Maria, shot four arrows from Takalaim to define Yoeme territory. Another story describes a Yoeme bowman's contest with the Spanish king to see who could shoot farthest. Shooting in the four directions, the Yoeme outdistanced the king and won the written title to their land (Evers and Molina 1989, 13). In tandem with the mythopoetic Testamento, Spicer suggests that the symbolic association of these crosses with land proprietorship developed during the late nineteenth century as a response to tribal displacement and pueblo revitalization (1980, 174). Hence the crosses that structure the Sunday kontim offer another example of Yoeme-Jesuit collaboration, continuing processes of societal change, and the distinctive local history of the pueblo.

As I previously noted, Spicer understood the military society's "most important function" as leading the Sunday processants (governors, church societies, and villagers), wearing the Coyote Society headdress of fox skin, carrying their bows, and carrying the image of their patroness, Our Lady of Guadalupe. Although his characterization seems simple enough, Spicer was articulating kontim as the fusion of precontact, socio-religious organizations with a post-Jesuit "new mythology" of divine territorialism. The precontact link to the kontim is most evident in the military society's leading role.

By wearing their headdresses and carrying their bows, the captains represent the Coyote Society, an aboriginal religious group that is affiliated with the aniam and the protection of all Yoemem. Coyote songs are similar to deer songs in subject matter, and coyote dances are somewhat similar to pahko'ola ceremonies in form. The captains of the military society are still referred to as bow leaders, the only military title in the Yoeme language. The coyote dances were associated with military action by both Mexican and Spanish witnesses (Evers and Molina 1989, 2; Spicer 1980, 182). This protective role remains paramount for coyote society members and for community members. When gifted a coyote society headdress once, I was told it would help me "work to protect Yoeme culture," although I also got the sense it was to remind me of the consequences of my irresponsibility. Throughout the year the society still supervises community activities and ceremonies as guardians. The sense among local community members is that the coyote society may enforce a more rigorous standard of cultural preservation. I have been told on many occasions not to bring a camera or recorder when we have spotted someone from the Coyote Society in the crowd. I have also seen my collaborators go talk to a coyote before giving me the go-ahead to take a picture of a church. The society members are charged with the duties of managing and protecting town territory, tribal lands, and the Yoeme people.

In Sunday kontim, these military captains demonstrate their commitment to both civic and territorial protection. The bows that they carry bring to mind the Yoeme bowman who, in some legends, won the title to the land from the king of Spain. As guards for the governors and administrators of Yoeme lands, the bow leaders are in service to civil authority and public welfare. Specifically, because the governors carry their canes of office (considered gifts from the king) and take them to the symbolic four corners of Yoeme land that were acknowledged by the king, the military society is fulfilling its responsibility to protect tribal territory in that one act of guarding the governors (Spicer 1980, 181, 209).

I described Spicer's characterization of the military society's significance in the kontim as also referencing a post-Jesuit "new mythology," since he reads Our Lady of Guadalupe as a Yoeme borrowing of Mexican Marian devotion from the mid-1800s (1980, 194). Spicer hypothesizes that Juan Banderas, a Yoeme military leader who attracted widespread support among Yoemem and other tribes in the 1820s, transformed the Virgin of Guadalupe from the Mexican patroness of revolting forces into the patroness of Yoeme soldiers and native resistance (Spicer 1980, 130–33, 183–84). We know that Our Lady of Guadalupe became a Creole-Indian mediator for many anti-Spanish sentiments at the beginning of the nineteenth century. These petitions were couched in terms of land, agricultural fertility, liberty, and equality (Ricard 1966; V. Turner 1974; Wolf 1965). We also know that during that same period Yoemem were reorganizing the highly Jesuit-influenced church and military societies in response to external pressures on territorial and town unity (Spicer 1980, 184). As Spicer argues, the convergence of these changes resulted in Yoemem relying more on rituals and myths that strengthen civil authority, involvement in ceremonial societies, and religious entitlement to land. Hence the Sunday konti develops more explicitly as a constant embodied retracing and singing of the boundaries sanctioned by Our Lady of Guadalupe. But what is it about this embodied retracing and singing that makes the Sunday konti the "fundamental ceremonial activity," as Spicer claimed?

In his study of public ritual in Santa Fe, New Mexico, Ronald Grimes explains that processions are usually interpreted in two ways: either as descriptions of its most general features, or through the selecting and reciting of a historical or mythical narrative. Grimes describes processions as typically composed of ordinary actions (walking, singing, carrying, praying) that take on "extraordinary symbolic significance" (1992, 62). As an example, Grimes notes that in the processants' traveling they bear witness to sites, possibly offering or reaffirming religious promises. Grimes also notes that movements to and through landscapes are acts of inclusion. The processants acquire physical relations with those "out there," as well as "up there" (1992, 68). In this shift toward understanding movement, Grimes's work parallels my study of kontim securely within a performance studies mode.

The Sunday kontim affirm Yoeme stewardship, religiously sanctioned, of their tribal territory. The processions also recognize that the territory has authoritatively established boundaries, signified by the four crosses. Surrounding the cemetery, the kontim relate Yoeme landownership to ancestral presence and the departed relatives to the living community. Led by church and society members, escorting symbols of religious (Our Lady of Guadalupe) and government authority (canes of office), the kontim demonstrate a collectively cohesive regard for pueblo and "homeland."[18] The weekly repetition of the konti circuit provides a constant public actualization of the postdiluvial singing of the boundaries and establishment of the Santam Liniam Divisoria, holy dividing lines. In this re-membered Testamento, we are shown how kontim are effective: singing over an area makes place. Accompanied by angels, prophets, and Our Lady of Guadalupe, Yoeme movement across land in song and prayer forever entrusts the demarcated ground to the people.

Nonliterate Cartography

Recalling my intention to study performance as nonliterate writing, I propose that Yoeme ceremonial activity generally and Sunday kontim particularly demonstrate a type of indigenous cartographic practice. I am not suggesting that Yoemem produce maps in these processions, but rather that their actions are a kind of mapping. I am obviously extending the metaphor of map making. As Denis Wood details in his critical analysis of Brian Harley's work, maps only exist in their inscription. Dances come from the sign system of dance; maps come from the sign system of cartography. I agree with Wood that mapping is not simply an externalization of a mental map but that the conventional sign system of mapping leads to the map discourse function. As he writes, "This situation will call for a story and that social situation will call for a dance and a third will call for a map. But this does not mean that stories and dance and maps are the same thing. It only means they vary with the discourse function they fulfill" (Wood 1993, 53). Where I differ from Wood is his move from this previous statement to his next deduction that "as the story exists in its telling, and the dance in its dancing, the map exists in its inscription. And it is this fine line of this inscription that differentiates something we might call mapping . . . from mapmaking" (1993, 53). Here Wood assumes that codes, signifiers, and functions are incapable of expressing more than one type of discourse. But what if a situation called for embodied acts of inscription that told a story yet left no artifact? Then a simple map wouldn't do, nor would a song, nor would a dance. You would have to practice all three discursive forms. Of course, Wood would always be able to define these acts as outside the object-oriented view of cartography (since maps are those things that can be measured repeatedly, shared as objects for study, perhaps used in courts of law).[19] But mapping in practice does not necessarily respect such definitions.

Some scholars have expanded the definition of writing to include systems of signified meanings (as opposed to signifying words) and discourse (as opposed to simply phonemic and morphemic) systems (Boone 1994; Gelb 1963; Hill 1967). What is needed now is an application of this expansion to other inscriptive acts, such as cartography.[20] How do non-Western mappings fit within or lie outside the Western assumption that maps are defined by their objectivity, transportability, scale, framing, selection, and coding? Can maps consist of settings, actors, and narrative? Can maps be so personal that they require embodiment? Let's imagine a map that appears only when danced, that realizes the mythology of our people, and that explains a community's past and future. As David Turnbull finds in his study of aboriginal Australian maps,

> If maps are seen as theories in the sense of fully articulated objective knowledge, then only one small group of maps appears to qualify as real maps — the supposedly accurate contemporary Western maps. We have seen that there are difficulties with that position. On the one hand, it fails to acknowledge the workability and potential power of maps from non-Western cultures, while on the other hand, it fails to acknowledge the contingent character of Western maps. The approach we are considering here, by recognising maps as embodying shared examples of practice, makes it perfectly reasonable to accept all maps as having a local, contingent and indexical character intimately tied to human purpose and action. (1989, 61)[21]

Turnbull has been at the forefront of scholarship on non-Western cartographic practices, examining various forms of graphic signs for their mapping significance. His work goes some distance in considering the ways people perform maps.

In my review of cartographic theory, only a few scholars take seriously mapping acts beyond the two-dimensional surface. For example, Wystan Curnow (1999) describes the use of embodied forms of mapping used by conceptual artists. Although still focused on physical maps, Mark Warhus (1997) provides further evidence that Western ideas of mapping, particularly a value on permanency, cloud our views of native cartography. He notes that "when a map was needed to show the way or convey a message, it would be drawn out on the ground, in the snow, or in the ashes of a campfire" (1997, 3). Warhus then expands on this description of map making in the earth and shows the complexities involved in such acts:

> Native American maps are always secondary to the oral "picture" or experience of the landscape. Routes, landmarks, sacred sites, and historical events formed a "mental map" that wove together geog-

raphy, history, and mythology. Lacking the artifice and conventions of western maps, these Native American maps are windows on a multidimensional landscape. Their richness is found in the unwritten texts of history, mythology, and spiritual belief. When viewed through the oral tradition, and what has been recorded of the peoples and individuals who are represented, it is possible to glimpse the different ways in which Native Americans perceived their land and how their cultures and technologies enabled them to share the universal human experience of place. (1997, 8)

By using words like *sophistication, richness,* and *technologies,* Warhus portrays indigenous mapping much as I argued that examining nonliterate writing processes might. Defying notions of "primitive" and "simplistic," native cartographic practices bring together contemporary politics, tribal myths, historic events, ancestral knowledge, and oral geography. To glean the "local" theory from these practices, we must first ask how such acts of mapping function within the specific societies. Turnbull argues this point effectively: "In the light of these considerations we should perhaps recognise that all maps, and indeed all representations, can be related to experience and that instead of rating them in terms of accuracy or scientificity we should consider only their 'workability' — how successful are they in achieving the aims for which they were drawn — and what is their range of application" (1989, 42). Perhaps more people will follow these authors' leads and look beyond Western cartographic theory and history to convey how indigenous peoples interpret mapping. One scholar who I believe accomplishes such work is Vishvajit Pandya.

Writing about the Ongees, a hunting and gathering group of Little Andaman, Pandya (1990) considers the relationship between the ordering of space and their patterns of movement. Pandya specifically moves beyond the Durkheimian symbolic analysis of space to demonstrate how the symbolic aspects of space are experienced by, derived from, and substantiated by individuals' actions. Ongee mythology, Pandya demonstrates, describes how the ordering of the cosmos depended on ancestral spirits categorizing the various ways that movements create space, i.e., birds and insects can fly and so they live in a world of light (sky), cats and lizards can climb up and down as well as swim and walk, thus they live in a world of shadow (land), and so forth. Except for the preborn, the deceased, and the religious specialist, all human movement, which is horizontal, is carefully considered in relation to spirit movement, which is vertical. Although deceased individuals or those not yet born may not yet be moving horizontally, they are still considered "human." Likewise, the spirits are considered to be human as well; they have either died or will be born. Thus it is not the relationship between spirits and humans that create demarcated space for interaction; it is their movements (Pandya 1990, 780). As Pandya's work shows, Ongee myth presents a map representing how movements create spatio-social order: "Ongee cosmology provides a model for how people think and is the source of their code of conduct. Ongee children learn to read the cosmological map while they learn their expected duties and tasks" (1990, 782–83). Pandya writes: "The conversion of myth into real day-to-day practice makes the Andamanese myth a map embodying and conveying knowledge of terrain, space, topography, and different forms of movement. The myth has a maplike quality in which movement orders spatial divisions" (1990, 782). In this detailed description of Ongee seasonal migrations, hunting paths, and concepts of spirit-human relations, Pandya allows us to follow one specific community's articulation of emplaced myth.

Pandya's attention to ethnocartography offers a productive way to view Yoeme ritual and cosmology. Since the Testamento describes the "original" formation of a Yoeme place in the world as a procession around territorial boundaries, Sunday kontim become recognizable as retracings of that map. Many Yoemem are clearly competent in literal map drawing and reading, and in fact they openly share their interest in maps of the *hiakim*. But this does not exhaust their "mapping" activity. As possessive acts, the kontim inscribe identity in socioreligious and spatial-performative terms. The order of the processants is constituted in terms of both societal rank and ritual functions, thereby demonstrating the interdependence and importance of the religious groups. Walking through the cemetery and circling the church, Yoeme movement reaffirms the deceased as a part of the local, living community that belongs to, as well as holds the "divine" title for, their land.

Similar to the Ongee narrative of ancestral cosmic ordering, the singing tree connects living Yoemem with their ancestors through the landscape. The Surem living in the oceans, hills, and mountains are related to Yoemem. The land is not simply a space to be sold for credit bailouts but, rather, the home of the Surem. Where they emerge and why they meet living Yoemem remain the heart and soul of the songs and dances. These songs and dances are modes of sustenance on which Yoeme identity continues. The Testamento exemplifies the performative way Yoeme religious processions create and maintain the boundaries around their land. The strongest Yoeme claim of sovereignty is not that they lived in a specific place the longest, but that they have been making that place their own through the human labor that constitutes all ritual activity. These are the intersections between performance and legal studies. Yoemem work the land, but they also work to make the land significant: their ceremonial acts affirm the community's value. We only get a slight sense of these relationships through papers and books.

Ethnographic Dialogue 6

DAVID SHORTER: When a person dies, the first thing that happens is that an elder or one of the oldest men in the community goes to ring the church bells.

RESPONDENT: Yes, that still happens.

DS: And they light bottle rockets immediately after the bells.

R: They do this before they ring the bells. When a person dies, like away from the town, whether it be in Obregón, Guyman, or Hermosillo, or another city at a hospital or clinic, when the car brings them back to their home here, the family lights three bottle rockets. The first one is to welcome them, the next is to announce their arrival home, and the third is to tell the town to come see them. Then the mourners go to the priest or church assistant and says, "Sir, I want you to do us a favor. We want the bells to ring, please, so that the town will know that our son, our family member, has died and is at home."

DS: Are the fireworks symbolic, or do they actually do something?

R: No, they are symbols, as you say. The first one welcomes the body, makes it known that they have arrived at your house.

DS: And because of the third one, the people come and watch over the body?

R: The third one is to call the attention of the people around town. After lighting the fireworks, they go see the priest so that they can ring the bells for the deceased. Then the priest says to the mourners, "You know that within an hour the *maehto* [lay priest] and the *kantooram* [female singers] are going to offer their prayers so that your loved one's soul can rest a little while waiting for the beginning of the wake." The prayers serve the deceased so that they do not fall into the hands of the demon, or so that they do not go into the darkness, but instead go to the light and to the one that gives eternal light to the deceased. It is a special prayer that they offer to those who have died or are dying.

DS: And at this time, only the godparents, the family, the singers, and the maehto are there?

R: No, at this moment the godparents are not there, just family. And after the maehto and singers pray, then the most respected family member who knows the language is going to tell the maehto, "We are now going to watch over the deceased." Then this respected family member goes to get the five pairs of godparents.

DS: So there are ten godparents?

R: Ten. And it is essential that you also have the people who baptized him, which makes twelve. The death godparents are always five pairs, no more. And if a person's childhood godparents die first, that person has the honor of visiting their bodies because he was a godchild of theirs. So when my father's godparents died, he went to watch over the bodies, accompanying their families, taking candles to the novenas, and bringing groceries to those families to help during the wake.

DS: What if the body is that of a baby? Is it true they take the body to the house of the birth godparents?

R: Currently, it is not like this all of the time. As soon as a child dies in a house, or in a hospital away from the town, or in a city, they bring them directly home. But as soon as they come home, the parents have to contact their godparents and tell them: "You know what, *kompae*? I am very sorry that your godchild has just died, and I want you to go get them." These are the ways of the Yoemem. Then they take the body to the godmother's or godfather's house, where they watch over them. The family members of the baby accompany the godparents to their house. Then the godfather has the obligation of making a celebration with *pahko'olam*, *matachines*, the kantooram, and the maehto. The godparents have to supply the food; they have to supply everything. And for the day when they bury the baby, the godparents have to make the little paper flowers. They are like papier mâché, or fine Asian paper, with the shapes of wings, extending into the air. Thus they put these little wings with the rosary and the little flowers and bury them with the baby in green or black cloth. Just as there are five mysteries on a rosary, there have to be five little flowers signifying the child's rosary.

DS: And for each person that dies, a separate gravestone is made close to a family plot?

R: When burying bodies, we cannot have a space of more or less than ten inches from another coffin, or sometimes we bury them as did the ancestors without a coffin, without anything except a sheet around them. We wrap them in the cloth and put them into the ground. And after the official prays over them, he gives them a blessed burial. Then the godparents are given permission to bury them. And the godparents offer the first words to those who are burying the body. Then the people pick up a bit of earth, and they throw it as a blessing, saying, "I am giving you a holy burial like the Master so that God forgives you. And wherever you are, may God gather you so that he has you." That is what we say at the peak of the burial.

DS: After the burial, they invite people to the house. Do they also bring out their book of the dead, their *anima*?

R: Yes, yes, it is there. Each family has a little book where they write the names of the people who have died, all of their relatives. If an uncle dies in Vicam, or in La Loma, or in Wuiviis, and even if they cannot go visit them, they put those names in the little books, called "*animam.*" And on the day of a burial, they put that little book on the table in the houseyard, and the maehto comes and opens up the book and reads the names of all those who have died. It is like a small Mass for the body lying there.

DS: Do you think it is possible to say that there are two sides of a houseyard at this time: one side for church activities like the kantooram, the singing, and this little Mass?

R: Yes, yes.

DS: And do they dress the body in the manner of the person's position in society? Do they dress a captain's body as a captain?

R: Yes and no. It is like an abbreviation of their position.

DS: Like a sort of sign of who they are.

R: Yes, a real sign. That is what they give him.

DS: Is it true a pahko'ola receives a note from the maehto explaining that he is a pahko'ola?

R: Yes. "He is a pahko'ola."

DS: Still they do this?

R: Yes. And they still make a pahko'ola mask for him. And they put it on top of the head.

DS: Okay. And all bodies receive a rosary?

R: All bodies.

DS: And all are wrapped in a white sheet?

R: They are often laid in a white sheet for the visitations.

DS: The visitors all see the body?

R: Yes, all the guests, all the celebrants.

DS: All the neighbors, friends, and family come and see the body?

R: Yes, yes. Everyone can. It is the last good-bye: "au emo

hiokoewame" (asking forgiveness for anything done in their lifetimes), they greet them in their last dwelling place.

DS: Is it true that it is okay to cry, but when a child dies, a baby, one should not cry because the baby is going directly to La Gloria?

R: Well, the thing about crying is that they cry for everyone that dies, old or young, whether they had a respected position or not. They cry because they had a lot of love, they loved them a lot, and they cry from these feelings, from seeing that these families have lost a loved one.

DS: I have read that in older times, before now, the family had to change houses when a person died in the house. The family could usually move. But today that isn't normal, is it?

R: Well, it is still something like this, but not how you asked it. They rearrange those houses when someone dies in a house that he built with his own hands. But if they didn't make it with their own hands, there isn't a problem. The house stays the same, the things as they are. It goes on the same. They will change the knots in some weavings, or they will rearrange the patio that he made in his life, because they say that if things are not rearranged, then his soul will not be able to rest in peace comfortably. They have to change these things before the ninth day passes so that the deceased can rest tranquilly.

DS: Are the clothes of the dead person burned?

R: No, they have never burned them. They give the buried person one or two styles of clothes because they continue to matter. They have a double life: here and in heaven or hell. Therefore, the people who die, being children or adults, have to be given one or two types of clothes so that they can use them wherever they go. I cannot say what they wear in heaven, since no one has experienced this type of situation. It is a saying, like only a legend.

DS: The books say that if a man dies, his wife cannot brush her hair for fifteen days. Have you heard this?

R: Your wife has a phase of not grooming for nine days. On the tenth or eleventh day, she can groom her hair or groom as she always did, just without soap. In the history of our tribe, the Yoeme, soap is very bad because of its whiteness. They call it *hiowam*. Hiowam is what befalls the eyes when one is not even old because he or she did not take precautions to uphold a rule when a family member died.

DS: I have heard that during these nine days, it is not good to eat meat or sweets or to drink milk.

R: Milk is not prohibited anymore. Sweets? No, not sweets. Well, milk and cheese are okay. But not meat, because I have heard people still say that eating meat within the nine days is like eating the body of someone you just buried.

DS: And after the nine days?

R: Afterwards, one can eat meat and sweets.

DS: After someone dies, I have heard that some families use smoke in the house.

R: To bless it.

DS: With smoke?

R: With incense, but not that much here in Potam Pueblo. They use blessed water. They put that water where the deceased lived: in the bedroom, in the hallway, where they sat, in the bathrooms. They do this so that he is not suffering and so that he will let go of his house and move in another direction and that he leaves his family comfortably tranquil. Although the family hurts to have lost him, that dear one, there is nothing more they can do for him.

DS: Do they avoid using the name of the person?

R: No, just the opposite. A son or grandchild may be named after the person who has died. "I am going to name my son after my uncle, who rests in peace, and he will carry his name."

DS: Somewhere I read that Yoemem in Arizona told an anthropologist that godparents give a new name to the person who died.

R: Yes, they do that here. The five couples, the five pairs of godparents, give a godparents' name to the deceased. These names are given in front of the cross of forgiveness. These are also rules for the person widowed: they have particular regulations. For instance, they cannot eat seafood, deer, or pork.

DS: For nine days?

R: No, for an entire year.

DS: In an older book, it says that Yoemem think that the soul of a person who does not have a spouse will go immediately to heaven. But a person that has a spouse will wait in the house for three days. Have you heard something like this?

R: No, that isn't true. Yes, they say that the deceased are waiting for their family members to join them. If the husband dies first, he will wait for his wife, and vice versa. They will wait for an indefinite amount of time until the spouse dies, if they were married by the church. If they were not married by the church, then there is not such a thing. They say that people married by the church are with a light, and they walk and play where one can see them. But when a child is born out of wedlock, then they are crying in the darkness. It is like a sense of salvation where you have to be married to have a saved soul. There is no hope of reuniting when the union was not blessed.

DS: There was a famous Yoeme poet named Refugio Savala who said that spirits, or souls, float near the house for nine days. But the majority of Yoemem, would they agree?

R: Well, from my point of view and from my knowledge of the elders, of my parents who rest in peace, and other elders to whom I have listened, this is true. The spirit will be present for nine days in the house without bothering anyone. No one will see them. And when the nine-day period has passed, they are given permission to go to heaven.

DS: In 1720, a Jesuit wrote that all the Yoemem associated souls with where the body is buried. For this Jesuit, it was an aboriginal Yoeme feeling that there is a relationship between the soul of the person who has died and where the body was buried near the church.

R: Well, not precisely. The tribe, they were Catholics, so they preferred to be buried in the hallowed ground, in a cemetary near the church. This was verified at the level of the eight pueblos that every church had its cemetery. But it is not because some people came and said, "We are here. Make this and make that." They do not have a test, or a person, who can say what happened when people arrived to the Yoemem. We did not even speak Spanish! It is as if I were to speak with an American. He would speak to me in English, and I would speak to him in Yoeme. Well, he wouldn't understand me, nor I him. How am I going to teach myself to speak English? In a yearlong course? Perhaps these days one can speak English in a year, or whatever language, with current methods. Those that exist in these times. If the Yoemem had the ability to defend their own territory, Mexicans also had the means. In those times it was kill or be killed. They didn't have confidence in their parents, not in priests, not in bishops. How are they going to have relations with people who were like dogs and cats. I believe it is not possible. In the first place, they do not understand what it is that they are trying to say. If they don't know when the other says, "Give me a glass of water," and the other does not know what to say back, well, instead of giving him water he throws a stone at him and kills him for saying something he did not understand. Or, better yet, what if he takes it as offensive what was said to him? Being of good heart like the Jesuits, the San Franciscans, they may say something, but really one does not understand. Is he saying this? Is he saying that? Back then, you would simply kill someone who was not of your own race. "What's wrong with this guy? Well, we must kill him!" In those times, there was just killing. That was the way of life. Even the Yoemem would kill people they encountered on the roads, and others did the same. For this reason, I say that perhaps it is not true what they said about Yoeme ways of life before the Jesuits. Much later, during the early times of our Catholicism, they were able to look back and amend the things we did before. But I doubt very much, I'm simply not very sure about, what they said about our ways of life. That's my point of view.

DS: You don't think that the souls of deceased people live in the pueblo all year?

R: No.

DS: Only in October, for *anima miika*?

R: Anima miika. The day of the dead is the first day of October. That is when the dead arrive from heaven. We Yoemem have verified it with noises. At four in the morning on October 1, in your house you hear noises, or you hear steps. We are familiar with these moments, and we know that our ancestors, our dear ones, come to visit us only for one month. At four in the morning on November 2, they begin their return back. It is when they say that we must give food and put out a small table. We do not give some bread or one plate, not something small, but with a lot of what they ate in life. We make it as an offering on the little table. And for those that have been dead less than a year, they do not come back in that first year. They are not allowed to come here.

DS: The family has twenty-four hours to bury the body after death?

R: Not precisely. Historically, the elders used a salve, like a bath, on their dear ones with branches from this area. And this would preserve the body so that it did not deteriorate.

DS: And there is a procession with the body?

R: To the church.

DS: And after the burial there is a *pahko*?

R: On the ninth day. Then, one year later, they have the *lutu pahko*.

DS: Isn't there a pahko on the day of the burial?

R: No.

DS: Okay. After the procession to the church with the body, there is not a pahko'ola dance?

R: No.

DS: Okay. And presently, in contemporary times, bodies are never buried in the *huya ania*?

R: No.

DS: Not even for a pahko'ola?

R: No.

DS: In much older times, do you think the bodies were cremated? Edward Spicer says they only began to bury bodies after the Jesuits arrived.

R: No, they never cremated bodies.

DS: Do families try to bury their dear ones near the bodies of their godparents who passed away before them?

R: No. What they try to do is bury them as close as possible to a relative.

DS: Sometimes that is impossible?

R: Yes.

DS: The bodies are always buried with their feet toward the church?

R: Yes, every time. No one is buried with the head toward the church.

DS: And all are sprinkled with blessed water?

R: Yes.

DS: By the godparents?

R: No.

DS: It is a bit odd how on so many of these matters the books have it wrong.

R: Yes.

DS: It is interesting at least. Is it true that the family of the person who died cannot look at or visit the burial procession?

R: That is also a lie.

DS: After the burial, the whole group then returns to the house for a dinner?

R: No. After burying them, they give thanks at the Cross of the Pardon, and then only the family returns to the house. From there, they simply thank the relatives and remind them of the novena nine days later.

DS: And is it always exactly nine days later?

R: Yes, nine days.

DS: And then they have a big meal.

R: Yes.

DS: So I understand now. Immediately after the buriel, there is nothing special.

R: No, there isn't anything. Only sorrow.

DS: You said last week that it is not true that Yoemem always use blue crosses for the grave marker. Is it only a matter of money?

R: The tombs, they are of all sizes: big, some adorned with saints, some have the luxuries of coffins, but none of this is necessary. The people who do these things have money. If you don't have these things, it is the same. It is not necessary to build such things.

DS: Have you seen that cemetery with Asian pogodas as tombs?

R: Yes.

DS: In Pitihaya, a town closer to the sea, a professor in 1945 saw lots of graves marked with shells. Is it simply because it is closer to the sea and so they use shells?

R: Yes, they are using them as adornment.

DS: In Wuivisiim, which is a community with very few Mexicans, the crosses are all made of wood, not concrete. Is this simply an issue of money?

R: Yes.

DS: A year after death, there is a lutu pahko. Is there always a deer dance at these?

R: Yes.

DS: Are the lutu pahkom organized and arranged by the godparents of the deceased?

R: No.

DS: They have an altar at the lutu pahko?

R: It is like a table, usually black.

DS: And it has the family's book of the dead?

R: The book must be there.

DS: And one lays out the woven cane matts for the kantooram to sit and lie upon?

R: Yes, one must do that.

DS: And on the othe side of the cross, is the area exclusively for the pahko'olam and deer?

R: Yes, and the musicians.

DS: Do they ever say a formal rosary?

R: No.

DS: The family wears the black cords around their necks at this point?

R: Yes, around their necks. That is the lutu pahko.

DS: Does the lutu pahko always culminate on a weekend? Or could you have one that ends in the middle of the week?

R: Well, they are modernizing it to do it at the end of the week. Before, we had it on the exact date of the person's death, one year later.

DS: It was the exact day?

R: Exactly and without exception. If it fell on a feast day, like on Holy Trinity Day, you had to do it on that day. But today they have changed it because, like this conversation, here we only have a short period of time. The dancers have to work. They cannot miss work because the person throwing the pahko cannot pay them that day to miss their work. Unavoidably, they have to let them work and then just do it on Saturday. That way, they don't have to work, and they can attend the party.

DS: The books say that they cut the cords on the day following the lutu pahko. And then these cuttings go into a cup of some sort?

R: Yes, a clay bowl. And they have a song. The maehtom have to sing it to the people as they are cutting the cord around their neck.

DS: And that's when they place the clay bowl at the foot of the cross?

R: Yes. And after they cut them from all the relatives, they take them to the front of the rama where there is this cross and right behind the cross they burn these pieces of cords.

DS: Do they always make *wakavaki* [Yoeme stew] for the guests?

R: Always, and another dish with meat and beans and red chile for the padrinos.

DS: The book say that the Yoemem do not believe the spirit of the person is at the lutu pahko. What do you think is normal among Yoemem?

R: Yes, it has to be there.

DS: Oh, it is possible?

R: Yes.

DS: And you think most Yoemem know this to be this way?

R: Yes.

DS: Okay. In October, for animam miika, they say that the souls return for the entire month.

R: Yes, for a month.

DS: Have you heard that people can see the spirits in the form of white dogs or in some other form? Or perhaps as the person?

R: No. You can't see anything, just hear the noises, footsteps that they are here. And all that we offer them in the ceremony, when we make that small Mass with the maehto and kantooram, the departed are the ones taking these things that we put out for them, our dear ones.

DS: There are some Yoemem in Tucson that I've heard say that after putting the food on the tables, the souls can eat the food through its aroma. Have you heard this?

R: This is still in our community, but not by the aroma. It is by the vapors that leave the food. *Hawa* in Yoeme. *Hawa* is the vapor. For the family of those for whom we are putting the table out, our dear ones, we have to take the food immediately from the oven or the stove so that the plate is still steaming. Then we take it to the table for the deceased to eat the steam.

DS: The books of the dead, the animam — does each family have one?

R: Yes, every family has them.

DS: And you mean every single one?

R: Yes, it is an obligation.

DS: It is simply a part of life for Yoemem.

R: Yes, for everyone.

DS: Your wife and all of her family members?

R: Yes, all of her family.

DS: So what about when a person has two families, like your daughter, who is married into another family now?

R: They will have them apart from each other. But God does not care how it works out, just that it is in a book.

DS: I understand. A person like your daughter can have the

animam miika with one book in the house of her family, and then go to her spouse's family for another little Mass with their book?

R: Yes. Or we could say it like this: She lives now with her in-laws. The day that I die, she will not be living here. But in their books over there, they have to note me when they are honoring their dead, lowering it onto the little table, putting that prayer out there for me.

DS: In 1954, Edward Spicer was living in Potam and wrote that the books of the dead were the property of the oldest woman in the house. Do you think this is correct now?

R: No. This is certainly not true.

DS: Okay. Can you write in the book yourself, or can only the *maehto* write in it?

R: Only the maehto. Other people are not able to do so.

DS: I have seen these books with drawings and paintings inside. Do you think that is normal?

R: Like symbols?

DS: Yes, symbols.

R: Of crosses, of a table, an altar. At the front of the book, they must have a cross on the first page.

DS: Are there also prayers in there in Spanish or Latin?

R: Yes, but in Yoeme. They use the Yoeme dialect more so.

DS: In the 1930s, an anthropologist said that Yoemem in Potam take these small books of the dead to the church with them every Sunday. Is that true?

R: No.

DS: Here is the book that says there are kontim every Sunday. Is that true?

R: Yes.

DS: The same kind of konti that I was in that Easter? Is it that big?

R: Yes, it is as big as that one.

DS: Are they exactly the same then?

R: No, no. It is only from the church to the cross of forgiveness. [Draws it on a piece of paper.] Here is the door. Here is the cross of the plaza. They leave from here and return to here. Here is the cross, and the people go around them like so. Here is where we were the other day on that path. Here we stopped. I don't know if you know that they have names: Bobedas, the Heart of Jesus, and then this one is called Alleluja, and then there is this other cross here, and then this other one, and then you return around this one. And then you enter into the church through here. Each Sunday.

DS: At what time?

R: Around 11 a.m. or noon.

DS: In the old histories of the indigenous people of Mexico, the Spaniards wrote that there were indigenous processions, not exactly like the kontim, but definitely an act of moving in a group in a direction, perhaps carrying things. This seems to be indigenous to Mexico and not just a Catholic addition. For example, we have talked before about the toad.

R: Yes, the frog.

DS: Do you think these processions preceded the Jesuits' arrival?

R: Yes.

DS: And because of this, we could say that the konti are very traditional, very ancient?

R: Well, those Yoemem already had their own culture and their own traditions before the arrival of the Jesuits. They worshipped all of these things, like the god of lightning, the god of food, the gods of the yo ania, and so the tribe had their own gods. Then they say the Jesuits came to evangelize them, but I don't know if it is true or false. But if they didn't know how to speak the same language, then how could they learn about each other? And this was the time of fighting. These people were raised in a time of war. So then they are going to let these strange people learn about them? I believe in this time there would have been fear of your own shadow. In these days, you wouldn't know who was who.

DS: And in the kontim each Sunday, they have the military societies, the governor, the pahko'olam, and the community members walking in procession.

R: We have all of them.

DS: And the figure of the Virgin of Guadalupe?

R: Yes.

DS: And Coyote Society members.

R: Yes.

DS: With their arrows?

R: Yes.

DS: Each Sunday?

R: Yes, each Sunday, with matachinim as well.

DS: And the governor of the pueblo.

R: Yes.

DS: And all of them are in a particular order?

R: Yes, it has to be that way.

DS: And flag bearers?

R: Yes, there are flag wavers from the church group, then the societies, and the Coyote Society.

DS: Do you think that on your normal Sunday konti there are approximately seventy or eighty people?

R: Sure. That is possible.

DS: It is possible. And these Sunday kontim circle around these three or four crosses?

R: Yes.

DS: So do you think that these crosses are symbolic of Yoeme territory?

R: No, no, no. I don't think so. I do not belive it. These processions are what our ancestors did in a particular manner. I will ask other elders to see if they think it is possibly both a procession and symbolic of land possession. After I verify these things, I will tell you if it is true and whatever else they may tell me.

DS: One of the first Europeans that came through Yoeme territory, Pérez de Ribas, said that the Yoemem had crosses before he arrived with his.

R: Yes, yes.

DS: So then the cross is a Yoeme thing, you would agree?

R: There is a history told in the tribe that I believe. In very early times, before the sixteenth century, as the legend goes, God caused a Yoeme to meet a non-Yoeme to see what would happen. The non-Yoeme immediately started searching for the Yoeme money. Instead of going to protect the money, the Yoeme went to get his cross. This coincides with what you just said to me. It is better spiritually that God enables us to see things this way.

Conclusion

POTAM PUEBLO ENACTED

March 8, 2001. As usual, the days before leaving for the pueblo are filled with so many errands, so much anxiety. I feel as though the crossing of the U.S.–Mexico border begins weeks before the actual physical movement: ordering pesos from the bank; purchasing auto insurance for Mexico coverage; preparing gifts for the family in Potam; buying film, batteries, audio cassettes, notebooks. Mentally, I'm already crossing the border between my life in the United States and my life in Mexico and the pueblo. I have come to know my way through Sonora and the eight villages well enough. But the fear remains of not being able to pass without delays or problems: my possessions still get inspected at the various checkpoints by border patrols, state of Sonora police, or federales. My identity changes with the context: I am sometimes a student, sometimes a professor, sometimes a waiter just visiting Mexican relatives in Obregón. I tell the inspectors what I think will get me through with the least hassle.

The U.S.–Mexico border in Arizona feels like a zone, since billboards in Spanish begin to appear miles north of the border. Just south of Tucson, the state highway signs change from miles to kilometers. Pesos are accepted at the Safeway and Chevron on the U.S. side of Nogales. Coming toward the end of U.S. territory, I drive between high concrete walls covered with barbed wire. The plotted neighborhoods behind the walls become crowded shantytown constructions along the hillsides. Floodlights sit atop the mountain peaks, sometimes accompanied by vans and trucks that patrol both sides of the bordered desert. Pulling up to the red light that faces my lane, I stop while the video cameras and guards behind one-way glass read my license plate, my vehicle, my body. Luckily, this time at least, the light changes to green. I don't get inspected at this checkpoint. During the five miles between the border and the "Sonora Only" visa registration complex, I notice the familiar taco carts, the roadside shrines, and the huddled figures warming themselves around burning trash piles. I've come to see my passing as a privilege since, so far at least, I can freely cross back to el otro lado while my collaborators and friends in the Hiak Vatwe don't have the means and rights to do so.

Unlike the U.S.–Mexico border, the Yoeme territory is unmarked from the highway. However, driving through San Carlos, a knowing eye will recognize Takalaim Mountain on the water's edge. Many Yoemem consider this mountain a landmark of the northwest point of their aboriginal homeland, although it lies outside President Lázaro Cardenas's 1937 "Zona Yaqui." Some Yoemem still consider Takalaim the place where those souls go who committed incest while alive. For most Mexicans in the area, Takalaim provides a backdrop for San Carlos and the beaches that attract Mexican as well as American spring breakers and sand dune racers. Takalaim is the first of a series of mountains that rise up from Yoeme history. Passing Guaymas, Totoitakuse'epo (hill of the rooster) and Maso Kova (deer's head) are visible to the east. I wonder which hills to the west are the ones formed by the severed body of the giant snake, killed during the time of the Surem. Along the freeway, images of deer dancers are shaped from huge metal plates attached to columns, marking not Yoeme land exactly but a general Sonoran state symbol. Many license plates on Sonoran vehicles show a deer dancer silhouetted by the sun. While I have some clues as to how this Uto-Aztecan performer specifically figures in northern Mexican identities, I personally see these images as I do the large metal sculptures along the highway, Takalaim, and Totoitakuse'epo. I understand them as marking a "field" where I do ethnographic "work." In my research, I share with many Yoemem the perspective that this region is marked by distinct histories that reach cosmological scale, though conjoined in many ways with the physical border between nations (Mexico/United States) and states (Sonora/Arizona).

Reaching the middle of the Zona Yaqui, I pull off the highway and head for Potam. At the center of the pueblos, Potam is the largest of the eight pueblos in terms of Yoeme population and accordingly is considered to have the biggest ceremonial performances. The road curves between lush green *fields and deep irrigation canals. An occasional Yoeme man rides on horseback, keeping the cattle under his care from standing in my vehicle's path. I pass the technical school that sits at the entrance of the pueblo. The pavement ends, and the dirt road becomes Avenida Central, the main strip of Potam. Driving slower now, I remember the ways I am watched by the locals — Mexican market owners; Yoeme women with their rebozos covering their heads and shoulders; people of all ages walking or riding bikes, talking outside bars or homes. I pass a male elder wearing large-framed sunglasses and a cowboy hat. We tip our hats to each other. Around this road, adobe and brick homes sit along perpendicular roads.*

Passing the medical clinic, I drive into the vast opening of space around the church. The graves in front of the church are marked by light blue and white crosses, or in the case of Mexican burials, large concrete gravestones and shrines. The church and the cemetery sit in the middle of a large expanse of fine powdered dirt. Outside of that space, to the east and recently to the west, are the older cane and mud-thatched houses, often surrounded individually by tall fences of cane woven through horizontal wires. The differences between these "traditional" dwellings and the more permanent structures near the main strip hint at the rarely expressed division between two types of Potam Yoemem: those who went to the mountains to resist Mexican colonization, and those who stayed and sometimes sided with the Mexican troops (Spicer 1954, 20). Driving east across the plaza onto one of the small pathways between the fences, I park in front of my kompae's campo. The children, recognizing my truck, are the first to run out of their house, followed shortly by their parents. I cross myself at the tevat kus *(patio cross), then shake everyone's hand and offer my greetings, paying special attention to my* vato'o asoam *(godchildren).*

I am offered a seat under the large ramada, *and the women begin warming a cup of coffee and a meal for me over the open fire near the wall of the house. As I sit and talk about recent happenings with my kompae, I again begin to sense consciously the place of Yoeme households: the large earthen olla on its tribranched mesquite stand, the washtub toward the back fence, the clothesline to the side of the house. I realize something is different about the campo space. Fence and house walls have shifted since my last trip; doors are now where walls had been. Demonstrating the malleability of these constructions, another*

family member removes a section of the fence so I can pull my truck into the
campo, away from the neighbors' view. After I park inside the fence, this same
man rebuilds the fence within a matter of minutes. He then says that I must
be tired as he begins constructing a cot for me. He spreads a large gunny sack
open and attaches the sides to wooden posts, which he then lays over a pair
of crossed posts that support the horizontal and taut fabric. I am amazed by
the seemingly easy reconstitution of space. They move fences and walls in no
time, and the ramada will frame our talking, then eating, and then later my
resting. A chicken pecks at my shoelaces. A puppy lifts his head to smell the
beans and fresh flour tortillas being set before me. The children chase each
other around the tevat kus, trying not to be too obvious about stealing glances
into my truck, hoping for gifts or perhaps imagining my life as evidenced by
my possessions. This is how I have come to know a Yoeme place, by leaving
my "home" in the United States, traveling across the international border, and
passing through mountains and images of Sonoran Indianness; by entering
a particular neighborhood (Santemea) within a particular pueblo (Potam);
by the faces, voices, smells, sounds, and tastes of my kompae's house. If only
we could make maps that had all the sensuality of place.

Spatial relations are a primary means of orientation. Constituted in
both myth and ritual, Yoeme worldview has been shown throughout
this book in a variety of particularly spatial ways. Looking at deer and
pahko'ola, Yoeme elder Don Jesús Yoi Lo'i described deer songs as originating with the Surem and the various *aniam*, the worlds from precontact
times to the present. Many Yoemem clearly continue to perceive aniam
as the active, living realms of their cosmos. The *huya ania*, or wilderness
world, surrounds Yoeme villages and continues to sustain Surem communities in the mountains, caves, and bodies of water. Nondomestic
animals, plants, and other-than-humans live in the huya ania. The *sea ania*
is the huya ania in bloom, the place of the deer. The sea ania is danced
into the present (a postcontact realm called the "pueblo") when and
where Yoeme have a *pahko* and are thus sharing in the sacrificial nature
of the deer's life and of an individual's ceremonial labor. The *yo ania*,
or respected world, is the actual home of the deer and the realm from

which knowledge of and skill for deer and pahko'ola can still be obtained. Sometimes experienced as a space in caves where Surem host visitors, or even the location of some dreams, the yo ania is considered present at those places where powerful animals and people once appeared or are known still to appear.

Like everyone else, contemporary Yoemem have diverse and sometimes complicated notions of the universe of possible relations. Although the ethnographic literature and my personal research offer few examples of Yoemem referring to hell, and even fewer to purgatory (Painter 1986, 89–91), many Yoemem consider heaven very real. Yet a distinction between the pueblo, aniam, and the Catholic world remains: while the aniam are accessible, geographically situated sources for ritual knowledge, the Catholic realms of heaven and hell are only reachable after death. Heaven is referred to in sermons, descriptions of holy week, and perceptions of the afterworld. The aniam are mentioned in stories about precontact life, dreams, hunting, and the meanings and makings of religious acts. The Catholic spaces of Yoeme life (the church, the left side of the pahko ramada, the pueblo plaza) extend into the daily world, not to mention into the dreams and ceremonial calendar. The combination of precontact and Catholic cosmographies has led to some cross-references, such as heaven being like sea ania and yo ania being hellish. Many Yoemem understand Jesus as having walked among the pueblos in pre-Jesuit times. This localization of Christian stories joins other aboriginal ones of the mountains in the Yoeme territory being formed by the cut-up body of a giant snake. Together these ways of understanding the landscape demonstrate the syncretic nature of Yoeme worldview and the ontological, ethical, and intellectual possibilities that are available to Yoemem in this universe of being.

I remember my first trip to the Hiak Vatwe with Felipe. Walking along the river in Torim, Felipe and his kompae, Ignacio Sombra, talked while I followed. Every few minutes Ignacio stopped, bent down, and pointed out a particular plant in the ground cover. He dusted off the leaves, traced the veins with his weathered fingers, and supported any blooms or stems that he thought Felipe

12. White paint on the rock gives searchers a clue to finding the footprints of Jesus in the Hiak Vatwe.

should take notice of. Felipe acknowledged him with a "heewi" or two. Felipe then looked at me as if we had just been given a priceless gift from another land, from another time, as if we were to carry this gift back to other people, to remember what we saw, to share it with others.

I didn't understand much of what they were saying, even after Felipe translated Ignacio's ethnobotanical stories. Actually, my mind was mostly on something else. I was eagerly anticipating seeing the footstep of Jesus, who was rumored to have walked along the river before Yoemem lived here. Many of Felipe's friends had been telling us about these tracks for days. When we arrived at the rocky riverbank, Ignacio raised his head and began a story of a different sort. Felipe translated that the footprint was on a rock. In my head, I imagined Jesus stepping from rock to rock, surrounded by the green grass, perhaps wading in the cool water.

Ignacio, speaking in Yoeme, then Felipe in English, said the footprint had been seen as recently as the previous spring by people on their way to the Holy Cross celebration. I wondered how Jesus' footprints would look and if they would photograph well. Searching for fifteen or twenty minutes, Ignacio spoke again, and although I couldn't understand his words, I felt a sense of abandon-

ment. Felipe's voice seemed to amplify the sentiment, telling me that sometimes the water level rises above the footprint and sometimes the rock moves of its own accord, into and out of view as was appropriate for the particular seekers. Felipe and Ignacio began heading back to the truck. I said that I wanted to take some pictures of the trees to stall them while I continued my private search. Who knew when I would be at this spot again, so close? Felipe and Ignacio agreed to wait while I photographed the horses, the bend of the river, anything to continue looking for Jesus' footprints. Perhaps I wanted to prove that Jesus walked across this respected Yoeme land. If his footprint moves, and moves away from me, is he still walking? Perhaps I wanted to commit a richer experience to my memory by staying longer. As if the smell of the plants, the coolness of the water, the contrast of the rocks and grass, and Ignacio and Felipe's voices were not enough.

I unfolded in this text a Yoeme cosmological map through an examination of deer and pahko'ola performances. As nonliterate cartographies, the deer and pahko'olam dance and sing the Yoeme-Catholic places into view. Epistemologically grounded in the embodiment of *lutu'uria* (truth), ritual demonstrates Yoeme place-making: Yoemem situate themselves on a specific area of land, in relation to aniam and the traditional Catholic realms. Yoemem ritually map their history in distinctly spatial ways.

Of course, the picture of Yoeme cosmology that slowly emerges is incomplete without consideration of the talking tree mythology. I brought the talking tree story into focus as, first, a means to understand an example of Yoeme historical consciousness and, second, as a tool by which to evaluate ethnohistoric representations of Yoeme agency in the early period of Spanish/Jesuit contacts. In the talking tree stories we find the most fundamental aspects of Yoeme religious identity. Armin Geertz wrote that Hopi myths were "not very interested in how everything was first created" but that "the main interest by far is with the Emergence" (1984, 218). I, too, found in my survey of Yoeme mythology a lack of widespread storying of original creation. Rather than talking about how life began on earth, the vast majority of Yoemem reflect back on the time when the Surem community evolved into a Yoeme community. The storytellers sometimes disagree on the translator's name, the location of the tree, or the details of the prophecy. Yet collectively, they agree that the people were once unitary, and due to internal disagreement, not external forces, they decided to divide into two groups: those receptive to Christianity stayed and became Yoemem, and those unreceptive moved into the earth and remained immortal. The tree does not function exactly as an *axis mundi* (Eliade 1954; Geertz 1984), as one might assume. However, its location is within the pueblos, and it provides a fused time-space of social transformation that remains central to Yoeme mythology. Almost every time I visit the Hiak Vatwe, I'm asked if I want to go there, do I understand its significance, and so on. The talking tree story provides an example of what James Fox (1997) has termed "topogeny," the creation of places.

Sharing talking tree stories provides a fundamental realization that, although divided, the Surem and Yoemem are related as one people. The community may be split in terms of location, but they avail themselves to each other as kin. It could be said that this division supplies the model by which Yoemem on the south side of the border understand northern Yoemem as jointly responsible for the welfare of all Yoemem, as members of one tribe. Moreover, the Surem/Yoemem split leads to a localizing of Yoeme identity. Their ancestors and sources of tribal knowledge are ever-present in the aboriginal land base. Besides decentering the role of Europeans as primary agents of change, by representing the conquest as a precontact, internal *konkista*, stories of the talking tree ground Yoeme history and identity within a specific place. James Weiner observed similar phenomena among aboriginal communities in Australia and Papua New Guinea: "We can begin by observing that the songs and myths that are the salient form of attachment to land and to the constitution of the person through the terrain are not just texts 'about' land or placedness. Rather they are the fundamental vocal and verbal dimensions of landedness, the form that this relation takes in people's embodied consciousness" (2001, 234). Together with ritualized and storied references to aniam and relating how Jesus walked in the Hiak Vatwe, sharing stories of the talking tree further emplaces Yoemem within a particular geography, history, and cosmology.

We see Yoemem making a place for themselves by circulating the Testamento. The Testamento defines Yoeme land rights in terms of divine sanction. During the flood, certain Yoeme were kept safe atop rising hills within the *hiakim*, or Yoeme homeland. Then the prophets and angels came down from heaven, declared that the land belonged to Yoemem, and warned of non-Yoeme encroachment. Singing the "Dawn Song," the surviving people walked around the land, delineating tribal borders. This procession established the Eight Pueblos and created the holy dividing line between Yoeme and non-Yoeme territory. Many Yoemem consider the Testamento a documentation of their aboriginal land. The Testamento defines a central component of Yoeme identity: the maintenance and interdependence of multiple pueblos at the center of their larger land base.

Yoemem in the Hiak Vatwe create a sense of locality, distinct from other people and landscapes, through oral and embodied performances: repeating stories of aniam, acting out Catholic dimensionality, searching for signs of Jesus in the hiakim, telling anthropologists about the talking tree, and writing versions of the Testamento. Working ethnographically from the standpoint of Igarapé Guariba, an Amazonian community, Hugh Raffles sought to answer a seemingly basic question: how does a place specifically get to be? In the process of addressing the question, Raffles demonstrated that places "come-into-being" through a combination of multiple place-making practices. He showed how historicizing such practices and discerning a particular place's distinctiveness requires focusing on "local" theory," the perspective that resides in the biographical complexities of a place's inhabitants. Raffles outlines the benefits of such an approach: "Reading locality through narratives of nature and person, tracing its imbrication in the multiple practices of place-making, searching for 'local relations' through which to draw understanding out of lived immediacies — these strategies help us recover a sense of the complex and unpredictable density of locality" (1999, 350). Raffles's project, as outlined succinctly in this quotation, relates directly to my research. I have attempted here a particular scholarly practice, what Raffles terms "a methodology of locality" (323).

Drawing a line in the sand in 1533, Yoemem defined their physical territory in the face of Spanish imperialism. After over a hundred years of "missionization," the geographically accessible aniam remain constitutive of a particular Yoeme cosmology, which also includes heaven, hell, Jesus, Mary, and the saints. Despite, and because of, the Mexican government's displacement and subjugation of Yoemem, the notion of the Eight Pueblos' divine right to aboriginal lands is central to the Testamento. Southern Yoeme "locality" is a composition of multiple histories — with Spanish explorers, other tribes, Jesuits, Mexican colonialists, mining companies, North American developers, Mexican bankers, non-Yoeme employers, and sorts of anthropologists. Because of these movements to and from others and others' places, these varying inclusive and exclusionary relations, Yoeme place-making entails the designation, maintenance, and permeability of boundaries. Geographic, cultural, cosmological, and ethnic identities define any ethnic community because, as Fredrik Barth shows, boundaries delimit the criteria for determining membership and often the signaling of such membership (1998, 15, 38). By looking at how two Yoeme ritual acts construct borders, boundaries, and crossings, we sense more of "local" Yoeme identity, learning where and why communities draw the line (and ease it, on occasion) between self and otherness. This line drawing and erasing, perhaps the central act of place-making, is evident in funerary practices and Sunday *kontim*.

In *Culture, Power, Place*, Akhil Gupta and James Ferguson (1997) respond to the widespread anthropological assumption that while "localness" is natural, global communities and regional territories develop through multiple histories and complex political negotiations. Such conceptual divisions, they demonstrate, continue the long-standing notion that "native" cultures are unitary and somehow pristine and that they are stationary and therefore more resistant to the external influences of global economics. Further, the local is often held in opposition to the global in order to evaluate rates of social change and capacities for internal difference. Gupta and Ferguson critically survey the ethnographic literature and find it mostly lacking analyses of communities and localities that are historically and discursively constructed. They propose another direction: "How are understandings of locality, community, and region formed and lived? To answer this question, we must turn away from the commonsense idea that such things as locality and community are simply given or natural and turn toward a focus on social and political processes of place-making, conceived less as a matter of 'ideas' than of embodied practices that shape identities and enable resistances" (1997, 6). I have aimed throughout to follow this call and demonstrate how and why communities understand their own places. I soon discovered, when focusing on a specific place, that one must pay attention to the ways people make places by making boundaries, however permeable. Yoeme ritual spatialization reflects their social solidarity and specific historical and mythical relations, while also defining internal and external boundaries.

We have explored how place-making entails boundary setting, much as other scholars have in their studies of group identity. Fredrik Barth explains that while boundaries are essentially social, they have territorial counterparts (1998, 15). Although used to signal membership and exclusion, boundaries are compromised in cross-border exchanges without disintegrating ethnic differences (9–10, 25). This "porousness of boundaries," as Edward Casey described it, is essential to place: "A place could not gather bodies in the diverse spatiotemporal ways it does without the permeability of its own limits. The sievelike character of places might well be regarded as another essential structure of place, one that could be called 'elasticity'" (1996, 42). Speaking directly to this issue of community resilience despite cultural changes, Anthony Cohen argues that the symbolic expression of collective unity and group boundaries increases in importance as the geosocial boundaries are challenged. Cohen offers as proof the role of ritual as reconstitutive in communities where members have been dispersed (1985, 50). These positions are clearly supported in my study of worldview, Testamento, talking tree stories, deer and pahko'ola dances, funerary ceremonies, and kontim.

In various ways, Yoemem set boundaries of differing degrees of "elasticity" in cosmological, civic, and interethnic ways. Cosmologically, the boundary between living and dead community members seems porous, although the fireworks and journeying associated with the souls' travels suggest a distant place for the deceased. The line between indigenous and Catholic worldviews is at times nonexistent and at other times demonstrative. Aniam and heaven can coexist in Yoeme thought. Yet the house cross and altars divide the patio into two sides, one for the church groups and the other for nonchurch groups. Evidenced by the *maehto* notes attached to deceased pahko'olam describing their ceremonial affiliation, these divisions seem to be recognized in the afterworld. The Coyote Society carries Our Lady of Guadalupe around the locally present deceased, as they salute crosses symbolizing the boundaries set by prophets. The lay priests read Masses for the Dead on the house patio, next to where the pahko'olam dance. In terms of civic organization, the divisions between military, government, and church groups are clearly firm. Yet in most Yoeme rituals, their collaboration is essential. Somewhat expressing interethnic boundaries, many Yoemem perceive their ceremonies for the deceased as part of their Catholic devotion, a standard some say that Mexicans fail to meet. Additionally, the link between kontim and the singing of the boundaries gives religious sanction to the holy dividing line that defines Yoeme land apart from the surrounding Mexicans. As a weekly performative embodiment of the Testamento, in Sunday kontim Yoemem re-member the lines traced through the earth in resistance to encroachment, thereby reflecting active dialogue with a local history of dispersal. All of these acts of place-making show an indigenous Catholic syncretism that Yoemem express through long-established inscriptive practices and historical consciousness.

Notes

1 There is no doubt that the Yoeme language is endangered. Both in north-ern and southern pueblos, children are rarely taught Yoeme in the schools. The language is used more frequently in the southern pueblos and almost exclusively during religious ceremonies and by their elders. The northern Yoemem with whom I have spoken on this matter fear that the language will be lost in a few generations, although I have not yet found research quantifying contemporary language use in any Yoeme community.

2 Mini Valenzuela Kaczkurkin now publishes under the name Herminia Valenzuela. Note her use of both "Yoeme" and "Yaqui."

3 This, of course, would mean that Yoemem knew Spanish during "first contacts."

4 One of my collaborators has pointed out that in an older way of speak-ing, a Yoeme dialect that only elders use and understand, Yoemem uti-lized *samaim nusmeam* to refer to themselves. I have not found any refer-ences to these words in any Yoeme dictionary.

5 For translations of the town names and a listing of other Yoeme com-munities, see Evers and Molina 1987, 195–96. In his annotations to the recently translated *History of the Triumphs of Our Holy Faith* (Pérez de Ribas 1999, 371n63), Daniel Reff lists "Abasorin" as one of the original eight pueblos but does not say how he came upon this information. I have not encountered that word in any of my textual, archival, or field research. Evelyn Hu-DeHart reminds us that Pérez de Ribas never mentioned their exact names (1981, 113n31). Edward Spicer describes Yoeme moves from these "original" eight pueblos to nearby communities and then their return to build new towns: Pitahaya, Copas, Lomas de Bacum, Batacon-sica, and Torocoba (1980, 225–27). He also comments on the importance of the eight pueblos to Yoeme collective identity (310–11).

6 For various examples of indigenous agency in controlling rates and effects

of colonization, see also Axtell 1985, 2001, Burnett 2002, Fowler 1987, Harrod 1995, Sahlins 1981, and White 1991.

7 Figuring the populations of tribes during the early years of contact remains a difficult task. I am relying on Hu-DeHart 1981, Pérez de Ribas 1999, and Reff 1991.

8 Spicer argues that Yoemem consciously unified Catholic and precontact mythology in the nineteenth century in order to provide divine sanction for their defense of land, religion, and government (1980, 164–74).

9 The fifty-year period directly before Jesuit expulsion contains not only frequent changes in Yoeme and Jesuit leadership, but also a pantribal revolt in 1740 and some indication of Spanish involvement in Jesuit corruption. The complex history is detailed more carefully by Spicer 1980, 32–58. An overview of landholding categories is available in both Zendejas and de Vries 1995 and Bartra 1993. For a history and detailed description of encomiendas, see Simpson 1950.

10 Stedt 1994 offers a basic history of the discovery of silver, the use of indigenous labor forces, and the relationship between the Spanish economy and the "new" resources in northern New Spain.

11 For a contrast to Spicer's work on ethnic identity maintenance in mixed-raced communities, Sands suggests Despres 1975.

12 The ontological category of "other-than-human persons" remains the most accurate and cross-tribal reference for those beings (animals, rocks, dream presences, etc.) that exercise will, intelligence, and agency. See A. Irving Hallowell's "Ojibwa Ontology, Behavior, and Worldview" (1975).

13 Drawing from and contributing to a large body of scholarship on religious change and continuity, my work demonstrates how Yoeme expressive culture embodies aboriginal ethics and logic. In terms of change and continuity, see Deloria 1994, Treat 1996, and Vecsey 1990, 1991. For an introduction to the topic of native conversion, see Cervantes 1994; Jansen, Van Der Loo, and Manning 1988, and Langer and Jackson 1995.

14 *Kompae* has been translated simplistically as "godfather" in earlier ethnographic works. Molina defines the terms as designating a "ceremonial kinship" that is separate from but related to the godparent kinship. If a person is a godparent to a child, that same person is a kompae (male) or a komae (female) to the child's parents, and the parents are then kom-

pae and komae to the child's godparent. Gudeman 1972 offers an extensive overview of the godparent systems across Latin America and the Indigenous communities therein.

1. GEOGRAPHY OF YOEME IDENTITIES

1 In using "re-member" in contrast with "remember," I aim to draw attention to the bodily and not simply mental production of memories. See Connerton 1989; Fentress and Wickham 1992; and Lipsitz 1990.

2 The scholarship on "place" and worldview seems never-ending, although several texts make particular use of these combined notions: see Allen and Schlereth 1990, Casey 1996, Feld and Basso 1996, Redfield 1960, Soja 1989, and Tweed 2006.

3 Felipe Molina, personal communication.

4 According to some of Painter's collaborators, the entire world of the Surem is known as the yo ania; see Painter 1986, 9–10. In my own fieldwork, some collaborators have used *yo ania* to refer to the larger collection of aniam.

5 I suspect that the speaker's use of *supernatural* is indicative of the American Indian tendency to relate indigenous concepts in unintentionally misleading terminology. For why "supernatural" is misleading, see Morrison 1992a, 1992b, and Shorter 2001. My suspicions have been supported in conversations with Yoeme language specialists, including Felipe Molina.

6 We know that Savala was collaborator number 55; see Davids 1988, 12, and Painter 1986, 28. Davids demonstrates that most of Savala's input tends to be heavily unbalanced, evidencing more of a polemical Catholic interpretation. Spicer also noticed these moralistic differences among Yoeme views (1981, 12).

2. PUTTING WORLDS INTO WORDS

1 Valenzuela quoted above in Evers 1981b, 205. Herminia Valenzuela is also known professionally as Herminia "Mini" Kaczkurkin.

2 The news of the tribe "in distress" made great fodder for the press across northern Mexico and in Arizona. See Ayoub and Hurtado 1999, Bolón 1999a, 1999b, Bolón and Esparza 1999, González and Ponce de León 1999, Hartman 1994a, 1994b, and Ponce de León and Wong 1999.

3 An example of this formalized speech can be found in my introduction and chapter 1 above, and in Ignacio Sombra's talks below. Also see Maaso, Molina, and Evers 1993.

4 Using "one word," bringing the collective voice to agreement, the eight governors of the pueblos historically came to decisions regarding issues confronting the larger tribe; see Giddings 1959, 44.

5 Giddings, "Folk Literature," (1945). The copies of these transcribed myths are located in ASM Accession 2000–175, box 6, folder 353, "Myths-Rahum, Juan Valenzuela."

6 Spicer, field notes 1942, file A-505-a.

7 Giddings, "Myths-Rahum, Juan Valenzuela," my emphasis.

8 Giddings, "Myths-Rahum, Juan Valenzuela," my emphasis.

9 According to Evers and Molina, McGuire argues that historical seminars in Potam where people discussed the singing of the boundaries must be a thing of the past (1992, 54).

10 I use the translated words provided by Giddings, god and kings, with some hesitation, since no one has previously attempted to discern pre-Christian Yoeme worldviews from the mythological records. Further work could be done in this difficult area of research.

11 Hardly exhaustive, such a list would contain the works of Barbara Meyerhoff, Peter Furst, William Merrill, many of the authors listed in this chapter, and, dare I mention, Carlos Castaneda.

12 For more direct analyses of dialogical ethnography, see Briggs 1993, Clifford 1988, and Dennis Tedlock 1979. Harvey Feit 1991 also shows how anthropological fieldworkers "constructed" Algonkian hunting territories by choosing to interpret the indigenous history selectively.

3. LISTENING TO THE TREE AND HEARING HISTORY

1 Spicer struggles throughout his writing on the Yoemem with the largely absent details of precontact Yoeme life. He often states that the earliest reports we can rely on are Spanish Jesuit descriptions after 1533, while occasionally drawing inferences from nearby tribes.

2 I do not include in my analysis the various versions by Refugio Savala, since Kathleen Sands extensively examines his interpretations in her article "The Singing Tree." However, the thirteen versions of the myth

that I include are representative of the variation and similarity that exists among the renditions with which I am familiar.

3 Granted, a complete study of each variable (the storyteller's role in the community, his background, the audience of the story, the context of the interview, and so on) would provide a great deal of information about the story's mythopoetics. Unfortunately, such information simply does not exist. The best we can do is detail the differences and similarities among the wide variety of versions, keeping in mind that the most basic factor of their transmission seems to be the context of an interview, often with a cultural outsider.

4 In version 4, where the tree taps like a telegraph, and in versions 2 and 12, where the tree is branchless like a telephone pole, the storytellers use analogies to modern technologies to describe the precontact tree.

5 Version 2's spelling, "Yomumuli," matches what was told to me in my own fieldwork. In a conversation with Yoeme scholars Felipe Molina and Mini Valenzuela on September 26, 1994, they translated her name to mean "enchanted little bee," which resonates well with the Tree's humming sounds as well as with her special labor for her community.

6 For a cross-cultural analysis of "great flood" myths, see Dundes 1988. We can also find talking trees in Papago stories according to Densmore 1929, and the Tepecanos tell stories of half of their tribe being opposed to and leaving before baptism in Mason and Espinosa 1914. I relegate this surely truncated list of comparisons here in the end notes in hopes of maintaining a Yoeme centered analysis.

7 My use of the category "other-than-human persons" proceeds from the works of several scholars: Gill 1977, Hallowell 1975, Lokensgard 1993, Mills and Slobodin 1994, and Morrison 2000.

8 Versions 3, 4, and 7 mention her father, but do not name him. Highlighting kinship and family responsibility undoubtedly reflects the values of both male and female storytellers.

9 Both of these types then reflect a parallel with the stories of the Aztec woman cultural translator and transformer, Malinche.

10 Although different interpretations can be found in Beals 1943, Giddings 1959, and Painter 1986, I have also heard that Yoemem, before European contact, acknowledged one creator who lived in the sun. Herminia Valenzuela, conversation with author, June 21, 1996.

11 Throughout the ethnographic works of Spicer and Painter, Yoeme infor-
    mants and collaborators offer cultural interpretations that vary from
    being quite non-Christian to the opposite perspective of thinking that,
    as they see them, precontact religious views are evil and hindrances to
    good Catholic lives. This spectrum is most evident in Painter's book *With
    Good Heart*. Painter directly quotes a large number of Pascua community
    members and often lists their contradictory statements side by side. As
    an ambitious senior project, Brent Michael Davids was able to decipher
    Painter's numeric codes for her informants and detail their roles in the
    community and, often, their tendency toward more pre-Catholic
    assimilationist perspectives (Davids 1988). I compared Davids's results
    with Painter's list of collaborators, which is kept in the Arizona State
    Museum, and found a high degree of accuracy. I should also note the
    heavy Christian tenor of one of the self-proclaimed spokesmen for
    the Yoeme, Refugio Savala, whom Painter relies on heavily and actually
    names as "informant" number 55 (Painter 1986, 28). See also his 1980
    book *Autobiography of a Yaqui Poet*. All of this is to say that Yoeme religion
    offers its practitioners a wide range of interpretive freedom in terms of
    Catholic or precontact tradition: Yoeme Catholicism is thus as polyvalent
    as other native/Christian religious syncretisms found elsewhere, if not
    more so.

12 Spicer, field notes, March 2, 1942.

13 Spicer, field notes, March 11, 1942.

14 Vicente L. Rafael's *Contracting Colonialism* (1993) shows that *conquista*
    was defined by the Spanish as "the forcible occupation of a territory and
    the act of winning someone's voluntary submission and consequently
    attaining his or her love and affection." Rafael then demonstrates that
    conversión literally means the changing of one thing to another. In this
    way, Rafael argues that conversion and conquest both mean exchanging
    another's desires for your own (xi). By these definitions, most Yoemem
    never converted.

15 Herminia Valenzuela and Felipe Molina told me in 2000 that "the Talk-
    ing Tree tradition goes back before the 1800s" and that some parts of
    the prophecy (origination?) are "not told to non-Yoemem."

1 Mallon acutely historicizes many of the goals of subaltern studies, particularly within the scholarship on Latin America. I have attempted in this book to provide a study of Yoeme performance without falling into an often-exclusionary conversation about theoretical approaches: postcolonialisms, poststructuralisms, subaltern theories, etc. That said, my work grows from and, I hope, contributes to many of those conversations.

2 In their 1994 study of the Battle of Little Bighorn, Welch and Stekler offer an excellent example of how ethno-ethnohistories might proceed. Several books stand out for rereading indigenous histories from internal sources: see Cruikshank in collaboration with Sidney, Smith, and Ned 1990, Brown and Vibert 1996, and Fienup-Riordan 1990, 1991.

3 Many scholars have examined the complex ways that Europeans predetermined their relationships with "New World" inhabitants. A good place to start is with Berkhofer 1978, Crosby 1972, Dussel 1995, Fitzhugh 1985, and Todorov 1984.

4 Carroll Riley argues that we should not put too much emphasis on slave raiding in this region as explanatory for wide and general diaspora. See her 1981 essay, "Sonora and Arizona in the Protohistoric Period."

5 Hu-DeHart takes this quote from "Proceso del Marquéz," 1871, 325–28.

6 James Clifford warns that "first-contact" stories often suppress the possible experiences of prior unrecorded contacts, and they usually place uneven attention on the traveler's "discovery" of the indigenous peoples (1997, 154). In the Yoeme case, I have found no evidence in the secondary literature or in field conversations of prior meetings with Spanish travelers.

7 These maces may have been symbols of respect, since Spicer notes that the governors of the Yoeme towns (thus in post-Jesuit times) held "canes of office" that were ordinarily topped with embossed silver (Spicer 1980, 28–29). I, too, have seen canes of office held by Potam officials during ceremonial seasons, but I would hardly consider them elaborate or macelike. Because Spicer later writes that the canes are clearly a Spanish contribution to Yoeme insignias of office, I am not quite sure what to make of the turquoise-studded gift given to Guzmán. Several Yoemem

have directly asked me if I have found at least one of these actual clubs supposedly in the Smithsonian.

8 I am hesitant to use terms such as *supernatural* or *divine*, since they both imply a Western system of categorizing human/nonhuman relations that in most cases fails to account adequately for indigenous worldviews, ontologies in particular. The significance of such issues plays out in the debate over Captain Cook's reception on the Hawaiian Islands in 1778. The famous Marshall Sahlins–Gananath Obeyesekere debate rests on both scholars using the non-Hawaiian notion of "divinity" to make sense of Hawaiian attitudes toward Cook. For a history of the debate and a comprehensive listing of the relevant literatures, see Adam Kuper 1999, 177–200. Two other inquiries into the hermeneutical problems with these categories are Axtell 1988 and Hefner 1993, 3–44, although a detailed analysis of these categorical failures can be found in Morrison 2002.

9 Hu-DeHart quotes Hammond and Rey for Obregón's statements (1928, 257–60).

10 According to Obregón, the Yoeme costume for celebration was the same as for war, which must have led to hesitancy on Ibarra's part. This observation, however, may have been designed solely for the Ibarra party when considering Ibarra's departure (discussed below) from Yoeme territory. For an interesting interpretation of native celebrations for intruders, see Pratt 1992, 80.

11 Daniel T. Reff argues that the decline in Yoeme population was due to smallpox. Various scholars counter Reff's analyses (1987, 1991), e.g., Larsen and Milner 1994, R. Jackson 1994, Pérez de Ribas 1944, and Verano and Ubelaker 1992.

12 A close tribal collaborator disagrees strongly with this list, saying that the Uparos, Opatas, and Apache were never close enough to be either enemies or friends of the Yoemem. He would, in their place, add the Pimas, Guarajillos, Tarahumaris, and Mochikawis as historic enemies turned friendly neighbors.

13 Alegre 1841–42, 234, 351; Beals 1943, 40–41; Beals 1945, 48–49; Hammond and Rey 1928, 164, 259–60; Hu-DeHart 1981, 19–20.

14 Hu-DeHart writes his name as "Anabailutei," though Felipe Molina informed me in 2000 that his proper name was Aniabailutek, which would translate as "the world ended by water/flood."

15 Hu-DeHart states that "he raised an auxiliary force of 2,000 Indians," but only accounts for "50 mounted and 400 Indian foot soldiers" retreating; Hurdaide and 25 others were caught on the hill. Perhaps only 450 of the Indian fighters joined Hurdaide on this particular assault?

16 The bullets would have led to a higher production of saliva, the cavorting to a higher state of Spanish humiliation.

17 The consensual nature of Yoeme intertribal actions is described in several ethnologies and supported by my own fieldwork as well as that of Mahoney 1994, 15. For textual references to the historic and contemporary Yoeme political collectives, see Beals 1943, 40; 1945, 53; McGuire 1986, 146; and Spicer 1980, 214–15.

18 The Jesuit Order had a very efficient and complex method of expanding across the Americas, including entering new areas only after previous native settlements were reorganized economically and politically. They never used Spaniards as catechists in the newer pueblos, only members of already missionized tribes with similar languages or natives from the new tribe who had previously received instruction at missionary schools in Culiacán (Decorme 1941; Dunne 1951; Jacobsen 1938; González de Cossío 2007).

19 Edward Fischer offers a similar interpretation: "Since contact was inevitable, better it be mediated by the Jesuits, who would bring novel farming techniques and Spanish goods along with a new God, not a militia" (1992, 7). His work is similar to that of my own or Spicer's, since Fischer leans toward asserting Yoeme agency. He includes a talking tree story. He does so only to interpret Yoeme acceptance of Jesuit ideas; he does not relate the tree to other European contact in the sixteenth and seventeenth centuries or to larger questions regarding Yoeme historiography.

20 Pérez de Ribas's *Triunfos* has been republished in English by the University of Arizona Press. For the corresponding page number, please see Reff, Ahern, and Danford, trans., 1999, 332–34.

21 As with the two thousand loads of maize given to Guzmán and gang, we might consider Yoeme terms of engagement more closely, asking, "Why wouldn't they use poisonous arrows if they had them?" Yoeme generosity seems to suggest compassion as well as control.

22 For some examples of this area of research, see Brown, Eccles, and Held man 1994, 57–64, 94–96; Trigger 1985, 126–28; and White 1991, 94–104.

1 Las Casas admitted that the indigenous peoples of the Americas lacked literacy, but still argued for an appreciation of their intelligence (Mignolo 1995, 129). For other descriptions of Las Casas's view of indigenous cultures, see also Hanke 1974 and chapter 4 of León-Portilla 1990.

2 Many authors have written volumes on exactly how those technologies were introduced in Native communities and the effects that learning to write has on their bodies, worldviews, epistemological functions, social memories, etc. See, among others, Adorno 1982; Connerton 1989; Diringer 1962; Fentress and Wickham 1992; Finnegan 1988; Foucault 1979; Goody 1987; Goody and Watt 1963; McLuhan 1967; Mignolo 1995, 2000; and Wolf 1982.

3 The Nisga'a Indians' cases are described in further detail in Berger 1981 and Tennant 1990.

4 A straightforward appreciation of Derrida's work in terms of nonliterate forms of communication in indigenous cultures is Elizabeth Hill Boone's 1994 "Writing and Recording Knowledge."

5 Mignolo argues elsewhere that Derrida should be avoided when attempting to interpret writing and cultures in the New World; see his afterword to *Writing without Words*, "Writing and Recorded Knowledge in Colonial and Postcolonial Situations" (Boone and Mignolo 1994).

6 On performance studies: Ben-Amos and Goldstein 1975; Benamou 1977; Briggs 1993; Conquergood 1991; Crumrine 1979; C. Geertz 1983; Harris 1993; Lincoln 1989; Phelan 1993; Rappaport 1999; Reinelt and Roach 1992; Schechner 1985; Schieffelin 1985; J. Z. Smith 1987; and V. Turner 1982a, 1982b.

5. HUNTING FOR HISTORY IN POTAM PUEBLO

1 See Beals 1943, 13; 1945, 13; Evers and Molina 1987, 47–48, 134–35, 137–38, 142, 150–54; Painter 1986, 120–21, 272–80, 282, 293–94, 297–302; Savala 1980, 188–90.

2 Muriel Thayer Painter collected numerous warnings and requirements regarding deer-human relationships, many of them analogous to those applying to curers who transmit power through their eyes and warnings not to blow on hot medicines (1986, 272–80).

3 The pahko'ola regalia are analyzed in Robinson 1992, 2–18. As noted in the introduction, my ability to describe, much less interpret adequately, the role of women in the ceremonies pales in comparison to those of the male groups. For descriptions of the female societies, see Painter 1986, 144–50; Erickson 2000, 227–52; and Erickson 2008.

4 Some of the more detailed can be found in the following works: Burton 1990; Evers and Molina 1987; Maaso, Molina, and Evers 1993; Montell 1938; Padilla 1998; Spicer 1980; E. Turner 1990; Valencia, Valencia, and Spicer 1990; Wilder 1963.

5 For more information on how Redfield, Spicer's thesis director, came to the quoted conclusion, see Edward H. Spicer, letter to Robert Redfield, 11 Feb. 1940, "Unprocessed Correspondence between Edward Spicer and Robert Redfield," ASM, folders 92–94.

6 Spicer's interpretations may have reflected a comment that Juan Valenzuela made one afternoon in conversation: "The pascolas don't come from the people of the enchantment. They just make jokes about coming from somewhere before they begin to dance" (Spicer, field notes 1942).

7 James Clifford notes, "Polyphonic works are particularly open to readings not specifically intended" (1982, 52).

8 For a detailed study of Spicer's modernist tendencies to categorize pahko'olam as profane, see Carsten 1993, 43. Thomas McGuire (1989) notes that Spicer viewed the rituals as both symbolically important and simply entertaining.

9 The types of animals addressed vary among pahko'olam. The practice of addressing these animals supports dialogic relations with the wilderness world, or huya ania. In this case particularly, lizards, toads, and other desert animals that walk close to the ground may be addressed due to their close connection with bringing rain in Yoeme cosmology. Herminia Valenzuela and Felipe S. Molina, conversation with the author, 21 June 1996.

10 This view of the shared culture of colonization is also taken up by Morrison 1979; Scott 1985, 1990; Trigger 1985. For descriptions of how power relations are mutually shared dynamics between groups of more and less power, see Gramsci 1973 and Thompson 1963.

11 I have found Richard Trexler's work very informative in regard to how

the Spaniards conceived of the cross as an effective tool in converting the indigenous populations of Central Mexico (1987, 481–83).

12 George Barker has written that "the climax of the Yaqui Easter Ceremony is not the Crucifixion but rather the final overcoming of the evil spirits." Barker 1957a, 141.

13 See also Morrison 1992a and 2002. A well-developed critique of Eliadian thinking throughout religious studies is Dudley 1977.

14 The "big headed" or masked monsters of the fariseos group belong to a secret society whose name, I am warned, should not appear in print outside of Lent. As a respectful gesture, I will use circumlocution regarding these performers.

15 Along this line of questioning, I am intrigued by the work of other scholars working with native hunters. Tim Ingold 2004, Sylvie Poirier 2004, and Adrian Tanner 2004 provide both the case studies and the theoretical models that may enable a better understanding of the importance of hunting to indigenous ontology and epistemology.

6. YOEME PLACE-MAKING

1 The main contention of the space-place debates is whether humans make indistinguishable spaces into constructed places, or do places shape our experiences of all senses of space? Edward Casey succinctly argues that since perception and knowledge rely on experience, and since experience is previously shaped by cultural constructions, the people never find themselves in unmarked, temporally independent spaces (1996, 44). Edward Relph 1985 and Miles Richardson 1989 contribute another perspective, that humans make spaces into places.

2 Beals 1943, 53–33; Beals 1945, 81; Holden et al. 1936, 55–66; Savala 1980, 174; Wagner 1972, 49–50, 57, 58.

3 One of the most focused descriptions of a Yoeme funeral was written by Chas. A. Guy, a newspaper correspondent on Holden's expedition. Unfortunately the writer's stereotypes and sensationalism cast doubt on most of his observations. See Guy 1972.

4 For previous accounts of burial activities, see Beals 1945, 77; Fabila 1940, 184; Wagner 1972, 59.

5 Also, there are only vague or general references to "angels" as inhabitants

of an other-than-earthly place: see both Painter 1986, 83–84, and Spicer 1980, 129.

6 The nine-day interpretation is found in Guy 1972, 186–87; Moisés, Kelley, and Holden 1971, 42, 66; and Painter 1986, 82, 88, 316. Yoeme views of afterlife become more complex when considering the widespread description of Yoeme views of ghosts; see Beals 1943, 55; Beals 1945, 81; Kelley 1971, xxx–xxxi, xxxiv; Painter 1986, 32–33, 67–68, 87–88; Wagner 1972, 24. For information on reincarnation, see Beals 1943, 55; and Beals 1945, 81.

7 For more information on the ever-present hand-touching ritual, see Spicer 1984, 234–35.

8 For an interesting description of how burial objects reflect complementary, not oppositional, concepts of Navajo ceremonial society membership and postmortem dimensions, see Cunningham 1993.

9 I asked one of my Yoeme friends if it is possible to draw a clear distinction between Mexican burials and Yoeme burials, and she told me that the use of wooden crosses for Yoeme burials continues, perhaps without exception.

10 See, e.g., Francaviglia 1971 and Sopher 1967.

11 I have gained much from reading the burial studies of Barber 1993 and Linden-Ward 1986.

12 For the categorization of the "death awareness" movement as a response to early twentieth-century anthropology, see Huntington and Metcalf 1979.

13 After the death of an immediate family member, individuals are often excused from ceremonial commitments for one year.

14 See J. B. Jackson (1967) for a contrasting view of American graveyard activities showing a private regard for the deceased, who are conceived as belonging to a separate community from the living.

15 Spicer notes elsewhere that the direction of west was "mythically" associated with a "land of the dead" and dangerous monsters (1980, 210). One of my main collaborators strongly disagrees with this notion.

16 Among others, see George C. Barker 1957a, 1957b; Richard Schechner 1997; and Edward Spicer 1958.

17 I am grateful to Don Brenneis for bringing my attention to the similarities between kontim and Rogationtide. Clearly, more work can be done in this area.

18 Spicer argued that this sense of "homeland" must be undeniable, since communities in Arizona have been less active in konti maintenance (1954, 205; 1980, 174).

19 Wood specifically admits that writing societies seem to develop in relation to mapping societies, thereby serving the power elites (1993, 53).

20 The concomitant relationship between writing and mapping societies is drawn out by Wood (1993), but also see Olson 1994, chapter 10. My thoughts on mapping in this section grow fruitfully from reading Cosgrove (1999).

21 For a concise analysis of the ways that all maps are subjective expressions of scale, symbol, and projection, see Monmonier 1991. For another description of the ways maps serve varying interests, see Wood 1992.

References

Adorno, Rolena, ed. 1982. *From oral to written expression: Native Andean chroniclers of the early colonial period.* Syracuse NY: Maxwell School of Citizenship and Public Affairs.

Alegre, Francisco Javier. 1841–42. *Historia de la Companía de Jesús en Nueva Espania.* México, D.F.: J. M. Lara.

Allen, Barbará, and Thomas J. Schlereth. 1990. *Sense of place: American regional cultures.* Lexington: University Press of Kentucky.

Anderson, Jeffrey D. 2001. Northern Arapaho conversion of a Christian text. *Ethnohistory* 48 (4): 689–712.

Ashcroft, Bill, Gareth Griffiths, and Helen Tiffin, eds. 1995. *The post-colonial studies reader.* London: Routledge.

Axtell, James. 1985. *The invasion within: The contest of cultures in colonial North America.* New York: Oxford University Press.

———. 1988. *After Columbus: Essays in the ethnohistory of colonial North America.* New York: Oxford University Press.

———. 2001. *Natives and newcomers: The cultural origins of North America.* New York: Oxford University Press.

Ayoub, Carlos Días, and Sandra Hurtado. 1999. Urge solucionar conflicto Yaqui. *El Imparcial*, October 4, Hermosillo ed.

Barber, Russell J. 1993. The Agua Mansa Cemetery: An indicator of ethnic identification in a Mexican-American community. In *Ethnicity and the American cemetery*, ed. Richard E. Meyer. Madison WI: Popular Press.

Barker, George C. 1957a. Some aspects of penitential processions in Spain and the American Southwest. *Journal of American Folklore* 70 (276): 137–42.

———. 1957b. The Yaqui Easter ceremony at Hermosillo. *Western Folklore* 16 (4): 256–62.

Barth, Fredrik, ed. 1998. *Ethnic groups and boundaries: The social organization of culture difference.* Prospect Heights IL: Waveland Press.

Bartra, Roger. 1993. *Agrarian structure and political power in Mexico*. Trans. Stephen K. Ault. Baltimore: Johns Hopkins University Press.

Basso, Keith H. 1996. *Wisdom sits in places: Landscape and language among the western Apache*. Albuquerque: University of New Mexico Press.

Beals, Ralph L. 1943. The aboriginal culture of the Cáhita Indians. *Iberoamericana* 19: 1–244.

———. 1945. *The contemporary culture of the Cáhita Indians*. U.S. Bureau of American Ethnology Bulletin 142. Washington DC: Government Printing Office.

Ben-Amos, Dan, and Kenneth S. Goldstein, eds. 1975. *Folklore: Performance and communication*. The Hague: Mouton.

Benamou, Michael, ed. 1977. *Performance in postmodern culture*. Milwaukee: Center for Twentieth-Century Studies, University of Wisconsin Press.

Berger, Thomas R. 1981. *Fragile freedoms*. Toronto: Clarke and Irwin.

———. 1991. *A long and terrible shadow: White values, native rights in the Americas, 1492–1992*. Seattle: University of Washington Press.

Berkhofer, Robert, Jr. 1978. *The white man's Indian: Images of the American Indian from Columbus to the present*. New York: Knopf.

Bhabha, Homi. 1985. Signs taken for wonders: Questions of ambivalence and authority under a tree outside Delhi, May 1817. *Critical Inquiry* 12 (1): 144–65.

Bogan, Phoebe M. 1925. *Yaqui Indian dances of Tucson, Arizona: An account of the ceremonial dances of the Yaqui Indians at Pascua*. Tucson: Archeological Society.

Bolón, Francisco González. 1999a. Amenazan Yaquis con subir presión. *El Imparcial,* October 4, Hermosillo edition.

———. 1999b. Buscan no imponer decisiones a Yaquis. *El Imparcial,* October 12, Hermosillo edition.

Bolón, Francisco González, and Analilia Esparza. 1999. Piden Amparo Nueve Yaquis. *El Imparcial,* October 7, Hermosillo edition.

Boone, Elizabeth Hill. 1994. Writing and recording knowledge. In *Writing without words: Alternative literacies in Mesoamerica and the Andes,* ed. Elizabeth Hill Boone and Walter D. Mignolo. Durham NC: Duke University Press.

Braden, Charles S. 1966. *Religious aspects of the conquest of Mexico*. 1930; reprint, New York: AMS Press.

Brandt, Elizabeth A. 1996. The fight for Dzil Nchaa Si An, Mt. Graham: Apaches and astrophysical development in Arizona. *Cultural Survival Quarterly* 19 (4): 50–57.

Briggs, Charles L. 1993. Metadiscursive practices and scholarly authority in folkloristics. *Journal of American Folklore* 106: 387–434.

Brill de Ramirez, Susan Berry. 1999. Sherman Alexie: Fancydancer. *Poets & Writers* 27 (1): 54–59.

Brown, Jennifer S. H., W. J. Eccles, and Donald P. Heldman, eds. 1994. *The fur trade revisited: Selected papers of the Sixth North American Fur Trade Conference, Mackinac Island, Michigan, 1991*. East Lansing/Mackinac Island: Michigan State University Press and Mackinac State Historical Parks.

Brown, Jennifer S. H., and Elizabeth Vibert, eds. 1996. *Reading beyond words: Contexts for native history*. Ontario: Broadview Press.

Brown, Joseph Epes. 1977. *The spiritual legacy of the American Indian*. New York: Crossroad Press, 1977.

Burnett, D. Graham. 2002. "It is impossible to make a step without the Indians": Nineteenth-century geographical exploration and the Amerindians of British Guiana. *Ethnohistory* 49 (1): 3–40.

Burton, Susan. 1990. Malichi, the flower fawn: The symbolism of the Yaqui deer dance. MA thesis, Texas Women's University.

Capps, Walter Holden, ed. 1976. *Seeing with a native eye: Essays on native American religion*. New York: Harper and Row.

Carsten, Cynthia G. 1993. Modernist versus post-modernist trends in ethnography: The case of the Yaqui. MA thesis, Arizona State University.

Casey, Edward S. 1996. How to get from space to place in a fairly short stretch of time: Phenomenological prolegomena. In *Senses of place*, ed. Steven Feld and Keith H. Basso. Santa Fe NM: School of American Research.

Cervantes, Fernando. 1994. *The devil in the new world: The impact of diabolism in New Spain*. New Haven: Yale University Press.

Chakrabarty, Dipesh. 1995. Provincializing Europe: Postcoloniality and the critique of history. *Cultural Studies* 6 (3): 337–57.

Christensen, Kathleen. 1982. Geography as a human science: A philosophic critique of the positivist-humanist split. In *A search for common ground*, ed. Peter Gould and Gunnar Olsson. London: Pion Limited.

Classen, Constance. 1993. *Inca cosmology and the human body*. Salt Lake City: University of Utah Press.

Cliff, Michelle. 1985. *The land of look behind*. Ithaca NY: Firebrand Books.

Clifford, James. 1982. *Person and myth: Maurice Leenhardt in the Melanesian world*. Berkeley: University of California Press.

———. 1988. *The predicament of culture: Twentieth-century ethnography, literature, and art*. Cambridge: Harvard University Press.

———. 1997. *Routes: Travel and translation in the late twentieth century*. Cambridge: Harvard University Press.

Clifford, James, and George E. Marcus, eds. 1986. *Writing culture: The poetics and politics of ethnography*. Berkeley: University of California Press, 1986.

Clendinnen, Inga. 1987. *Ambivalent conquests: Maya and Spaniard in Yucatan, 1517–1570*. New York: Cambridge University Press.

Cohen, Anthony P. 1985. *The symbolic construction of community*. London: Tavistock.

Connerton, Paul. 1989. *How societies remember*. New York: Cambridge University Press.

Conquergood, Dwight. 1991. Rethinking ethnography: Towards a critical cultural poetics. *Communication Monographs* 58 (2): 179–94.

Cosgrove, Denis. 1999. *Mappings*. London: Reaktion Books.

Crosby, Alfred. 1972. *The Columbian exchange*. Westport CT: Greenwood Press.

Cruikshank, Julie, in collaboration with Angela Sidney, Kitty Smith, and Annie Ned. 1990. *Life lived like a story: Life stories of three Yukon native elders*. Lincoln: University of Nebraska Press.

———. 1998. *The social life of stories: Narrative and knowledge in the Yukon Territory*. Lincoln: University of Nebraska Press.

Crumrine, N. Ross, ed. 1979. *Ritual symbolism and ceremonialism in the Americas: Studies in symbolic anthropology*. Greeley: Museum of Anthropology, University of Northern Colorado.

Crumrine, N. Ross, and Rosamond B. Spicer. 1997. Summary and
conclusions. In *Performing the renewal of community: Indigenous
Easter rituals in North Mexico and southwest United States,* ed.
Rosamond B. Spicer and N. Ross Crumrine. Lanham MD: University
Press of America.

Cunningham, Keith. 1993. The people of Rimrock bury Alfred K. Lorenzo:
Tri-cultural funerary practices. In *Ethnicity and the American
cemetery,* ed. Richard E. Meyer. Bowling Green OH: Bowling Green
University Popular Press.

Curnow, Wystan. 1999. Mapping and the extended field of contemporary
art. In *Mappings,* ed. Denis Cosgrove. London: Reaktion Books.

Davids, Brent Michael. 1988. Beginning analysis of the range of Yaqui
reality in Painter's *With good heart.* Manuscript. Arizona State
University.

de Certeau, Michel. 1988. *The writing of history.* Trans. Tom Conley. New
York: Columbia University Press.

Decorme, Gerard. 1941. *La obra de los Jesuitas Mexicanos durante la epoca
colonial, 1572–1767.* México, D.F.: Antigua Libreria Robredo de José
Porrua e Hijos.

Deloria, Vine, Jr. 1994. *God is red: A native view of religion.* 1973. Golden
CO: Fulcrum.

Densmore, Frances. 1929. *Papago music.* U.S. Bureau of American
Ethnology Bulletin 90. Washington DC: Government Printing Office.

Derrida, Jacques. 1974. *Of grammatology.* Trans. Gayatri Chakravorty
Spivak. Baltimore: Johns Hopkins University Press.

Despres, Leo. 1975. *Ethnicity and resource competition in plural societies.* The
Hague: Mouton.

Diamond, Stanley. 1974. *In search of the primitive: A critique of civilization.*
New Brunswick NJ: Transaction Books.

Diringer, David. 1962. *Writing.* New York: Dover, 1962.

Dirlik, Arif. 2000. Is there history after Eurocentrism? Globalism,
postcolonialism, and the disavowal of history. In *History after the
three worlds,* ed. Arif Dirlik, Vinay Bahl, and Peter Gran. Lanham MD:
Rowman & Littlefield.

Dirlik, Arif, Vinay Bahl, and Peter Gran, eds. 2000. *History after the three*

worlds: Post-Eurocentric historiographies. Lanham MD: Rowman and
Littlefield.

Dubisch, Jill. 1995. In a different place: Pilgrimage, gender, and politics at a
Greek island shrine. Princeton: Princeton University Press.

Dudley, Gilford, III. 1977. Religion on trial: Mircea Eliade and his critics.
Philadelphia: Temple University Press.

Dunbier, Roger. 1968. The Sonoran Desert: Its geography, economy, and
people. Tucson: University of Arizona Press.

Dundes, Alan, ed. 1988. The Flood Myth. Berkeley: University of California
Press.

Dunne, Peter Masten. 1951. Andrés Pérez de Ribas: Pioneer black robe of
the West Coast, administrator, historian. Edited by John J. Meng.
New York: United States Catholic Historical Society.

Dussel, Enrique. 1995. The invention of the Americas: Eclipse of "the other"
and the myth of modernity. Trans. Michael D. Barber. New York:
Continuum.

Eliade, Mircea. 1954. Cosmos and history: The myth of the eternal return.
Trans. Willard Trask. Princeton: Princeton University Press.

Erasmus, Charles J. 1967. Culture change in northwest Mexico. In
Contemporary change in traditional societies 3: Mexican and Peruvian
communities, ed. Julian H. Steward. Urbana: University of Illinois Press.

Erickson, Kirstin C. 2000. Ethnic places, gendered spaces: The expressive
constitution of Yaqui identities. PhD diss., University of Wisconsin,
Madison.

———. 2003. "They will come from the other side of the sea": Prophecy,
ethnogenesis, and agency in Yaqui narrative. Journal of American
Folklore 116: 465–82.

———. 2008. Yaqui homeland and homeplace: The everyday production of
ethnic identity. Tucson: University of Arizona Press.

Evers, Larry. 1981a. On the power of Yaqui deer songs. Telescope 2: 99–109.

———, ed. 1981b. The south corner of time: Hopi, Navajo, Papago, and Yaqui
tribal literature. Tucson: University of Arizona Press.

Evers, Larry, and Felipe S. Molina. 1987. Yaqui deer songs/Maso Bwikam:
A native American poetry. Tucson: Sun Tracks and University of
Arizona Press.

————. 1989. *Wo'i Bwikam = Coyote songs.* Tucson: Chax Press.

————. 1992. The holy dividing line: Inscription and resistance in Yaqui culture. *Journal of the Southwest* 34 (1): 3–46.

Fabila, Alfonso. 1940. *Las tribus Yaquis de Sonora.* México, D.F.: Departamento de Asuntos Indigenas.

Farrer, Claire R. 1991. *Living life's circle: Mescalero Apache cosmovision.* Albuquerque: University of New Mexico Press.

Farriss, Nancy M. 1984. *Maya society under colonial rule: The collective enterprise of survival.* Princeton: Princeton University Press.

Feit, Harvey. 1991. The construction of "Algonquian Hunting Territories." In *Colonial situations: Essay of ethnographic knowledge,* ed. George Stocking Jr. Madison: University of Wisconsin Press.

Feld, Steven, and Keith H. Basso, eds. 1996. *Senses of place.* Santa Fe NM: School of American Research.

Fentress, James, and Chris Wickham. 1992. *Social memory.* Boston: Blackwell.

Fienup-Riordan, Ann. 1990. *Eskimo essays: Yup'ik lives and how we see them.* New Brunswick NJ: Rutgers University Press.

————. 1991. *The real people and the children of thunder: The Yup'ik Eskimo encounter with Moravian missionaries John and Edith Kilbuck.* Norman: University of Oklahoma Press.

Finnegan, Ruth. 1988. *Literacy and orality: Studies in the technology of communication.* Oxford: Blackwell.

Fischer, Edward F. 1992. Yaqui voices and Spanish texts, or inquiries into Yaqui history, 1533–1740. *Human Mosaic* 26: 4–11.

Fitzhugh, William W. 1985. *Cultures in contact: The impact of European contacts on Native American cultural institutions, AD 1000–1800.* Washington DC: Smithsonian Institution Press.

Folgelson, Raymond D. 1974. On the varieties of Indian history: Sequoyah and Traveler Bird. *Journal of Ethnic Studies* 2: 105–12.

Foucault, Michel. 1976. *The archaeology of knowledge.* New York: Harper.

————. 1979. What is an author? Trans. Josué V. Harari. In *Textual strategies: Perspectives in post-structuralist criticism,* ed. Josué V. Harari. Ithaca NY: Cornell University Press.

Fowler, Loretta. 1987. *Shared symbols, contested meanings: Gros ventre culture and history, 1778–1984.* Ithaca NY: Cornell University Press.

Fox, James J. 1997. Place and landscape in comparative Austronesian perspective. In *The poetic power of place: Comparative perspectives on Austronesian ideas of locality*, ed. James J. Fox. Canberra: Department of Anthropology, published in association with the Comparative Austronesian Project, Research School of Pacific and Asian Studies, Australian National University.

Francaviglia, Richard W. 1971. The cemetery as an evolving cultural landscape. *Annals of the Association of American Geographers* 62: 501–9.

Franklin, Wayne, and Michael Steiner, eds. 1992. *Mapping American culture*. Iowa City: University of Iowa Press.

Geertz, Armin W. 1984. A reed pierced the sky: Hopi Indian cosmography on Third Mesa, Arizona. *Numen* 31 (2): 216–41.

———. 1994. *The invention of prophecy: Continuity and meaning in Hopi Indian religion*. Berkeley: University of California Press.

Geertz, Clifford. 1983. *Local knowledge: Further essays in interpretive anthropology*. New York: Basic.

Gelb, I. J. 1963. *A study of writing*. 2nd ed. Chicago: University of Chicago Press, 1963.

Giddings, Ruth Warner. 1945. Folk literature of the Yaqui Indians. MA thesis, University of Arizona.

———. 1959. *Yaqui myths and legends*. Ed. Harry Behn. Tucson: University of Arizona Press.

———. Myths-Rahum, Juan Valenzuela. Accession 2000–175, box 6, folder 353. Tucson: Arizona State Museum Archives.

Gill, Sam D. 1977. Prayer as person: The performative force in Navajo prayer acts. *History of Religions* 17 (2): 143–57.

———. 1982. *Beyond "the primitive": The religions of nonliterate peoples*. Englewood Cliffs NJ: Prentice.

———. 1998. *Storytracking: Texts, stories, and histories in central Australia*. Oxford: Oxford University Press.

Gledhill, John, Barbara Bender, and Mogens Trolle Larsen, eds. 1988. *State and society: The emergence and development of social hierarchy and political centralization*. Boston: Unwin Hyman.

Goldie, Terry. 1995. The representation of the Indigene. In *The post-colonial* studies reader, ed. Bill Ashcroft, Gareth Griffiths, and Helen Tiffin. London: Routledge.

Goody, Jack. 1987. *The interface between the written and the oral*. Cambridge: Cambridge University Press.

Goody, Jack, and Ian Watt. 1963. The consequences of literacy. *Comparative Studies in Society and History* 5: 304–45.

González, Candelaria, and Gerardo Ponce de León. 1999. Preparan Bloqueos Los Yaquis. *El Imparcial*, October 5, Hermosillo edition.

González de Cossío, Francisco. 2007. *Crónicas de la compañía de Jesús en la Nueva España*. México, D.F.: Universidad National Autónoma de México.

Gramsci, Antonio. 1973. *Letters from prison*. Ed. Lynne Lawner. New York: Harper.

Griffith, James S., and Felipe S. Molina. 1980. *Old men of the fiesta: An introduction to the Pascola arts*. Phoenix: Heard Museum.

Gudeman, Stephen. 1972. The compadrazgo as a reflection of the natural and spiritual person. *Proceedings of the Royal Anthropological Institute for 1971*, 45–71.

Grimes, Ronald L. 1992. *Symbol and conquest: Public ritual and drama in Santa Fe*. Albuquerque: University of New Mexico Press, 1992.

Gupta, Akhil, and James Ferguson. 1997. Culture, power, place: Ethnography at the end of an era. In *Culture, power, place: Explorations in critical anthropology*, ed. Akhil Gupta and James Ferguson. Durham NC: Duke University Press, 1997.

Guy, Charles A. 1972. Here's how it happened: Charles A. Guy's newspaper accounts of the Yaqui expedition. In *Chronicles of the Yaqui expedition*, ed. Jimmy M. Skaggs, Fane Downs, and Winifred Vigness. Lubbock: West Texas Museum Association, 1972.

Hallowell, A. Irving. 1975. Ojibwa ontology, behavior, and worldview. In *Teachings from the American earth: Indian religion and philosophy*, ed. Dennis Tedlock and Barbara Tedlock. New York: Liveright.

Hammond, George P., and Agapito Rey. 1928. *Obregón's history of sixteenth-century explorations in western America*. Los Angeles: Wetzel.

Hanke, Lewis. 1974. *All mankind is one: A study of the disputation between Bartolomé de Las Casas and Juan Ginés de Sepúlveda on the religious*

and *intellectual capacity of the American Indians.* De Kalb: Northern
Illinois University Press.

Haraway, Donna. 1988. Situated knowledge. *Feminist Studies* 14: 575–99.

Harris, Max. 1993. *The dialogical theater: Dramatization of the conquest of
Mexico and the question of the other.* New York: St. Martin's.

Harrod, Howard L. 1987. *Renewing the world: Northern Plains Indian
religion.* Tucson: University of Arizona Press.

———. 1995. *Becoming and remaining a people: Native American religions on
the Northern Plains.* Tucson: University of Arizona Press.

Hartman, Pamela. 1994a. Yaquis in crisis. *Tucson Citizen,* November 24,
Home edition.

———. 1994b. Yaqui tribe's factional dispute turns bloody. *Tucson Citizen,*
November 25, Home edition.

Hartsock, Nancy. 1984. *Money, sex, and power: Toward a feminist historical
materialism.* Boston: Northeastern University Press.

———. 1987. Rethinking modernism: Minority vs. majority theories.
Cultural Critique 7 (Fall): 187–206.

Hassig, Ross. 1993. Foreword to *The conquistadors: First-person accounts of
the conquest of Mexico,* ed. and trans. Patricia de Fuentes. Norman:
University of Oklahoma Press.

Hefner, Robert. 1993. *Conversion to Christianity: Historical and
anthropological perspectives on a great transformation.* Berkeley:
University of California Press.

Hertz, Robert. 1907. *Mélanges de sociologie et de folklore.* Ed. Marcel Mauss.
Paris: Alcan.

Hill, Archibald A. 1967. The typology of writing systems. In *Papers in
linguistics in honor of Leon Dostert,* ed. William A. Austin. The Hague:
Mouton.

Holden, William Curry. 1972. General introduction. In *Chronicles of the
Yaqui expedition,* ed. Jimmy M. Skaggs, Fane Downs, and Winifred
Vigness. Lubbock: West Texas Museum Association.

Holden, William Curry, C. C. Seltzer, R. A. Studhalter, C. J. Wagner,
and W. G. McMillan. 1936. Studies of the Yaqui Indians of Sonora,
Mexico. *Texas Technological College Bulletin* 12 (1): 55–66.

Hu-DeHart, Evelyn. 1981. *Missionaries, miners, and Indians.* Tucson:
University of Arizona Press.

———. 1984. *Yaqui resistance and survival.* Madison: University of Wisconsin Press.

———. 1995. *Historia de los Pueblos Indígenas de México.* Juárez, Mexico: Centro de Investigaciones y Estudios Superiores en Antropología Social.

Hultkrantz, Åke. 1979. *The religions of the American Indians.* Berkeley: University of California Press.

———. 1981. *Belief and worship in Native North America.* Ed. Christopher Vecsey. Syracuse NY: Syracuse University Press.

Huntington, Richard, and Peter Metcalf. 1979. *Celebrations of death: The anthropology of mortuary ritual.* Cambridge: Cambridge University Press.

Icazbalceta, Joaquín García. 1866. *Colección de documentos para la historia de México.* 2 vols. México, D.F.: Antigua Librería.

Idinopulos, Thomas A., and Brian C. Wilson, eds. 1998. *What is religion? Origins, definitions, and explanations.* Leiden: E. J. Brill.

Ingold, Tim. 2004. A circumpolar night's dream. In *Figured worlds: Ontological obstacles in intercultural relations,* ed. John Clammer, Sylvie Poirier, and Eric Schwimmer. Toronto: University of Toronto Press.

Irwin, Lee. 1994. *The dream seekers: Native American visionary traditions of the Great Plains.* Norman: University of Oklahoma Press.

Jackson, J. B. 1967. From monument to place: The vanishing epitaph. *Landscape* 17 (Winter): 22–26.

Jackson, Kenneth, and Camilo José Vergara. 1989. *Silent cities: The evolution of the American cemetery.* New York: Princeton Architectural Press.

Jackson, Robert H. 1994. *Indian population decline: The missions of northwestern New Spain, 1687–1840.* Albuquerque: University of New Mexico Press.

Jacobsen, S.J., Jerome V. 1938. *Educational foundations of the Jesuits in sixteenth-century New Spain.* Berkeley: University of California Press.

Jansen, Maarten, Peter Van Der Loo, and Roswitha Manning, eds. 1988. *Continuity and identity in Native America: Essays in honor of Benedikt Hartmann.* New York: E. J. Brill.

Kaczkurkin, Mini Valenzuela. 1977. *Yoeme: Lore of the Arizona Yaqui people.* Tucson: University of Arizona Press.

Kelley, Jane Holden. 1971. Introduction to *The tall candle: The personal chronicle of a Yaqui Indian*, by Rosalio Moisés, Jane Holden Kelley, and William Curry Holden. Lincoln: University of Nebraska Press.

———. 1978. *Yaqui women: Contemporary life histories*. Lincoln: University of Nebraska Press.

Klor de Alva, J. Jorge. 1982. Spiritual conflict and accommodation in New Spain: Toward a typology of Aztec responses to Christianity. In *The Inca and Aztec states, 1400–1800: Anthropology and history*, ed. George A. Collier, Renato I. Rosaldo, and John D. Wirth. New York: Academic Press.

Kroeber, Alfred L. 1927. Disposal of the dead. *American Anthropologist* 29: 308–15.

Kugel, Rebecca. 1998. *To be the main leaders of our people: A history of Minnesota Ojibwe politics, 1820–1998*. Ann Arbor: Michigan State University Press, 1998.

Kuper, Adam. 1999. *Culture: The anthropologists' account*. Cambridge: Harvard University Press, 1999.

Kusch, Rodolfo. 1963. *América profunda*. Buenos Aires: Hachette, 1963.

Ladner, Joyce. 1971. *Tomorrow's tomorrow*. Garden City NY: Doubleday.

Langer, Erick, and Robert H. Jackson. 1995. *The new Latin American mission history*. Lincoln: University of Nebraska Press.

Larsen, Clark Spencer, and George R. Milner, eds. 1994. *In the wake of contact: Biological responses to conquest*. New York: Wiley-Liss.

León-Portilla, Miguel. 1990. *Endangered Cultures*. Trans. Julie Goodson-Lawes. Dallas: Southern Methodist University Press.

Lévi-Strauss, Claude. 1977. *Tristes tropiques*. [1973.] Trans. John and Doreen Weightman. New York: Modern Library.

Leyva, Alfonso Florez. 1992. Testamento. *Journal of the Southwest* 34 (1): 73–106.

Lincoln, Bruce. 1989. *Discourse and the construction of society: Comparative studies of myth, ritual, and classification*. New York: Oxford University Press.

Linden-Ward, Blanche. 1986. Putting the past under grass: History as death and cemetery commemoration. *Prospects* 10: 279–314.

Lipsitz, George. 1990. *Time passages: Collective memory and American popular culture*. Minneapolis: University of Minnesota Press.

Lokensgard, Kenneth. 1993. Medicine bundle persons: Blackfoot ontology and the study of Native American religions. MA thesis, Arizona State University.

Maaso, Miki, Felipe Molina, and Larry Evers. 1993. The elders' truth: A Yaqui sermon. *Journal of the Southwest* 35 (3): 225–317.

Madsen, William. 1957. Christo-Paganism: A study of Mexican religious syncretism. *Middle American Research Institute Publications* 19: 105–80.

Mahoney, James Michael. 1993. Yoeme testamento: Original compact, contemporary interpretation and implementation in the Rio Yaqui, Sonora, Mexico. Manuscript. Arizona State University.

———. 1994. The sacred trust: Basic policies of wilderness conservation in the Yaqui indigenous community, Sonora, Mexico. MA thesis. Arizona State University.

Mallon, Florencia. 2000. The promise and dilemma of subaltern studies: Perspectives from Latin American history. In *History after the three worlds: Post-Eurocentric historiographies,* ed. Arif Dirlik, Vinay Bahl, and Peter Gran. Lanham MD: Rowman and Littlefield.

Mason, J. A., and A. M. Espinosa. 1914. Folk-tales of the Tepecanos. *Journal of American Folklore* 27: 148–211.

McCutcheon, Russell. 1998. Redescribing "religion" as social formation: Toward a theory of religion. In *What is religion? Origins, definitions, and explanations,* ed. Thomas A. Idinopulos and Brian C. Wilson. Leiden: E. J. Brill.

McGuire, Thomas R. 1986. *Politics and ethnicity on the Rio Yaqui: Potam revisited.* Tucson: University of Arizona Press.

———. 1989. Ritual, theater, and the persistence of the ethnic group: Interpreting Yaqui Semana Santa. *Journal of the Southwest* 31 (2): 159–78.

McLuhan, Marshall. 1967. *Understanding media: The extension of man.* London: Sphere Books.

Merrill, William L. 1988. *Rarámuri souls: Knowledge and social process in northern Mexico.* Washington DC: Smithsonian Institution Press.

Meyer, Melissa. 1994. *The white earth tragedy: Ethnicity and dispossession at a Minnesota Anishinaabe reservation, 1889–1920.* Lincoln: University of Nebraska Press.

Meyer, Richard E. 1993. Ethnic cemeteries in America. In *Ethnicity and the American cemetery*, ed. Richard E. Meyer. Bowling Green OH: Bowling Green State University Popular Press.

Mignolo, Walter. 1994. Afterword. In *Writing without words: Alternative literacies in Mesoamerica and the Andes*, ed. Elizabeth Hill Boone and Walter D. Mignolo. Durham NC: Duke University Press.

———. 1995. *The darker side of the Renaissance: Literacy, territoriality, and colonization*. Ann Arbor: University of Michigan Press.

———. 2000. *Local histories/global designs: Coloniality, subaltern knowledges, and border thinking*. Princeton: Princeton University Press.

Mills, Antonia, and Richard Slobodin, eds. 1994. *Amerindian rebirth: Reincarnation belief among North American Indians and Inuit*. Toronto: University of Toronto Press.

Mills, Kenneth. 1994. The limits of religious conversion in mid-colonial Peru. *Past & Present* 145: 84–132.

Moisés, Rosalio, Jane Holden Kelley, and William Curry Holden. 1971. *The tall candle: The personal chronicle of a Yaqui Indian*. Lincoln: University of Nebraska Press.

Molina, Felipe S. Personal interview. September 21, 1994.

———. Personal interview. February 15, 1996.

———. Personal interview. March 14, 1996.

———, and Mini Valenzuela. Personal interview. September 26, 1994.

———. Personal interview. June 21, 1996.

Molina, Felipe S., and Larry Evers. 1998. "Like this it stays in your hands": Collaboration and ethnopoetics. *Oral Tradition* 13 (1): 15–57.

Molina, Felipe S., and David Leedom Shaul. 1993. *A concise Yoeme and English dictionary*. Tucson: Tucson Unified School District.

Molina, Felipe S., Herminia Valenzuela, and David Leedom Shaul. 1999. *Yoeme-English/English-Yoeme standard dictionary*. New York: Hippocrene Books.

Molina, Felipe S., Octaviana Salazar, Mini V. Kaczkurkin. 1983. *The Yaqui: A people and their place — A history*. Phoenix: Pueblo Grande Museum.

Monmonier, Mark. 1991. *How to lie with maps*. Chicago: University of Chicago Press.

Montell, Gösta. 1938. Yaqui dances. *Ethnos* 3 (6): 145–66.

Morrison, Kenneth M. 1979. Towards a history of intimate encounters: Algonkian folklore, Jesuit missionaries, and Kiwakwe, the cannibal giant. *American Indian Culture and Research Journal* 3 (4): 51–80.

———. 1992a. Beyond the supernatural: Language and religious action. *Religion* 22: 201–5.

———. 1992b. Sharing the flower: A non-supernaturalistic theory of grace. *Religion* 22: 207–19.

———. 2000. The cosmos as intersubjective: Native American other-than-human persons. In *Indigenous religions: A companion*, ed. Harvey Graham. London: Cassell.

———. 2002. *The solidarity of kin: Ethnohistory, religious studies, and the Algonkian-French religious encounter*. Albany: State University of New York Press.

Nabokov, Peter. 1996. Native views of history. In *The Cambridge history of native peoples of the Americas, part one*, ed. Bruce G. Trigger and Wilcomb E. Washburn. New York: Cambridge University Press.

Nandy, Ashis. 1983. *The intimate enemy: Loss and recovery of self under colonialism*. New Delhi: Oxford University Press.

Niranjana, Tejaswini. 1992. *Siting translation: History, post-structuralism, and the colonial context*. Berkeley: University of California Press.

Norrell, Brenda. 1998. Indian passports. *Indian Country Today*, May 22, 47.

Olson, David R. 1994. *The world on paper: The conceptual and cognitive implications of writing and reading*. Cambridge: Cambridge University Press.

Ortiz, Alfonso. 1977. Some concerns to the writing of "Indian" History. *Indian Historian* 10 (1): 17–22.

Padilla, Stan. 1998. *Deer dancer: Yaqui legends of life*. Summertown TN: Book Publishing Company.

Painter, Muriel Thayer. 1986. *With good heart: Yaqui beliefs and ceremonies in Pascua village*. Tucson: University of Arizona Press.

Painter, Muriel Thayer, Refugio Savala, and Ignacio Alvarez, eds. 1955. A Yaqui Easter sermon. *University of Arizona Social Science Bulletin* 26 (6).

Pandya, Vishvajit. 1990. Movement and space: Andamanese cartography. *American Ethnologist* 17 (3): 775–97.

Patterson, Thomas C. 2000. Archaeologists and historians confront civilization, relativism, and poststructuralism in the late twentieth century. In *History after the three worlds: Post-Eurocentric historiographies,* ed. Arif Dirlik, Vinay Bahl, and Peter Gran. Lanham MD: Rowman and Littlefield.

Pérez de Ribas, Andrés. 1944. *Triunfos de Nuestra Santa Fé entre Gentes las mas Bárbaras y Fieras del Nuevo Orbe.* Vols. 1–3. 1645. México, D.F.: Editorial Layac.

———. 1999. *History of the triumphs of our holy faith amongst the most barbarous and fierce peoples of the new world.* Trans. Daniel T. Reff, Maureen Ahern, and Richard K. Danford. Tucson: University of Arizona Press.

Phelan, Peggy. 1993. *Unmarked: The politics of performance.* New York: Routledge.

Pickles, John. 1985. *Phenomenology, science, and geography: Spatiality and the human sciences.* Cambridge: Cambridge University Press.

Poirier, Sylvie. 2004. Ontology, ancestral order, and agencies among the Kakatja of the Australian Western Desert. In *Figured worlds: Ontological obstacles in intercultural relations,* ed. John Clammer, Sylvie Poirier, and Eric Schwimmer. Toronto: University of Toronto Press.

Pollock, Della, ed. 1998. *Exceptional spaces: Essays in performance and history.* Chapel Hill: University of North Carolina Press.

Ponce de León, Gerardo, and Diego Wong. 1999. Está tranquila situación. *El Imparcial,* October 5, Hermosillo edition.

Powers, William K. 1987. *Beyond the vision: Essays on American Indian culture.* Norman: University of Oklahoma Press.

Pratt, Mary Louise. 1992. *Imperial eyes: Travel writing and transculturation.* London: Routledge.

Proceso del Marquéz del Valle y Nuño de Guzmán y los adelantados Soto y Alvarado, sobre el descubrimiento de la Tierra Nueva (Año de 1541). 1871. *Collección de documentos inéditos relativos al descubrimiento, conquista y organización de las antiguas posesiones españoles de América y Oceanía, sacados de los archivos del de Indias* 15. Madrid: Impr. De José María Pérez, 300–408.

Rabasa, José. 1993. *Inventing America: Spanish historiography and the formation of Eurocentrism.* Norman: University of Oklahoma Press.

———. 2000. *Writing violence on the northern frontier: The historiography of sixteenth-century New Mexico and Florida and the legacy of conquest.* Durham NC: Duke University Press.

Rafael, Vicente L. 1993. *Contracting colonialism: Translation and Christian conversion in Tagalog society under early Spanish rule.* Durham NC: Duke University Press.

Raffles, Hugh. 1999. "Local theory": Nature and the making of an Amazonian place. *Cultural Anthropology* 14 (3): 323–60.

Ramsey, Jerold. 1977. The Bible in western Indian mythology. *Journal of American Folklore* 90: 442–54.

Rappaport, Roy. 1999. *Ritual and religion in the making of humanity.* New York: Cambridge University Press.

Redfield, Robert. 1960. *The little community and peasant society and culture.* Chicago: University of Chicago Press.

———. 1984. Foreword to *Pascua: A Yaqui village in Arizona,* by Edward H. Spicer, 1940. Tucson: University of Arizona Press.

Reff, Daniel T. 1987. Old world diseases and the dynamics of Indian and Jesuit relations in northwestern New Spain, 1520–1660. In *Ejidos and regions of refuge in northwestern Mexico,* ed. N. Ross Crumrine and Phil C. Wiegand. Tucson: University of Arizona Press.

Reff, Daniel T. 1991. *Disease, depopulation, and culture change in northwestern New Spain, 1518–1764.* Salt Lake City: University of Utah Press.

Reff, Daniel T., Maureen Ahern, and Richard K. Danford, trans. 1999. *History of the triumphs of our holy faith amongst the most barbarous and fierce peoples of the new world: An English translation based on the 1645 Spanish original.* Tucson: University of Arizona Press.

Reinelt, Janelle G., and Joseph R. Roach, eds. 1992. *Critical theory and performance.* Ann Arbor: University of Michigan Press.

Relph, Edward. 1985. Geographical experiences and being-in-the-world: The phenomenological origins of geography. In *Dwelling, place, and environment: Towards a phenomenology of person and world,* ed. David Seamon and Robert Mugerauer. Dordrecht: Martinus Nijhoff.

Ricard, Robert. 1966. *The spiritual conquest of Mexico: An essay on the apostolate and the evangelization methods of the mendicant orders in New Spain, 1523–1572.* Trans. Lesley Byrd Simpson. Berkeley: University of California Press.

Richardson, Miles. 1989. Place and culture: Two disciplines, two concepts, two images of Christ, and a single goal. In *The power of place: Bringing together geographical and sociological imaginations,* ed. John A. Agnew and James S. Duncan. Boston: Unwin Hyman.

Riley, Carroll L. 1981. Sonora and Arizona in the protohistoric period: Discussion of papers by Sheridan, Reff, Masse, and Doelle. In *The protohistoric period in the North American Southwest, AD 1450–1700,* ed. David R. Wilcox and W. Bruce Masse. Tempe: Arizona State University.

Robinson, Alfred Eugene. 1992. Beneath the mask of the Pahkola: Survival, continuity, and renaissance in the body of Yaqui tradition. MA thesis, University of California, Los Angeles.

Rosaldo, Renato. 1993. *Culture and truth: The remaking of social analysis.* Boston: Beacon.

Ross, Ellen. 1991. Diversities of divine presence: Women's geography in the Christian tradition. In *Sacred places and profane spaces: Essays in the geographics of Judaism, Christianity, and Islam,* ed. Jamie Scott and Paul Simpson-Housley. New York: Greenwood Press.

Ruíz Ruíz, María Trinidad, and Gerardo David Aguilar. 1994. *Tres procesos de lucha por la sobrevivencia de la tribu Yaqui: Testimonios.* Hermosillo: Universidad de Sonora.

Rumsey, Alan, and James Weiner, eds. 2001. *Emplaced myth: Space, narrative, and knowledge in Aboriginal Australia and Papua New Guinea.* Honolulu: University of Hawai'i Press.

Sahlins, Marshall D. 1981. *Historical metaphors and mythical realities: Structure in the early history of the Sandwich Islands Kingdom.* Ann Arbor: University of Michigan Press.

———. 1985. *Islands of history.* Chicago: University of Chicago Press, 1985.

———. 1994. Goodbye to Tristes Tropes: Ethnography in the context of modern world systems. In *Assessing cultural anthropology,* ed. Robert Borofsky. New York: McGraw.

Sands, Kathleen M. 1983. The singing tree: Dynamics of a Yaqui myth. *American Quarterly* 35: 355–75.

Sarris, Greg. 1994. *Mabel McKay: Weaving the dream*. Berkeley: University of California Press.

Savala, Refugio. 1980. *The autobiography of a Yaqui poet*. Ed. Kathleen M. Sands. Tucson: University of Arizona Press.

Schechner, Richard. 1985. *Between theater and anthropology*. Philadelphia: University of Pennsylvania Press.

———. 1997. Waehma: Space, time, identity, and theater at New Pascua, Arizona. In *Performing the renewal of community: Indigenous Easter rituals in north Mexico and southwest United States*, ed. Rosamond B. Spicer and N. Ross Crumrine. Lanham MD: University Press of America.

Schieffelin, Edward L. 1985. Performance and the cultural construction of reality. *American Ethnologist* 12: 707–24.

Scott, James C. 1985. *Weapons of the weak: Everyday forms of peasant resistance*. New Haven: Yale University Press.

———. 1990. *Domination and the arts of resistance: Hidden transcripts*. New Haven: Yale University Press.

Seamon, David, and Robert Mugerauer, eds. 1985. *Dwelling, place, and environment: Towards a phenomenology of person and world*. Dordrecht: Martinus Nijhoff.

Sheridan, Thomas E. 1981. Prelude to conquest: Yaqui population, subsistence, and warfare during the protohistoric period. In *The protohistoric period in the North American Southwest, AD 1450–1700*, ed. David R. Wilcox and W. Bruce Masse. Tempe: Arizona State University.

———. 1988. How to tell the story of a "people without history": Narrative versus ethnohistorical approaches to the study of the Yaqui Indians through time. *Journal of the Southwest* 30 (2): 172–86.

Shorter, David. 2001. Binary thinking and the study of Yoeme Indian lutu'uria/truth. Paper presented at the annual meeting of the American Anthropological Association, Washington DC, November 28–December 3.

———. 2002. Santam liniam divisoriam/holy dividing lines: Yoeme

Indian place-making and religious identity. PhD diss., University of California Santa Cruz.

——. 2003. Binary thinking and the study of Yoeme Indian lutu'uria/ truth. *Anthropological Forum* 13 (2): 195–203.

Shorter, David. 2003. *Vachiam eecha/Planting the seeds: Yoeme culture and language.* New York: Hemispheric Institute of Performance and Politics, *http://hemi.nyu.edu/cuaderno/yoeme/content.html.*

Simpson, Lesley Byrd. 1950. *The encomienda in New Spain: The beginning of Spanish Mexico.* Berkeley: University of California Press.

Skaggs, Jimmy M., Fane Downs, and Winifred Vigness, eds. 1972. *Chronicles of the Yaqui expedition.* Lubbock: West Texas Museum Association.

Slagle, Allogan. 1990. The Native-American tradition and legal status: Tolowa tales and Tolowa places. In *The nature and context of minority discourse,* ed. Abdul R. JanMohamed and David Lloyd. Oxford: Oxford University Press.

Smith, Bruce R. 1999. *The acoustic world of early modern England: Attending to the O-factor.* Chicago: University of Chicago Press.

Smith, Linda Tuhiwai. 1999. *Decolonizing methodologies: Research and indigenous peoples.* New York: Zed Books.

Smith, Jonathan Z. 1978. *Map is not territory.* Chicago: University of Chicago Press.

——. 1982. *Imagining religion: From Babylon to Jonestown.* Chicago: University of Chicago Press.

——. 1987. *To take place: Toward theory in ritual.* Chicago: University of Chicago Press.

Soja, Edward W. 1989. *Postmodern geographies: The reassertion of space in critical theory.* London: Verso.

Sombra, Ignacio. Personal interview. October 30, 1995.

Sopher, David Edward. 1967. *Geography of religions.* Englewood Cliffs NJ: Prentice.

Spence, Jonathan D. 1984. *The memory palace of Matteo Ricci.* New York: Viking Penguin.

Spicer, Edward H. 1942. Field notes, file A-505-a. Tucson: Arizona State Museum Archives.

———. 1943. Linguistic aspects of Yaqui acculturation. *American Anthropologist* 45: 410–26.

———. 1954. *Potam: A Yaqui village in Sonora.* Menesha WI: American Anthropological Association.

———. 1958. Social structure and the acculturation process. *American Anthropologist* 60 (3): 433–41.

———, ed. 1961. *Perspectives in American Indian cultural change.* Chicago: University of Chicago Press.

———. 1962. *Cycles of conquest.* Tucson: University of Arizona Press.

———. 1980. *The Yaquis: A cultural history.* Tucson: University of Arizona Press.

———. 1981. Southwestern healing traditions in the 1970s: An introduction. In *Ethnic medicine in the Southwest,* ed. Edward H. Spicer. Tucson: University of Arizona Press.

———. 1984. *Pascua: A Yaqui village in Arizona.* 1940. Tucson: University of Arizona Press.

———. 1988. *People of Pascua.* Tucson: University of Arizona Press.

———. 1992. Excerpts from the "Preliminary report on Potam." *Journal of the Southwest* 34 (1): 111–28.

———. 1997. Yaqui holy week in Potam. In *Performing the renewal of community: Indigenous Easter rituals in North Mexico and southwest United States,* ed. Rosamond B. Spicer and N. Ross Crumrine. Lanham MD: University Press of America.

Spicer, Rosamond B., and N. Ross Crumrine, eds. 1997. *Performing the renewal of community: Indigenous Easter rituals in north Mexico and southwest United States.* New York: University Press of America.

Spivak, Gayatri Chakravorty. 1988. Can the subaltern speak? In *Marxism and the Interpretation of Culture,* ed. Cary Nelson and Lawrence Grossberg. Urbana: University of Illinois Press.

———. 1996. How to teach a "culturally different" book. In *The Spivak reader: Selected works of Gayatri Chakravorty Spivak,* ed. Donna Landry and Gerald MacLean. New York: Routledge.

Stedt, Pauline Gertrude. 1994. Syncretic religions — merging symbols. PhD diss., University of California, Riverside.

Stratton, Jon. 1990. *Writing sites: A genealogy of the postmodern world.* Ann Arbor: University of Michigan Press.

Street, Brian V. 1984. *Literacy in theory and practice.* Cambridge: Cambridge University Press.

Sullivan, Lawrence E., ed. 1989. *Native American religions.* New York: Macmillan.

Tanner, Adrian. 2004. The cosmology of nature, cultural divergence, and the metaphysics of community healing. In *Figured worlds: Ontological obstacles in intercultural relations,* ed. John Clammer, Sylvie Poirier, and Eric Schwimmer. Toronto: University of Toronto Press.

Taylor, William B. 1996. *Magistrates of the sacred: Priests and parishioners in eighteenth-century Mexico.* Stanford: Stanford University Press.

Tedlock, Dennis. 1979. The analogical tradition and the emergence of dialogical anthropology. *Journal of Anthropological Research* 35 (4): 387–400.

———, trans. 1985. *Popul vuh: The definitive edition of the Mayan book of the dawn of life and the glories of gods and kings.* New York: Simon and Schuster.

Tennant, Paul. 1990. *Aboriginal peoples and politics: The Indian land question in British Columbia, 1849–1989.* Vancouver: University of British Columbia Press.

Thompson, E. P. 1963. *The making of the English working class.* New York: Pantheon.

Todorov, Tzvetan. 1984. *The conquest of America.* New York: Harper.

Tonkin, Elizabeth. 1992. *Narrating our pasts: The social construction of oral history.* New York: Cambridge University Press.

Treat, James, ed. 1996. *Native and Christian: Indigenous voices on religious identity in the United States and Canada.* New York: Routledge.

Trexler, Richard C. 1987. *Church and community, 1200–1600: Studies in the history of Florence and New Spain.* Rome: Edizioni di Storia e Letteratura.

Trigger, Bruce G. 1985. *Native and newcomers: Canada's "heroic age" reconsidered.* Montreal: McGill-Queen's University Press.

Turnbull, David. 1989. *Maps are territories: Science is an atlas.* Chicago: University of Chicago Press.

Turner, Edith. 1990. The Yaqui deer dance at Pascua Pueblo, Arizona. In *By means of performance: Intercultural studies of theatre and ritual,* ed. Richard Schechner and Willa Appel. Cambridge: Cambridge University Press.

Turner, Victor. 1974. *Dramas, fields, and metaphor: Symbolic action in human society*. Ithaca NY: Cornell University Press.

———. 1982a. *From ritual to theatre: The human seriousness of play*. New York: Performing Arts Journal Publications.

———, ed. 1982b. *Celebration: Studies in festivity and ritual*. Washington DC: Smithsonian Institution Press.

Tweed, Thomas A. 2006. *Crossing and dwelling: A theory of religion*. Cambridge: Harvard University Press.

Valencia, Anselmo, Heather Valencia, and Rosamond B. Spicer. 1990. A Yaqui point of view: On Yaqui ceremonies and anthropologists. In *By means of performance: Intercultural studies of theatre and ritual*, ed. Richard Schechner and Willa Appel. Cambridge: Cambridge University Press.

Valenzuela, Herminia. Personal interview. 21 June 1996.

Van Gennep, Arnold. 1909. *Les rites de passage*. Paris: Emile Nourry.

Vansina, Jan. 1985. *Oral tradition as history*. Madison: University of Wisconsin Press.

Vecsey, Christopher. 1990. *Religion in Native North America*. Moscow: University of Idaho Press.

———. 1991. *Imagine ourselves richly: Mythic narrative of North American Indians*. San Francisco: Harper, 1991.

Verano, John W., and Douglas H. Ubelaker, eds. 1992. *Disease and demography in the Americas*. Washington DC: Smithsonian Institution Press.

Voss, Stuart. 1981. Review of *The Yaquis: A cultural history*. American 38 (1): 143–45.

Wagner, Charles J. 1972. The Yaqui trip: The diary of Charles J. Wagner. In *Chronicles of the Yaqui expedition*, ed. Jimmy M. Skaggs, Fane Downs, and Winifred Vigness. Lubbock: West Texas Museum Association.

Warhus, Mark. 1997. *Another America: Native American maps and the history of our land*. New York: St. Martin's.

Weiner, James F. 2001. Strangelove's dilemma; or, What kind of secrecy do the Ngarrindjeri practice? In *Emplaced myth: Space, narrative, and*

knowledge in Aboriginal Australia and Papua New Guinea, ed. Alan
Rumsey and James Weiner. Honolulu: University of Hawai'i Press.

Weismann, Elizabeth Wilder. 1985. *Art and time in Mexico: From the conquest to the revolution.* New York: Harper.

Welch, James, and Paul Stekler. 1994. *Killing Custer.* New York: Norton.

West, Robert C. 1993. *Sonora: Its geographic personality.* Austin: University of Texas Press.

White, Richard. 1991. *The middle ground: Indians, empires, and republics in the Great Lakes Region, 1650–1815.* New York: Cambridge University Press.

Wilcox, David R., and W. Bruce Masse, eds. 1981. *The protohistoric period in the North American Southwest, AD 1450–1700.* Tempe: Arizona State University.

Wilder, Carleton Stafford. 1963. *The Yaqui deer dance: A study in cultural change.* U.S. Bureau of American Ethnology Bulletin 186. Washington DC: Government Printing Office.

Williamson, Ray A. 1984. *Living the sky: The cosmos of the American Indian.* Boston: Houghton Mifflin.

Wolf, Eric R. 1965. The virgin of Guadalupe: A Mexican national symbol. In *Reader in comparative religion: An anthropological approach,* ed. William A. Leesa and Evon Z. Vogt. New York: Harper.

———. 1982. *Europe and the people without history.* Berkeley: University of California Press.

Wood, Denis. 1992. *The power of maps.* London: Guilford Press.

———. 1993. The fine line between mapping and mapmaking. *Cartographica* 30 (4): 50–60.

Zendejas, Sergio, and Pieter de Vries, eds. 1995. *Rural transformations seen from below: Regional and local perspectives from western Mexico.* Transformation of Rural Mexico Series. San Diego: Center for U.S.–Mexican Studies.

Index

commandments of, 74; of
hell, 151; precontact, 48, 91–92,
150–52, 200, 239, 251, 304; son
of, 241, 249; Yoeme relationship
with, 34, 50, 77, 99, 102, 105,
132, 184, 195, 250, 291, 322n10;
Yoeme terms for, 37, 82. *See
also* baptism; Jesus; religious
syncretism

Goldie, Terry, 201

Goljota, 70

Grimes, Ronald, 283

Guadalupe AZ, 10, 87, 171, 172, 173,
195

Guarajillo, 150

Guaymas, 71, 134, 186, 192, 249, 308

Gupta, Akhil, 316–17

Guzmán, Diego de, 157–59, 161–66,
325–26n7, 327n21

Hallowell, A. Irving, 320n12

Hammond, George P., 173, 326n9

Harley, Brian, 284

Hartsock, Nancy, 244

Hassig, Ross, 166

heaven, 24, 29, 30, 45, 46, 47, 58,
66, 76, 127, 132, 163, 231, 239, 240,
254–55, 256, 259–60, 269, 271,
293, 295, 296, 297, 311, 315, 316,
318

hell, 24, 30, 45, 46, 47, 66, 151, 231,
271, 293, 311, 316

Hertz, Robert, 264

Hiak Vatwe (Yaqui River, or Yoeme
homeland), *95, 312*; aboriginal

relationships with, 91–92; and
agriculture, 7–9; as homeland,
5–7, 24, 25, 28, 55–56, 59, 69, 315;
human re-creation in, 90; maps
of, 287; in Mexican politics, 94,
95, 97; and migration, 10, 37,
148, 171; redirection of, 7–8, 95.
See also cosmology; history;
identity; pueblos

history, interpretations of: as
change and continuity, 8, 13,
16, 17–18, 22, 24–25, 37, 68, 82,
84, 86, 93, 95–96, 97, 114, 116,
128, 129, 138, 145, 175, 177, 178,
215–16, 232–37, 263, 281–82,
314, 316, 317, 320n13; colonial,
77, 98, 131, 156, 170, 201–2; as
ethno-ethnohistory, 10, 157,
242; as ethnohistory, 25, 111,
166, 170, 174–75, 213, 214, 242;
oral tradition as, 5, 16, 55–56,
68, 80, 81, 97, 167, 179, 204;
performance and, 5, 15, 16,
198, 205, 207, 215–16, 221, 225,
228, 231, 232–43, 251, 254, 264,
274, 277–83; writing and, 197,
198, 200–201, 202, 203, 208–9,
271–74; as Yoeme historicity,
2–6, 13, 22, 24, 131, 132, 143, 160,
177, 179, 180, 208, 243, 315. *See
also* embodiment; indigenous
agency; interpretation; myth;
orality; performance; writing

Holden, William Curry, 81, 253

holy: animals as, 230, 231; as authoritative sanction, 2; Catholicism as, 1, 248, 278, 291; time as, 51, 52, 53, 59, 64, 74, 148, 150, 153, 210, 211, 214, 239, 240, 241, 246, 272, 301, 311, 312. *See also* cross; heaven; pueblos; sacred and profane; Testamento

Hu-DeHart, Evelyn, 12, 22, 116–17, 156–57, 161–65, 167–71, 173–75, 177–80, 319n5, 320n7, 326n14, 327n15

Hurdaide, Diego Martínez de, 167–70, 174–77, 180, 327n15

huya ania (wilderness world): agency of, 43; associated with Surem life, 35; and Catholicism, 83, 237–38, 259–60; dialogic relations with, 329n9; physical locale of, 46; and other *aniam*, 36–39; as the wilderness world, 35, 37, 217, 219, 310. *See also* aniam; pahko'olam

Ibarra, Diego de, 157, 164

identity: contemporary ethnography of, 22–23, 27, 29, 307; and everyday life, 5, 11–12, 18, 30, 47, 98, 129, 215; internal contestation of, 129; military struggle for, 10, 160, 165–66; multidimensionality of, 4, 20, 25, 30, 37–38, 55, 56, 130, 271, 314; religious, 3, 4, 12, 14, 15, 37, 273, 287; ritual and, 30,

323n8; transnational, 9, 25, 114, 130, 225. *See also* boundaries; Catholicism; conversion; cosmology; deer dance; embodiment; emplacement; history; indigenous agency; knowledge; memory; myth; performance; religion

indigenous agency: as adoption of culture, 47, 198, 206, 209, 232, 233–34, 236, 237; ethnohistoric representations of, 313; as historical consciousness, 13, 15, 81, 112–13, 115–16, 122, 156, 170, 313–14, 318, 343, 364; and tribal sovereignty, 8, 10, 15, 22, 56, 81, 86, 94, 130, 176, 177, 198, 202, 213, 288. *See also* boundaries; history; identity; religious syncretism; ritual

inscription, 5, 15, 21, 23–25, 56, 69, 76, 82, 198, 202, 205–9, 229–31, 244, 284, 278, 318. *See also* cartography; orality; writing

interpretation: and archival, field, and ethnographic study, 4; as collaboration, 3–4, 8, 14, 15, 25–27, 29, 33–34, 37, 46, 48, 57, 64, 69, 77, 91, 93, 96, 113, 125, 203, 213–14, 217, 220, 226, 227, 229, 232, 244, 253, 256, 258, 272, 281, 308, 321n6, 324n11; and dichotomous thinking, 19, 23, 38, 83, 198–99, 201, 205–6, 208, 216, 225, 229, 231, 238; and direct historical approach, 12–13; to expand writing and history, 4–5, 13, 22–24, 81–83, 93, 111, 197–99, 283, 284, 286, 328n5; and geography, 5, 24, 28–56, 187, 264, 286, 314; and hermeneutics, 205, 206, 326n8; limitations of, 26–27; of missionization and conversion, 9, 20, 25; and non-Yoeme written sources, 12; of place and space, 253; as related to previous ethnographies, 5; as romantic and spiritualized representation, 21; and self-reflection, 1, 2–3, 13–14, 28–29, 30–35, 51–55, 72–75, 84–86, 113–15, 123–26, 159–61, 210–11, 222–24, 260–62, 275–77, 307–10, 311–31. *See also* conversion; history; identity; inscription; knowledge; sacred and profane; stories, writing; subaltern studies

Jackson, Kenneth, 263–64

Jesuit missionaries: accounts of the Yoemem by, 7, 322n1; as actors in conquest, 130; collaboration with Yoeme by, 9, 10, 208, 229, 233, 281; deities and ritual of, 176, 236, 241; and indigenous language, 153; and influence on religious societies, 282; and lack of understanding, 152; ritual and processions, 279, 304; and revolt of 1740, 320n9; sacred authority

of, 82–83; and schools, 8–9, 81, 236–37; Yoeme invite, 8, 10, 167, 170, 175, 176, 177, 178, 180, 236. *See also* conversion; cosmology; gods; indigenous agency; Jesus; literacy; Mary; myth; New Spain; religion; religious syncretism; ritual; Talking (Singing) Tree; Testamento

Jesus: as benefactor, 29; cross as Heart of, 304; death of, 145, 153, 238; deer and, 241–42; as flower person, 239; footprint and handprint of, 30–33, 312–13; as healer, 32, 239; image of, 102, 221; and life at *hiakim*, 28–29, 31–32, 47, 56, 238–39, 311, 314, 315; and older views of ritual sacrifice, 216; passion play of, 218, 237–40, 276, 278; precontact presence of, 83; and Yoeme kin solidarity, 23. *See also* cross; Easter Ceremony; gods; Mary; religious syncretism

kinship: deer as brother, 36, 37, 216, 217, 223–24; with godchild, 290–91, 309; of godparents, 26, 255, 256–59, 261, 265–67, 275, 276, 290–91, 295, 298–300, 320–21n14; and obligations, 217–18, 302, 323n8; *pahko'olam* as, 241; as solidarity, 23, 27, 130; with other-than-humans, 348. See also *animam miika*; deer; *pahko'olam*; Surem

Klor de Alva, J. Jorge, 232

knowledge, modes of: as alternative to Western thought, 4, 19, 80; as autoethnography, 3, 33, 205; as communication, 205–6; gift of, 3; local character of, 4, 5, 15, 16, 22, 24, 25, 56, 81, 84, 208, 253, 265, 273, 278, 281, 286, 311, 314–18; as truth-making, 55; and verbal arts, 35. *See also* cosmology; embodiment; history; interpretation; literacy; *lutu'uria*; memory; myth; performance; *tekipanoa*

kontim (processions), 13, 24, 27, 68, 75, 77, 80, 85, 152, 154, 155, 198, 205, 207, 231, 239, 240, 246, 250–52, 256, 257, 261, 272, 275–83, 287, 288, 298, 299, 303–6, 315–18, 331n17, 332n18. *See also* cartography; Catholicism; dance; religious syncretism

Kukut, Jose, 42–45, 88

language: of *aniam*, 119, 222; and *animam*, 264; and communication, 52, 119, 129, 296, 304; of deer, 217, 241, 243; as endangered, 6, 172, 319n1; formal instruction in, 171–73; of the *huya ania*, 128, 222; and incommunicability, 19, 34, 35, 113, 119, 128, 296, 321n5; indigeneity and, 243; and knowledge of worldview, 172;

of missionaries, 9, 154, 236, 296, 304; and ritual usage, 255, 275, 290; and telepathy, 122; and watching over the deceased, 255, 264, 275, 290. *See also* inscription; interpretation; literacy; orality; performance; religious syncretism; writing

Lautaro, Juan, 167, 169

León-Portilla, Miguel, 232, 328n1

Lévi-Strauss, Claude, 197–200, 204

Leyva, Alfonso Florez, 77–80, 82

literacy, 78, 80, 82, 97, 198, 206, 271, 328n1. *See also* cartography; inscription; orality; writing

lutu pahko, 126, 189, 214, 224, 249, 265–77, 298–301. *See also* death; food

lutu'uria, 18, 23, 35, 44, 48–51, 53, 55, 66, 80, 90, 100, 106, 125, 179, 207, 215, 216, 231, 244, 313

Maaso, Miki, 48–53

Madsen, William, 232–33

Mahoney, James, 7, 87–88, 90, 93, 222

Mallon, Florencia, 156–57, 325n1

Marana Pueblo, 21, 25, 159

Mary: as benefactor, 29; ceremonial society of, 13–14, 150, 152, 240, 256, 258, 291, 305; as flower, 238–39; as Itom Ae, 28, 82; and kinship solidarity, 23; and life on earth, 28, 29, 47, 56, 83; power of, 234; as Virgin of

Guadalupe, 102, 239, 279, 281–83, 305, 318

masks, 26, 150, 211, 217, 220, 222, 228, 239, 240, 246, 255, 275, 276, 277, 292, 330n14

Maso Kova, 308

McCutcheon, Russell, 98

McGuire, Thomas, 89, 322n9, 329n8

memory: as collective ritual embodiment, 23–24, 25; deer dance as, 35, 39, 215, 229; and focus on places and movements, 30; folklore as, 159; and identity, 35, 68; and maintaining Yoeme culture, 48; as reassertion of Yoeme knowledge, 3; as transformation of space, 29; scholarship on, 321n1; and semi-official rememberers, 80–81; as word and deed, 68; and worldview, 56; writing as, 22, 199. *See also* cartography; cosmology; emplacement; history; identity; inscription; knowledge; performance; ritual; stories; writing

Merrill, William, 216, 232, 322n11

Mexico: beliefs and religions in, 134; and conquest, 77, 135, 166; Cárdenas's favorable policy on, 15; hostile relations with, 9, 66, 94–95; nineteenth-century Yoeme policy on, 9, 10, 14; and Yoeme factionalism, 70–71, 73; and race relations, 123, 296,

309; revolution in, 94; and territorial encroachment, 17, 45, 94, 95, 130, 182, 188–92; war of independence in, 14; in Yoeme history, 229, 241. *See also* Alvaro Obregón Dam; boundaries; credit banks, conquest; history

Meyer, Richard, 264

Mignolo, Walter, 204–6, 328n1, 328n5

Moisés, Rosalio, 133–34

Molina, Felipe, 1, 2, 6, 15–16, 19, 25–26, 29, 30–33, 34, 35, 36, 38, 39, 42–45, 46–48, 51–53, 55, 58, 69, 71–73, 76–79, 80, 81, 82, 84–85, 87, 88, 89, 90, 93, 113–14, 115, 118, 119, 124, 128, 159–61, 210, 219–20, 222, 224, 229, 241, 243–45, 260–61, 274–76, 278, 311–13, 320n14, 321n3, 321n5, 322n9, 323n5, 324n15, 326n14, 329n9

Morrison, Kenneth, 15, 179, 216, 233, 234–35, 238, 321n5, 323n7, 326n8, 329n10, 330n13

music, 26, 30, 33–34, 40, 41, 42, 121, 124, 126, 155, 204, 211, 221–24, 240, 266, 268

myth: as Christian, 77, 253, 276; and community, 68; as distinctly religious, 17, 97; as ethnohistorical representation, 5; as form of historical consciousness, 15, 25, 29, 37, 91, 98, 234, 252–53, 314, 317; as geographical map, 285–86; in myth (*cont.*)

indigenous studies, 15–20; as mythistory, 68, 131, 179–80; and mythopoesis, 16, 93, 280, 323n3; and writing, 204. *See also* cosmology; history; performance; prophecy; religious syncretism; ritual; stories; Surem; Talking (Singing) Tree; Testamento; writing

Nabokov, Peter, 17–18
Namu, 91–92, 150
Nandy, Ashis, 232
New Pascua, 87
New Spain: indigenous syncretism in, 232–33; Jesuit expulsion from, 9; and policy toward indigenous peoples, 157; and slave raiding, 14; Yoeme defense against, 75; Yoeme engagement with, 166. *See also* Jesuit missionaries; religious syncretism; Talking (Singing) Tree; Testamento
Niranjana, Tejaswini, 202

Obregon, Alvaro, 94
Obregon, Balthasar de, 164–65, 326n10
Old Pascua, 210–11
Ometeme Kawi, 113, *114*, 118, 122, 137, 139, 144,
ontology: as categorical challenge,

326n8; and mythistory, 179; and other-than-human persons, 19, 320n12; and the Yoemem universe of being, 311
orality, 4, 13, 14, 16, 18, 21–23, 34, 35, 51, 66, 68, 71, 76, 78, 80, 81–84, 86, 90, 93, 97, 112, 116, 128, 130, 156, 157, 170, 177, 180, 198, 200, 203, 204–6, 208, 216, 218, 272, 273–74, 285–86, 315
Ortiz, Alfonso, 81, 88–89

pahkom (ceremonies): and church activities, 51, 83, 210; church/ *aniam* divide in, 259, 300, 311, 318; blessings of, 230; as negotiated knowledge, 245; as nonliterate inscription, 208–9, 229–30, 242, 313; as performed ethnographies, 244; and spatialization, 39, 230, 238, 310; of the Surem, 40, 129. *See also* deer dance; embodiment; inscription; *lutu pahko*; music; *pahko'olam*; performance; ramada; ritual
pahko'olam (ceremonial performers): animal helpers of, 214, 229–31, 251, 329n9; as clowns, 210, 218, 220–21, 224, 227–28, 231, 251; and the devil, 231; and flower, 220, 231, 238; funeral of, 255, 292, 298, 318; and goats, 41, 49, 220; and *huya ania*, 83; kin relations with, 241;

manager of, 222, 229; oration of, 249–50; organic historicism of, 242–45; otherness of, 35, 42, 43, 48, 229; performance of, 220, 222–24, 240–41; power and talent of, 39, 41, 226, 228, 230; as precontact performers, 152, 213, 221; as "profane," 227, 329n8; regalia of, 329n3; and Yoeme Catholicism, 208, 211. *See also* cosmology; deer dance; *lutu'pahko*

Painter, Muriel Thayer, 36–37, 38, 40, 41, 45–46, 47, 48, 90, 122, 123, 127, 208, 216, 226–28, 242, 256, 271, 278, 279, 321n4, 324n11, 328n8

Pandya, Vishvajit, 286–87

Pérez de Ribas, Andrés, 7, 173, 174, 175, 180, 236, 237, 253, 279, 306, 319n5, 327n20

performances: as civic events, 224–25; as embodied action, 13, 14, 23, 30, 315, 320n13; as expressive culture, 12, 30, 278, 320n13; as history, 13, 23, 16, 198, 207–8, 232, 242; and identity, 23, 39, 215, 225; as knowledge- and truth-making, 18, 244; oral, 13, 51, 76, 78, 81, 315; and place, 14–15, 37, 39, 221, 255, 265, 288; as place-making, 4, 5, 23–25, 51, 252–54, 313; precolonial logic of, 216; as "profane," 216, 225, 227–29, 231, 238, 242, 329n8; as

re-membering, 29, 35, 37, 39, 51, 231, 318, 321n1; and sovereignty, 81, 198, 288; as spatial practice, 17, 29, 30, 34–35, 39, 56, 198, 207, 228, 230, 238, 253, 257, 258, 264, 267, 271–73, 274, 287, 310, 313, 315–18; as transformation, 230; and Yoeme writings, 13, 76, 78, 206, 208–9, 283, 313. *See also* embodiment; emplacement; *lutu'uria*; *pahkom*; *pahko'olam*; ritual; writing

Pilem, 42–45, 56

poetics. *See* deer dance; Elders' Truth; sacrifice; stories

Pollock, Della, 207–8

power: and *aniam*, 37, 48; as beings, 33, 37, 91, 122, 129, 186, 171, 176, 219, 230, 241, 252, 259, 266, 310; for communicating, 127; and cures, 102, 104, 228, 248, 328n2; performance as, 208, 228; political, 9, 17, 21, 39–40, 48, 50; 114, 132, 156, 161, 165, 166, 173–74, 176, 179, 180, 197, 204, 208, 316–17, 329n10, 332n19; of ritual, 230, 231, 237; and *seataka*, 58, 65, 99, 101, 106, 136, 217, 219, 247; Yoeme terms for, 58, 99–110

Powers, William K., 234

processions. See *kontim*

prophecy: and linear history, 128, 131; as conceptual weapon, 17–18; as efficacious, 70; and establishment of tribal territory, prophecy (*cont.*)

    15; and factionalism, 70–71; and indigeneity, 178–79; and preparation for European contact, 118; and relationship to myth and religion, 15–20; and Yoeme truth claims, 179. *See also* indigenous agency; myth; stories; Talking (Singing) Tree; Testamento

pueblos: Catholic spaces in, 311; and consolidation of precontact population, 8; and divine right to aboriginal lands, 316; and factionalism, 70–71, 73; formation of, 15, 29, 36, 68, 75, 89, 90, 92, 97, 115, 130, 134, 142, 164, 175–76, 236, 315; governors of, 71, 72, 73, 87, 147, 191, 246, 249, 279, 281, 282, 305, 322n4, 325n7; as holy, 1, 2, 7, 8; Jesuit schools in, 81; Mexican destruction of, 7–8; Mexican occupation of, 94–95; names of, 319n5; patron saint of, 47, 75, 218; precontact and Catholic mythology in, 252–53; repopulation of, 10; and revitalization, 281; social reciprocity in, 251; as synonymous with Yoeme people, 2; Testamento boundaries of, 77, 79; versus wilderness, 83

purgatory, 30, 46, 66, 271, 311

Rabasa, Jose, 202

Rafael, Vicente L., 216, 235, 324n14

Raffles, Hugh, 315

ramada (*rama, santo heka*), 36, 37, 51, 52, 84, 210, 211, 218, 220–24, 229, 230, 240, 249–51, 258–59, 265–70, 273, 276, 278, 283, 293, 300, 301, 309–11, 318. See also *pahkom*

Ramsey, Jarold, 16

Redfield, Robert, 12, 225–26, 329n5

Reff, Daniel, 319n5, 326n11, 327n20

religion: definitions of, 18–19; as belief, 16, 18, 19, 134, 153, 177, 200, 225, 227, 232, 264, 286; non-supernatural, 238; as ultimate transcendence, 29, 229, 243; and Yoeme history, 9, 13–14, 21, 244. *See also* cosmology; gods; Jesus; *lutu'uria*; knowledge; Mary; religious syncretism; ritual; sacred and profane; tradition

religious syncretism: as colonial semiosis, 205–6; as continuity and adaptation, 22; deer dance as, 216, 221, 242; as fusion of worldview and Catholicism, 9, 29, 47, 231–33; as individual sin, 29; *kontim* as, 278; myth and ritual in, 204; new deities and ritual in, 176; *pahko'olam* as, 231, 242; of precontact worldview and Catholic cosmology, 8, 45–48; prophecy as explanation of, 16; as radical conversion,

29; as religious change, 23, 24, 30, 45–46, 56, 115, 126–27, 158, 215, 229, 233–34, 237, 238, 267, 274, 313, 315; and religiously transformed space, 29, 252, 311, 318; ritual mediation of, 25; as shift from spatial to temporal, 29, 47; varying Yoeme views of, 47–48, 243, 256, 321n6, 324n11; and writing 82. *See also* conversion; cosmology; flower; history; indigenous agency; interpretation; Jesus; *kontim*; Mary; prophecy; ritual; Talking (Singing) Tree; worldview

ritual: as affirmation of the community's values, 25, 288; as autoethnography, 205, 208, 241, 244; as blessing, 31, 140, 218, 222, 229–31, 258, 259, 272, 273, 291, 294, 295, 298; Catholic, 2, 19, 23, 24, 47, 81–82, 158, 208, 209, 215, 216, 221, 234, 236, 238, 241–42, 243, 252, 267, 274, 296, 304, 313, 315, 318; and ceremonial calendar, 51, 237, 238, 241, 311, 325n7; and ceremonial error, 256; and ceremonial regalia, 220, 226, 255, 259, 329n3; and ceremonial restraints, 265, 331n13; cost of, 96–97, 189, 211, 226, 266, 269, 299–301, 306, 329n6; and enduring cultures, 12, 225; as exorcism, 104; and hand-touching, 331n7; as historical

consciousness, 5, 15, 24, 198, 208, 232, 234, 243; Holy Cross Day, 51–53, 272, 312; humor in, 227–28, 231; and land rights, 21, 71, 73, 77, 86, 97, 315; precontact, 8, 9, 19, 29, 37, 91, 93, 111, 118, 163, 179, 213, 216, 220, 221, 234, 235, 237, 241, 253, 279, 281, 310, 311, 314, 320n8, 322n1, 323n4, 324n11; Running of the Old Man, 85; women in, 329n3; and writing, 206, 242, 271; as Yoeme religious obligation, 244, 267, 279, 291, 302. See also *animam miika*; baptism; books of the dead; Easter Ceremony; funeral; *kontim*; *lutu pahko*; *pahkom* boundaries; ceremonial societies; cosmology; cross; deer dance; embodiment; flower; history; identity; indigenous agency; Jesus; knowledge; memory; *pahko'olam*; performance; religion; religious syncretism; *tekipanoa*; writing; worldview

Rosaldo, Renato, 243

Sands, Kathleen, 11, 16, 113, 116, 123, 165, 320n11, 322n2

sacred and profane, 19, 38–39, 216, 225, 231, 234, 238, 242

sacrifice, 36, 37, 40, 162, 213, 216, 219, 229, 238–41, 248, 310. *See also* deer; flower; food; Jesus; Mary; Saint Michael

9, 86, 91, 237, 321n10; and
religious syncretism, 47–48,
56, 157, 230, 236, 276, 311, 318;
and ritual, 29, 42, 51, 218, 225,
226, 244, 273, 314, 315, 316;
and Talking Tree, 117. *See also*
Catholicism; cosmology;
knowledge; memory; religious
syncretism
writing: and arche-writing, 204,
328n4; and ethnography, 4;
evolutionary views of, 23,
198–202, 206, 332n19; and
history, 5, 13, 23, 81, 131, 198,
203, 208–9; performance as,
22, 204, 206, 242, 283; Yoeme
examples of, 24, 76, 78, 81–83,
93, 112, 207, 271–72, 315. *See
also* cartography; history;
inscription; interpretation;
language; memory; myth;
orality; performance; religious
syncretism; ritual; Testamento

Yaqui Irrigation Commission, 9,
95, 182

Yaqui River. *See* Hiak Vatwe
Yaquis: and nationalist discourse,
10; origin of, as Yoeme name,
10–11; Edward Spicer's usage of,
9. *See also* Yoemem
yo ania (respected world): agency
of, 39–41; association with
God, 48; as "enchanted," 38–39;
and evil, 45–48; location of,
37–39; presentness of, 46, 52,
231, 271, 311, 314. *See also* deer
dance; deer song; Elders' Truth;
pahko'olam; power; Surem
Yoemem: autoethnography of, 7,
33, 40, 205; as baptized ones, 6;
bi-national identity of, 14, 15, 31;
contact population of, 8, 320n7;
defined, 9; poverty of, 30, 71,
73, 96–97, 181–96, 226, 260,
269, 299–301, 306. *See also* Hiak
Vatwe; identity
Yoi Lo'i, Don Jesús, 35, 310
Yomumuli, 119–20, 123, 134–43,
323n5
Yo Va'am, 139